MW01013178

No Barrier Can Contain It

Envisioning Cuba

Louis A. Pérez Jr., *editor*

Envisioning Cuba publishes outstanding, innovative works in Cuban studies, drawn from diverse subjects and disciplines in the humanities and social sciences, from the colonial period through the post–Cold War era. Featuring innovative scholarship engaged with theoretical approaches and interpretive frameworks informed by social, cultural, and intellectual perspectives, the series highlights the exploration of historical and cultural circumstances and conditions related to the development of Cuban self-definition and national identity.

No Barrier Can Contain It

Cuban Antifascism and the Spanish Civil War

· ·

ARIEL MAE LAMBE

The University of North Carolina Press Chapel Hill

© 2019 The University of North Carolina Press
All rights reserved
Set in Charis by Westchester Publishing Services
Manufactured in the United States of America

The University of North Carolina Press has been a member
of the Green Press Initiative since 2003.

Library of Congress Cataloging-in-Publication Data
Names: Lambe, Ariel Mae, author.
Title: No barrier can contain it : Cuban antifascism and the
    Spanish Civil War / Ariel Mae Lambe.
Other titles: Envisioning Cuba.
Description: Chapel Hill : University of North Carolina Press, [2019] |
    Series: Envisioning Cuba | Includes bibliographical references and index.
Identifiers: LCCN 2018055505 | ISBN 9781469652849 (cloth : alk. paper) |
    ISBN 9781469652856 (pbk : alk. paper) | ISBN 9781469652863 (ebook)
Subjects: LCSH: Anti-fascist movements—Cuba. | Spain—History—Civil War,
    1936–1939—Influence. | Cuba—Politics and government—1933–1959. |
    Anti-fascist movements—Spain. | Fascism—Spain—History—20th century.
Classification: LCC JC481 .L295 2019 | DDC 320.53/309729109041—dc23
    LC record available at https://lccn.loc.gov/2018055505

Cover illustration: Detail from Henry Glintenkamp's *Club Julio A. Mella
(Cuban Workers' Club)*, 1937. © Estate of Henry Glintenkamp, gift of Walter P.
Chrysler Jr., Chrysler Museum of Art. Used with permission.

I dedicate this work to my parents, Richard and Karen Lambe,
for their extraordinary generosity and support of my education
at every level.

Contents

Graphs and Tables

Graphs

Tables

Acknowledgments

I begin by expressing my gratitude for the institutional and financial support that made this project possible. The University of Connecticut's policy of granting a semester of junior faculty leave provided an extremely valuable period of time for finalizing the manuscript, and History Department start-up funds covered vital research and editing expenses. Columbia University's Richard Hofstadter Faculty Fellowship and Teaching Scholars Fellowship, as well as a summer research field grant from Columbia's Institute of Latin American Studies, funded the primary research phase of this project and early writing work on the manuscript. So, too, did the U.S. Department of Education's Foreign Language and Area Studies (FLAS) and Javits Fellowships.

During my time researching in Cuba, Spain, and the United States, I received critical assistance from many librarians, archivists, and fellow scholars, all of whom I appreciate. I am particularly grateful to Fernando Rovetta Klyver of the Centro de Estudios y Documentación de las Brigadas Internacionales at Universidad de Castilla–La Mancha in Albacete, Spain, and to Ana Suárez Díaz of the Centro Juan Marinello in Havana, Cuba, for their extraordinary hospitality and generosity.

For key assistance with specific research tasks for the book, I am indebted to Yesenia Barragan, Elizabeth Schwall, and Ana Suárez Díaz. For reading and giving productive feedback on part or all of the manuscript at various stages of its development, I am grateful to Carolyn Arena, Yesenia Barragan, Barry Carr, Jason Oliver Chang, John Coatsworth, Anne Eller, Temma Kaplan, Jose Moya, Melina Pappademos, Pablo Piccato, Elizabeth Schwall, many helpful scholars at various conferences and workshops, and two anonymous readers for the University of North Carolina Press. For extensive stylistic editing, I thank Kim Singletary of Humanities First. I am grateful to Erin Davis and the staff at Westchester Publishing Services for copyediting, to Margaretta Yarborough for proofreading, and to Roberta Engleman for indexing. All errors remain solely my own.

I am deeply appreciative of Elaine Maisner—my editor at the University of North Carolina Press—and Envisioning Cuba series editor Lou Pérez for their enthusiasm for my project, their encouragement, and their expert guidance. I extend my thanks to the entire editorial team at UNC Press for their help in turning this book into a reality.

Each day I am thankful to be part of an intellectually and academically engaged and encouraging History Department at the University of Connecticut, a truly excellent group of colleagues. For mentorship and support in my department, I am particularly indebted to Jason Oliver Chang, Chris Clark, Judy Meyer, and Melina Pappademos. Additionally, I am grateful for the History Department staff, the Waterbury Campus staff, and all the other employees of the university, whose labor makes the faculty's work possible. Thank you.

I benefited tremendously from the instruction, mentorship, and friendship of my teachers and advisers at Columbia, including Chris Brown, Eric Foner, Natasha Lightfoot, Nara Milanich, and particularly those with whom I worked most closely: John Coatsworth, Jose Moya, Pablo Piccato, and Caterina Pizzigoni. Those from other fields of history were generous to take an interest in my work and my scholarly development; those in Latin American history made up the most accomplished, supportive, engaging, and fun advising team a graduate student in the field could hope for. To all of them I extend my sincerest thanks. Also at Columbia, I was fortunate to be aided in my academic endeavors, professional development, and day-to-day necessities by the dedicated staff of the History Department, excellent librarians, the interdisciplinary Institute of Latin American Studies, an innovative teaching center, a supportive career services office, and all the other hardworking staff at the university. I appreciate the efforts of all these people. Additionally, I am thankful to have been part of a collegial community of graduate students in history and related fields at Columbia. For friendship and mutual aid, I am particularly grateful to fellow history graduate students Carolyn Arena, Hannah Barker, Yesenia Barragan, Eric Frith, Toby Harper, Julia del Palacio, Elizabeth Schwall, and Andy Whitford.

I would not have chosen to become a historian were it not for the encouragement of three practitioners of the trade during my final undergraduate year and the three years following my graduation from college. Jennifer Klein helped me connect my academic interests to professional work in labor organizing, and then bring the valuable experiences of that work back to my scholarship and teaching. Gil Joseph demonstrated to me that academic eminence and sincere kindness need not be mutually exclusive and helped coax me back from the brink of law school. It was Seth Fein whose extraordinary commitment to teaching and advising most changed the course of my trajectory. Though I was already a history major when I met Seth at the beginning of my senior year, I did not become a historian until I began to work with him. So compelling was the enthusiasm of his intellectual engagement with history and with his students that I was inspired by his example to pursue a PhD in history. I cannot thank him enough.

I wish also to thank all the many superb teachers with whom I learned during my primary education. From the earliest age, I was fortunate to have teachers who recognized and nurtured my twin loves of history and writing, as well as many other endeavors. In particular, I thank the late Robin L. Crawford, the late William Thomas, and K. Kelly Wise of Phillips Academy Andover for leading me past the limits I imagined for myself.

The completion of this book would not have been possible without the efforts of a smart, thoughtful, and compassionate medical team dedicated to keeping me healthy enough to do the work I love. I thank each of my medical professionals for their excellent care.

I offer my sincerest appreciation to all my wonderful friends—the "village" of family friends who helped raise me, my childhood and adolescent companions, kindred spirits I met during my higher education and early work years, and my current community of fellow parents in greater New Haven—for their love, camaraderie, and encouragement. For particularly vital and sustaining support over the past few years, I am profoundly grateful to Yesenia Barragan and Kate Nesin.

I am enormously appreciative of my husband, Kevin Mercik, for more than I can possibly summarize. Our love, our partnership, and our home are the core of my life. I admire deeply the fact that, like many of the protagonists of this book, Kevin is guided in his life's work by the conviction that a better world is possible. I am grateful to both of our delightful daughters, Bridget Aurore Mercik, born in 2013, and Noelle Geraldine Mercik, born in 2018, who have enriched my life immeasurably, and to Bridget in particular for having so obligingly shared her mother's attention during her early years with her textual sibling, this book.

Finally, I dedicate this book to my parents, Richard and Karen Lambe, who—in addition to being truly excellent parents—have been exceptionally generous in every possible way in their support of my education and academic career.

Thank you, all.

Abbreviations in the Text

AABI Asociación de Amigos de las Brigadas Internacionales (Association of Friends of the International Brigades)

AANPE Asociación de Auxilio al Niño del Pueblo Español (Association of Aid to the Child of the Spanish People)

ABC ABC (revolutionary society)

AIE Ala Izquierda Estudiantil (Student Left Wing)

AMB American Medical Bureau

ANAPE Asociación Nacional de Ayuda al Pueblo Español (National Association of Aid to the Spanish People)

ASE Ateneo Socialista Español (Spanish Socialist Athenaeum)

CFE Centro Federalista Español (Spanish Federalist Center)

CNE Comité Nacionalista Español de Cuba (Spanish Nationalist Committee of Cuba)

CNOC Confederación Nacional Obrera de Cuba (National Worker Confederation of Cuba)

CNT Confederación Nacional del Trabajo (National Confederation of Labor)

CPUSA Communist Party of the United States of America

CES Círculo Español Socialista (Spanish Socialist Circle)

CTC Confederación de Trabajadores de Cuba (Cuban Confederation of Workers)

DEU Directorio Estudiantil Universitario (University Student Directorate)

FAI Federación Anarquista Ibérica (Iberian Anarchist Federation)

FDE Frente Democrático Español (Spanish Democratic Front)

FEU Federación Estudiantil Universitaria (University Student Federation)

FGAC	Federación de Grupos Anarquistas de Cuba (Cuban Federation of Anarchist Groups)
FJLC	Federación de Juventudes Libertarias de Cuba (Federation of Cuban Libertarian Youth)
FOH	Federación Obrera de La Habana (Worker Federation of Havana)
IB	International Brigades
JONS	Juntas de Ofensiva Nacional-Sindicalista (Councils of the National-Syndicalist Offensive)
LAI	Liga Anti-Imperialista de Cuba (Anti-Imperialist League of Cuba)
NAACP	National Association for the Advancement of Colored People
OCC	Oposición Comunista de Cuba (Communist Opposition of Cuba)
ORCA	Organización Revolucionaria Cubana Antiimperialista (Cuban Anti-imperialist Revolutionary Organization)
PAN	Partido Agrario Nacional (National Agrarian Party)
PBL	Partido Bolchevique Leninista (Bolshevik-Leninist Party)
PCC	Partido Comunista de Cuba (Cuban Communist Party)
PCE	Partido Comunista de España (Spanish Communist Party)
POR	Partido Obrero Revolucionario (Revolutionary Worker Party)
POUM	Partido Obrero de Unificación Marxista (Workers' Party of Marxist Unification)
PPC–O	Partido del Pueblo Cubano—Ortodoxo (Cuban People's Party—Orthodox)
PRC–A	Partido Revolucionario Cubano—Auténtico (Authentic Cuban Revolutionary Party)
PSOE	Partido Socialista Obrero Español (Spanish Socialist Worker Party)
PUR	Partido Unión Revolucionaria (Revolutionary Union Party)
UGT	Unión General de Trabajadores (General Union of Workers)
UN	Unión Nacionalista (Nationalist Union)
UNIA	Universal Negro Improvement Association

No Barrier Can Contain It

Introduction

Antifascism for a New Cuba

· ·

Reflecting on her participation in the fight against Cuban president-turned-dictator Gerardo Machado, Teresa "Teté" Casuso described Machado's fall in 1933 as a dam breaking. Dismissing the "peaceful solution" orchestrated by U.S. special ambassador Sumner Welles to remove Machado through a negotiated coup d'état, she commented, "As always happens when there is total ignorance of a people's deepest problems, those responsible for this neat 'arrangement' . . . suddenly found themselves confronted by a broken dike." U.S. officials trying to avoid revolution, she argued, had "only suc-ceeded in filling the dam till it burst."[1] Chaos ensued, and despite a brief hopeful period of change, Fulgencio Batista soon rose to power as a new strongman promising order. The fight continued until Batista's forces crushed a massive general strike in March 1935. With this victory, he achieved the peace and quiet that U.S. officials had desired in 1933, but it was, Teté wrote bitterly, "the peace of the absent and the quiet of the dead."[2] The dike broken in 1933 was rebuilt, the revolutionary waters once again contained. Choosing quiescence or exile, many activist Cubans stepped out of the reservoir behind that dam.

Teté and her husband, activist intellectual Pablo de la Torriente Brau, were two of those who fled to exile in New York City. In the record-breaking heat of midsummer 1936, Pablo began to daydream of water. Bored and dis-dainful of glittering trivialities in the big city, he lamented that he got swept away by the "nocturnal river of Broadway" that "at the door of each burlesque, of each movie theatre . . . makes whirlpools." The vitality of a Union Square rally for the Spanish Republic against rebel general Francisco Franco jolted Pablo from languid tedium, redirecting his activist impulse into transnational antifascism. He decided to travel across the ocean to par-ticipate in the conflict recently begun in Spain, imagining that there he would be swept away by the "river of revolution" and "be close to the great silent whirlpool of death."[3] Most importantly, he would learn lessons appli-cable to the fight back home. The Spanish Republican struggle, Pablo wrote, would teach Cubans "that when a people wishes to fight to the death for its ideals and necessities, *there is no barrier that can contain it*."[4]

As the global fascist threat loomed ever larger and more menacing, many Cuban activists, like Teté and Pablo, reinterpreted their domestic fight as antifascism.[5] Their general goals for Cuba remained the same as they had been for years: an end to strongman governance and U.S. neocolonialism, economic and social progress, and some form of democracy and/or revolution. Often Cubans summarized this set of goals with the idea of a "New Cuba."[6] This concept covered as many disparate viewpoints as did antifascism itself, and the exact nature of the goals differed from one person or group to another. Nevertheless, diverse Cubans—nationalists and internationalists, moderates and radicals—found a crucial degree of unity in their shared desire for a New Cuba. Likewise, many Cubans unified around antifascism, which they defined as not only *against* fascism but also *for* a New Cuba. Thus, Cuban antifascism served as a crucial continuity of domestic activism during times of severe repression—vital activism that would change Cuba between 1935 and 1940.

Frustrated by multiple setbacks culminating in Batista's violent breaking of the general strike in March 1935, activists for a New Cuba continued in the face of defeat by refusing to view their political goals as confined to the island. They moved across borders and oceans both physically and symbolically, cultivating networks and building solidarity. They defined their struggle for a New Cuba as connected to antifascist efforts in countries around the world, including Ethiopia and especially Spain. Self-identified Cuban antifascists believed that it was through these ostensibly foreign fights that they would achieve their political goals at home. They acted transnationally—making connections, spreading propaganda, contributing monetary and material aid, and even volunteering to fight on foreign soil— to sustain their fight for a New Cuba in a different form. Their redefined understanding of the island's political arena as transnational forces us to reimagine Cuban activism during an era previously regarded as a lengthy, defeated lull. The presence of diverse and vibrant Cuban antifascism reveals significant personal resilience and a continuity of struggle heretofore underappreciated.

Writing about the impact of the March 1935 general-strike defeat, scholars of Cuban history have emphasized calamity, drawing on documentation of deep despair and disillusionment to assert that this historical moment was "the last revolutionary surge of the first republican generation" and "the end of an era."[7] To the extent that scholars have acknowledged Cuban antifascism, they have interpreted it as (1) a foreign endeavor of young Cuban men who physically traveled to Spain as volunteers to fight for the Republic; (2) a Communist endeavor imposed from without by Communist International (Comintern) Popular Front policy; and/or (3) a moderate liberal endeavor during World War II that resulted from Cuba's joining the Allies and was therefore both imposed from without and largely separate from Cuban domestic politics before 1941.[8] Expanding the analysis in terms of scale, geography, and time frame uncovers a much broader and more diverse Cuban antifascism than these characterizations suggest, one that was firmly located on the island and within Cuban communities abroad, inclusive of Communist projects alongside many others, and significantly intertwined with Cuban popular politics long before Cuba's powerful neighbor to the north embraced an antifascist stance during World War II. Bringing the antifascist movement more meaningfully into Cuban history builds on established scholarship of 1930s popular politics and shifts interpretation of the aftermath of the general strike in March 1935 from an emphasis on defeat to an analysis of continued activism.

Before considering the case of Cuban antifascism, it will be useful to look briefly at a broad definition of fascism and then specifically at fascism in Spain—which, to the majority of Cuban antifascists, was unquestionably the most important incidence of fascism after Cuba itself.[9]

Fascism, the Vaguest of Political Terms

That antifascism is against fascism seems a straightforward assertion, but it leads directly into a notoriously difficult task: defining fascism. Fascism "remains probably the vaguest of the major political terms," in the words of Stanley G. Payne.[10] The purest definition of fascism confines it to Fascism, the political movement begun in Italy in 1919 by Benito Mussolini. A broader and widely accepted definition within fascism studies includes German Nazism, despite its many significant distinctions from the Italian case.[11] Beyond these two "classical fascisms," however, the question of which regimes should be deemed fascist is vigorously contested. Scholars must glean from the Italian and German examples some formula flexible enough to be applied to various specific locations while rigid enough not to include every conceivable dictatorship with any passing resemblance.[12] Attempting to distill an essence of fascism from multiple historical cases is not within the scope of this study. Yet since this book explores the definitions of fascism offered by Cuban antifascists, it is worth attempting a general working summary of our own, with full acknowledgment that we are treading in extremely contentious territory.

To synthesize expert summaries, fascism begins with the sense that a national community of "chosen people" under attack must be defended and vindicated, and a nation in decline, regenerated and reborn.[13] In the 1930s the capitalist economic crisis of the global Great Depression fueled the sense of attack and decline and therefore buoyed fascist growth. As a solution, fascism offers an energetic, unifying, revolutionary nationalism, genuinely supported by large numbers of people, who coalesce into a militant party with an activist political style and a charismatic authoritarian male leader.[14] The leader and party do not offer a unified ideology in the sense of a coherent system of thought or a strict adherence to a set of stated policy goals; rather, emotional and sensual experience through theatrical ritual inspires enthusiasm for and unity around moral, cultural, and spiritual renovation, as well as a drive toward totalitarian and often corporatist control of economy and society. Fascists position themselves against liberals and leftists (especially Marxists), and collaborate uneasily and intermittently with traditional conservatives. The fascist party abandons and attacks democratic practices and institutions, creates parallel operations and governing bodies, and celebrates violence as the means by which to redeem the nation in victory over its internal and external enemies and through wars of territorial expansion and empire.

What foreign fascism did Cuban antifascism attack? Of the two foreign cases considered by Cuban antifascists in this study, Ethiopia is clearer. Mussolini's Italy was the prototype of fascism, and its 1935 attack on the African nation was a quintessential war of territorial expansion that proudly used overwhelming violence against a people whom Italy's leaders considered inferior. Whether or not there was fascism in Spain, on the other hand, is highly contested—some scholars consider fascism to have existed there, while others see only a separate variety of authoritarian regime: the military dictatorship. For our purposes in this book, we will assume there was fascism in Spain for two reasons. First, for Cuban antifascists, fascism existed meaningfully in Spain because they believed it did according to their own definitions. Second, the history of Spain from the First Republic through the Nationalist attack on the Second Republic shows fascism developing and functioning in that country.

Spain's short-lived First Republic was declared in 1873 following a crisis of monarchy that began in the late 1860s. A lack of national unity doomed the experiment, and the monarchy was restored in 1875. Spain experienced tumult at the turn of the century, as it lost its remaining colonies—the Philippines, Puerto Rico, and Cuba—to the United States. It remained neutral during World War I and enjoyed some prosperity due to increased trade, but these gains quickly disappeared at the war's end, and unrest increased. Adding military insult to economic injury, the country suffered defeat in a war in Morocco in 1921. Dictator Miguel Primo de Rivera (ruled 1923–30), backed by the king and the military, viewed Mussolini as "his inspirer and teacher," though he denied imitating fascism.[15] He mobilized conservative, Catholic, middle-class Spaniards in a civic movement for modernization and prosperity, social and economic reforms, increased influence abroad, and, above all, renewed patriotism. Despite some notable successes, many Spaniards ultimately saw the Primo de Rivera dictatorship as a failure. The Great Depression hit Spain hard, and Primo de Rivera resigned in January 1930. Frustrated expectations for reforms led Spaniards to establish the Second Republic in April 1931: after municipal elections in which Republicans won a number of majorities, King Alfonso XIII, in power since 1902, abdicated and left the country. The Republic's constitution of 1931 guaranteed new rights, severely restricted the special privileges of the Catholic Church and nobility, and paved the way for significant reforms. Progressive reforms of the Republican government under moderate liberal Manuel Azaña, combined with popular unrest, pushed many political, economic, and religious elites to the right. Meanwhile, many on the left felt that the Azaña government failed to go far enough in addressing Spain's ills. The embattled leader lost power in September 1933, though he would serve as prime minister again in 1936. Between 1933 and the start of the Spanish Civil War in 1936, violence increased as forces on the right and left struggled for power.

During this time of political unrest, various groups espousing fascist or fascist-like ideas existed in Spain. The group with the most clearly defined fascist characteristics was founded in 1931: Juntas de Ofensiva Nacional-Sindicalista (Councils of the National-Syndicalist Offensive, or JONS). The organization's influence increased substantially in 1934 when it entered into association with José Antonio Primo de Rivera—son of the late dictator and a well-connected and savvy leader—and his group, Falange Española, founded in 1933.[16] José Antonio, as he is commonly known, founded the Falange at a time when he was enraptured by Mussolini.[17] He conceived of the Falange as fascist by his own definition, which at the time "seemed to amount to a radical and authoritarian nationalism with a modern social and economic program of radical reformism, audacious and modern in culture but still somehow in harmony with Catholicism and traditionalism, and ready to employ whatever violence was necessary," according to Payne.[18]

Over the next couple of years, the combined Falange and JONS attempted to increase its strength, negotiate alliances and understandings with other political groups in Spain, and develop a platform.[19] Despite being small and politically weak, the new group raised concerns among leftists, traditional conservatives, and the Republican government, who subjected it, respectively, to hostility, disdainful criticism, and repressive force.[20] Early in 1936 the Falange failed miserably in what would turn out to be the final elections of the Republic—the Republican Popular Front of moderates and leftists won narrowly—showing, Payne argues, that at that historical moment, "categorical fascism was weaker in Spain than almost anywhere else in western or northern Europe."[21] Following the elections, however, when left–right violence intensified across the country during the Tragic Spring of 1936, the popularity of the Falange began to soar as its paramilitary forces engaged in armed struggle in the streets against the Spanish Left. Falange leadership had been plotting against the Republican government for months. These efforts raised enough alarm that Falange leaders were imprisoned and some even executed; the Republican government banned the organization in April 1936. Meanwhile, waves of new adherents strengthened the organization.[22] By the time the rebellion led by Franco began, the Falange *was* Spanish fascism.[23]

In July 1936, beginning in Morocco, right-wing Nationalists rose up in military insurrection against the Republican government and its loyalists, sparking civil war. Germany and Italy quickly offered aid to the Nationalists, and right-wing forces unified behind Franco. Falange members would make up at least 55 percent of civilian volunteers for Franco during the war, serving in combat and repression capacities. Once José Antonio had been executed in prison in November 1936, Franco began to make use of his political program, his movement, and even his identity as the central martyr figure of the Nationalist cause.[24] Nationalists soon overwhelmed those loyal to the government in a number of Spain's key regions.

Republicans hoped for aid, but they were disappointed when Britain, France, the United States, and others chose to abide by the newly created Non-Intervention Agreement—which prohibited partisan foreign participation in the Spanish conflict—in the belief that by doing so, they might avoid a larger war in Europe. The Republican side did receive aid from Mexico and, more significantly, the Soviet Union, which sent war materiel and approximately two thousand men.[25] However, that assistance was no match for that of the Germans and Italians to the Nationalists, in flagrant violation of the Non-Intervention Agreement. Germany contributed training, weaponry, and bombers; Italy sent military planes and 100,000 soldiers. Foreign fascist military intervention resulted in unprecedented levels of civilian casualties due in large part to the bombing of population centers. German and Italian aid was widely credited as one of two central factors responsible for winning the war for Franco's forces. The other was the fact that the Nationalist side included most of Spain's formal military and was thus better trained and equipped even before receiving foreign aid. It is estimated that more than 580,000 people died in the Spanish Civil War from bombings, executions, malnourishment, disease, and battle. Within this prolonged horror, pro-Republican forces—including more than thirty thousand foreign volunteers—fought tenaciously, often keeping Nationalists at bay and regaining territory despite the overwhelming military power of their opponents. And as they did so, they had little doubt that what they were fighting was fascism—Spanish as well as foreign.

The immediate causes of the conflict were largely domestic Spanish concerns. One central problem was frustration and anger directed at traditional power holders—the monarchy, the military, the Catholic Church, and the oligarchy of the nobility—as well as an ascendant capitalist class. A second problem was the need for land reform in a country that was still largely agricultural. A third issue was militant organizing by both peasants and industrial workers in response to extreme economic inequity. Finally, Spain was destabilized by the general sense that the country was weighed down by tradition, anti-modern and backward, and "barely touched by the industrial and liberal revolution that succeeded in transforming the old Europe," in the words of Pierre Broué and Emile Témime.[26] In addition to these clear domestic factors, many participants and observers interpreted the struggle in international terms as one of antifascists against fascists. As Fredrick B. Pike summarizes, the conflict "was in many ways a homegrown struggle," but "it was also a reflection of the struggle between the defenders and critics of modernity, which, having originated in the late nineteenth century, threatened during the 1920s and 1930s to destabilize all of Europe."[27] In other words, the Spanish political arena was both domestic and foreign, national and transnational; the same was true in Cuba.

Toward Cuban Antifascism

No Barrier Can Contain It takes Cubans at their word in their claim to be fighting fascism abroad and at home. During the 1930s, Cuban domestic popular politics became encompassed by transnational antifascism. In the words of Francisca López Civeira, "The ascent of Nazi-fascism had imposed new analyses that helped to interpret the national situation from new perspectives."[28] The diversity and complexity of the antifascist movement as it played out in Cuba provided space for a loose unity of many conflicting views and goals, which proved vital to the effort to shape a New Cuba. Antifascism came to encompass Cuban popular politics in the 1930s because of the perception of a clear and present threat of foreign fascism both at home and in general, as well as a tradition dating back to the 1920s of conflating Cuba's domestic problems with fascism.

Antifascism began in Cuba in the mid-1920s against Italian Fascism and against Machado, whom activist Julio Antonio Mella dubbed a "Tropical Mussolini" in 1925. This assertion came long before most Cubans began to have a problem with their then democratically elected president, but the characterization rang true enough by 1931 to make its way to the cover of *Time* magazine.[29] Tenacious, too, was Mella's understanding of the close connection between fascism, dictatorship, and imperialism.[30] From the beginning, the Cuban conception of fascism was as a conglomerate of Cuba's two greatest ills—dictatorship and imperialism—against which activists struggled to create a New Cuba. Mella embodied this connection as a principal instigator of Cuban antifascism and the struggle against Machado. His efforts against the dictator are well known and discussed in chapter 1, but his antifascist organizing has received less attention. One example took place in September 1924, when an Italian ship arrived in Havana on what activists perceived to be a fascist propaganda tour. Militant students led by Mella joined forces with organized workers in street protests and rallies near the docks and in front of Italian diplomatic offices. Years later, labor activists José López Rodríguez, a tobacco worker, and José Rego, a cigar maker, recounted that the antifascist outpouring was so intense, it caused the ship to depart Cuban waters earlier than planned. In addition to being a victory for Cuban students and workers generally, López Rodríguez and Rego recalled, the fascist ship's early departure was a clear demonstration of Mella's character and abilities as an organizer.[31]

Mella did not live to see Machado's downfall and the Revolution of 1933, but his tradition of conflating antifascism and the fight for a New Cuba carried on. The April 1931 establishment of the Spanish Second Republic took place in the midst of intense domestic agitation in Cuba, and Cubans found inspiration in Spain and a great deal of support from the Spanish community on the island. Cuba's Círculo Republicano Español (Spanish Republican Circle) was founded shortly thereafter, and its periodical, *República*, disseminated Spanish Republican news and ideas to Cuban and Spanish Cuban readers. Other groups of pro-Republican Spaniards living on the island and their Cuban allies did the same, including the Izquierda Republicana Española (Spanish Republican Left) and the Centre Català (Catalan Center).[32] Cuban students in September 1933 told a visiting U.S. reporter that their nascent revolutionary government—the short-lived government between Machado's downfall and Batista's rise—"compare[d] most closely with the new revolutionary republic of Spain." Additionally, the students said that their government was "both intensely nationalistic and socialistic," but they objected to "being called 'National Socialist,' because they oppose[d] fascism," the correspondent reported. In his words, the influences of the Spanish Republic and antifascism on these Cuban student activists factored centrally in their conception of a New Cuba as "a completely sovereign State with fundamental political, economic and social reforms."[33] The students' commentary makes clear how Cuban antifascism formed around Mella's original assertion about dictatorship and imperialism, a close connection drawn between revolutionary governments in Cuba and Spain, and a strong sense of the need for reforms.

As Cubans witnessed the rise of U.S.-backed military strongman Batista in 1934, the world witnessed the threatening advance of fascism in Europe. The Liga Anti-Imperialista de Cuba (Anti-Imperialist League of Cuba, or LAI) observed those developments in Cuba and Europe side by side and analyzed their connections from leftist and Communist-influenced perspectives—not all members of the LAI were Communists, but the organization generally followed the party line. Linking Cuba's struggles against dictatorship and imperialism to the fight against fascism, LAI writers followed Mella's lead and continued his work building on the foundation of an authentically Cuban antifascism. The LAI's 1934 definition of *fascism* as "the terrorist dictatorship of the most reactionary, most chauvinistic, and most imperialist elements of financial capital" would echo in discussions of antifascism on the island throughout the 1930s.[34] This resonance of the LAI's early outlines of Cuban antifascism is hardly surprising considering that multiple authors who edited or wrote for the LAI's periodical *Masas*—such as Joaquín Cardoso, Mirta Aguirre, and Alberto Moré Tabío, as well as the more well-known Pablo de la Torriente Brau, Emilio Roig de Leuchsenring, and Juan Marinello—would go on to report on the Cuban efforts in support of the Spanish Republic in such Cuban periodicals as *¡Ayuda!* (Help!), *Facetas de Actualidad Española* (Facets of Spanish news), and *Mediodía* (Midday).[35]

On 1 August 1934, the National Congress against War, Intervention, and Fascism took place in Havana. This secret meeting included two hundred geographically and racially diverse Cuban delegates organized by the LAI for the purpose of formulating strategy.[36] Resolutions from the National Congress encompassed a number of issues and causes, both foreign and domestic, that would become parts of Cuban antifascism: support for Cuban workers and the *"masas populares"*; antagonism toward the island's political elite; outcry and pushback against Cuban government repression; anti-imperialism directed against U.S. officials and economic interests; denunciation of racism against Cubans of African descent; desire to organize and mobilize the Cuban peasants; solidarity with Cuban organizations abroad (such as the Club Cubano Julio Antonio Mella in New York City) and with people of other Latin American countries (such as those fighting for Puerto Rican independence); support for the Red Army, the people of China, and the Soviet Union; and concern for besieged workers and antifascists in all countries. The resolutions made clear that Cuban antifascism existed for the purpose of supporting people in other countries *and* advancing the domestic fight for a New Cuba.[37] The LAI sought to build transnational solidarity by showing that Cubans were part of the fight against fascism around the world. For example, Cubans faced the same problems as people oppressed by fascism elsewhere, the National Congress claimed. Control by the Cuban elite and U.S. imperialists meant "illiteracy, hunger, misery, terror, fascism and war," which caused the deaths of thousands of poor Cuban men, women, and children.[38] Furthermore, as an article in *Masas* a few months later pointed out, Cubans employed the same tactics against oppression as did the anti-Hitler underground.[39]

Like the LAI, the island's anarcho-syndicalists kept a close watch on both fascism and Cuba's domestic situation in 1934. For inspiration, they reported on workers fighting against the fascist threat in various European nations. Domestically, their central belief was that Cuba's workers needed to be unified in struggle.[40] An anonymous anarcho-syndicalist author wrote in *Nuestra Palabra* (Our word) that Cubans must exterminate fascism or it would exterminate them, and that little by little Cubans were realizing this fact. From the anarchist perspective, the "stupid and idiotic political revolution against Machado" had raised hopes for justice and better material conditions, but instead, Cubans were left with a "regime of crime."[41] Batista's strongman tactics, wrote another anarchist in ¡Tierra! (Land!), were like those of Hitler's Germany, "much more refined" than those used during the Machado era.[42] Havana's anarchist youth called on the Cuban proletariat to take up arms against fascism in February 1935.[43]

Cuban anarcho-syndicalists saw many of the same ills in fascism as were expressed in *Masas* and at the LAI's National Congress but also bitterly denounced Soviet Communism.[44] Tensions between anarchist antifascism and Communist antifascism would only grow going forward, but already in 1934 it was possible to see the way the two would operate: both would fight against fascism, but they would do so using different methods and seeking different ends, and all the while at each other's throats. One example occurred during the LAI's National Congress, when Armando Ramírez—delegate to the gathering from the Club Cubano Julio Antonio Mella in New York—was detained by police in Havana. Both anarchists and Communists protested for Ramírez's freedom, but anarchists claimed that the "communists" (in quotation marks implying that they were not real communists) were hypocrites to call for his freedom because workers in Russia were not free.[45] Furthermore, they denounced the National Congress itself, claiming that it was a farce.[46]

One central cause of the fighting between these two groups on the island was the struggle to control organized labor, which constituted by far the largest collectivity in protest in Cuba during 1934. That these two ideologically leftist groups were working to lead the protest of a mass of Cuban workers across the island put them in a position of significant influence over a large number of people. And both were engaging simultaneously with the threat of global fascism and with Cuba's domestic problems. As a result, anarchists and Communists outlined antifascism as authentically relevant to Cubans of both domestic and transnational identities and experiences, and transmitted this relevance to working-class Cubans specifically. Additionally, through writings, speaking engagements, and conferences, leftists were able to convey the importance of antifascism to students, intellectuals, and professionals sympathetic to their messaging. By the time the March 1935 general strike took place, an antifascist spark had been lit in the minds of countless Cubans by leftists as well as nationalists. After the defeat of the strike, Cubans continued their domestic fight, reimagined as antifascism, in whatever ways they could, but they increasingly turned their antifascist attention toward transnational concerns.

Upon Italy's invasion of Ethiopia in October 1935, transnational networks delivered news and analysis of the attack to the island, and what had been a general watchful eye on the development of fascism in Europe became an active antifascist impulse among some Cubans. Cuban Communists officially supported that impulse, as did some notable individuals, such as poet Nicolás Guillén and Freemason and anarchist Antonio Penichet. It was particularly resonant with Cubans of African descent, many of whom identified with a conception of Ethiopia as a symbolic "homeland" in need of protection by all members of the black diaspora.[47] Interpreting Mussolini's invasion as a project of colonization, black Cubans and their antifascist allies appealed to their compatriots based on a historically informed sense of anticolonial solidarity. Yet while there was significant criticism of Mussolini and Fascist Italy, Ethiopia's fight failed to attract truly widespread commitment on the island.

With Franco's July 1936 rebellion against the elected government of Spain, however, antifascism exploded into Cuban consciousness. A greater number of Cubans identified with the Spanish revolutionaries and Republican loyalists fighting Franco than with any other antifascist effort worldwide. They defined their Spanish enemies as fascists for three reasons: Italian and German alliance with Franco and the Nationalists; Franco's co-option of the Falange; and the widespread belief that the Nationalists represented a reactionary, backward, and regressive "Old Spain," associated with the Inquisition and colonization. Assessing the fascist threat to Cuba in similar terms, Cuban antifascists feared direct Italian and German influence, the role of the Falange, and a revival of the colonizing forces of Old Spain. They also opposed a broader fascism defined in Cuban terms, one that encompassed strongman governance and U.S. neocolonial control— dictatorship and imperialism in the tradition of Mella—as well as economic and social injustice.

Fascist Italy and Nazi Germany did directly threaten Cuba. During the 1920s and 1930s, Fascists and Nazis worked to exert political, military, economic, and cultural influence on the Western Hemisphere. They dispatched agents, intellectuals, and travelers throughout the Americas to gather intelligence and spread propaganda, and they developed organized structures for recruiting Italian and German expatriates and descendants abroad.[48] At many points in the history of the Americas, Cuba's location and geographical characteristics made it of special interest to all those with designs on the region, from empires to pirates. It seemed entirely likely to many observers, Cuban and otherwise, that fascists would seek to occupy Cuba as a logistical entry point to the Americas—or, at the very least, that they would infiltrate the island covertly to aid fascist ascension and victory.[49] By the time the United States and many other countries of the region joined the Allies in World War II, there were urgent concerns about the possibility of Axis agents in Cuba radioing U-boats in the Caribbean.[50] Nazi spy Heinz August Lüning, alias Enrique Augusto Luni, was captured in Havana in 1941. That the case generated popular fervor sufficient enough to have him executed by Cuban firing squad despite the misgivings of prominent island elites—and despite the fact that he had been a remarkably inept and disappointing spy—indicates the degree of fear surrounding fascism in the populace during the early 1940s.[51] A counterintelligence program involving Cuban, U.S., Mexican, and British-Bermudian collaboration—as well as a private intelligence service made up of eighteen Spanish Republican exiles and poorly led by writer Ernest Hemingway—operated in Cuba during World War II.[52]

A central figure in fascist attempts to garner support in both Spain and Spanish America was General Wilhelm von Faupel, appointed by Hitler as the director of the Ibero-American Institute in Berlin early in 1934 and the first Nazi diplomat to Nationalist Spain from November 1936 to August 1937. Faupel had lived and worked in Spanish America for two decades before assuming his first Nazi post, and he sought to establish intelligence and paramilitary operations in every country of the region. He believed that the key to German seizure of Spanish America was Spanish imperial influence, which he felt could be revived with Nazi assistance.[53] Once in a position to act on this idea, he sought to use the Falange to spread Nazi influence throughout Spain and use the Iberian nation as a platform from which to launch movements and governments favorable to Germany throughout the Americas.[54] There is evidence that, to a limited extent, Fascists and Nazis, in a plot to gain influence in the Western Hemisphere, sought to use or at least influence the Spanish Falange in the Americas as a friendly entry point.[55] Even after he was recalled from Spain as a German diplomat, Faupel continued to host and train Falangists at the Ibero-American Institute in Berlin.[56]

As Cuban antifascists were well aware, the Spanish Falange was more powerful and influential in the Americas than were Italian Fascists or German Nazis. The Falange served as the most potent form of foreign fascism in much of Spanish America, where it counted Spanish immigrant communities and Spain-oriented Spanish Americans as its members.[57] A transnational organization that operated in a carefully structured hierarchy in multiple countries, the Falange abroad published periodicals and distributed propaganda in other media such as radio to spread Nationalist ideas and rhetoric; engaged in charitable efforts; encouraged the establishment of pro-Nationalist organizations, such as the Comité Nacionalista Español de Cuba (Spanish Nationalist Committee of Cuba, or CNE); pursued aggressive measures to force existing Spanish clubs and associations to declare their loyalty to Franco or cease their claim to Spanish identity; and, through these various efforts, garnered support for Franco in the form of aid— monetary, material, and human—to the Nationalist cause. Consuelo Naranjo Orovio estimates the number of Falange affiliates in Cuba before the start of World War II at 1,550.[58] As was true elsewhere in Spanish America, the majority of Cubans engaged with the conflict in Spain sided with the Republic.[59]

Though it had support among both immigrant and native populations, there was an intense outcry against the Falange by antifascists in Cuba and the Americas more broadly. Hemingway, familiar with struggles in both Cuba and Republican Spain, broadcast his fear of the Falange on the island, which he considered to be a particularly ominous fascist threat.[60] Antifascist U.S. journalist Allan Chase examined the threat to the entire hemisphere in his 1943 investigative book *Falange: The Axis Secret Army in the Americas*, which captured the imagination of readers.[61] Exposés such as Chase's, while based on information available at the time, were exaggerated for political purposes and contributed to anti-Falange "hysteria."[62] Journalistic exaggeration aside, Cuban and other antifascists had no doubt that Spanish fascism was acting pervasively and effectively on their island and elsewhere in the hemisphere.

The Falange presence had clear postcolonial resonance for Cubans, whose compatriots had fought Spain for independence just a few decades prior. They viewed the Spanish Civil War as a conflict between Old Spain, which colonized and enslaved people throughout the Americas—a return of the Spain of the historic Black Legend of Spanish infamy[63]—and a New Spain, embodied in the formation of the Republic and encompassing all that was best about both Hispanic tradition and modern, progressive Spain. Spanish antifascists conceived of fascism as "reactionary"—a term common among Communists—or, in the conception of one Spanish anarchist periodical in 1933, as a new enemy composite of all the enemies of the past.[64] Cubans asserted that Falangists and Nationalists were direct descendants of brutal and exploitative Spanish colonial authorities, and that the Old Spain fascists sought to reestablish was precisely the rapacious Spain against which

Cubans had fought for thirty long years during the nineteenth century in three wars of independence (1868–98). For example, Franco was a reincarnation of Valeriano Weyler, the infamous villain in the final Cuban War of Independence (1895–98), whose devastating program of *reconcentración*— which killed hundreds of thousands of Cubans when they were forcibly moved into densely packed makeshift accommodations—resembled the concentration camps later established in Europe. Just as during the wars of independence, Cubans had to beware the forces of Old Spain and their traitorous island allies, to fight both foreign and domestic threats. The fascist vision for revitalization of the Spanish Empire in the Americas was a mirror image of the Cuban antifascist vision for revitalization of Cuban sovereignty: "Never again!," Cuban antifascists asserted against the Spanish Nationalists, with no sense of paradox at conflating historical Spanish colonialism with present fascism. Thus, they turned domestic popular politics into geopolitics, and the local into the international, in a manner that defied definitions and delineations.[65]

Traditionally, antifascism has been defined by scholars as a phenomenon limited to the resistance to regimes and groups such as Fascists, Nazis, and the Falange in Europe during the interwar period.[66] Increasingly, however, scholars of antifascism are opening up the field geographically and chronologically.[67] Instead of cutting off the study of antifascism at a geographic boundary, a historical era, or a particular set of characteristics, these broader studies consider antifascism as an adopted identity, a transnational movement encompassing disparate but often interconnected threads, and a stance that was *for* a broad set of values and goals as much as, if not more so than, it was *against* fascism(s).[68] Antifascism brought together extant transnational organizations, identity groups, and other collectivities, some officially constituted in institutions and others more diffuse, including, in no particular order: liberals, democrats, socialists, anarchists, Communists, Trotskyists, anti-imperialists, trade unionists, feminists, members of the black and Jewish diasporas, and Freemasons. Each of these collectivities had its own background, beliefs, and aims; some overlapped, and others famously clashed. Their preexisting networks facilitated building solidarity, as did the circulation of people, materials, funding, ideas, and symbols. Antifascist experiences built antifascist identities and eventually an antifascist culture.[69] Rather than being a traditionally structured movement, antifascism existed in flux and encompassed multiple goals in addition to defeating fascism. It included "different and changing proposals for, and repertoires of, action."[70] And not only proposals and repertoires but also arenas and scales: antifascism began in particular, nation-based resistances against Fascism and Nazism, spread to other sites, and grew into a transnational whole. Hugo García, at the forefront of expanding antifascism studies, summarizes that antifascism "remained diverse, across nations, regions and political cultures—a meeting place for various strategies, visions and discourses rather than a unified movement. These contradictory elements can only be reconciled by paying attention to the complex interplay between the individual, local, national and global dimensions of antifascism."[71]

The methodology implied by this understanding of antifascism works fruitfully in the Cuban case. Indeed, the broadening of antifascism studies makes this book possible. Within antifascism's framework of transnational solidarity, conflicts across multiple nations became part of the same worldwide effort according to antifascists, and this imagining expanded the Cuban political arena during the 1930s. The domestic fight for a New Cuba joined and gained strength from the global fight against fascism without losing its content or its specifically Cuban character. Once the fight for a New Cuba had become antifascist, it could not be contained—it could move across borders and oceans proclaiming itself freely, or it could erupt right at home on the island, under oppressive circumstances coded in the new language and symbols of the global struggle. Transnational solidarity facilitated a continuity of activism that is difficult to detect when Cuban political history is confined to the national scale. Viewing antifascism as a Cuban phenomenon requires connecting geopolitics and domestic popular politics. It necessitates tracing multiple components of the struggle for a New Cuba into antifascism, including individual and organizational participants, historical memory, activist symbols and metaphors, relationship and network links, paths of migration, and sites of exile. It requires analyzing the specific ways one movement flowed into the other and considering the opinions, emotions, and experiences of Cuban antifascists to assess how and why they interpreted antifascism as a continuation of their fight for a New Cuba. Human stories reveal the ways in which antifascism served to inspire Cuban political actors and revitalize Cuban groups, both of which had been badly shaken in 1935. Therefore, this book takes a narrative approach, one that follows the sources closely and studies activists' lives carefully. Since self-definition is vital to understanding the values and goals of antifascism, taking antifascists' words and experiences seriously is key; thus, the book uses a lived definition of antifascism voiced by the antifascists themselves. To understand Cuban antifascism's persistence in particular, the book considers activists' personal resilience and interpersonal relationships. Combining biography with political history in a transnational context allows *No Barrier Can Contain It* to uncover a heretofore underappreciated continuity of Cuban activism in the form of antifascism.

Postcolonialism, Diasporas, and "Special Relationships"

Though transnational antifascism is sometimes reductively assumed to have functioned primarily ideologically—as a global left or, more specifically, as a project of the Comintern—the Cuban case demonstrates the equally important role historical and cultural identities played in its formation. The two most significant "special relationships" that informed and facilitated Cuban antifascism were postcolonial pan-Hispanic identity (*hispanismo* or *hispanidad*) and black diasporic identity understood as pan-Africanism. The latter is discussed in depth in chapter 2's consideration of the antifascist defense of Ethiopia. The former warrants an introduction here.

Spain and Spanishness were absolutely central to Cuban antifascism, and Cuban antifascists sometimes went so far as to suggest that Spain and Cuba were still one and the same. There were a considerable number of Spaniards living in Cuba during the decades between the Cuban War of Independence and the Spanish Civil War; *peninsulares* (people from the Iberian Peninsula) not only remained in Cuba after independence but also increased their numbers on the island significantly. In 1899 approximately 8 percent of the total Cuban population (130,000 out of 1.6 million people) were Spaniards. Between 1902 and 1916, over 400,000 more Spanish immigrants flooded the island's population and labor market. The presence of Spaniards in Cuba in the first few decades of the twentieth century was not uncomplicated, especially because they dominated economically desirable positions, much to the frustration of Cubans.[72] Yet it did substantially strengthen the enduring cultural and familial ties between the countries.

The line between Spain and Cuba was most thoroughly blurred in the idea of *hispanismo* or *hispanidad*. Many Cubans believed that there was a special relationship between Cuba, Spain, and the rest of Spanish America. This belief stemmed from the long history of the Spanish Empire and was reinforced by projects to promote the concepts of a pan-Hispanic identity and "a transatlantic Hispanic family, community, or *raza* (race)."[73] Proponents of the idea espoused the belief that Spaniards transmitted their culture, traditions, and identity to the indigenous people they met and subjugated in the Americas, the Africans who accompanied them or whom they transported by force, and the resultant descendants of mixed ethnic and racial heritages.[74] In other words, *hispanismo* or *hispanidad* applied to Spanish Americans regardless of racial background. Proponents sought to rehabilitate Spanish history in the Americas, counteracting the Black Legend and emphasizing the positive nature of Spain's legacy.[75] At various times during the nineteenth and twentieth centuries, the concept of pan-Hispanic identity was mobilized in attempts to reinforce the national character of individual Spanish American countries, formulate a sense of solidarity across national borders in the region, and harness those national and regional identities as strength against the incursions of non-Hispanic interlopers, especially the United States.

Spain's loss of Cuba and Puerto Rico in 1898 was a significant moment for Spain and for Spanish America, as the former lost its final colonial possessions and the latter, though finally free from Spain altogether, was forced to confront the imperialist threat of the United States unleashed by the Spanish-American War. The most famous pan-Hispanist response was the 1900 essay *Ariel* by José Enrique Rodó, which reaffirmed Spanish America as spiritual and aesthetic in contrast to the materialist and utilitarian United States.[76] Even more important for Cubans was the legacy of the late Cuban independence leader José Martí, who, though he died before the U.S. intervention in the Cuban independence movement, had carefully considered the issues of breaking with Spain and defending against U.S. encroachment.[77] Famously, Martí asserted the existence of "Our America"—the Hispanic America in contrast to Anglo-America—and laid out what Pedro Pablo Rodríguez calls "a continental strategy of national liberation against imperialism."[78] A man of action as well as ideas, Martí worked tirelessly on Cuba's anti-Spanish fight while living in the United States. The Cuban child of Spaniards, university educated in Spain, and a great admirer of Spanish culture, as well as a longtime resident of the United States, Martí had nuanced views of both countries and their relationships with Cuba. He analyzed the pros and cons of the philosophies, politics, and societies of both. He also carefully examined and critiqued multiple countries of Spanish America in developing his own sense of *hispanismo* or *hispanidad*. Ultimately, he fought against Spain from within the United States while crafting a unifying pan-Hispanic vision for Spanish America in opposition to U.S. influence.[79] In such instances of pan-Hispanic identity mobilized against U.S. intervention as those of Rodó and Martí, Spanish Americans did not seek to reunite politically with Spain or reconstruct the Spanish Empire, though some regional elites did maintain that dream. Rather, pan-Hispanic Spanish Americans looked to Spain as their symbolic motherland and their independent Spanish American neighbors as brother or sister republics.

Cuban antifascists mobilized this conception of pan-Hispanic identity, which was powerful both because it was an effective tool for building solidarity and because it defied efforts to define pan-Hispanic identity in Spanish Nationalist terms. Over time, Miguel Primo de Rivera, the Falange, and Franco developed a conception of *hispanismo* or *hispanidad* into a national policy based on Hispanic tradition, Catholicism, anticommunism, and a neo-imperialism that claimed that Spain was destined to lead a fascist Spanish America of the future.[80] Like previous iterations, this pan-Hispanic identity claimed religious, spiritual, and aesthetic supremacy—but instead of directing this sense of superiority primarily against the powerful external enemy of U.S. imperialism, fascist *hispanismo* or *hispanidad* turned against perceived internal enemies conceived of as the *antipatria*: liberals, socialists, communists, Freemasons, and Jews.[81] In Nationalist hands, pan-Hispanic efforts resembled a twentieth-century *Reconquista*, a territorial reclamation and ethnic reassertion. When Cuban antifascists referenced the special relationship they felt with the motherland during the Civil War, then, they were fighting for contested rhetorical territory. Fascist, pro-Nationalist Cubans sparred with antifascist, pro-Republican Cubans over the meaning of Spain and of *hispanismo* or *hispanidad*. The dramatic political and ideological polarization that would rend Spain in two during the 1930s was reflected not only in Spanish American nations but also within pan-Hispanic thought. *Hispanismo* or *hispanidad*, like Spain and Cuba, was not fascist or antifascist; it remained to be claimed and defined.

Chapter Outlines

Cuban popular political leader Julio Antonio Mella originated the fight for a New Cuba and Cuban antifascism in the 1920s. *No Barrier Can Contain It* begins with him, and his life intersects with the topics and themes covered in chapter 1. The chapter sets the stage for the discussion of antifascism by following Cuban popular politics from the crisis of 1920 through the election of Gerardo Machado, his devolution into a strongman, and his overthrow, to Fulgencio Batista's rise to power and victory in breaking the March 1935 general strike. The chapter introduces activists Teté Casuso and Pablo de la Torriente Brau as central figures and guides throughout the book. Chapter 2 picks up chronologically where chapter 1 leaves off and examines Cuban responses to Mussolini's invasion of Ethiopia in 1935, focusing on Communists and people of African descent. Distinctions between these two groups as well as their overlap introduce the diversity of Cuban antifascism and its possibilities for conflict and solidarity. The chapter analyzes the impact of shifting Comintern policy, asserting that the Cuban Communist Party's response to the Ethiopian invasion was a barometer of change. It explores antifascism in the African diaspora, Cuban participation in this transnational network, and attempts by Cubans of color to reconcile the diaspora with their Cuban nationalism in the context of antifascist struggle. It concludes with a look at how black Cubans made a gradual and troubled transition from supporting the Ethiopian cause to supporting the Spanish Republican cause.

Chapters 3 through 6 deal with Cuban antifascism in relation to the Spanish Civil War, and chapters 3 and 4 feature Torriente and Casuso, respectively. Chapter 3 follows Torriente from where we left him in chapter 1, examining his path from the Cuban domestic struggle into exile and then on to a combat death on the Spanish front in December 1936. His trajectory illustrates at an individual human scale the meaning of transnational antifascism for Cuban activists. The chapter studies recruitment in New York City and Havana for the Cuban volunteers inspired by Torriente, and considers the logistics of the recruitment effort. It examines notable Cuban martyrs in the Spanish conflict as well as their symbolism, especially with regard to the pursuit of Cuba's domestic struggle abroad. The chapter discusses Cubans' belief that Spain would offer "countless lessons that will benefit our people" in the fight back home.[82] Chapter 4 begins with Casuso in the aftermath of her husband's death in Spain, when she founded Havana's Asociación de Auxilio al Niño del Pueblo Español (Association of Aid to the Child of the Spanish People, or AANPE), the central organization of the Cuban campaign to assist Republican children during the conflict. Composed of children, women, and men from all over the island and Cuban communities abroad, the AANPE was part of the international campaign to aid Republican children but was nonetheless unmistakably Cuban. One of its most powerful organizing mechanisms was the argument that the blood of Spanish children ran through Cuban veins. Fostering this sense of familial and cultural solidarity and billing itself as a nonpartisan charity served the association well for much of the war, helping it to achieve impressive successes in collecting aid. That its pro-Republican stance was deemphasized indicates mobilization of a subtle solidarity, in which the cause was obscured to garner broader popular support.

Chapter 5 returns to Cuban volunteers in Spain to explore the function and significance of their transnational identities and experiences. Due to colonialism, neocolonialism, and migration, Cubans were transnational—shaped by movement, connection, and exchange across borders and oceans. In particular, Cuba had ties with Spain and the United States, which gave Cuban volunteers special roles as translators and network builders and made them especially valuable to Spaniards and English-speaking volunteers. Another fundamental characteristic of volunteers was political and ideological diversity, which also characterized antifascism on the island. Chapter 5 studies two domestic groups whose commitment to the Spanish Republic did not rest primarily on leftist ideology but rather on other types of transnational identifications tied to domestic concerns: Cubans of African descent and Freemasons. Examining these two groups along with the Cuban volunteers, chapter 5 explores the connection between transnationalism and continuity from Cuba's struggle to Spain's.

Chapter 6 considers the antifascist perspectives and goals of a number of leftist individuals and groups on the island. Tension and overlap and conflict and collaboration between groups characterized the antifascism of the Cuban Left. The factionalism of the era is readily apparent, but so, too, is significant unity and solidarity building. Unity and solidarity—even if limited and imperfect—are notable not only in the various leftist internationalist groups well known to have fought among themselves but also between those ideological cohorts and Cuban domestic political actors and groups not affiliated with internationalist ideologies. Ultimately, to demonstrate that there was a continuity in the fight for a New Cuba in Cuban antifascism, chapter 6 illustrates the ways in which the defense of the Spanish Republic on the island involved the same people, groups, relationships, networks, ideas, goals, rhetoric, and tactics as did the Cuban struggle. The Spanish Civil War caused each group to reckon with its own existence, role, values, and aims. The conflict reenergized these groups and provided the impetus for unity, which was vital for the continuation of struggle at home and abroad.

In the end, Franco's Nationalists overthrew the Republican government of Spain, and Cuban antifascists suffered yet another defeat. The conclusion of *No Barrier Can Contain It* details how Cuban activists continued antifascist efforts during World War II as antifascism went "mainstream." There was no greater symbol of the official position antifascism attained in Cuba than Batista himself; the book suggests that the fight for a New Cuba achieved substantial success in antifascism in part because it influenced Batista, at least for a time. Taking a longer-term view, a postscript examines the legacy of antifascism and the Spanish Civil War in Cuban politics and historical memory during the early years of the Cuban Revolution that triumphed in 1959. The postscript returns to Teté Casuso during the struggle of the 1950s, when she helped Fidel Castro, and afterward, when she broke with the Revolution and left once again for exile in the United States. It addresses selective memory and forgetting of Cuban antifascists such as Casuso in revolutionary Cuba's official accounts of antifascism and the Generation of the Thirties. Also, it connects Cuban antifascism to the present by discussing the Antifa movement across time and space.

1 Hope and Despair

The Fight for a New Cuba, 1920–1935

From the perspective of many activists on the island, Cuba's 1930s began on 10 January 1929 in Mexico City. Then and there, Cuban popular political leader Julio Antonio Mella was murdered. Circumstances of the crime proved controversial. Was it a love triangle gone wrong, or were agents of the Mexican government scared of destabilization by foreigners? Was it a Stalinist hit leveled at a Communist who was too independent-minded or an act of political repression by henchmen of Cuba's strongman government? A complex and transnational web of personal and political motivations, the possibility of double agents, and the involvement of prominent figures—politically active artists Tina Modotti and Diego Rivera, and especially the mysterious Vittorio Vidali, alias Carlos Contreras, an international Communist operative and Mella's alleged romantic rival—may always cast doubt on the circumstances of Mella's death. This uncertainty has resulted in the controversy's remarkable resiliency, but a number of scholars of various nationalities share the same belief as that held in Cuba: that Mella died at the hands of the government of Gerardo Machado, which had already attacked, imprisoned, and exiled him for his leadership of dissent on the island.[1] The Cuban activists who made Mella into their most celebrated martyr for the cause of a New Cuba after his death believed—or at least asserted—that Machado was at fault. None of the other explanations allowed for Mella's use as a powerful symbol in the anti-Machado struggle.

Mella died a transnational death—pursued by the Cuban dictator across a border and a sea, exiled but still unsafe. Transnational movement and struggle were familiar to the young Cuban activist. Indeed, much of the mystery surrounding Mella's death resulted from a life lived transnationally.[2] Mella's identity was, like many Cubans of the era, transnational in terms of both genealogy and migration. He and his brother were the illegitimate sons of an Irishwoman who had lived in the United States, then Cuba, and a man born in the Dominican Republic, who had lived in France before settling in Cuba. The boys went with their mother when she returned to the United States, but they came back to the island to live with their father and stepmother when their mother's new husband forbade her children from living in his household.[3] Mella's experience straddling countries and navigating disparate identities endowed him with flexibility and adaptability—his identity was transnational, and that served his activism, as transnational identities would later serve Cuban antifascists. He consciously became Cuban when he changed his given name, Nicanor McPartland, to Julio Antonio Mella. As a Cuban activist, Mella would be known for the way in which his political thought and activism encompassed various efforts of earlier Cuban revolutionary thinkers and leaders from multiple ideological camps and organized multiple constituencies, from middle-class university students to veterans of Cuba's nineteenth-century wars of independence to Havana's working class. A widely beloved leader whose good looks, charisma, and athletic prowess enhanced the adoration of his followers, Mella had become a nucleus of the movement for change and one of its most iconic leaders by the late 1920s. His death, then, ended one decade of possibility and left his *compañeros* to begin the next chapter of struggle for a New Cuba.[4]

There were two Old Cubas, each corresponding to a different historical era. One Old Cuba involved centuries of Spanish colonial rule, characterized by exploitation and slavery. Cubans ended Spanish rule after thirty years of intermittent fighting against Spain during three late nineteenth-century wars of independence, but it nevertheless cast a long shadow over the Republic. Cuba's anticolonial struggle against Spain remained in the 1920s and 1930s in the form of living veterans, in popular memory and legends, and in the writings of independence thinkers—especially José Martí, embraced by a new generation of activists. According to the activists seeking change, the other Old Cuba was the Republic itself, powerfully overshadowed by U.S. control, enjoyed by an elite few, and characterized by instability and injustice. Struggle against the second Old Cuba existed in multiple complex and often conflicting forms throughout Cuba's Republican period. For example, there were those Cubans who opposed codifying U.S. control in independent Cuba's first constitution by way of the Platt Amendment; the members of the Partido Independiente de Color (Independent Party of Color) who were massacred fighting for racial justice in 1912; and the activists of the 1920s and 1930s, who are the subject of this chapter. The activists of the 1920s and 1930s created multiple competing and complementary visions of a New Cuba during two decades characterized by ideological and political tension and confusion. We begin with the 1920s, a decade that would prove to be, in the words of Robert Whitney, "a time of crisis and transformation and hope and despair."[5]

A Movement Begins, 1920–1924

By 1920 the global context in which Cuban popular politics operated was characterized by flux. The Great War destabilized imperialism around the world, calling into question its inevitability and permanence. The Mexican (1910) and Russian (1917) Revolutions challenged the established order and demonstrated to revolutionaries elsewhere that they might create new political, economic, and social systems.[6] In Latin America a number of key political thinkers, activists, and popular movements espoused revolutionary regionalist, nationalist, anti-imperialist, race-based, and leftist beliefs, all of which resonated in Cuba during a time of turmoil. The people of Cuba suffered a wild ride between the end of World War I and 1924, as Cuba's economy cycled from extraordinary wartime prosperity to a precipitous decline in 1920 and then on to comfortable recovery. Economic instability led to political and social instability. When the "very bottom dropped out of Cuba" in 1920, the devastating economic crisis that followed affected the entire population and sparked severe political and social crises, including a government shutdown, labor strikes, student protests, and popular discontent verging on armed conflict.[7] The aforementioned international examples suggested militant, radical, and revolutionary solutions to many Cubans, and activism surged.[8] A disputed presidential election contributed to the chaos and unrest. In October 1920 the United States intervened—as it had done under the authority of the Platt Amendment in 1906–9, 1912, and 1917—and the U.S. State Department appointed a "Special Representative of the President" to decide the elections and clean up government corruption. Alfredo Zayas stepped into the presidency, and the special representative—General Enoch H. Crowder—stayed on the island for more than two years, forcing sweeping governmental reforms in exchange for approval of a much-needed loan to Cuba. Unable to force Zayas into full compliance, General Crowder issued a series of reform ultimatums and appointed a cabinet of key government ministers in the spring of 1922. Shortly thereafter, Cuba was approved for a $50 million loan.[9]

By 1923 the economy had improved and the government deficit was brought under control—in part because of the loan and in part because of a good sugar harvest combined with improved sugar prices—but four key factors resulted in continued discontent among the Cuban people. First, many on the island desired political change. As soon as Cuba received its coveted loan, the Zayas government reversed the reforms U.S. officials had implemented and resumed pilfering public resources.[10] The president's methodical exploitation of the island's political system for his personal gain and that of his family and cronies followed similar behavior by his predecessors, but due to the extremity and timing of his offenses, he became the iconic corrupt Cuban president.[11] There was widespread disappointment about his reversal of the clean-government reforms. Additionally, many members of the economic elite were furious about being excluded from political power. Discontent across the socioeconomic spectrum led to calls for political change. Second, the economic crisis had laid bare both the financial instability all Cubans faced and the dramatic wealth inequality that left the majority of Cubans in tenuous or desperate conditions. In response, the island's working class engaged in the strongest labor organizing in Cuba since the late nineteenth century. Holding national labor congresses in 1920 and 1925 and building federations of unions—including the influential anarcho-syndicalist Federación Obrera de La Habana (Worker Federation of Havana, or FOH)—Cuban workers and labor activists fought for basic needs as well as broader economic justice. Third, calls for Cuban sovereignty against U.S. interference gained strength in various sectors of society during the early 1920s. Cubans of many different backgrounds and stations in life blamed U.S. power and interference for all of the island's ills, so when they protested against anything, it was also against U.S. presence and those elite Cubans who benefited from neocolonialism. Fourth, identity organizations, such as those organized by women and people of African descent, fought for nationalism and simultaneously for their place in the Cuban nation. Thus, discontent was political, economic, and social, directed against U.S. neocolonialism and Cuban elites in power. Dissent and calls for reform came from throughout the populace, all over the island.[12]

The most unifying activist theme in Cuba was nationalism against U.S. interference. Cubans of various identities, including some elites, joined the call for increased national sovereignty and, more specifically, the abrogation of the widely loathed Platt Amendment. Forced into the Cuban constitution following U.S. intervention in the island's final war of independence, the amendment formalized substantial U.S. control over Cuba's government, foreign relations, economy, public health, and territorial integrity. Cubans opposed to it called it "imperialism" and "neocolonialism."[13] Doing away with the Platt Amendment was probably the only policy proposal on which all Cubans could agree, argues Louis A. Pérez Jr.: "Nothing aroused as much collective Cuban indignation as the amendment did. A source of enduring injury to Cuban national sensibilities, it quickly became the focal point of growing nationalist sentiment."[14]

Nationalism could unify many Cubans in sentiment, but effective organizing would be necessary to unify them into a movement. An important precedent for this movement came in 1923, when veterans of Cuba's wars of independence along with various political leaders organized a reformist protest movement of veterans and patriots. With the prestige of the veterans at its helm, the slogan "For the regeneration of Cuba," and a fundamentally reformist platform, the movement appealed to elite and middle-class Cubans alike. It united old and young activists—energizing the former and legitimizing the latter—against a corrupt and ineffective national government and neocolonial exploitation by U.S. officials and capitalists. The Veterans and Patriots Movement called for measures to clean up the government, protect Cuban workers over foreigners, and grant political rights to women. It lacked, however, effective organizing skills and therefore widespread support beyond the elite and the middle class. Thus, when the Zayas government responded to the movement's demands with unexpected severity, it easily defeated the group with infiltration, denunciation, and help from the United States. As its meetings were disrupted and its leaders imprisoned, the Veterans and Patriots Movement became increasingly radical. By the time it staged an armed rebellion in April 1924, however, there had been too many arrests and too many flights into exile, and the uprising failed. Humiliated and disappointed, many activists of the independence generation gave up. Many of the younger activists in the movement, however, got angry instead, becoming more militant and radical. They came to identify as their goal a complete overhaul of Cuba's politics, economics, and society— in other words, a truly New Cuba.[15]

This movement to regenerate Cuba was a steady stream, a mighty river, an overwhelming flood. It might be dammed, rerouted, or forced underground, but inevitably the pressure would build, the waters rise, the dike burst. It might branch off into tributaries or encompass multiple currents, but despite every seemingly insurmountable difference or faction, it was all one sea of change. The symbolism of Cuban popular politics as water was so ubiquitous that it lingers in the words of historians. Capturing the mindset of so many actors in Cuban popular politics of the 1920s and 1930s, Pérez uses the metaphor to describe the mechanism of activist continuity in the wake of the defeat of the Veterans and Patriots movement: "The reform surge had been contained, at least for the time being. In the course of the next decade the tide of pressure for political change would be channeled into different currents, and Cuba would not be the same."[16]

The Rise of the Machadato, 1924–1930

In 1924, Liberal Party candidate Gerardo Machado ran for president to succeed the unabashedly corrupt Alfredo Zayas. A veteran of Cuba's independence struggle, Machado attempted to channel popular discontent and desire for a New Cuba into electoral politics—and his own campaign. He called his agenda the "Platform of Regeneration," promising many of the reforms the Veterans and Patriots Movement supported, and more. Despite having made a fortune in business with U.S. companies, Machado championed nationalism and called for abrogation of the Platt Amendment. He fully adopted the Cuban rhetoric of reform while reassuring U.S. officials and capital interests that he would ensure a clean government, a safe environment for business, and order on the island, necessary components of the U.S. agenda in Cuba. Order coupled with reform sounded good to many Cubans, too. In a climate of economic instability, political uncertainty, popular agitation, and rising nationalist sentiment, Cubans elected Machado as a reformer who would bring calm and assert Cuba's sovereignty. Immediately, Machado embarked on implementing programs of industrial and agricultural diversification and building infrastructure, and on adjusting important economic policies, such as tariffs. Many Cubans believed that Cuba had found the conduit to reform through electoral politics and that true change was taking place.[17] As leftist Carleton Beals, a U.S. observer who was no fan of the Cuban president, noted in 1933: "The Machado program jibed four-square with popular demands: administrative honesty, public works, no increase in the public debt, no reelection." There was no doubt, Beals admitted, that "Gerardo Machado was the honest choice of the Cuban people" when he was elected. However, after a couple of years, he abandoned his campaign promises and, in Beals's estimation, committed "crimes" against his own people.[18]

The timing of Machado's administration did not bode well for his ability to lead. Economic tremors of the coming global Great Depression hit Cuba shortly after Machado assumed the presidency, draining his ability to succeed in implementing his program of reforms. Starting with sliding sugar prices in 1926, economic crisis on the island spread steadily to sectors beyond the sugar industry. Unemployment went up, wages went down, retail sales slowed, and the government payroll—which had, for better or worse, sustained Cubans in an entrenched system of patronage politics—thinned.[19] Having felt a sense of hope about Machado's reforms, Cubans were disappointed when economic downturn brought the reform momentum to an end, and the elected President Machado transformed into the increasingly vicious strongman Machado. At first, disappointment led to a pause in activism for a New Cuba. Whitney writes of the years 1926–29: "Mass mobilization during these years was at a low ebb in comparison to 1923–24."[20] During the dry spell, "a few idealistic students maintained a rebellious spirit," but outside the Universidad de La Habana (University of Havana), little dissent or activism took place.[21] Workers and the elite political opposition engaged only in small, sporadic acts of protest.[22] The lull in activism, however, was temporary; as economic devastation increased, so, too, did discontent.[23]

Among those maintaining a rebellious spirit was Mella. He was one of the young people who had joined the Veterans and Patriots Movement, only to be frustrated. His disappointment spurred him into greater action. Mella got his start in politics at the University of Havana. In 1922 he led a campus occupation during which students demanded such reforms as free tuition, the firing of bad faculty, and university autonomy from the government.[24] As a university student, Mella believed that the university was a good place to start the renovation of all of Cuba, and he was in large part responsible for making it a vital center of broader activism—yet such change could not come from students alone. Convinced that the agents of change would have to be all types of laborers, Mella sought to unite students, intellectual and professional workers, and manual and service workers in a common cause. Following government repression of the Veterans and Patriots Movement, he led the Universidad Popular José Martí (José Martí Popular University), in which activists from these groups came together from 1923 to 1927 in a collaborative teaching and learning effort that closely resembled long-standing traditions of anarchist education on the island.[25] Mella's political development was characterized by influence from various leftists who had mentored and collaborated with him, including anarcho-syndicalist Alfredo López—his partner in leading the Universidad Popular—and socialist Cuban nationalist Carlos Baliño.[26] In 1925 Mella was one of the founders, along with Baliño, of the Partido Comunista de Cuba (Cuban Communist Party, or PCC). In his embrace of Marxism, however, Mella did not fall easily into step with the PCC and would famously go on to have disputes with Communist leaders and policies. Neither was he ideologically representative of most Cubans of his day in his leftist ideology and commitment. Rather than relegating him to the fringe, however, his inability to fit neatly into any one ideological group made him relatable to many and allowed him to act as a point of connection in the politically diverse movement for a New Cuba. Through his intellect, charisma, and activism, Mella "played a decisive role in creating a Marxist and radical leftist subcurrent within the larger stream of Cuban radical nationalism," writes Whitney.[27] Mella embraced anti-imperialist nationalism to garner the widest possible popular support for the movement for a New Cuba across many potentially factious lines of class, race, ideology, and Cuban geography and to connect the movement to a global swell of anticolonial sentiment that would bolster the Cuban cause with transnational solidarity.[28] Mella's transnational identification set an important precedent. A few years later, *Masas*—the journal of the Liga Anti-Imperialista de Cuba, produced by Mella's professed admirers—would exemplify the ways in which discussions of Cuban domestic problems came to meld with concerns in other countries through transnational solidarity. As discussed in the introduction, its pages would also show the early emergence of antifascism within this Cuban transnational engagement.

Though organizing efforts lacked widespread popular adherence at first, Mella and his *compañeros* kept alive the spirit of struggle, maintaining the current of activism during this dry season in Cuban popular politics. Whitney states that the years 1926–29 "proved to be the calm before the storm."[29] In 1927, in opposition to Machado, student activists organized the Directorio Estudiantil Universitario (University Student Directorate, or DEU); because the government controlled the university administration, they were promptly expelled. The swift defeat quieted the students temporarily, but the strongman's next move aroused their ire and that of the Cuban population in general.[30] Using corruption and intimidation, President Machado maneuvered his way into a new term in office in 1928.[31] Many, including those in the political class, were disgruntled by his antidemocratic power grab, but unrest remained minimal at first. The following year, however, true economic devastation struck as the full force of the Great Depression hit the island, which was already beset by economic malaise. The United States worsened Cuban conditions in 1930 with the Hawley-Smoot Tariff Act, increasing the duty on the island's sugar. The double economic blow resulted in the destruction of Cuba's economy. As the desperation and misery of the Cuban people grew, so did their struggle and revolutionary fervor.[32]

On 10 January 1929, at the start of the year in which the Cuban people would begin to dissent en masse, Mella was assassinated in Mexico City. Out of his violent end, a new generation of student, professional, and intellectual activists emerged, who, feeling the loss of Mella's thoughtful and charismatic leadership, stepped forward to continue the fight for a New Cuba. Mella became a foundational martyr of the cohort of young activists that would come to be known as the Generation of 1930 (or the Generation of the Thirties). Even his physical remains would play a role in popular politics in 1933. True to Mella's character as an organizer and his legacy of working to connect student and intellectual activism to organized labor, this new generation had a genuine—though inevitably imperfect—commitment to diversity in the movement. It was a matter of necessity, not idealism, to connect with Cubans of different classes and race identities and with organizations such as labor unions. Students and intellectuals would make up only one small part of the broad protest that was about to explode across the island.

Discontent had built up over the final years of the 1920s, and a significant anti-Machado popular politics erupted from mid-1929 through 1930 due to extreme economic devastation coupled with increasingly authoritarian governance. Economic downturn and unpopular leaders were both known quantities in Cuba; what was rarer was the widespread agitation that rapidly began to flood the island. No longer just "a few idealistic students," the ranks of popular politics swelled to include impressively large numbers of urban and rural workers, professionals, women's organizations, and even some members of the military. Cuban popular politics at the time was characterized by three general segments. The first was the student movement, which had been fighting since the early 1920s—initially for rights specific to the university but progressively for broader political demands—and was closely connected to urban intellectuals and professionals. The second encompassed organized labor, which retained significant anarchist influence despite a general trend of decline in anarchism on the island, and leftist groups, including the young Communist Party. The third was the traditional political class in opposition to Machado, formalized in 1927 into the Unión Nacionalista (Nationalist Union, or UN) by Liberal Carlos Mendieta, who had been an important leader in the Veterans and Patriots Movement, and including former Cuban president Conservative Mario G. Menocal and his followers.[33] The year 1930 was characterized by the organizing efforts and actions of all three groups.

It was at the beginning of 1930 that the cruelest cuts and blows of the Great Depression began to be felt on the island; at the same time, the Machado government decreed any demonstrations by unregistered organizations as illegal. By March, unrest exploded. The Confederación Nacional Obrera de Cuba (National Worker Confederation of Cuba, or CNOC)—founded with the support of 128 unions at the third National Labor Congress in 1925—organized a general strike, in which an estimated 200,000 workers participated. The strike, directed by the prominent intellectual and activist Rubén Martínez Villena, paralyzed the island before it was broken by government violence. It was not long, however, before workers were once again demonstrating and striking in both urban and rural locations across the country, most notably in a particularly bloody clash at a May Day celebration in Regla. On 19 May a clash between police and thousands of Cuban men, women, and children attending a Unión Nacionalista rally in Artemisa left eight attendees dead and hundreds wounded when soldiers opened fire on the crowd before the event had even begun. The government immediately imprisoned or forced into exile nearly all UN leaders, dramatically weakening the elite opposition's primary organization. However, the economic hardship and state repression experienced by workers, the middle class, and many elites fueled an ever-greater sense of outrage and motivation to fight. Multiple segments of society came together in bloody, desperate solidarity. Throughout 1930, the island's political arena expanded as diverse Cubans increasingly became involved in the fight for a New Cuba.[34]

A Revolutionary Romance in the Fight for a New Cuba, 1930–1935

Pablo de la Torriente Brau and Teté Casuso, a couple in life and in activism, were two of the young Cubans inspired by Mella to fight for change on the island who became ardent antifascists. Interconnected with many people and organizations, Pablo and Teté participated in the anti-Machado, anti-imperialist, anti-Batista, and antifascist movements as activists, thinkers, commentators, and fighters. Their intertwined personal and political experiences in the struggle, and the rich record of thoughtful and passionate writing they left behind, make them worthy guides. Tracing their stories—his largely unknown outside Cuba and hers hardly known at all—through the familiar chronology of Cuba's 1933 revolution and its aftermath illustrates how personal resilience, interpersonal relationships, carefully sustained solidarity, and networks of individuals and groups made possible activist continuity through the tumult and strain of victories and defeats. Study of their trajectory reveals the mechanisms by which the movement for change continued to flow over, around, and under the barriers blocking the way to a New Cuba.

Torriente and Casuso first met in Oriente Province when he was seventeen years old and she, seven. He was, she remembered many decades later in 1961, "an extraordinary boy both physically and mentally" who would tell epic stories, such as those of Homer, to Casuso and other children, and read them works by José Martí. Torriente courted Casuso from the time she was eleven or twelve, at which point her family was living in Havana and Torriente was a student at the university. In her memoir, she stated that Pablo was "like a son" to her parents and remarked on his "offensive of books, poems, and flowers. No girl could have long resisted such a charming courtship, and for me he was a magician who rendered everything beautiful and noble." The courtship was not only charming but also lengthy; they married many years later, when both were adults.[35] Torriente was responsible for shaping Casuso's identity; in fact, he gave her her nickname, Teté, in the first book of stories he published, dedicated "to Teté Casuso, *muchacha*." Writing decades later, Casuso commented: "Many people in Cuba still call me 'Teté Casuso, *muchacha*,' remembering those days when Pablo and I were together."[36] This intimate relationship, built in childhood, served as the architecture of their activism.

Torriente had a genealogy and childhood that symbolized Cuba's old Spanish colonial heritage, its relationship with Spain, and its relationship with Puerto Rico, partner in both late Spanish colonial status and U.S. intervention. Though he identified himself as Cuban, Torriente was born in Puerto Rico, the son of a man born in Spain, Félix de la Torriente Garrido, and a Puerto Rican woman, Graciela Brau. Pablo's maternal grandfather was Salvador Brau, a Puerto Rican writer, politician, and historian who wrote the first history of Puerto Rico. When Pablo was a young boy living in Cuba, his grandfather Brau sent him a copy of Martí's work *La Edad de Oro* (*The Golden Age*) (1889). Brau was Martí's contemporary and, like Martí, an eminent intellectual figure and important proponent of his country's autonomy from Spain.[37] Brau's influence had a strong effect on Pablo, shaping the development of his intellect, talent, morality, and patriotism.[38]

Like his son's, Félix de la Torriente Garrido's nationality was divided between countries. He was the "son of a Cuban and Cuban himself in his sentiments," but he had been born and raised in Spain until the age of five. In 1898, Félix moved from Cuba to Puerto Rico to become secretary to the last Spanish governor of Puerto Rico. On 12 December 1901, Pablo was born in San Juan. From then until 1909, when the family settled in Santiago de Cuba, the family's life was characterized by frequent travel and migration between Puerto Rico, Cuba, and Spain.[39] Pablo had a multinational background, a migratory childhood, and an intellectual and professional-class family scattered among three countries. These attributes would fundamentally shape his character, beliefs, and political trajectory.

Casuso was a child of the economically unstable segment of Cuba's landowning elite. Her father owned a tobacco estate in Pinar del Río and undertook railroad and residential development projects in Oriente. She was born in a small village near Havana, and her early life was rural and migratory around the island, surrounded by nature, agriculture, peasants, and foreign laborers. She recalled hearing "the beat of the bongos" and the sound of "haunting Moorish laments, the *décimas*," echoing across the countryside. She prided herself on being able to ride any horse, no matter how lively, fearlessly and without being thrown, an experience she linked to her later courage in political activism. She described her family's dwelling in Oriente as a "house of cedar" and the one in Pinar del Río as an "old, oversized mansion." Her parents wanted her to study for a professional career, she wrote, "because of the recurrent sugar crises and my father's financial worries." The family arrived in Havana when Teté was eleven, and she enrolled in private school to complete the grades she had missed while living in places without elementary schools. Her parents' fears were realized as another sugar crisis gutted the country's economy and the ensuing recession destroyed the family's fortune. To pay for Teté's school, her father took a government engineering job.[40] The timing of Casuso's chronology and of Cuba's sugar crises indicates that these events took place during the economic downturn that began in 1926, meaning that, to make her continued education possible, her father went to work for the Machado government, which she would devote herself to fighting just a few years later.

Both Torriente and Casuso began to engage with political activism as children. When he was nine years old, Pablo published an article in his school's student magazine in which he expressed his "great ambition: to become a sailor, attain the rank of admiral, direct a large squadron, go to Puerto Rico, and throw out the North Americans who were subjugating the nation," in the words of his sister Zoe.[41] Just about a decade into life and the twentieth century, young Pablo understood U.S. neocolonialism as a central political problem faced by both Puerto Rico and Cuba and envisioned himself as a heroic leader in the struggle against it. Teté saw herself more modestly in terms of her childhood political activism. In the midst of

Machado's scandalous reelection, he made a trip to the United States and, when he returned, ordered all schoolchildren in Havana to greet his ship. Casuso's school, too, was expected to greet Machado, but "the students of the University of Havana had visited the schools and indicated that such an order ought not to be obeyed, and I did not go. It was my first act of civic rebellion," Casuso wrote.[42] As children, then, Pablo and Teté positioned themselves differently in the struggle: he as heroic leader, she as reliable follower. To a great extent, these activists' respective self-images would endure, despite the fact that Casuso would prove her husband's equal in leadership, independent thinking, and courage.

As they fought alongside each other in the early 1930s, Casuso and Torriente were among those who organized at and in connection with the University of Havana, among students, intellectuals, and professionals. While Casuso was a student at the university, Torriente was integrated into the intellectual and professional elite of Havana, having worked since 1923 as a secretary for the eminent Cuban intellectual Fernando Ortiz. Torriente was part of a group of men in their twenties and thirties affiliated with Ortiz—including Rubén Martínez Villena, Juan Marinello, and Raúl Roa—who had similar political and ideological affinities. The same men played important roles in an infamous event that would come to symbolize the leadership of the student-intellectual-professional segment of Cuban popular politics in the anti-Machado struggle.

In the autumn of 1930, university students, many of whom had been expelled for protesting against Machado in 1927, reorganized the DEU and held clandestine organizing meetings. Historical accounts vary, but it is clear that the students were inspired by the courageous public stand taken in an August interview by prominent elder intellectual Enrique José Varona against imperialism and the Machado government. The students wanted to stage an event in Varona's honor, but the government sought to stop them, in part by altering the university's academic calendar. On the day of the planned event, September 30, 1930, the university was fully surrounded and barricaded by police and soldiers, as if they were preparing for battle. Approximately one hundred students protested, joined by some intellectuals and workers. As the protesters began to chant against the regime, the police advanced; the students hurled rocks, and the police retaliated with clubs and guns.[43]

Casuso remembered: "The students ran through the streets shouting protests until the police wagons arrived and began carting them off. None of the students was armed, for at that time we did not dream of such things."[44]

While Teté downplayed the threat of violence from the students, Pablo's sister Zoe emphasized the students' throwing rocks at police officers and shouting "Death to Machado!" and "Down with tyranny!" They did not have firearms, she confirmed, but they put their faith in the fists of the strongest among them, including Pablo. Torriente's friend Raúl Roa commanded his *compañeros* to knock down any police officer who touched them. In an instant, Pablo heard gunshots and fell to the ground. Only when he saw student leader Rafael Trejo González next to him bleeding out did he realize that he had not been shot. A mounted police officer, however, had left him with a serious head wound. Though he lost a great deal of blood, Torriente resumed his life after a month in the hospital; seriously injured worker Isidro Figueroa also recovered. Trejo, however, died the next morning.[45]

Trejo's death was a turning point in the anti-Machado struggle. Though there continued to be multiple contenders for leadership, students moved to the fore. There was a power vacuum created by the decimation of the elite UN in May. The students had fought Machado's dreaded police and sustained injuries and a death, which gave them legitimacy and prominence in the eyes of the wider Cuban population. The 30 September battle at the university brought students down from its hilltop campus and into the national political arena once and for all, making them sympathetic and admirable to the general public. The following day, Machado suspended constitutional guarantees, but the measure failed to silence widespread dissent in the wake of Trejo's death. All over the island, Cubans expressed their support and pledged their solidarity with the students. Their popular outcry fueled unrest, escalating tension.[46]

Not long after leaving the hospital, Torriente published a rousing piece, "¡Arriba muchachos!" ("Up, boys!"), in the student publication *Alma Mater*, calling on the youth of his generation to rise up in revolution. Connecting his words to the popular outrage over Trejo's death, he intended the article to agitate other Cubans into action: "Trejo fell in the streets of Havana . . . Fell, no. He rose up taller than an immense statue, and from the height of a granite pedestal, wrought by his valor and the cowardice of his assassins, he delivers a powerful cry to wake all sleeping consciences: DOWN WITH TYRANNY AND OPPRESSION! . . . DOWN WITH THE REGIME OF ASSASSINATION IN THE BACK! . . . DOWN WITH THE MONOPOLY OF THEFT! . . . DOWN WITH THE DISGRACE THAT CORRUPTS US! . . . This is how the dead speak, those who fall, with their chests facing forward, toward the rough path of dignity and of honor."[47] Using metaphors of fire and water, Pablo imagined a river of revolutionary youth and a flame of revolution. Rise up, he ordered, to clean, "with the pure and rushing torrent of our youth, this, our Republic which they have rotted and sold to the foreigner." Forward, he commanded, "to put all our unmarred spirit into the furnace in which must be forged, by the fire of revolution, the new era of liberty and justice!"[48]

In October 1930, the DEU published a political program that sought to channel popular outrage after Trejo's death and assert its members as leaders. In November the government prohibited a memorial ceremony for Trejo, and protest increased. The government suspended constitutional guarantees and declared a state of siege. Acts of sabotage—such as burning sugarcane, attacking the railroads, cutting communication wires, and ambushing outposts of the Cuban Rural Guard—became commonplace in the countryside. The military patrolled cities and towns and replaced civilian provincial governors. The university and schools across the island were closed. Several prominent newspapers and periodicals were forced to suspend publication, editors were arrested, and government censors monitored those publications still in production. The government shut down the exclusive Havana Yacht Club for allegedly harboring activists, an indication that even elites posed a threat to Machado. In January 1931, the entire membership of the DEU was arrested and imprisoned.[49]

In the summer of 1931, the political elite opposition tried to regroup and make its final attempt at ridding Cuba of Machado. After a legal challenge to the strongman in the Supreme Court failed in June 1931, many on the island looked to elite leaders Mendieta and Menocal to orchestrate a coup or revolution. In August the generation of the wars of independence waged battle one final time. The Rebellion of Río Verde was an armed insurrection carried out by Unión Nacionalista with the intent of provoking the United States to remove Machado. The effort proved to be poorly led, uncoordinated, disorganized, and lacking proper training. The revolt lasted four days and was an utter failure. Dispersed uprisings—one of them led by Antonio Guiteras, who would become an important leader over the next two years—were easily defeated, and both Mendieta and Menocal were captured in Pinar del Río. The mainstream opposition was finished. With many of their leaders among the four hundred arrested after Río Verde, moderate elites quieted their calls for coup or revolution. Many of those disillusioned after the defeat were radicalized, and those who had never believed in moderate solutions in the first place were bolstered in their resolve. The moderate path and the moderate leaders were fatally weakened, and this change opened the way for those who envisioned a different path with different leadership. The possibility of a political settlement to the crisis was thoroughly discredited; calls intensified for overthrowing not just the strongman Machado but the entire system.[50]

One activist organization that gained prominence as the moderate elite opposition lost influence was the Ala Izquierda Estudiantil (Student Left Wing, or AIE, but often called simply the Ala). The group, which counted among its members Torriente and Roa, split off from the DEU to adopt a more radical position, especially with regard to the issue of U.S. imperialism.[51] As some moderates continued to consider U.S. intervention as a possible solution to Cuba's problems after the Río Verde fiasco,[52] the Ala asserted a strong stance against both Machado and U.S. imperialism. In a July 1931 "call to arms" published in the AIE periodical *Línea* (Line) and directed at both students and the general public, Roa made explicit the connection between anti-imperialism and the movement against Machado as it was understood by Ala members. The revolutionary student movement attacked not only Machado, Roa stated, but also "the social classes and foreign interests that maintain and profit from him."[53] Roa's rhetoric was in keeping with the Ala's manifesto from earlier that year—"signed" by imprisoned *compañeros* Roa and Torriente as well as five others in prison and thirty-four *en libertad*—which had called for the overthrow of the "dictatorial government of Machado, faithful servant of Wall Street."[54] Reasserting their anti-imperialism just as elite moderates lost legitimacy—in part for courting U.S. assistance—the students, intellectuals, and professionals of the AIE fully assumed the leadership role that had opened for them after Trejo's death.

Young Cuban activists had formed the AIE in the swell of revolutionary outrage and momentum following Trejo's death; one year later, they were still riding the wave of discontent. In September 1931, Roa wrote a commemorative piece titled "Rafael Trejo y el 30 de septiembre" (Rafael Trejo and the 30th of September) from inside the Castillo del Príncipe prison. Roa used an image of new growth amid barrenness to illustrate the revolutionary movement. He imagined the event of that day as revolutionary and as a "magnificent spring shoot among the desolation and the shadows of an endless winter of horrors." That day was just the beginning, a tender green sprout of revolution that would grow. Trejo's "martyrdom" would be used for the purposes of revolution. "His name is and will be," stated Roa, a "flag of combat we will hoist to all winds."[55] Trejo would not be forgotten. Both Roa and Torriente used the concept of martyrdom expressed by the phrase "Hasta después de muertos somos útiles" (Even after death we are useful) to argue that even after a revolutionary like Trejo or Mella died, he or she would continue to serve the revolutionary cause.[56]

The students actively cultivated Mella's memory to propel their momentum, the martyr serving as an engine and a guide. The Ala manifesto echoed Mella's statements.[57] Casuso, like other participants and observers, attributed the students' involvement in Cuban politics from 1923 to Mella, writing that he had agitated his fellow students by proclaiming in manifestos and at public meetings the truth of Cuba's politics and its colonial position, and demanding autonomy for the university.[58] Torriente's sister Zoe sought to connect her brother to Mella's legacy by asserting decades later that Pablo had contributed money to the fund that paid for Mella to escape Cuba for exile in Mexico.[59] If Mella was top martyr to the student activists, Trejo was a close second. These men served as banners under which activists united. They could be used by their survivors to rally support for the cause—energizing activists, inspiring new participants, and making their deaths serve the continuity of their struggle.

Many activists would die anonymously, however, never to be known widely, let alone celebrated. The suspension of rights, censorship of the press, closure of institutions, and mass surveillance of the populace were accompanied by frequent and widespread arrests, kidnapping, torture, disappearances, and extrajudicial executions. Members of Machado's secret police, the Porra, were often referred to as "henchmen," a term indicative of the fear they induced. Hunting anti-Machado activists like prey, they left blood, bodies, and terrifying absences in their wake, often operating under the so-called *ley de fuego*, or "law of fire," shooting whichever prisoners they pleased by claiming that they were "trying to escape."[60] In some cases, such as that of influential anarcho-syndicalist and Mella collaborator Alfredo López, disappeared individuals' physical remains stayed unrecovered for years. (López was kidnapped and executed by Machado's forces in 1926, as many radical working-class activists—especially anarcho-syndicalists like López, who were leaders in powerful networks of organized labor—had been persecuted by the Machado government long before other, more elite Cubans.) By 1931 it became evident that the treatment of anarcho-syndicalists and other committed non-elite radicals early in Machado's presidency had been a preview of what was to come for the broader populace.[61]

Summarizing the conditions on the island, Pérez writes that "Cuba assumed the appearance of an armed camp, and terror became the principal means of government. The government physically eliminated opposition, real and suspected."[62] Activists like Torriente and Roa, who were, in Casuso's words, "in the thick of the political agitation to clean up the government and free Cuba from its colonial status," moved repeatedly from the fight to prison to exile and back again.[63] As they traveled between locations, they worked to maintain the struggle. In New York City, for example, a group of Cuban political exiles—including Torriente, according to his sister—formed the Club Cubano Julio Antonio Mella, which would serve as an important center of Cuban organizing for years to come.[64] Though they were imprisoned and forced into exile, often multiple times, activists fought back against Machado at every opportunity, demonstrating their resilience in the face of defeat after defeat. As the government's violence increased, so, too, did that of the opposition. Destruction and bloodshed escalated, and the struggle took on the character of war across the island, in cities, towns, and rural areas. As the warlike conflict intensified, it appeared more and more certain that it would result in a radical, revolutionary end and that any moderate political solution would be drowned by the currents of discontent.[65]

As the economic and social crisis of the Great Depression created increasing chaos and desperation in Cuba and as the revolutionary movement gained momentum, Machado began to lose control of the country. Meanwhile, U.S. president Franklin Delano Roosevelt replaced former U.S. president Theodore Roosevelt's "Big Stick" policy with his own "Good Neighbor" policy. In May 1933, he sent Sumner Welles to Cuba as a special ambassador to "try to mediate the convulsed country toward a 'peaceful solution' that would avoid the outburst of revolution," as Teté put it.[66] On behalf of the United States and in the Plattist tradition of U.S.-Cuban relations, Welles would attempt to shuffle Cuban elites—with or without Machado—to restore order.[67] Mediation began in late spring of 1933, in which U.S. officials attempted to separate those they considered the "responsible" opposition and avoid revolution.[68] These mediations included representatives of the Machado government and the traditional political elite, the Unión Nacionalista, and many middle-class anti-Machado groups, including secret armed cells such as the revolutionary society known as the ABC, which was a powerful and violent organization of the middle-class nationalist opposition with considerable popular support. Due to its adherence to terrorist attacks as a methodology, the elitism of some of its members, and its rejection of both leftist and liberal positions, the ABC has garnered a characterization as "proto-fascist" from some, especially Marxist intellectuals in revolutionary Cuba. Already in 1932, ABC leaders had felt it necessary to clarify that they were "neither Communists nor fascists" but simply Cubans. ABC participation in U.S.-led mediations, however, did not help to endear the society to other Cuban activist groups, despite its bona fide anti-Machado credentials.

Indeed, participation caused a schism in the society, leading to the exit of some members and the formation of the ABC Radical.[69] To those who did not participate in the mediations—the students (both DEU and AIE), the leftists (including anarchists and the Communist Party), and organized labor—acquiescence to U.S. meddling was treasonous and undesirable even if it might result in Machado's removal. To those left out, the true struggle was against the Cuban dictator *and* U.S. imperialism; a solution that did not do away with both was unsatisfactory.[70] Popular protest would not be easy to contain.

Unrest continued as the mediations took place. Over a two-month period in the spring of 1933, ongoing conflict between students and police left thirty-two students and thirteen police officers dead. Activists for women's rights protested and demanded the vote.[71] In late July, police violence against striking transit workers in Havana inspired sympathy strikes that quickly spread. Soon the capital city was paralyzed by a widespread general strike, and as further police violence led to mounting casualties, the strike began to evolve into a revolutionary confrontation with the government.[72] Communists; Trotskyists; anarchists; long-standing and newly formed worker organizations; women's groups; non-ideological local and regional power holders (*caudillos*); black Cuban groups, some of which were influenced by Garveyism; and radical students, intellectuals, and professionals all contributed to the tumult across the country.[73] No one group or organization could take charge.

Nevertheless, both Cuban and U.S. authorities and the Communists wanted to credit the Communist Party with leadership of the uprising.[74] Machado offered the Communists release of political prisoners, union recognition, and party legality in exchange for ending the strike. Party leaders, believing similarly that they were in charge, jumped at the opportunity and made a deal with the dictator. The Communists were not in charge of the strike, however, and proved powerless to stop it. Their deal with the dictator wounded their reputation and did little for them or for him.[75] From the anarchist perspective, the Communists had betrayed the workers and the people of Cuba. The Federación de Grupos Anarquistas de Cuba (Cuban Federation of Anarchist Groups, or FGAC) issued a manifesto denouncing the Communists as traitors, and the non-Communist FOH, which had anarchist and Trotskyist leadership, kept fighting as part of a general strike propelled by workers who would not give up. Armed conflict between anarchists and Communists followed, marking a serious rupture in the cautious collaboration between Cuba's embattled established leftists and its energetic ascendant ones.[76] This schism would reverberate in the island's popular politics for years, especially during the antifascism of the late 1930s.

Welles made a series of calculated moves to hasten Machado's departure and control its aftermath, convincing the political elites of the traditional parties that their best chance at preserving their position was to follow his lead. Fearful of social revolution from below, many in the moderate opposition chose the path Welles charted. As it turned out, however, the widespread popular unrest was in many ways out of the control of radicals, moderates, and Cuban and U.S. officials alike. The special ambassador succeeded in negotiating a coup with Machado, and the dictator left the country on 12 August 1933. The leader of Machado's army took over the presidency but, just a few hours later, passed it on without incident to Carlos Manuel de Céspedes, son of the famous Cuban independence hero of the same name, but otherwise largely unknown and politically unaffiliated and unvetted.[77] A telegram from Welles to the U.S. secretary of state sent that afternoon was optimistic: "The next few days will probably be difficult but I now have confidence that the situation has been saved and that no further action on the part of the United States Government will be necessary."[78] The forces of order, those who sought to contain popular politics, seemed ascendant. Welles appeared to have obtained the "peaceful solution" he had sought, Casuso remembered. "Then something went wrong."[79]

Machado's departure did little to assuage widespread unrest on the island—indeed, it seemed only to have opened the sluice gates fully. Though Céspedes as a figure was essentially neutral, the situation was anything but. The presidential succession did not result in significant changes in Cuba's political structure and brought no relief from the economic hardship of the Great Depression. Worker occupations and strikes spread. Members of the radical opposition—those who had fought for an end to both Machado's dictatorship and U.S. neocolonialism, such as the student activists and the leftists—rejected the new government's legitimacy and resolved to keep fighting. Victims of the strongman sought revenge and retribution for their suffering, anti-Machado activists meted out vengeance against former Machado officials, and looting and lynching characterized the earliest days of the new administration.[80]

As unrest swelled in the first few days of the Céspedes government, Welles's confident and calm tone became increasingly strained. In a 15 August telegram to the secretary of state, he complained that "utterly lawless student groups" were making the situation difficult to control. "The exiles who are now returning from the United States are unfortunately doing a great deal to increase agitation. They are taking the attitude that a triumphant revolution has placed the Government in power and that they are consequently entitled to dictate the policies of the Government. Furthermore the student group which is the most pernicious element in Cuban public life is constantly issuing inflammatory proclamations and making speeches of the same character over the radio."[81] The special ambassador was referring to young activists like Pablo and Teté. Earlier that year, in May and June alone, two thousand Cuban exiles returned from the United States to the island.[82] Torriente was one of the exiles who had rushed back to Cuba from New York "at the first hint of Machado's fall," in Casuso's words.[83] Radical students, intellectuals, and professionals turned the university into a central location of national politics and attempted to make use of the moment as an opportunity to further their agenda. They held large assemblies to discuss, debate, and vote on issues having to do with the Cuban government and the economy.[84]

The spark that led to the final conflagration of 1933, however, did not come from the students. It did not come from the leftists or the workers or the moderate opposition, though all these groups were responsible for the presence of ample tinder. The ignition came from a group of disgruntled low-ranking members of the Cuban military. A meeting on 3 September to discuss troops' grievances led to a list of demands. When the demands were rejected by officers who abruptly departed the military camp, the sergeants, corporals, and enlistees found themselves unexpectedly in a state of mutiny. One sergeant took command and instructed the troops to hold out for negotiations with officers in a standoff that came to be known as the Sergeants' Revolt. Learning of the mutiny, students and other radical activists hurried to the barracks the next morning and persuaded the soldiers to expand their protest from seeking to negotiate their grievances within the military to overthrowing the Céspedes government. It was this cooperation between military and civilian elements that would prove effective in achieving substantial change—at least for a time.[85]

In the middle of the overthrow, Casuso and Torriente went to the presidential palace, which was occupied by hundreds of students. While there, Casuso saw an army sergeant "curled up and sound asleep" on a Louis XV sofa. He was "disheveled and very thin, with sunken cheeks and a look of utter exhaustion." The man, she noted with a sense of foreboding, was Fulgencio Batista.[86] He was the sergeant who had taken command during the mutiny, refusing to back down until officers negotiated with the soldiers, and the man who led the soldiers into the alliance with the students.[87] Upon that act of bravery turned revolution, Batista would go on to build a powerful, multidecade political career. Many of those who embraced him on 4 September 1933 would soon turn the ire, organization, and activism that had constituted the anti-Machado fight into a fight against Batista.

First, however, there would be the so-called Government of 100 Days. At one o'clock in the morning on 5 September 1933, a revolutionary leadership group formed. Named the Agrupación Revolucionaria de Cuba (Revolutionary Group of Cuba), it issued a proclamation declaring, in part, the intent "to commence the march toward the creation of a new CUBA founded upon the immovable foundations of justice and of the most modern conception of democracy."[88] By that afternoon, the collapse of the Céspedes government was complete. The U.S. special ambassador reported, "Very little disorder took place. Immediately thereafter the Committee of five members of the revolutionary group took possession of the Palace as the executive power of the Cuban Republic." One member Welles described as a radical, two as extreme radicals, one he ignored, and the last member he described as "a supposedly conservative business man of good reputation who is being used as window dressing."[89] In fact, the five members of the provisional government, known as "the Pentarchy," were well-regarded nationalists of differing political stances. The students did not take charge, but their involvement was ubiquitous and their influence undeniable.[90] In Casuso's view, they were "going to be the government's principal support." Roa, Casuso noted, deemed the government an "ephebocracy," or government by teenagers. Due to the many factions of the struggle, however, students were not the only constituency to which the new government was beholden. A vast array of Cubans had been mobilized to overthrow Machado and Céspedes, so for the new government to live up to its mandate, it would need to address the concerns of a multitude. Decisive action was required, and within a week, the Pentarchy proved too unruly to act decisively.[91] Thus, it dissolved on 10 September in favor of a single executive, Ramón Grau San Martín, a professor close to the students.[92]

Teté summarized the optimism felt during this transition by members of the radical opposition and many other Cubans: "Everything connected with mediation was swept away. We were going to have what Mr. Welles and the officers who had helped Machado to flee had tried to prevent. We were going to have a renewal of Cuba, sanctions against the late dictatorship's wrongdoers, improved conditions for labor, autonomy for the university, freedom and equal rights for all."[93] Indeed, while it lasted, the Grau government worked to make sweeping, systemic reforms that, taken together, could have constituted a political, economic, and perhaps even partial social revolution: abrogation of the Platt Amendment, minimum wages, agrarian reform, women's suffrage, university autonomy, and a nationalist labor law requiring 50 percent Cuban citizenship in the workforce.[94] True to the radical opposition out of which they emerged, decision makers in the Government of 100 Days defined the New Cuba they sought in terms of both domestic regeneration and total sovereignty for the island through an end to U.S. imperialism. Though short lived, the brief attempt at a Cuban nationalist government under Grau from September 1933 to January 1934 was hardly insignificant; it marked the first time in its history when the Cuban government answered to neither Spain nor the United States, and represented a jubilantly welcomed moment of hope for some of those who sought a New Cuba.[95]

Buoyant promises of change did not quell the island's chaos, however. The economy remained in shambles, and labor unrest increased after Grau assumed the presidency. Welles's presence in Havana quickly became a great source of tension that delineated factions of the conflict. Army officers, backed by groups that had taken part in the mediation, faced off against the mutinous soldiers led by Batista at the Hotel Nacional, where Welles was staying along with several hundred members of the Machado government. The standoff precipitated the arrival of sixteen U.S. warships in the island's waters, leading many Cubans to fear an invasion.[96] Casuso remembered that marines arrived in the waters of Havana harbor but did not land, succeeding only in rousing anti-imperialist sentiment. "The population of Havana poured out on the quay," Casuso recalled, "shouting 'Get out! Go back to your country! You have no business here!'" Someone fired a revolver at the battleships in a "gesture [that] was ridiculous but symbolic, and was much commented on in the newspapers and in the streets." The confusion of those days is evident in Casuso's recollection: "I was present," she remembered of the confrontation, "though I hardly know how I got there or with whom."[97]

Entering the chaos as if they were a metaphysical benediction upon the struggle, Mella's remains returned to Cuba from Mexico in September 1933. The homecoming had deep significance for many Cubans, especially those who had been personally connected to the murdered activist. In predictably exultant prose, Torriente anticipated the event in an article for the AIE publication *Línea*. Mella, he wrote, was their "precursor, hero, and martyr." He was the first "to insult with word and with action the slobbering senile monster Machado." Mella's remains would be "received by frenetic throngs that applaud[ed] him as a living hero." Victory over the dictator was achieved in Mella's honor. Now the workers and the students could build him a great national monument that, no matter how beautiful it was, would never "shine as much as his simple name, united in a pool of blood with a universal idea: sacrifice for 'the poor of the world,'" wrote Pablo.[98] Anticipation of Mella's return marked a hopeful moment; with Machado gone, possibility ruled the day. In reality, however, on 29 September, at the rally in Mella's honor, the police and the army forced rally participants to disperse.[99] The revolution was not turning out as the activists had planned.

The exhausted army sergeant Casuso saw on the sofa in the presidential palace had not stayed asleep in the halls of power for long. Batista began to position himself as a new strongman leader: he gradually consolidated his power within the military and increasingly allied himself with foreign corporations against workers in the labor unrest that was ongoing in the fall of 1933, then turned his attention to extending control over the police force. In a continually chaotic situation with no end in sight, Batista's growing power and his promise to bring order, stability, and peace positioned him for a classic strongman ascent. Meanwhile, civilian leaders in the new government found themselves embattled, mistrusted, envied, and feared. The old political class—organizations of the moderate opposition such as the Unión Nacionalista—ousted military leaders, and foreign interests denounced Grau's government as too radical, while labor organizations and leftist political groups attacked it as too moderate. The government began to form into factions: centrists and moderates around the president, and radical nationalists and some leftists around his minister of government, Antonio Guiteras (though Guiteras had a troubled relationship with many on the left). Batista was part of the government, but it became increasingly apparent that he was organizing against it. His skillful jockeying for power coupled with divisions among potential opponents brought down Grau.[100] As the fallen president departed for Mexico, throngs of fervent Cubans gathered to see him off.[101] As leader of the Partido Revolucionario Cubano—Auténtico (Authentic Cuban Revolutionary Party, or PRC-A), established in 1934 and commonly known as the Auténticos, Grau would go on to become president of Cuba again from 1944 to 1948. First, however, Batista would control the government through a series of civilian presidents before formally taking office in 1940. Batista made clear that he was exerting power as a new strongman when he precipitated Grau's fall, appointing former opposition leader Carlos Mendieta as president in January 1934 and shifting the allegiance of the armed forces from Grau to the UN head, which the United States quickly sanctioned with an official recognition of the new government.[102] Batista's government encompassed elements of the old opposition, including some leaders of the traditional political parties, the UN, and the ABC—but those factions fought among themselves and chafed against Batista.[103] Outside the new government, many outraged activists for a New Cuba returned to fighting once again.

Not long after the end of the Government of 100 Days, Casuso was part of a group of about twenty student leaders occupying the university, surrounded by Batista's military and police forces. The unarmed youth decided that the armed forces "would have to kill us all if they tried to occupy our alma mater." Soldiers and police fired tear-gas shells at them from nearby roofs, and the students "held out by tying handkerchiefs soaked in vinegar over [their] noses like masks."[104] Casuso's story demonstrates the way in which the political and the personal melded for her and Torriente; her narrative of the university occupation is half revolution, half romance: "Pablo heard of what was happening and came rushing over to share whatever fate was in store for us, to protect me, as he always did in his lifetime. He sprinted between two soldiers and came racing up the great stairway, over a hundred meters high, and reached us safely, gasping, 'Where is Teté?' It is a marvel that he was not shot. I think it was surprise, plus the fact that the soldiers and police thought the university was stacked with arms and ammunition—which was not true—that held them back."[105]

The students won that battle. Sensing perhaps that giving them the coveted victory of university autonomy might weaken their motivation to interfere in the larger political arena, the government capitulated to the students, as it did also in the case of some labor demands. To both students and workers, the government meted out repression while simultaneously claiming to enact the reformist decrees of the Grau administration.[106] Regardless of the government's duplicity, the students celebrated attaining university autonomy, a goal they had long sought. Imagining that she acted in the name of the fallen martyrs, Casuso gave an emotional account of carrying the government decree from the presidential palace to the university, where thousands of students awaited: "I think that that has been for me the most solemn and important occasion of my life. During the automobile ride from the palace to the university I held that scroll in my hand as if I were carrying the sacred fire of a beautiful temple. What I was carrying represented a twelve-year struggle that had begun with Julio Antonio Mella; a struggle during the course of which many dear friends had died, like Mella, without seeing victory."[107] She arrived at the university amphitheater, and *compañeros* pulled Casuso from the car, joyfully shouting, "Teté is bringing the Decree of Autonomy!" Carrying her on their shoulders, the students entered the arena full of excitement. As Casuso wrote, "After prolonged applause and happy laughter, and shouts, and cheers, someone made the announcement that I was going to read the document. Instantly the silence was so profound that the reading resembled a religious ceremony. With what pride did I read that document that meant so much to us! It was the most truly radiant morning of my life."[108]

· · · · · ·

The triumphant wave of Casuso's prose in that section of her memoir crests with her marriage to Torriente in "a lovely church wedding in a hermitage on a hill." It is as if the young Teté on the page is floating, almost literally, with joy: "My immense veil of white tulle was like a cloud." Amid cheers and congratulations, the newlyweds headed off to their life together under a shower of rice—but their moment of happiness did not last. Mid-sentence, politics and struggle reentered Casuso's story and put an end to the honeymoon: "We had a beautiful little apartment . . . in which we spent just one month of our hazardous marital life. After that we were in constant flight from the police and had to sleep in the houses of friends like escaped prisoners."[109] The ellipsis, present in the original, is pregnant with meaning. The reader can imagine Teté pausing as she composed her memoir in 1961, lifting her hands from her typewriter or suspending her pen midair, and contemplating, "What if . . . ?" What was the road not taken; the normal life, free from activist struggle and revolution, from countless disappointments and defeats; the long, happy, married life she and Pablo could have spent and the home they could have made together if not for the role they chose to play? What could have been? Without their personal resilience and that of so many of their *compañeros*, the movement for a New Cuba could not have been sustained over time as it needed to be. Activists like Pablo and Teté made enormous personal sacrifices for the greater political good.

The government's gesture of granting university autonomy, regardless of its intent, did not change much. University autonomy was important for the young activists, but it did not improve the situation of Cuban people generally, so the fight against Batista went on. The students continued to run through the streets, shouting protests against the government and organizing public meetings. These meetings came to be called "hit and run," in honor of the hails of bullets with which they were often met.[110] Batista was intent on returning order to Cuba and used force against not only the student revolutionaries but also the new political threat represented by Grau's Auténticos, the followers of Guiteras who organized the underground group Joven Cuba (Young Cuba), various leftist groups, and, more broadly, the thousands and thousands of workers who struck across the country during 1934 and early 1935.[111]

Backed by Batista's forces, President Mendieta's government immediately confronted the challenge of widespread labor unrest. During the first three months of 1934 alone, there were more than one hundred strikes of sugar mill workers, tobacco workers, miners, railroad and other transportation workers, telephone employees, dock workers, public school teachers, medical professionals, journalists, students, and others, as well as three general strikes of over 200,000 workers each during the year after Grau's fall. In response, the government issued a suite of labor decrees meant to discipline labor while simultaneously upholding—or maintaining the appearance of upholding—the promised positive labor reforms of the Grau administration. Early in 1934, for example, Mendieta implemented an arbitration process overseen by the Ministry of Labor, which Grau had initially created; and early in 1935 Mendieta resurrected Grau's labor exchanges to facilitate employment generally as well as union-based hiring. The government's anti-labor measures, however, were severe. Strikes were legally constrained and then outlawed altogether. Some strikebreakers were members of President Mendieta's UN, former opponents of Machado. Legal measures were put into place to repress and deport "communist" and "foreign" agitators, who were arrested in large numbers. Rights guaranteed by the nation's constitution were revoked. Organized labor interpreted these measures as hostile while continuing to feel the strain of extreme economic peril, and agitation only intensified.[112] Though the government resistance to and repression of labor were severe, the extent of the unrest and organizing was so great that workers were, in a number of cases, able to make progress through collective bargaining and labor-management agreements over the course of 1934. As spring turned to summer and then fall, five thousand Havana bus drivers went on strike, followed by postal workers, federal employees of multiple ministries, and Havana municipal workers. Employers relied, in many cases, on the government or the army to provide and protect the replacement workers they needed to keep their businesses and offices running, but worker activism threatened to overwhelm Mendieta and Batista. The military occupied the island's two biggest cities, but each severe government measure being met by ongoing worker resistance made the government look weak.[113]

Organized labor and leftist groups struggled with a central weakness of their own. A fundamental obstacle potentially more fatal than government, military, and employers was factionalist disunity. The battle workers waged failed to bring labor and leftist activists into a unified force. The Communists and the CNOC, which they controlled by 1934, faced off against the FOH, which Trotskyists and anarchists led. All other non-Communist leftists, reformists, and smaller groups fought for their place in organized labor on the island.[114] Though anarchists were past their peak in Cuba by the 1930s, the influence of anarchist ideology, strategy, tactics, and education were undeniably still widespread, as was the respect they commanded.[115] In some cases, anarchists partnered with dissident Communists. As the struggle against Machado had unfolded, so, too, had a fight within Cuban communism. Prominent black Cuban unionist and CNOC leader Sandalio Junco, one of Mella's *compañeros* in exile, became a vocal critic of the PCC. He challenged especially the disconnect between Comintern assumptions and imperatives on the one hand and Cuban realities on the other, then a weak point for Cuban Communists. Junco was a founder of the Trotskyist Oposición Comunista de Cuba (Communist Opposition of Cuba, or OCC), in which substantial labor organizations—including the formidable old FOH, of which he became an important leader—collaborated with some members of the Ala Izquierda Estudiantil. The OCC evolved into the Partido Bolchevique Leninista (Bolshevik-Leninist Party, or PBL), Cuba's Trotskyist party founded in Havana in September 1933.[116] Joining Trotsky's followers in other countries, the leaders of the PBL proclaimed themselves independent from the Cuban Communist Party. In opposition to the Communists but also embedded in Cuba's domestic political realities, the PBL aimed to proceed with the workers' struggle toward socialism while integrating the Cuban fights for national sovereignty in alliance with the middle class, and agrarian revolution in alliance with the peasantry.[117] In 1934 the PBL grew to approximately six hundred members—large for a Latin American Trotskyist party at that time—and had ideological and strategic influence in Cuban activism.[118] Cuban Trotskyists were influential for a number of reasons, one of which was the weight of their movement internationally. Another source of their influence was their success at gaining leadership within the labor movement and allying with other Cubans. During the early 1930s, their position in favor of collaboration better positioned them to address Cuban concerns than did Comintern policy during its Third Period, which forbade alliance with non-Communists. Specifically, control over the FOH and allies within the Ala contributed to the Trotskyists' impact in activism. Another important source of their influence was their partnership with Guiteras's Joven Cuba, though the latter, while strengthening the PBL for a time, would ultimately factor prominently in the party's dissipation by absorbing much of its leadership. Additional sources of Trotskyist influence were the threat they posed to the Communists, and the Communists' reaction against them. The violence of the schism within organized labor and the left exploded on the evening of 27 August 1934 when a group of armed Communists who had assembled at CNOC headquarters went to the FOH building. A fight ensued in which one person was killed and several more were wounded. Other violent confrontations took place between the Communists and the Trotskyists, especially in the capital city.[119]

Violence was a common experience for activists during the post-Grau period, when resilience and even survival were challenges. Pablo and Teté lived in fear for their lives during those months, moving from place to place while continuing to organize and fight. Meanwhile, Casuso tried to finish school and start her new married life with Torriente. "It was not easy to concentrate on one's studies in 1934, 1935," she stated. "I would go home, to wherever we were staying at the time, without knowing where my husband was, and sit down with a textbook to study for examinations." One day she got home to study for a test in biology just half an hour after she had seen a murdered friend on the steps of the university: "I opened the book and read a sentence of Claude Bernard's: 'Death is a phenomenon of perfection.' My eyes still filled with the image of my friend's corpse as it had been carried still warm to the university hospital, I threw the book from me violently. Our comrade's death was a phenomenon of absurdity! He had been gentle, intelligent, useful, loved, full of life and illusions. What perfection could his death hold? What did the science of all that stuff know?"[120] Clearly, it was difficult to focus on one's studies under such circumstances.

There would be one last forceful, organized attempt at Cuban revolution by the Generation of the Thirties during that decade. On 19 February 1935, university students went on strike, beginning an action that would rapidly expand to include as many as 500,000 Cubans in the largest general strike in the island's history.[121] Teachers and university employees soon joined the students, and over the next few days, the education strike spread rapidly. By the beginning of March, a range of unions across the country had joined in, and the action had become a general strike encompassing the efforts of middle-class nationalists and reformers, radical leftists, and the organized working class. Leadership of the strike consisted of a body called the Committee of Proletarian Defense. Control over this organization was diverse:

the student movement, the Auténticos, Joven Cuba, the FOH, the Trotsky-ists, and other activist groups all jockeyed for influence. The Communists and the CNOC supported the strike but decided to organize separately from the Committee of Proletarian Defense.[122] Much of the country came to a halt—Santiago de Cuba was shut down completely—and the government teetered on the brink of collapse. Split leadership was indicative of both factionalism and an overall lack of planning and coordination, which would prove to be fatal weaknesses. Also, Batista was determined to crush the massive uprising—stating publicly that the strikers would "fail totally"[123]—and he did not hesitate to do so with every measure of force at his disposal. He ordered the military to take over public transportation, the university, and the postal service, and instructed them to protect replacement workers taking strikers' jobs. He suspended constitutional rights, declared unions illegal, and had workers locked out of their workplaces.[124]

Batista's forces used violence in their strikebreaking. Casuso recalled a report being made to the student leaders by a young man returning from what was to have been a secret worker meeting. He had arrived at the apartment where the meeting was to be held, only to find the door open and the apartment empty—it was "as if buckets of blood had been poured over those floors," Casuso remembered the man saying. "We never knew how many people had died there," she wrote. Those with ties to revolutionary movements were hunted. Torriente, Casuso, and many of their fellow activists were constantly moving during the strike to avoid being caught. Despite the number of strikers and the extent of participation, the uprising collapsed and Batista was victorious. Using language suggesting biblical proportions, Casuso registered the defeat: "And so it came about that Cuba was bathed in blood, and that a newly consolidated dictatorship was able to last another ten years." Zoe shared her sister-in-law's sadness, remembering "the failed strike of March 1935, that fill[ed] the entire citizenry with discouragement." The activists were defeated, at least for the time being. Batista knew that "the energy to resist was exhausted," Casuso conceded. "The ruthless suppression, the collapse of the strike, the closing of the university[,] made it pointless for the more active and known among us to stay[,] and the survivors of that Generation of the Thirties fled to Mexico and the United States." Zoe recalled that with the prisons full and political persecution ongoing, Pablo had to abandon Cuba. "He did not leave until he himself saw that, for the time being, there was nothing to be done in Cuba," Teté concluded. "He was one of the last to go."[125]

These types of activist statements have led scholars to a narrative of rupture, and there are plenty of them to serve as evidence. The story of Pablo Torriente and Teté Casuso, however, is representative of so many who, though defeated and bitterly disappointed in March 1935, were back in action in a matter of months and moved their activism for a New Cuba into transnational antifascism. The personal resilience of these people made possible a political continuity of Cuban activism as antifascism.

2 Support the Brother People of Ethiopia

The Italo-Ethiopian War and Development of
Antifascism in Cuba, 1935–1936

• •

Although undoubtedly distracted by the general strike underway on the island, Cubans reading the popular weekly magazine *Bohemia* in late February and early March 1935 could, if they chose, turn their attention to learning
about Italian Fascist leader Benito Mussolini and his designs on Ethiopia.
Presented without commentary, a piece authored by Il Duce and accompanied
by various images of him—some solemn, others triumphant—proclaimed
fascism to be "the new civilization" and celebrated its solutions to economic crisis in Italy and beyond. The piece might well have left some Cuban readers with a favorable impression of the Italian leader, but such an
opinion would be challenged the very next week, when *Bohemia* followed up
with biting, sarcastic criticism of Mussolini's aggression toward Abyssinia,
as Ethiopia was often called at the time.[1]

Against the backdrop of the general strike and its collapse, a change took
place. On 3 March *Bohemia*'s cover showed the University of Havana's statue
of Alma Mater draped in garland and wreath, and proclaimed: "The Cuban
Student Body Is Standing Up." The cover's subheading enumerated Cuban
grievances and commended the striking students on their "vigorous protest movement" against the government. On 10 March, as the general strike
approached its apex, the magazine's cover showed a different group of young
people on the move: Mussolini's soldiers embarking from Naples on their
way to East Africa as part of a gradual troop and munitions buildup.[2] Over
the previous months, *Bohemia* had primarily covered Cuban domestic concerns, including the recent history of the island, as there was plenty of material for reporting and commentary. During the island's general strike,
however, space devoted to domestic popular politics declined, while space
given to coverage of European fascism's rise expanded dramatically. Mussolini and Hitler became protagonists in *Bohemia*, where Blackshirts and
Nazis marched through its pages.

On 24 March, with the general strike broken and a violent crackdown
underway, *Bohemia* published a weary-sounding editorial. "A summary of

this national moment might be expressed by saying that a great moral and spiritual exhaustion pervades us all," it stated. Cubans were "tired of the futile fight, tired of endless struggle, tired of fruitless efforts. And it is against this fatigue precisely that we must react." Both governors and the governed, the editorial urged, must abandon violence and build a "comprehensive statement of standards and principles adequate to the level of civilization and progress which every free nationality views as a target." Cuba needed peace, but without civic progress, social justice, economic liberation, and spiritual affirmation, any peace achieved would be "fictitious." Thus, while acknowledging the listless disappointment of yet another defeat—this one particularly substantial—the editorial suggested that the struggle should continue. Precisely how it should continue was left up to the reader.[3] Surrounding pages offered scant overt assistance: a photograph of Hitler playing with his dog; another showing a large rally in Nazi salute; a collage proclaiming, "Over the map of Europe the bloody phantom of war casts its tragic shadow"—and among this serious fare, an incongruous photograph showing the purported "world's heaviest child," a three-year-old weighing 125 pounds.[4] The following week, there was more of the same.[5] *Bohemia*, it seems, had little to say—or could say little in an atmosphere of intense repression—about Cuba's popular politics in late March 1935.

The heft of fatigue and pessimism felt by Cubans about political prospects both domestic and global is palpable in these pages, yet the weight or emphasis had subtly shifted. During and immediately following the general strike, as *Bohemia* toned down its reporting on the struggle at home and placed greater importance on foreign fascism, it exemplified a stance that would become widespread among Cubans in the months and years ahead. Amid scant domestic reporting, a full special issue devoted to jubilant celebration of the Spanish Republic's fourth anniversary hinted at the direction this turn would ultimately take.[6] First, though, Mussolini's invasion of Ethiopia would inspire Cuban antifascism to expand.

Cuban Communists in Defense of Ethiopia

The Partido Comunista de Cuba condemned the Italian invasion of Ethiopia, which began early in October 1935.[7] Cuban Communists had already been monitoring fascism, and the buildup to the invasion had been taking place for months, so Il Duce's move came as no surprise. The invasion's timing, however, handed Cuban Communists a propitious opportunity. It came only weeks after official endorsement of the Popular Front policy at the Communist International's Seventh World Congress (July–August 1935) and seemed the perfect rallying point around which to build the antifascist unity new Comintern policy encouraged. Founded in 1925, the relatively young PCC was working to grow and strengthen its influence. Accepting collaboration with Machado during his final days amid the July 1933 general strike seriously harmed Communists' ability to work with other Cubans. Additionally, during the revolutionary struggle against Machado up through the general strike, Cuban Communists had been constrained in their organizing efforts by the Comintern's Third Period policy, which both rejected collaboration with moderates and other leftists and asserted that individuals such as Grau and Guiteras were "social fascists." Third Period policy had deeply harmed Communists' ability to work with other Cubans. For nearly a decade, then, the PCC had struggled to reconcile directives from Moscow with the realities of Cuban life. As opportunities to develop Cuban antifascism emerged following the Comintern's Seventh World Congress, however, Cuban Communists finally found themselves in a position in which international Communist policy and Cuban domestic activism aligned. They were determined not to miss the chance to connect Communism with the goals and aspirations of Cuban activists and the Cuban general public. Accordingly, they advocated their definition of fascism, portrayed it as relevant to Cuban history and present realities on the island, and conceived of antifascism that was both genuinely Cuban and internationalist.

In their published condemnations of Mussolini in Ethiopia, the PCC presented a description of fascism that would become familiar to Cubans over the coming years: Italian Fascists were barbaric, killed women and children, assassinated workers and intellectuals, destroyed the people's rights and freedoms, brought with them crime and terror, reversed progress, and robbed Ethiopia to benefit the powerful Italian capitalists whom Mussolini served. Italian Fascism was expansionist, its action in Ethiopia was imperialist war, and it sought to install "the yoke of slavery" in the African nation despite claiming to have a civilizing mission. Fascist "civilization" was in fact "death and destruction."[8] Such claims not only shocked on a human level but also connected a conflict on the other side of the world to Cuban history, values, and frustrations. Indeed, Communists attempted to explicitly assert ways in which the conflict in Ethiopia was specifically relevant to Cubans and the Cuban domestic political situation. The heroic Ethiopian people, though "weak and poorly armed," were defending their nation against powerful foreigners. They "rose en masse against the fascist invader with the same valor and the same contempt of death with which rose our people in 1895 against the Spanish yoke," the PCC wrote, promoting anti-colonial solidarity. To defend Ethiopia against fascism was to defend its independence and sovereignty against foreign control, a struggle with which Cubans were all too familiar. Communists compared the expansionism of Italian Fascism in Ethiopia not only to Spanish colonialism in Cuba's past but also to the "Yankee imperialism" in its present. The antifascist fight was one for national independence in both countries, against war and imperialism in general, and against Cuba's "dictatorship of Batista and Caffery"—the intertwined ills of strongman rule and U.S. neocolonialism.[9] The people of Havana, "hating imperialist interference in their territory," would come to the aid of the Abyssinian people, Communists claimed optimistically. Envisioning actions like those led by Mella in the 1920s, they hoped that Cubans would organize "mass protests in factories [and in] neighborhoods, with attacks on the embassy and large commercial houses, representatives of Italian fascism."[10]

In keeping with the new Comintern policy of leftist and moderate unity, the PCC attempted to use the Ethiopian cause to build a Cuban Popular Front, aiming its mobilization efforts regarding Ethiopia at Cubans of various political stances, including the Auténticos (followers of Grau, members of the Partido Revolucionario Cubano—Auténtico), Guiteristas (followers of the late Guiteras, members of Joven Cuba), and Agrarios (members of the National Agrarian Party [Partido Agrario Nacional, or PAN]). In statements ostensibly devoted to the cause of Abyssinia, Cuban Communists argued for democratic rights generally; against war, intervention, and fascism globally; against fraudulent elections and for a constituent assembly in Cuba; and for a "popular, revolutionary, anti-imperialist government," presumably in both Ethiopia and Cuba. With these types of goals, Cuban Communists sought to find common ground with domestic political groups.

At the same time, however, they did not neglect to glorify the Soviet Union, their ideological symbolic motherland. "The Soviet Union is the bulwark of world peace!" they proclaimed, "the only great country that does not possess colonies or enslave people." With urgency they wrote that "every man or woman, everyone who loves freedom and hates the barbarism brought to Abyssinia by Mussolini, must be beside the people of Ethiopia, beside the Soviet Union, against the new world war, against fascism and imperialism."[11] (Unsurprisingly, the actual stance of the Soviet Union vis-à-vis the Italo-Ethiopian conflict was more complex than Communist slogans suggested, and equally unsurprisingly, the nature of its stance is contested in the historical literature.)[12] In addition to portraying the Soviet

Union as a worldwide guardian of oppressed peoples, Cuban Communists claimed Communism as the extension of this mission in Cuba: "The Communist Party launches its cry of alarm, and calls all the people to fight against the war and support the brother people of Ethiopia, a victim[,] like us, of imperialist rapacity." Alternating among the cause of Ethiopia, Cuban domestic concerns, and the Communist Party line, Cuban Communists attempted to weave the three together in a fight for people everywhere—a fight waged by Cubans at home directed by the PCC. Their goals, they believed, represented "the cause of our people and all oppressed peoples."[13]

In these Cuban Communist statements on Abyssinia, it becomes impossible to discern the point at which the cause of Ethiopia ends and that of Cuba begins. On the one hand, Communists expressed in these antifascist arguments a type of perfect solidarity, in which the struggles of Ethiopia and Cuba became intertwined in the noble fight against the oppression of dictatorship, imperialism, and fascism. On the other hand, however, Communists did not succeed in analyzing or presenting any specificity about the Ethiopian cause aside from an acknowledgment of the country's independent status on a continent nearly entirely consumed by European colonization. Most Cubans knew few specifics of Ethiopian history or the country's current condition. Communists did not offer such information in their antifascist proclamations concerning the African nation, which contributed to the Cuban population's lack of commitment to the Ethiopian cause. In contrast, black antifascists explained at length the history and the present situation of the country and thus became Cuba's most formidable voices regarding Mussolini's aggression against Ethiopia.

Cubans of African Descent in Defense of Ethiopia

The invasion of Ethiopia occurred during a period of renovation in activism and political participation by Cubans of African descent. During Cuba's republican period, the island's black elites—defined by Melina Pappademos as "those of African descent with significant actionable social, economic, or political power"[14]—established and led associations that acted as both social clubs and political organizations. For the elite Cubans of color able to access them, these black societies offered "uplift, respectability, cultural refinement, and intellectual pursuits," fostering prestige for their leaders and thus helping "privileged blacks generate a robust public presence."[15] Such civic identities, in turn, could translate into important assets for the island's community of color at large. Within republican Cuba's pervasive system of patronage politics, leaders reliably delivered the black vote to politicians in exchange for significant rewards, including access to employment, schools, land, contracts, and other valuable resources.[16] In so doing, they participated alongside other Cubans in a system in which ostensibly democratic electoral politics overlay the ubiquitous reality of dependence on political patronage and public office for employment and livelihood. The central, poorly concealed purpose of involvement in Cuban politics at any level was to distribute resources to one's people, however they were defined.[17] Black societies provided Cubans of African descent with entrance to the game all Cubans were playing.

Through the societies, black elites during Cuba's republican period sought not only material gains in the patronage political system but also inclusion in Cuban nationalism. They developed civic institutions as a means to assert their legitimacy in the island's political and social arenas and to fight racial discrimination and break barriers. Their presence and actions had the positive outcomes of both bringing more resources into the black community than would have arrived otherwise and creating a powerful counter-narrative to white racism in the Cuban public sphere.[18] Though significant, however, the achievements of black elites and their societies did little to advance equality and justice generally or to include Cubans of African descent more meaningfully in the nation. Deep inequality within Cuba's black population persisted, with the elites of the black societies—who represented only 3 percent of the total black Cuban population—"work[ing] very hard to distance themselves from the masses of black Cubans."[19] Thus, despite their achievements, black societies fostered the underlying discontent and tension that emerged in the 1920s and would grow more acute as the 1930s began amid the economic devastation of the Great Depression and the increasing oppression of the Machado regime.

Many Cuban activists of African descent rejected elite black leaders' links to first Machado and later Batista as well as their acquiescence as participants in a political system interpreted as exclusionary, corrupt, and a central source of the island's ills. Leaders of the established black societies, like other Cuban elites, found themselves under attack by new, more radical forces in the early 1930s.[20] Traditional black leaders declared a sense of responsibility to their brethren, but more militant black activists increasingly challenged them, calling into question their intentions and ties to corrupt politicians.[21] These activists accused eminent black organizations, such as the formidable Club Atenas (Athens Club), of having not only intimate ties to the crooked and oppressive government but also elitist pretensions. They organized a renovation of black Cuban activism, creating new societies, such as the Directorio Social Revolucionario "Renacimiento" (Social Revolutionary Directorate "Renaissance") and the Club Adelante (Forward Club). These groups shunned connection to the machinery of the political patronage system and claimed to be, in contrast to the established black societies, truly representative of Cuban people of color.[22] Furthermore, in attempting true representation, they emphasized their connection with the broader radical moment in Cuban politics. The "revolutionary mission of the black youth," stated black Cuban activist Serapio Páez Zamora in the periodical *Adelante* (associated with the club of the same name), consisted of education and indoctrination of the masses and "the recruitment of ethnic factors" to the cause of "common liberation."[23] These emergent black activists made up one important part of the powerful revolutionary current that included diverse Cubans, led to Machado's overthrow, and changed the island's political landscape.[24]

The new black Cuban activism of the 1930s was one realm in which Cuban antifascism grew robust. As they struggled toward a New Cuba not only for black Cubans but also for the island's *clases populares* more broadly, engaging in the domestic fight for "collective betterment,"[25] some of these Cuban activists of African descent came to identify their organizing agenda in antifascist terms, linking their fight at home to the fight against fascism abroad. For many black Cubans, the transnational experiences, networks, and ideas that first facilitated their developing antifascism were those of the African diaspora, in which antifascism flourished, especially directed against Mussolini's invasion of Ethiopia in 1935. Thus, black Cuban activists developed antifascism both as Cubans and as members of this transnational collectivity, and understanding their antifascism requires study of their interwoven cultural, national, and political identities and multilayered goals.

Due to their identification as pan-Africanists, politically active members of the African diaspora mobilized more quickly, more forcefully, more knowledgeably, and with a greater sense of history against Mussolini in Ethiopia than did the movements specific to Cuba's *clases populares*; it is probable that most antifascist Cubans of African descent arrived at their position first through their racial identification—with the possible exception of those who were members of internationalist leftist groups, such as the Communist Party. An understanding of black Cuban antifascism as diasporic, therefore, is fundamental to the study of black Cuban antifascism generally.

Pan-Africanist activists of the black diaspora—from Cuba, the United States, and elsewhere—built transnational antifascist solidarity around the defense of Ethiopia. Ethiopia had a particular resonance within the diaspora that was compelling to many black people regardless of nationality: it served in the diasporic role of symbolic ancestral homeland, more so than even the continent of Africa. Even though the ancestors of most people of African descent in the Americas had come from the western part of the continent, it was this eastern nation that members of the diaspora felt an ultimate duty to protect and renew, and from which they derived the greatest sense of their identity as descendants of Africa. Neither nationhood nor specific location were the most centrally important characteristic of Ethiopia's appeal; the concept of "Ethiopia" was symbolic of African or black identity in general and substantially distinct from the nationality of the country itself.[26] Ancient histories claiming Ethiopia as the progenitor of the magnificent and better-known Egyptian civilization, as well as its favorable references in the Bible, contributed to a sense of Ethiopia as the cradle of all civilization.[27] As one of the first places on earth to have adopted Christianity, Ethiopia signified an "African Jerusalem" to Christians in the African diaspora.[28] Furthermore, many throughout the diaspora believed that biblical prophecy foretold Ethiopia's redemption of the black race from white rule, which, in the historical context of the 1930s, meant European colonial rule.[29] Built on this powerful narrative, the idea of Ethiopia came to represent the dignity and freedom of black people worldwide. For many black people in 1935, protecting Ethiopia from Italy signified self-defense from colonialism and racism.

To point out Ethiopia's weighty symbolic importance is not to discount what some members of the diaspora knew about the realities Ethiopia faced as a nation. Some black Cuban activists elaborated on Ethiopian history and current events in a manner that showed concern for the actual Ethiopia in addition to the symbol. In these cases, though, the specific realities of the nation often served to reinforce its symbolic weight. Ethiopia was one of only two African nations able to maintain sovereignty during the late nineteenth and early twentieth centuries, as European powers divided the rest of the continent into colonies. Liberia also remained sovereign, but black Cubans commenting on Ethiopia often omitted it, claiming Ethiopia as "the only free nation of Africa."[30] The forces of Ethiopian Emperor Menelik II (ruled 1889–1913) defeated Italy's colonizing efforts in 1896, and this defeat of would-be white colonists by an African leader confirmed the strength of Ethiopia as a diasporic symbol. Many believed Ethiopia's redemptive antiracist potential preordained in the Bible had come to fruition. The white man might have conquered and colonized most of the rest of Africa, but in

Ethiopia, the African had fought back—and won. Would that Africans and people of African descent everywhere could assert themselves with similar success against racist oppression and exploitation, went popular thinking within the diaspora. In his 1935 "Ballad of Ethiopia," African American poet Langston Hughes celebrated Ethiopia as the place

> Where the mighty Nile's
> Great headwaters rise
> And the black man's flag
> In bright freedom flies.

According to Hughes and countless other pan-Africanists, Ethiopia *was* African freedom from European colonialism and, by extension, black freedom from racism globally.

In 1935 that sacred freedom was once again under attack. Immediately following jubilant celebration, Hughes turned his "Ballad" into a call for action:

> All you colored peoples,
> No matter where you be,
> Take for your slogan:
> AFRICA BE FREE!

> All you colored peoples,
> Be a man at last,
> Say to Mussolini,
> No! You shall not pass![31]

Ethiopia's symbolic weight—built by legend and history—and its compromised reality in 1935 combined to powerful effect in the black diaspora. The Italian invasion under Mussolini constituted a deep affront that sparked an "international confrontation with fascism that rocked the Pan-African world," argues Robin D. G. Kelley.[32] People of African descent in multiple countries took the Italian attempt to colonize Ethiopia personally, viewing it as an attack on the entire black race and, in some cases, even identifying Ethiopians as their endangered "kinfolk." These interpretations inspired an organized campaign to defend the symbolic homeland and sovereign African nation from a force understood as racist white colonialism.[33] Following Mussolini's aggression, prominent African American activists, such as A. Philip Randolph and W. E. B. Du Bois, contributed to the definition of fascism within the African diaspora as racism and colonialism.[34] With this definition, African Americans brought the fight against Mussolini home. Regardless of prior exposure to the concept of pan-Africanism or the history of African colonization, an African American could find solidarity with a distant people who shared the same race based on the idea of white aggression and oppression. James Yates—African American antifascist organizer and later volunteer for the Republic in the Spanish Civil War—recalled asking a man on the street in Harlem about a rally taking place and being told, "Why, man, don't you know? That Mussolini has invaded the homeland of Ethiopia!"[35] Activists were defining distant geopolitics as immediate and local, viewing the transnational as domestic, even familial and personal.

Cubans of African descent, too, constructed a concept of fascism as racism and colonialism. Perhaps more so than their African American counterparts, black Cubans felt the significance of Ethiopia's potential colonization as a powerful and mobilizing force for their antifascism. Cubans of African descent shared with African Americans the experience of racism but had a much closer view of colonization by a foreign power than did their North American counterparts. Cubans of African descent, along with other Cubans, were in the midst of a fight against U.S. neocolonialism. The immediacy of this domestic concern as a source of inspiration for black Cuban antifascism stood alongside the long-standing and profound symbolic weight of Ethiopia on the island.

At least as early as 1812, the idea of the African nation played a powerful role in the struggle of Cubans of African descent. Ada Ferrer details the deep significance of Ethiopia to the 1812 Aponte Rebellion, during which people of African descent in Cuba rose up to liberate slaves and imagined, in Ferrer's phrase echoing Alejo Carpentier, "the next black kingdom of their world."[36] In the black Atlantic context of the time, people of African descent in multiple locations—including the recently established nations of the United States and Haiti—invoked Ethiopia. The Cuban conspirators attempting their own great feats of change in 1812 imagined the African nation as "majestic and powerful," sovereign, not only Christian but in fact biblical, politically and spiritually mighty, ruled by a black monarch, protected by black armies, and able to send envoys to Europe as a respected ally.[37] Just like members of the black diaspora for many decades to come, early nineteenth-century people of African descent in the Americas claimed Ethiopia as their own, as fundamental to their personal identities, and honored it in the names of their organizations. Whites made a similar identification, calling people of African descent "Ethiopian"—particularly when they seemed threatening to white dominance.[38] In his struggle against slavery, racial subordination, and perhaps even colonial rule by Spain, José Antonio Aponte used Ethiopia as inspiration, a source of strength, and a goal. Just as it would be more than 120 years later, Ethiopia was for the rebels in 1812 a legendary past, a prideworthy present, and a deeply desired future.[39]

Later in the nineteenth century, Ethiopian and Cuban histories would parallel each other. In 1895, Cubans began their final war of independence against Spanish colonial rule; in 1898, they entered into a tense and complex relationship with the ascendant imperial power of the United States during the Spanish-American War, which would result in substantially compromised sovereignty for the newly independent Cuba. Meanwhile, in 1895 and 1896, Emperor Menelik II mounted his defense of Ethiopia's sovereignty against an Italian military offensive and colonial invasion. There were scores of differences between the two cases, some of them substantial, but from the perspective of Cubans several decades later, viewing Ethiopia from afar and looking to build solidarity with the African nation, the similarities were enough. The First Italo-Ethiopian War, like the Cuban War of Independence, pitted Goliath against David, a colonial aggressor against a country with fewer resources. Both Cubans and Ethiopians were noble, heroic underdogs. Cuba fought off its age-old colonial "motherland," with which it had much in common, while Ethiopia fought off a foreign would-be colonizer of a different race and culture. For Cubans of African descent, however, this distinction was less clear than it was for Cubans with only Spanish ancestry; considering both cases of anticolonial struggle, Cubans of color could envision black people fighting against white oppression.[40] For them (and some white Cubans), the nineteenth-century wars of independence had been in large part about the abolition of slavery, racial equality, and raceless blood-brotherhood.[41] This interpretation made the anticolonial struggle an antiracist struggle as well, bringing the Cuban–Spanish case closer to the Ethiopian–Italian one. The parallel of the Italian invasion of Ethiopia with the 1898 U.S. incursion into Cuba was perhaps even more obvious. Like the nations of Europe that were colonizing Africa, the United States was in an offensive rather than a defensive position. Indeed, increasing European colonization of Africa is cited among the reasons for U.S. action in Cuba in 1898; the newest player on the world stage wanted its own overseas colonies, too.[42] By intervening in Cuba's war with Spain, the United States frustrated thirty years of anticolonial struggle and significantly— though not single-handedly—set back the substantial antiracist efforts that had been integral to, if not universal within, the independence movement.[43] On this historical basis, Cubans of African descent could easily draw a comparison between their struggle and that of the Ethiopians, understood in terms of anticolonialism and antiracism.

According to one article in the periodical *Adelante*, histories of the two nations were linked directly around the turn of the twentieth century by the mysterious figure Guillermo Enrique Eliseo, a.k.a. William H. Ellis, a man of African descent. In "Menelik y Cuba," contributor José M. Saenz claimed that Ellis was a Cuban born in the city of Santiago de Cuba, who lived in the United States from the age of four, where he adopted an Americanized "psychology" and name and became a successful businessperson on Wall Street and in Mexico. His business interests extended to Ethiopia, Saenz stated, leading him to develop a friendly relationship with Emperor Menelik II and serve as a special envoy to Ethiopia for U.S. president Theodore Roosevelt. Ellis allegedly spoke so beautifully about Cuba to the Ethiopian emperor that Menelik said, "The description you give me of Cuba is so lovely that it must surely be the second country created by God, after Abyssinia."[44] The information presented by Saenz contradicts more recent works on Ellis. His origin is a mystery, and he was known to lie about his identity—though he did serve the United States in a diplomatic capacity in Ethiopia.[45] However, for Cubans, the significance of these stories was not diminished by the uncertainty surrounding Ellis. With evident pride, Saenz sought to present a strong connection between Ethiopia and Cuba, and Ellis provided one specific example of the link.

Some Cubans of African descent strengthened their connection to Ethiopia as symbol and to a pan-Africanist identity during the 1920s through participation in Garveyism, the transnational movement led by Jamaican Marcus Garvey. Native Cubans who joined Garvey's Universal Negro Improvement Association (UNIA) subscribed to the movement's pan-Africanist tenets of racial pride, black nationalism, and African redemption, but—as opposed to Garveyite West Indian immigrants in Cuba—Garveyite *cubanos de color* did so within a context of Cuba's historically based conceptions of "racelessness," Cuban nationalism, and domestic struggles on the island. They strove to fight for racial justice, foster cultural pride in black Cubans, and take part in pan-Africanism "without ceasing to be Cuban,"[46] just as Cuban antifascists of African descent would do ten to fifteen years later. These Garveyites chanted not only "Viva Africa libre!" but also "Viva Cuba libre!" They concerned themselves with the defense of the African "motherland" and of black nationhood in Africa against the colonizing aggression of Europe, conceiving of the defense as being in the interest of all people of African descent, including Cubans.[47] As Garveyites did elsewhere,

Cubans of African descent attending meetings and celebrations would sing "The Universal Ethiopian Anthem."[48] Even if the anthem were not translated into Spanish, as many UNIA materials were,[49] surely Spanish-speaking Cubans would recognize the words *Ethiopia* and *Africa* repeated throughout. "Ethiopia, thou land of our fathers," the song begins, and its chorus declares: "Advance, advance to victory! Let Africa be free!"[50] That this anthem was penned for the diaspora twelve years before the Ethiopian national anthem was created for the actual country of Ethiopia is a fitting reminder of how Ethiopia's symbolic weight was in tension with its reality. What might Ethiopians and other Africans have thought if they encountered Cuban Garveyite women who took on the names of African tribes and competed to be crowned "African Queen" or "Queen of Ethiopia"?[51] Just as had Aponte and his co-conspirators more than a century earlier, Cuban Garveyites venerating Ethiopia in the 1920s drew vital energy from their imagined roots unearthed in this far-off land. The symbolic motherland continued to inform present identities and struggles.

Like Cuban Garveyites of the 1920s, black Cuban antifascists of the 1930s cited Ethiopia's historical and present realities to ground the inspiration they drew from its symbolism. *Adelante*, a nucleus of antifascism among the new generation of black Cuban activists, served as a central platform for elaborating a vision for the defense of Ethiopia that was clearly built on the long tradition of Cuban engagement with the African country as both symbol and reality. Writers in *Adelante* defined fascism as exploitative—capitalist, colonial-imperialist, enslaving, racist—and a brutal menace violently attacking a noble but relatively weak nation. According to black Cuban antifascists, fascism, as a system of capitalist exploitation, served the Italian bourgeoisie seeking to invest in African plantations and mines. As the labor supply for such Italian capitalist endeavors, Ethiopians would work at starvation wages, oppressed and exploited. Capital investment and the acquisition of cheap labor were "economic necessities of capitalism," stated José Luciano Franco, a mixed-race antifascist intellectual, journalist, and activist, who was a member of the Cuban Comité Pro-Abisinia (Pro-Abyssinia Committee), along with poet Nicolás Guillén, a fellow antifascist writer and activist of color.[52] The parallel with Cuba's relationship to the United States— and the earlier relationships of all American countries with their European colonizers—was clear. Cubans were well acquainted with plantations, mines, exploited labor, and oppression in the service of foreign capital. To describe Italian Fascism in Ethiopia in these familiar terms served to render a specific far-off conflict easily intelligible for readers on the island and to build a definition of fascism that resonated with Cubans and connected to their own struggles.

The specific method of capitalist exploitation Italian Fascists sought to employ in Ethiopia was colonization, argued black Cuban antifascists. As a system of colonization, fascism would degrade the free African nation sacred to the black diaspora and strike another blow against freedom generally. The "ferocious war" waged by Italy was destroying the "relative liberty of Ethiopia," wrote Franco.[53] In his poem "Soldados en Abisinia" (Soldiers in Abyssinia), Guillén evoked the Roman Empire, calling Mussolini "son of Caesar," and imagined the fascist effortlessly claiming for Italy "a paper Abyssinia" off a tabletop map of Africa, the essence of overwhelming colonial domination from afar.[54] Cuban antifascists of African descent used the concept of foreign invasion and colonization in their attempts to mobilize broad support on the island for Ethiopia's defense against Mussolini. An anonymous piece in *Adelante* claimed that Italian Fascist attitudes and actions had "engendered lively popular revulsion in all countries because the spirit of justice revolts against a tragic, desperate struggle between a giant and a child, in which, moreover, the giant is wrong." No doubt overstated in its global reach, the claim of "lively popular revulsion" did certainly describe the reaction of some Cubans, especially black Cuban antifascists. Such revulsion was to be expected in Cuba, the article asserted, because the island's historic, economic, and social conditions allowed its people "to comprehend the intensity of the drama which Ethiopia lives today." Not only had Cuba fought heroic wars for liberty against Spain, a country vastly more powerful than itself—just as Ethiopia now did, without modern military capacity in the face of the Italian Fascists' "technical perfection"—but Cuba was, like Ethiopia, a nation "kept prisoner by the influence of great foreign capitals"—in the sense of both metropolises and financial interests—and might at any moment lose what compromised sovereignty it had. The island was "a small country, surrounded by ambitions, harassed by those who see in it, like Mussolini in Abyssinia, a necessary and easy prey."[55] Thus, just as black Cuban antifascists compared the defense of Ethiopia under Emperor Menelik to the Cuban struggles for independence in the 1890s, they compared Ethiopia's defense by Emperor Haile Selassie to their own fight for a New Cuba. Cubans engaged in rhetorical dialogue with the Ethiopian emperor himself. In his famous appeal to the League of Nations in June 1936, Emperor Selassie described "that unequal struggle between a Government commanding more than forty-two million inhabitants, having at its disposal financial, industrial and technical means which enabled it to create unlimited quantities of the most death-dealing weapons, and, on the other hand, a small people of twelve million inhabitants, without arms, without resources having on its side only the justice of its own cause and the promise of the League of Nations."[56] Cuban antifascists who celebrated the valiant actions of this relatively defenseless people against an immensely powerful adversary linked the events in Ethiopia to broader Cuban anticolonial identity.

Cuban antifascists extended the assertion of colonization to one of enslavement.[57] The contention was highly resonant with an African country, though Cuban antifascists would later apply it in the case of Spain. Latin American history taught that slavery was the necessary engine of colonization, and Cuba was a perfect example. When the high mortality of the island's indigenous people threatened to diminish the Spanish colonizers' wealth, wrote economist Alberto Arredondo in *Adelante*, the conquistadores brought slaves from Africa. As other European countries colonized the Americas, they, too, relied on enslaved African labor,[58] and now, similarly, multiple European countries sought to colonize Africa and exploit the labor of Africans. When they referred to slavery, black Cuban antifascists did not confine themselves to referencing enslaved Africans in the transatlantic trade. Rather, they called to mind what Carlos Baliño—a prominent socialist and friend of José Martí—had termed "Cuban slavery," not enslaved Africans brought to the island to labor in captivity but all non-elite Cubans under the yoke of U.S. imperialism, their livelihoods at the mercy of the foreigner exploiters and their Cuban accomplices. Baliño's broad definition of Cuban slavery was useful to black Cuban antifascists because it facilitated solidarity building and because it asserted that black Cubans were the most oppressed due to the harmful legacy of chattel slavery.[59] Black Cuban antifascists adopted this nested definition of slavery to encompass all of the colonized as oppressed and enslaved while giving special consideration to the legacy and the threat of black chattel slavery. They expanded the definition of slavery to build broader solidarity without ignoring the specific historical position of people of African descent. Functionally, concentric definitions of fascism served the same purpose.

If colonization and slavery were inherent to the Italian Fascist invasion of Ethiopia, then so, too, was racism. The expression of fascist racism was the so-called civilizing mission. Inverting the diasporic claim that Ethiopia was the "cradle of civilization," Italian Fascists asserted as their role the job of civilizing the African nation. To justify their colonial aspirations, Franco stated, Italian Fascists used "the absurd pretext of bringing civilization to

Africa's *tierras incultas*" (uncultivated or virgin lands), a notable phrase given the talk of developing plantations.[60] Land for the taking was coupled conveniently with people whose perceived need for education and indoctrination provided a pretext for exploitation. If taking a people's land and forcing them to labor on it were to be acceptable, the justification needed to be that those people were inferior. This process sounded all too familiar to Cubans. Spaniards in the Americas had claimed to "instill a new civilization in peoples of nonexistent, rudimentary, or radically different cultures than that which they brought with them," wrote Arredondo, when in fact Spaniards kept American indigenous peoples in "the most degrading servitude."[61] Exactly the same process was taking place in the European colonization of Africa, Cuban antifascists argued. Mussolini claimed to be bringing civilization (defined as European culture and society) to "savage," "barbaric," or "backwards" people in foreign lands, but the racist "civilizing mission" was purely cynical—a flimsy cover story for rapacious colonization.[62] The antifascist Cuban poet Tomás Borroto Mora expressed this view in a poem about Ethiopia titled "Sintesis" (Synthesis, 1935), written from the point of view of the Italians:

¡Más tierra! ¡más!	More land! More!
. . . la nuestra es ya pequeña,	. . . ours is now small,
¡Es preciso buscar gran extensión!	It is necessary to seek a great extension!
¡Hallad un punto débil! . . . la Etiopía,	Find a weak spot! . . . Ethiopia,
¿Un pretexto? . . . la Civilización.	A pretext? . . . Civilization.[63]

Making reference to the colonial division of the African continent, the poem concluded by pointing out that the non-fascist powers of Europe stood by during Italy's invasion of Ethiopia without intervening because "thieves who retain their plunder cannot handcuff another thief."[64] Antifascist sentiment in these discussions was not strictly directed against fascists only, though it certainly focused on them. Black Cuban antifascism, broadly defined, encompassed the fights against colonization and racism regardless of the perpetrator.

Another way that black Cuban antifascists refuted claims that invading Ethiopia was a civilizing mission was by flipping the narrative of barbarism and savagery on its head. They argued that such assertions were the most basic form of racism and that the fascists were much more barbaric and savage than the Ethiopians. Referencing the Capitoline Wolf from the founding myth of Italy's capital city, Borroto Mora's poem stated provocatively:

"In Rome, the Wolf howls and the Vatican is silent."[65] Condemning both fascist Italy's violence and the Catholic Church's acquiescence while making an accusation of a cynical pretext, Borroto Mora challenged the claims of the civilizing mission. As a grand European city, the center of world Catholicism, and the seat of the mighty Roman Empire of antiquity, Rome should have been a font of human civilization. Instead, it produced horrific violence, which antifascists defined as antithetical to true civilization. To make this point, Cuban antifascists countered fascist civilizing claims by condemning the use of violence against innocent human victims, as well as attacks on civilian targets, urban centers, and buildings of societal and cultural importance. Italian bombs were "destroying defenseless cities."[66] Ethiopia witnessed thousands of women, children, and the elderly "swept away by shrapnel"; decimated in "horrendous massacres conducted by plane," including chemical weapons attacks; and "decapitated by fascist bombs."[67] What savagery, what barbarism in the name of civilization! An illustration published in *Adelante* in February 1936 of a bomb attack from the air foregrounded an Ethiopian mother holding up her infant, blood pouring from its head, and looking to the sky in anguish or supplication or both. A caption identified the horrific scene as "Roman Culture."[68] In 1938 Lucas Pino described the horrors wrought by "crime" in Ethiopia—Italian Fascists "throwing incendiary bombs on defenseless civilians, killing children, the elderly and women, destroying civilization and peoples."[69]

As they accused Italian Fascists of being uncivilized due to such savage violence, black Cuban antifascists emphasized the Ethiopians' humanity and respectability. Ethiopians were not against civilization. The "civilization" they rejected was that of colonization and enslavement, the "alleged civilization of the Europeans" that brought fierce exploitation, the same "civilization" that Europeans gave "to our brothers the American Indians," wrote Vicente Martínez. The Ethiopians' struggle "to preserve their independence through the centuries," fighting "heroically" against the "imperialist pirates of Europe," made them "respectable in every respect."[70] Cuban activists knew they had to establish the humanity and respectability of the Ethiopians, but by proffering such a defense, they fell into dialogue with the fascists on fascist terms, taking the defensive position. For example, in order to cast the Ethiopians as uncivilized, their adversaries reported that they decapitated people and killed priests, and Cuban antifascists rushed to defend such actions.[71] "Every day," complained Martínez about Cuban opinion, "some periodical from the capital conveys gruesome news about alleged acts of barbarism committed by the soldiers of the Negus [King of Ethiopia] or just by some 'fierce' tribesman of Abyssinia." These types of reports, he noted, relied on Italian sources and were not only "intended to present the Abyssinian people as the most ferocious and barbarous in the world" but also "intended to justify the bloody fascist campaign."[72] Martínez wrote, "We admit unreservedly that a good Abyssinian gentleman, driven by a fierce hatred toward the invaders of his homeland, slaughters mercilessly the unfortunate who falls into his hands; we admit also that an Ethiopian 'tribe' beheads a holy soldier of the Pope determined to make them believe that the fascist bombs are blessed by the Heavenly Father and that they should submit meekly to the civilizing intentions of Mussolini."[73] Black Cubans—and Cubans more generally—could empathize in anticolonial solidarity, he suggested, with this "good Abyssinian gentleman" and his "tribe," as they were invaded, attacked, oppressed, and occupied by a foreign power. Violence in self-defense was understandable and justified. "What is more barbarous, to slaughter a Dominican priest or to massacre an entire defenseless people? What is more ferocious, to decapitate an Italian pilot or to cowardly bomb the hospitals and the trucks of the Red Cross, the defenseless villages?"[74] To black Cuban antifascists, the answers to these questions were self-evident.

In describing fascist and antifascist tension around assertions of civilization and barbarism, black Cuban antifascists once again engaged in conversation with the ideas of Haile Selassie, who spoke in terms of contrasting Ethiopian civilization with Italian barbarism. On Italy's use of deadly mustard gas, the emperor crafted an image of sophisticated savagery reaching genocidal proportions:

It was at the time when the operations for the encircling of Makalle were taking place that the Italian command, fearing a rout, followed the procedure which it is now my duty to denounce to the world. Special sprayers were installed on board [sic] aircraft so that they could vaporize, over vast areas of territory, a fine, death-dealing rain. Groups of nine, fifteen, eighteen aircraft followed one another so that the fog issuing from them formed a continuous sheet. It was thus that, as from the end of January, 1936, soldiers, women, children, cattle, rivers, lakes and pastures were drenched continually with this deadly rain. In order to kill off systematically all living creatures, in order to more surely to [sic] poison waters and pastures, the Italian command made its aircraft pass over and over again. That was its chief method of warfare.[75]

Fascist Italy was the clear aggressor in the conflict. Its warmongering against Ethiopia violated the 1928 Treaty of Friendship between the two countries, and its attack against a fellow member of the League of Nations violated various other agreements and norms. Additionally, the would-be colonizer was engaging in "the systematic extermination of a nation," in Selassie's words. Raining down fear and death over Ethiopia, he stated, the Italians honed the "very refinement of barbarism." Such savagery he contrasted with his record of having "never ceased to use all my efforts to bring my country the benefits of civilization, and in particular to establish relations of good neighbourliness with adjacent powers."[76] It seems that Emperor Selassie, too, thought of himself as having a civilizing mission in Ethiopia. Black Cuban antifascists do not appear to have engaged this contradiction with their conception of the emperor. Like Ethiopia itself, Haile Selassie was in many respects more powerful as an inspiring ideal and symbol than as a nuanced, complex reality. Part of the appeal and power of a broadly defined antifascism was its ability to smooth over any discrepancy or disagreement in the name of strength and solidarity against a common enemy.

The Defeat of Ethiopia and Transition to the Defense of the Spanish Republic

By May 1936, black Cubans expressed deep pessimism about events in Ethiopia. Each day the free African nation was losing its territory, while Great Britain, France, and the Soviet Union disappointed black Cubans with their responses. Fascist aggression and the inaction of the world's other powers were equally to blame for Ethiopia's fate, wrote black intellectual and *Adelante* administrator Mariano Salas Aranda. Ethiopia's fate, he argued, was one that foreshadowed world war: "In the end Italy will achieve its desires and Ethiopia will be one more colony in Africa, with the consent of the League of Nations, the Institution which was created for the establishment of peace, so that humanity would not again be plunged into the macabre spectacle of a new war."[77] In the eyes of black Cuban antifascists in 1936, fascist colonization and the complacency of global powers made a new world war inevitable.

It was with the avoidance of future war in mind that *Adelante* printed, over the course of four issues between August and November 1936, a series of declarations made by the exiled emperor Selassie to French scholar Marcel Griaule, translated into Spanish. José Luciano Franco, of the Cuban Comité Pro-Abisinia, oversaw this extensive publication effort, noting his own devotion to the Ethiopian cause, "which is that of the right and the just." The numbers of pages and months devoted to Selassie's words indicate a substantial commitment on the part of the black Cuban periodical to publicize the issue of Ethiopia's defeat at the hands of Italian Fascism. To relate the conflict to his readers, Franco drew a comparison between Ethiopia and the island: Mussolini called the Ethiopians bandits just as the Spaniards had called the soldiers of Cuban independence leaders Antonio Maceo and José Martí thieves. The "tragic and poignant" pages devoted to Selassie's words would bring to every Cuban home "the certainty that fascism, . . . shown in the butchery of our black brothers of Ethiopia, is the most terrible danger that threatens civilization." Franco wished to advertise the terrible truth about "what will be the future war, if the peoples do not stop in time the unleashed desires of all imperialisms." The Ethiopians, he assured Cubans in another statement, which would be echoed in reference to the Spanish Republicans, would keep fighting for their liberty and "for the right to command their own destinies."[78]

People's indifference both globally and in Cuba was also to blame for Ethiopia's plight, claimed prominent Cuban antifascist and Comité Pro-Abisinia member Antonio Penichet. An antifascist in his roles as both an anarchist and a Freemason, Penichet published a scathing incrimination of humanity and his fellow Cubans vis-à-vis Ethiopia's failed defense. Penichet, who was white, accused the world and the Cuban population of recognizing the threat of fascism only once it menaced non-black countries. It took atrocities committed by fascist forces against the civilian populations—and especially the children—of Spain and China for the world to comprehend "the barbarity of the procedure used against Abyssinia," Penichet asserted. Fascism had "razed" and "assassinated" Ethiopian children, youth, women, and the elderly without significant protest, he argued, accusing observers across the globe of "accepting Italy's 'civilizing' claim" and of wanting "to mitigate or conceal the crime and the theft committed against the Abyssinian people." The crime was committed with impunity before an unsympathetic world, he wrote. On the island, the Comité Pro-Abisinia had acted "in an atmosphere of hostile indifference," Penichet chastised fellow Cubans, even though "we had and have in Cuba so many motives to sympathize with Abyssinia." The Spanish case had proven necessary to make Cubans take notice of "the bloody biology of fascism." The plight of China fighting Japanese fascism, Penichet claimed, drew greater attention on the island than had the pain of the Ethiopian people, though it was far more distant.[79] Had fascism been contained in Ethiopia, he asserted, the "somber spectacles" of Spain and China would not exist to horrify public senti-ment.[80] By printing Penichet's article, the black Cuban editors of *Adelante* promoted his condemnation of the Cuban public's indifference.

Indeed, to remark that the volume of documents and number of words written about the Spanish conflict in Cuba far surpasses those about the de-fense of Ethiopia is to make a dramatic understatement. Nationalists' at-tack on the Spanish Republic in July 1936 awoke fervent popular antifascism among Cubans; black Cuban antifascists who had been laboring for the defense of Ethiopia had to decide, at a point when the cause of Ethiopia seemed lost and antifascism was swelling, whether they would switch their focus to the new fight in Spain. *Adelante* expressed concern for Ethiopia far more prominently and voluminously than it did for the Spanish Republic. Nevertheless, many black Cuban antifascists eventually embraced the Span-ish Republican cause; Penichet's rebuke, for example, is accompanied in the black Cuban publication by a poem celebrating Spain's role in advanc-ing the workers of the world.[81]

Black Cuban activists' transition from adherence to the Ethiopian cause to that of the Spanish Republic proceeded gradually. During the first few months of the Spanish Civil War, from August to November 1936, the lengthy declarations of Emperor Selassie featured prominently in *Adelante*, while the periodical generally ignored events taking place in Spain. As time passed and Selassie remained in exile, however, the publication's writers began to pay more attention to the Spanish conflict. Once they did so, they implic-itly declared themselves to be antifascists generally, as opposed to defenders of Ethiopia specifically. Thus, these black Cuban activists served to build up Cuban antifascism in 1935, alongside the Communists, who attempted to organize around the Ethiopian cause. Overlap in Communist Party and black activist concerns and rhetoric in this case was not a coincidence. De-scribing this overlap's transnational context, Alejandra Bronfman writes of the 1930s: "Marxism and communism became intertwined with black radi-calism in a variety of political and cultural movements. Internationally, this period witnessed a surge in mutual interest between people of African de-scent and Marxists."[82] The defense of Ethiopia was a central site of this mu-tual interest. After its defeat, many antifascists of African descent changed the focus of their struggle from Ethiopia to Spain, at times easily and at times with considerable tension.

Though Cuban Communists and others of leftist internationalist politi-cal ideologies had tremendous interest in the conflict in Spain, and though Cubans of Spanish heritage shared that interest for historical and cultural reasons, it was not immediately clear what connection Cubans of African descent and the black diaspora more broadly might have to the defense of the Spanish Republic. These identities were not necessarily mutually exclusive, and Cubans of African descent did, in many cases, support the Spanish Republic as leftists or as people who were partially genealogically or culturally Spanish—or both. However, there were likely some black Cubans who took the diasporic position explored by Kelley: that Spain was a proxy for Ethiopia, a chance for revenge. In fact, the Communist Party produced the slogan "Ethiopia's fate is at stake on the battlefields of Spain," a concept that some people of African descent attacked but many eventually embraced.[83] Since it was known widely that Italian Fascists—as well as German Nazis—were aiding the Spanish Nationalists, black antifascists had the chance to fight Ethiopia's invaders on Spanish soil, either literally as combat volunteers or figuratively through other means of support of the Republic. As William R. Scott put it, "Black volunteers saw in the Spanish conflict an opportunity previously denied them to take up arms against fascism in Ethiopia."[84] Indeed, approximately a dozen Ethiopians traveled to Spain to fight the Spanish Nationalists and their Italian and German allies, including at least one member of the Ethiopian royal family.[85] Kelley quotes this individual as expressing the opportunity for revenge posed by the Spanish conflict: "Madrid is not Addis Ababa. There we had nothing but our justified hatred. Here we have guns, tanks, and aeroplanes."[86] However, a poem written by African American poet Jay N. Hill and published in July 1937 in the *Crisis*—the journal of the National Association for the Advancement of Colored People (NAACP)—crafted an image of this same royal Ethiopian as a "silent man of the past," a reserved and exotic symbol rather than a strong and vengeful fighter, indicating that the tension between Ethiopia as symbol and Ethiopia as reality was ongoing.[87] Nevertheless, many in the black diaspora felt that they could, in reality, fight Ethiopia's war against Mussolini on Spanish soil. African American combat volunteer Oscar Hunter encapsulated this belief in a work of fiction he authored, in which a wounded black soldier explains his reason for volunteering in Spain: "I wanted to go to Ethiopia and fight Mussolini," he says. "This ain't Ethiopia, but it'll do."[88] For black Cuban antifascists, fighting in Spain served as a proxy not only for the defense of Ethiopia but also for their domestic struggle and the fight for a New Cuba.

3   **Cuba's Revolutionary Spirit and the Hopes of Free Spain**

Cuban Martyrs for the Spanish Republic

In the aftermath of the broken general strike of March 1935, Pablo de la Torriente Brau and Teté Casuso left Cuba for New York City. Through victories, defeats, and periods of hope that crested magnificently, only to be dashed upon the rocks of dictatorship and imperialism, they had been on a political and emotional roller coaster for five years. They had felt the jubilation of triumph in Machado's downfall and the intense energy of optimistic momentum during Grau's brief presidency. They had believed for a short time that they were finally going to achieve democratic governance, an end to U.S. neocolonialism, and substantial economic and social progress—a New Cuba. Then their victory fell apart. Batista's rise to power was a significant defeat for those who sought to remake Cuba, one that resulted in discouragement, disillusionment, even despair for many Cubans. It was as if the dam holding back Cuba's revolution, which had broken in 1933, had been rebuilt and the revolutionary waters once again contained.

Contained for the moment, perhaps, but not dried up. An inspiration to many who would come after him, Torriente turned to antifascism as a continuation of and framework for his native struggle. Unlike historians who have declared Cuban popular politics dead after March 1935, Pablo saw them as deadlocked. Though he acknowledged that there was little activists could do on the island for the time being, he asserted that in the end, time would be their "sincere ally." "And the marathon will continue," he wrote in July 1936.[1] If the fight could not take place in Cuba primarily, it would go on transnationally. The fight in Spain and transnational antifascism would give Pablo the opportunity to demonstrate that he and his *compañeros* would not be contained.

In New York, Pablo "worked at anything he could find"—including laboring in a factory, busing tables at the Harvard Club, and waiting tables at Columbia University.[2] After coming home each night exhausted and sore from an eleven-hour shift, he would write articles for publications across the Americas. Teté tried—and failed—to grow accustomed to life as a factory worker and took classes at Columbia.[3] In July 1935, Pablo, Raúl Roa, and other Cuban political activists in exile founded the Organización Revolucionaria Cubana Antiimperialista (Cuban Anti-imperialist Revolutionary Organization, or ORCA), which would operate in New York City, Philadelphia, Tampa, and Miami. ORCA's leadership was made up of Ala Izquierda Estudiantil veterans. The group, strongly influenced by Marxism but unaffiliated with the Communist Party, acted as an important network node, connecting multiple Cuban parties and organizations: the Partido Revolucionario Cubano—Auténtico, the Partido Comunista de Cuba, the Partido Agrario Nacional, and Joven Cuba; internationalist and U.S. leftist organizations, such as the International Labor Defense and the American Civil Liberties Union; U.S., Cuban, and other Latin American individuals concerned with Cuba's freedom from dictatorship and imperialism; and the Spanish American clubs in New York.[4] One such club was the Club José Martí, founded in October 1935 by many of the same Cuban exiles, where they gathered for political, cultural, and social events; participated in athletics; and raised money for ORCA's periodical, *Frente Único* (United Front), which they sent back to the island covertly.[5] Though they were far from home, and the period constituted a lull in mass political activity relative to the preceding years, Cuban activists in exile maintained contacts; organized new groups; planned events; published periodicals; and kept thinking, writing, and hoping. Teté remembered it as a peaceful time for her and Pablo, despite its hardship. "Although never poorer," she wrote, "I think I have never been more content or in better company." She believed it was their "real honeymoon."[6]

Pablo, however, grew frustrated. By the summer of 1936, he felt bored and discouraged. "I haven't told you about activity here," he wrote to Carlos Martínez, a fellow ORCA activist who was in Miami, "because really there isn't any. Anywhere. Everything is dead. And, consequently, we are, too."[7] Everyone was away for the summer, and the Club José Martí was vacant. Maybe he could resurrect it in the winter, when its members returned, but Pablo was beginning to doubt that he would still be in New York come winter.[8] He was irritated by his life there, feeling as though he was wasting his time on menial work. "Here, in a year and a half of political exile, I have done nothing but carry trays and wash dishes. It has made me stupid," he wrote to Juan Marinello.[9] Metaphors of water and fire used elsewhere to describe Cuba's struggle were sullied in New York. Instead of representing cleansing revolutionary change and renewal, water and fire came to signify distraction and inertia. Through the valley between the skyscrapers—"mountains ablaze with eternal fireworks"—a torrent swept Pablo away, spinning him in whirlpools.[10] This was not his river. In New York he was stuck—or, worse yet, had been pulled off course by a riptide.

In this context of feeling stuck in New York, the eruption of conflict in Spain grabbed his attention. The war in Spain, he wrote to Martínez on 28 July, "has had my imagination going full steam these last few days."[11] That same day, he heard that Miguel Angel Quevedo, director of the Havana periodical *Bohemia*, was coming to New York. Pablo had written for *Bohemia* before, and he jumped at the chance to write again. He went to see if Quevedo would publish an article about the repercussions of the Spanish conflict in New York. Quevedo asked him to send a story as soon as possible. Here was some excitement, some activity! That afternoon, he headed down to Union Square for a big rally in support of the Spanish Republic.[12]

As he noted in his article for Quevedo, everyone knew Union Square as the Red Plaza of New York. Men and women gathered there to talk revolution; workers and radicals held rallies. At this rally, Pablo was inspired by the cries of "Long live the Spanish Popular Front!" and the sentiments against Mussolini and Hitler, the red flags and banners in the air, the revolutionary newspaper sellers, and the four thousand people in attendance.[13] The international character of support for the Spanish Republic moved him. Recounting the participation of various political clubs, he remembered their diverse banners: "Not only of the Spaniards. Not only those of the Hispanic Americans. Also those of the German, Italian, Chinese, U.S., and French clubs. And the orators spoke like this also. Nobody understood them but everyone comprehended. There was one who spoke in German. Another in Hebrew. Another in Russian. When one began to speak in Italian, many people, in a friendly nature, exclaimed: 'That's Spanish!' And when the Spanish orators Garriga, García, and Alonso spoke there were giant ovations." One speaker, Pablo recalled, emphasized the significance of the fight for Europe and the world. Another "signaled the importance for Latin America, tied in all respects to Spain, that the revolution there would have and the courage it would give our peoples."[14] Thus, the rally connected with Pablo's core identity and values: it brought together leftist revolutionary activists, intellectuals, and workers; it stirred deep emotion; it had an international character; it concerned "the motherland," as he called Spain; and it demonstrated that the Spanish conflict would have transnational repercussions, including for Spanish American countries. With each of these elements a stick of kindling, Pablo's imagination erupted in flame, as he later described: "And so, remembering the fever with which I had been following the course of the fight in Spain, it was then that the luminous idea exploded in me of going to Spain, to the Spanish revolution, to march with the columns, to capture cities, to speak with the heroes, to see armed children and women."[15] In fact, he had already noted the idea in a 28 July letter, but conception of the plan in the midst of the jubilant rally had a greater literary quality.[16] More accurately, Pablo's transition from boredom to impulse happened as a process rather than in a particular moment, which he acknowledged: "The idea exploded in my brain, and since then it has been setting fire to the great forest of my imagination. But it didn't explode by means of a spark. It was even better, the way they used to set off bombs: by means of a long slow-burning fuse."[17] To enter a foreign war zone across a vast sea was a momentous decision; understandably, it took a little time.

Though the conflict was less than two weeks old when he struck upon the idea, Torriente chastised himself for not thinking of going to Spain earlier, blaming New York for trapping him.[18] Though adrift in exile and separated from Cuba's fight, the activist felt himself drawn gradually back into struggle. Torriente's writings suggest several motivations that drove his decision to go to Spain: a personal sense of duty as well as curiosity, adventure, and excitement; his desires to leave New York and to procure journalism work; the special relationship between Spanish America and "the motherland"; and the international threat of fascism. The endeavor was also partly a romanticized one. He wanted to take part in an event of world significance. He wanted an "opportunity to live" and "to be seen as a man" (which he emphasized despite remarking elsewhere on the heroic role of women in the conflict).[19] In Spain, he would be swept away by the "great river of revolution. To see a people in combat. To meet heroes. To hear the thundering of the cannon and feel the breeze of shrapnel. To contemplate fires and executions. To be close to the great silent whirlpool of death."[20]

Pablo was concerned about the spread of fascism in Europe, but he was particularly concerned about the threat of fascism in the Americas. He believed that if fascism won in Spain, a country with historic and economic ties to Spanish America, "reactionary forces" in Cuba and other Spanish American countries would come together in solidarity, allowing fascism to spread throughout the region.[21] In this interpretation, the fate of Cuba and other Spanish American countries struggling with strongman governments, neocolonialism, and "reactionary forces" depended directly on the outcome of the Spanish conflict. Military power was especially concerning to him. The struggle in Spain was the fight of a people against its army—he returned to this point again and again. And there existed, he exclaimed, "the possibility of the triumph of the people!" The young revolutionary saw this fact as particularly significant for the countries of Spanish America. If the people defeated the army in Spain, then the Spanish Republic would serve as a vital inspiration and model for the revolutionaries and peoples of Spanish America who needed to fight against their armies.[22]

Emphasizing the antagonism between the people and the armed forces, Torriente implied a comparison between Franco in Spain and Batista in Cuba. The ability of Spanish Republicans to put down the military uprising felt crucial in light of the situation in Cuba of rule by a military strongman. Pablo understood that the chances of the Cuban revolution, toward which he, Teté, and so many of their dear friends and compatriots had worked, were dependent on the outcome in Spain. Victory in Spain would be the "prologue" to Cuban revolution; the effort in Cuba would be delayed indefinitely if Spain were lost to fascists.[23] Regarding going to Spain, he wrote, "I believe firmly that I could do much for the Cuban revolution, since it seems clear that the Spanish revolution has profound repercussions for Cuba and there will be countless lessons that will benefit our people given its vibrant imagination."[24] Thus, one of Pablo de la Torriente Brau's most important reasons for participating in the pro-Republican fight in Spain was to learn from its example.

Given this significance of the Spanish conflict for Cuba and the Americas, and given Torriente's particular blend of talents, he envisioned a specific role for himself in Spain. "I go concretely and specifically to Spain for us," he wrote, to use his eyes and his *maquinita*—his little typewriter—to observe, learn from, and convey the lessons Spain had to teach transnationally.[25] As a writer with an identity that encompassed Spain and multiple countries of the Americas, Torriente was well positioned to play the role of a transnational activist-writer. His political convictions and experience would not only serve his writing but also guide his actions more broadly, ultimately leading him into the fight itself. Pablo went to Spain as a journalist and as a student of revolution, two roles that melded and became inseparable in his mind. War reporting was an "extraordinary opportunity" to perform "work of a revolutionary nature."[26] The experience in Spain would be a "course of 'specialization,'" an "apprenticeship" in which he would learn to be a better revolutionary for Cuba.[27]

Despite his belief in the importance of the Spanish conflict for Cuba and the Americas, Pablo still felt the need to justify his choice of switching activist arenas from Cuba to Spain, responding to criticism by those who did not see the continuity between the two that he did. "I do not dispute," he wrote to Ramiro Valdés Daussá, a militant student activist and dear friend, "that I could . . . be of more use in Cuba, for Cuba, today, than in Spain." However, the choice in Spain to accept or reject fascism was, he argued, a matter of life and death for the whole world, particularly "the colonial or semi-colonial countries."[28] It was a critical event in which he felt he must take part.[29]

It was decided: Pablo would go to Spain. There were some practical considerations to be addressed. First, there was Teté. Even before the Union Square rally, Pablo had grappled with how to get her to accompany him. He told Martínez of his plans: "I will try to dupe Teté for the trip there. Now she is finishing a course at Columbia University and in September she will go to Cuba. It might be that she would take advantage of this to visit the motherland, if I can convince her."[30] Teté had struggled emotionally with the violence and losses of the anti-Batista fight. It is possible she would have resisted the idea of reentering violent struggle so soon; her planned return to Cuba in September 1936 indicates as much. "Of course the return would have to be effected in a mood of submission—silently and with acceptance of the status quo that had been imposed by the new ruling caste, the army," she acknowledged. Pablo would not return to the island under such conditions, she stated, but apparently she was prepared to do so even before it was decided that her husband would go to Spain.[31] Having written on 28 July that he would try to convince her to go to Spain instead, Pablo implied on 6 August that Teté would not accompany him. She understood, he believed, "that it is a glorious duty to go there to learn and tell other peoples how liberty was victorious and fascism crushed."[32] When it came to fulfilling that duty, she realized, he wrote, "that when I think that something is a duty, there is no way to impede me from it."[33] He was determined to go, and she acknowledged that he would but she would not. Many years later, she would write of his departure: "He left New York in August, and I returned to Cuba to stay with my parents until he sent for me. In his first letter from Spain, however, he wrote that it was no place for me, and I must not think of going there for the time being."[34] Though his wife had participated side by side with him in the marches, rallies, and day-to-day work of political activism in Cuba for years, Pablo did not view the Spanish Civil War as an appropriate setting for her involvement. In the end, Teté did not make the trip to Spain, though she became a strong antifascist supporter of the Spanish people from afar.

Torriente's second major consideration was logistics, specifically time and money. He suddenly felt pressed for time. There was a boat leaving for Spain in less than two weeks, he wrote on 2 August, but faster boats would leave for France sooner. If he could scrape together the money in time, he would be on one of those.[35] He was trying to finish his novel, *Aventuras del soldado desconocido Cubano* (Adventures of the Cuban unknown soldier), he wrote to Roa on 4 August, and was working on several other projects.[36] One such project, a New York commemoration of the "third anniversary of the fall of the tyrant Machado," was advertised on a flyer promising "speakers who lived through those tragic moments." The event was scheduled for 12 August, which indicated that Pablo and Teté—who would both be featured— intended to remain in the city at least that long.[37] Torriente's letters, however, show that he would have gladly left for Spain before the commemoration. Fighting for Spain's future was more important to him at that moment than remembering Cuba's past, as the fervor of his correspondence indicates. "I have a feverishness bordering on madness about my idea to travel to Spain," he wrote to Roa on 4 August. "If I don't go, it will make me sick."[38] On 6 August he continued to worry about finding a boat to take him to Europe and money to pay for the trip: "I am restless, nervous, irritable. Because there is no boat. Nor have they answered me yet from Cuba, where I asked a periodical for money for the voyage." He tossed and turned at night, preoccupied: "In bed the hours pass . . . one, two, three, four. . . . And I never sleep."[39] Just a few days later, with his plans still unconfirmed, he complained: "I have lost four pounds this week. And if this uncertainty continues, I'll lose until I'm just bones."[40]

Said Roa of his friend: "The fever of the Spanish revolution had taken possession of him, absorbing all his capacity for service, his inexhaustible energy, and his heroic sense of life." Looking back in 1949 on the days described in Torriente's letters from New York, Roa remembered his friend's determination:

Pablo had decided to go to Spain and he was going to go. To impede him, to convince him otherwise, was impossible. In long hours of insomnia, in the momentary gaps [*huecos relampagueantes*] in the brutal work, he saw himself already on the front with the armed people, among *milicianos* [fighters for the Spanish Republic] without fear and without reproach, one more among them, soldier of Spanish liberty, which is to be a soldier of the liberty of the whole world. He guarded his meager savings with generous miserly zeal. He had no other aspiration or thought than collecting funds to pay for the trip.[41]

Torriente did not want to be dissuaded. "Write to me," he commanded poet Gonzalo Mazas Garbayo, his friend and coauthor, "but don't give me any cowardly advice."[42]

Torriente left New York on the ship *Île de France* on 28 August 1936.[43] He arrived in Madrid on 24 September after crossing the Atlantic and spending short periods of time in Brussels, Paris, and Barcelona. His arrival in Spain energized him tremendously. He worked without respite, sponsored by two Communist-affiliated periodicals: *New Masses* of the United States and *El Machete* (The machete) of Mexico. His friend and fellow Cuban exile in New York, Jaime Bofill, served as his interlocutor with the editors of *New Masses*.[44] As Torriente awaited instructions from Bofill, he worked of his own volition.[45] He walked the streets, took notes, and met and interviewed people. He sought and obtained interviews with important figures using his connections with other writers and journalists, such as those made at the Alianza de Intelectuales Antifascistas (Alliance of Antifascist Intellectuals) in Madrid.[46] What he liked best was simply talking with people.[47] In addition to the foreign periodicals that sponsored him, the Cuban magazines *Bohemia, Mediodía,* and *Noticias de Hoy* (Today's news) would publish Torriente's pieces on Spain during the conflict.

In one of his most widely read pieces, Torriente sought to present a seminal revolutionary lesson to his transnational readership: the differences between the Republican and Nationalist sides. The essay, published in both the United States and Cuba, framed the struggle for readers.[48] The piece was based on a strange occurrence. Torriente had traveled to the Sierra de Guadarrama with a column of soldiers led by Francisco "Paco" Galán. Once there, he received a "baptism by fire."[49] He attended meetings of the *milicianos*, suffered the daily shelling by Nationalists, and climbed the parapets. The parapet from which the Republicans fired was close enough to those of the Nationalists that, "as soon as it gets dark," Pablo wrote in October, "little by little speeches start that end with harsh insults." Each side would taunt the other. "Reds!" began the Nationalists, "have you eaten today? Have you smoked?" The Republicans responded: "Yes, fascist, we've got chicken left over." To this the Nationalists cried: "Reds, *hijos de puta!*"[50]

Whatever may have been the actual content of discussion among soldiers between the parapets, that there was discussion at all served as a literary device allowing Pablo to define for his readers the meanings of fascism and antifascism. For example, whereas many spoke from his group, only two or three voices emerged from the opposing parapet, demonstrating, in his view, "that there was less enthusiasm on the side of the enemy." The majority of the interchange was a discussion of the fight itself and the relative positions and merits of each side. Particularly interested in the subject of foreign aid, the enemy directed its attention to Pablo, calling on him to speak, saying, "Comrade, you who come from abroad should speak to tell us what you think of Spain." Torriente took the opportunity to describe the difference between the foreigners who helped the Republicans and those who aided the Nationalists. International support for both sides was a subject of intense debate, with each claiming legitimacy indicated by foreign endorsement. The Nationalists asserted that their foreign participants demonstrated international support: "Italians, Germans, and Moors come because we have the support of the whole world," a priest named Calvo, spokesperson for the Nationalists, stated in Torriente's account. Torriente countered that the foreigners on the Nationalist side were in fact mercenaries, "Italians and Germans, paid by their governments, sent by Hitler and Mussolini." The Italians and Germans who volunteered for the Republic, on the other hand, were those "who fight for the liberty of their countries," Torriente claimed. With the Republican side were the workers of the United States, France, Belgium, Canada, England, and Mexico—the workers of the world. Hispanic Americans, Torriente asserted, "have come here, and there collected money for the cause of the Spanish people, because we are against the Spain which you want to prolong, the old Spain of the exploitation of our people."[51]

Thus, Torriente integrated his Cuban identity into his mission in Spain, and his fierce anticolonialism into his burgeoning antifascism. For Torriente there existed the exploited and the exploiters—these were the real opposing groups, regardless of nationalities or sides in the conflict. Those Nationalists who "have calluses on their hands" would be welcomed "with open arms" by the Republicans if they defected, he said, while the "exploiters" should prepare for death because there was "no hope for them." The exploiters were the only ones truly supportive of the Nationalists, he believed. "The whole world is against you," Torriente told his opponents. "With you are the swine of the world." Conversely, the Nationalists envisioned all good people being with them and the supporters of the Republic as malcontents and troublemakers, in Torriente's account. Claiming that respectable Latin American governments were withdrawing their diplomats from Madrid and thus their support from the Spanish government, Calvo told Torriente: "The America that is with you is nothing but the bad America, which is equal to the bad Spain here."[52]

"You have to know governments are one thing, and people another," Torriente called to the Nationalists. The governments desired by their people—such as in Mexico and Russia—supported the Republic, he argued, while governments that were tyrannical supported the Nationalists. To Torriente, support from these different types of governments was entirely different. Calvo, the Nationalist priest, called Torriente a hypocrite: "You accuse us of using Italian planes and yet you brag that you shoot us with Mexican bullets?" His question gave Torriente the opportunity to expound on the difference between a government and its people, as well as to assert the validity of transnational solidarity and foreign participation in the Spanish conflict. The difference between an Italian plane and a Mexican bullet, Torriente claimed, was the difference between fascism and antifascism: "These Italian planes you are using are the same that bomb the defenseless population of Abyssinia," he stated. "They are the same that Mussolini uses in the name of civilization to crush and assassinate a people, the most heroic in the world." He went on: "You haven't hesitated to turn Spain into a new Abyssinia, and I know that you know what an Italian plane represents." He continued:

> But you don't know what a Mexican bullet represents, and I'm going to tell you. A Mexican bullet has never represented the conquest and the destruction of a people. A Mexican bullet has always represented a fight for the liberty of the people. A Mexican bullet represents for us, the Hispanic Americans, a constant, tireless fight against imperialism. For this reason, fascist, we feel proud to fire at you Mexican bullets, paid for by the Mexican workers, because they are bullets to liberate and not to oppress the people. And this is the difference between the Italian planes you use and the Mexican bullets we use.[53]

With this conclusion, Torriente wrote, the Nationalist parapet exploded with gunfire and angry cries: "Traitor, go back to your country. *Hijo de puta*! How much are they paying you?"[54] In Pablo's interpretation, the correctness of his position in the global fight against fascism was so firm that no further discussion was necessary or even possible.

Torriente claimed from the parapet that transnational solidarity helped to legitimize the Republican cause—certifying it with the approval and support of the working people of many nations. He reported on one concrete form of this solidarity: widespread monetary aid from the Americas to the Spanish Republic. His description emphasized that supporters included people and organizations from Latin America and Anglo-America as well as Spaniards living in those regions. He also asserted that fund-raising efforts were enthusiastic and rapid despite the risks. People in most of the countries of Latin America were managing to collect money for the Spanish cause despite their living under dictatorships. In Cuba, Torriente claimed, the people raised $27,000 in just two days.[55]

The clarity of understanding and purpose Torriente demonstrated in such optimistic assertions faltered as he increasingly faced the grim realities of war. Though there is no indication that his support for the Republic waned, his zeal and focus wavered after a couple of months in the war zone. In a late-November letter to Bofill, he remarked on hearing a piece of music by Chopin on a car radio in a military camp. He thought wistfully of a time when music, for him, consisted of more than "revolutionary hymns sung discordantly by marching companies." The man who had turned on the radio asked Pablo if he liked the piece. "I remember," Torriente wrote, "because the next night, on the same road, he disappeared, probably forever." A jovial man of brilliant wit, loved by all, was now lost in the chaotic fight, replicating experiences Pablo, Teté, and many other Cuban activists had had during their struggle on the island.[56] The sharp and strident idealistic absolutes of Torriente's rhetoric softened in response to the harsh daily experience he was living. A constant assault on Madrid of cannon fire and enemy planes, he wrote, was creating "a type of enraged resignation" in the general population. "I have been very close several times to places where inexpressible tragedies have occurred," he reported. He was standing, as had been his wish, "close to the great silent whirlpool of death." Suddenly, however, he found reporting difficult. He promised Bofill he would try to write another piece about the International Brigades (IB), but he pleaded, "Understand that in these moments it is extraordinarily difficult to write in a journalistic tone."[57]

By the end of November, Torriente was struggling personally, both to continue working and to stay optimistic. After fifteen days of writing no letters to his friends, his letter of 13 December betrayed his annoyance. He had not written because he did not have a spare moment, he stated, but also because he had gotten nothing in return for some time. Minimizing writing, the craft for which he had been known since childhood, he wrote: "And I do not like to write for the pleasure of doing it, because this is time I could spend doing other things." He stated in a terse tone that he had had "formidable war experiences" and that there was general pessimism about the fight. Nevertheless, he went on to describe positive elements of the situation, such as military advances, education efforts in the regiments, and improved discipline among the *milicianos*. He mentioned the weddings taking place among the revolutionaries, marriages affirmed for the time being with the statement: "By the powers invested in me by the laws of war and revolution." He worried he would freeze to death and wondered how he would endure the winter. And then he concluded: "Regards to everyone even though no one remembers to send me anything. I haven't learned anything of the Conference of Buenos Aires or of the latest American successes.[58] And of Cuba, political news, not one bit."[59] Pablo sounded discouraged.

He abandoned his pen and joined with the *milicianos*. It was not honorable, Roa wrote of his friend years later, "to fight with the pen when what was urgently needed was to have a confrontation with bullets."[60] With bombs falling on Madrid, Pablo wrote to Teté: "I cannot stay seated before a typewriter while the city is being bombed. I go out into the street and see the mangled bodies of women, children, beasts of burden. . . . On the radio two women, 'La Pasionaria' and Margarita Nelken, are calling pathetically for all able-bodied men to take up rifles and help defend Madrid. I am going to offer myself as a volunteer. I will fight beside the Spaniards. When the danger is past, I will return to my typewriter."

On 19 December 1936, Torriente was struck by a bullet and killed. He was thirty-five years old. "I learned of his death on the Madrid front in a newspaper," Teté remembered. His body spent three days behind enemy lines before being recovered, his sister Zoe wrote, but her narrative lost track of her brother's remains after this point. They were in a mass grave for dead Republicans, she implied, "awaiting an opportune moment for their final return to Cuba." She asserted that Pablo was "the first Hispanic American to cross the Atlantic to go to the Spanish Revolution, and he will remain there as a symbol of the human solidarity between America and Spain." Teté's conclusion was less grounded—and less hopeful—than her sister-in-law's. "On the fall of the Republic," she wrote, "his remains were carried out by a retreating Cuban, but they have never since been located, and Pablo, like Ignacio Agramonte, of whom he used to tell me when he was a youth of seventeen and I[,] a fascinated girl of seven, has no known grave."[61] Thus, both women acknowledged Torriente's transnationalism in death: Teté envisioned her husband as a kind of nationless ghost, lost in the unknown, while Zoe envisioned her brother as an embedded link between Spain and Cuba across the Atlantic.

It was the latter interpretation that came to define Torriente's legacy: the continuity of struggle from Cuba to Spain. Having died in combat, fighting for the Republic as a foreign volunteer before the majority of foreign volunteers arrived in Spain, Torriente was notable. Even the *Volunteer for Liberty*, the publication of the English-language volunteers in Spain, noted his death, albeit belatedly. In an October 1937 article on Madrid's Alliance of Antifascist Intellectuals, the *Volunteer* stated that some members of the alliance leave "to continue their work as fighters or artists at the front, and they do not come back again," and named Torriente as an example.[62] Cubans marked his battlefield death in commemorative events and published laudatory remembrances, honored him posthumously in poetry, and memorialized his name in the titles of organizations. At a gathering in April 1937 to remember him, several notable Cuban intellectuals and activists spoke: Roberto Agramonte, Emilio Roig de Leuchsenring, Lázaro Peña, Carlos Rafael Rodríguez, and Torriente's dear friend Roa.[63] The *homenaje* (tribute) took place just as the first group of Cuban volunteers from the island was preparing to leave. It was advertised in *Mediodía*, the periodical begun in June 1936, edited by Nicolás Guillén, and active throughout the Spanish conflict. Along with *Facetas de Actualidad Española*, begun in April 1937 specifically to bring news of the war to the island, *Mediodía* would serve as one of the central pro-Republican journalistic voices in Cuba. Both periodicals celebrated Torriente.[64] In a piece for *Facetas*, Roig de Leuchsenring called the Cuban volunteers, especially Torriente, "Creole heroes of liberty."[65] Like Mella and Trejo before him, Pablo became a martyr, his memory celebrated and used by those who survived him. "In your surname," a friend wrote to Zoe, "is rooted Cuba's revolutionary spirit and the hopes of free Spain."[66] Indeed, her brother was transformed in death into a powerful symbol of the struggles of both countries—and the connection between them. Torriente became an iconic figure and an inspiration to other Cubans to continue their fight by traveling to Spain for the defense of the Republic.

Hundreds of Cubans—those on the island and those in exile—followed Torriente's example and volunteered in Spain. Cuba sent more volunteers during the Spanish Civil War than any other Latin American country, volunteers who served in both the International Brigades and the Republican forces as well as in medical, transport, and other support positions. Two Cubans became lieutenant colonels, thirteen became commanders, twenty-seven became captains, and thirty-three became lieutenants. In addition, twenty-two Cubans served as political commissars (one of them Torriente).[67] Though conflicting claims, scattered and incomplete records, the use of pseudonyms and fake passports, and the diverse origin points of the volunteers' voyages make identifying a precise number impossible, estimates suggest that at least 1,067 Cubans participated in the Spanish conflict on the side of the Republic.[68] For comparison, the much larger United States sent only 2,800–3,300 volunteers, according to various estimates.

Although the Spanish Republicans did not receive formal international aid to nearly the same extent as did the Nationalists from Germany and Italy, their cause did attract foreign participation by numerous individual volunteers, the majority of whom served in the International Brigades. The IB were a project of the Comintern, which decided in September 1936 to organize foreign volunteers to aid the Spanish Republic and ordered the Communist Party of France to coordinate recruitment and mobilization. Estimates suggest that more than thirty thousand foreign volunteers arrived at the IB base in Albacete, Spain, over the course of the war. Initially, these recruits made up five International Brigades, traditionally identified by roman numerals: the XI, XII, XIII, XIV, and XV International Brigades. Later, a sixth IB formed and was given an arabic numeral: the 129th International Brigade.

Many Cubans and other Latin Americans served in the IB, particularly if they traveled to Spain from the United States. Cubans with non-Communist leftist affiliations—such as anarchists and Trotskyists—served in military units specific to those ideologies. Additionally, the Republican military invited Spanish speakers to serve in its regular military forces rather than the IB. Hispanic volunteers from the Americas were international, but they were not quite as foreign as other international volunteers. This distinction was especially true of volunteers from Cuba, which had a large Spanish population and a much more recent history as a colony of Spain than most of the other formerly colonized countries (with the exception of Puerto Rico, which also sent volunteers).[69] Thus, Spanish American and especially Cuban volunteers served an intermediary role between Spaniards and other international volunteers—still from abroad but more easily able to integrate.

That the Spanish Civil War was a conflict both Spanish and international placed Spanish American volunteers in a unique position relative to their comrades from non-Hispanic countries. On the one hand, the fight in Spain represented the global struggle between democracy and fascism; on the other, the war resulted from "peculiarly *Spanish* controversies," in the words of Mark Falcoff, such as land reform, the relationship between church and government, the relationship between military and society, and tension between ideals of progress and tradition.[70] While most foreign volunteers in Spain well understood the struggle's international significance, those from Spanish America empathized deeply with Spain's domestic problems, so similar to their own. Unlike most North American and northern European volunteers, "Spanish Americans did not 'discover' the criticality of Spanish issues in the summer of 1936," Falcoff writes.[71] Spanish American volunteers in Spain were better able than their international counterparts to comprehend the totality of the conflict's complex causes. They interpreted the struggle in Spain as one of significance globally, for Spain, and for their own countries. To fight for their homeland, defend "the motherland," and progress toward a better world, Cuban men and a few women crossed the Atlantic and entered a foreign war in which no one required them to fight.[72]

Getting to Spain: Recruitment of Cuban Volunteers and the Transnational Antifascist Network

According to his writings, Torriente came up with the idea of participating in the Spanish Civil War on his own, guided by his feeling of solidarity with "the motherland," his engagement in the leftist milieu of New York City, and his sense of revolutionary continuity from Cuba's domestic struggle; no individual or group recruited him actively. In turn, his involvement and death in the conflict inspired many other Cubans to volunteer. There were some Cuban volunteers who were already in Spain when the conflict broke out, and those who traveled there from elsewhere; the vast majority, however, came directly from the island or from the United States. Recruitment of Cubans to volunteer in Spain took place primarily in two closely linked places: Havana and New York City. Getting Cuban volunteers to Spain involved the same types of logistical challenges Torriente had faced. An organized support system assisted many of the Cubans who followed in Torriente's footsteps; its largest player was international Communism. Cuban Communists recruited and supported the most volunteers—both Communists and non-Communists—of any organization on the island. They coordinated with the efforts of the Comintern as well as Communist Parties from other countries, such as the United States, France, and Spain. The modest strength of the party on the island, compared to the weak Communist presence in many other Latin American countries, likely contributed to the larger number of volunteers from Cuba relative to other countries in the region. Furthermore, the Communists appear to have kept better records than many other organizations on the island, providing a much clearer view of their recruitment efforts than is available, for example, from the anarchists, who also sent volunteers to Spain.[73]

The Cuban Communist Party began its official engagement with the cause of the Spanish Republic in November 1936, following the lead of the Comintern. Long-standing party activist Ramón Nicolau González—a party member since 1926 and Central Committee member since 1929—took on the role of coordinating recruitment.[74] He described a dual intent behind the Cuban Communist Party's recruitment of volunteers to go to Spain. The internationally focused reason for recruitment efforts was to liberate the Spanish people from fascism and other reactionary forces in keeping with international Communist goals at the time. The domestic consideration was that participation in the Spanish conflict would provide military training to Cuban volunteers who would return to the island equipped to participate in "an eventual armed anti-imperialist fight in our country," Nicolau González stated.[75] The latter motivation echoes the argument, expressed by Torriente and others, that the Spanish conflict would teach Cubans lessons they could use in their own efforts.

The work of recruiting, supporting, and transporting volunteers on the island took place clandestinely and faced further difficulties internationally due to the Non-Intervention Agreement (1936)—the international accord meant to keep foreign countries from aiding either side in the Spanish conflict. On 3 December 1937, the Cuban government issued Decreto Presidencial No. 3411, a "decree of impartiality" that made illegal "the activities of associations constituted or which functioned fundamentally to help, morally or materially, belligerent contests in foreign countries."[76] The decree meant the closure of the Círculo Español Socialista (Spanish Socialist Circle, or CES), the Círculo Republicano Español, and the Izquierda Republicana Española on the Republican side, and the Falange Española on the Nationalist side.[77] Many on the Republican side, however, claimed that the decree was "of a fascist character" and, like the Non-Intervention Agreement with which it was meant to comply, targeted Republican supporters while ignoring the Nationalist side.[78] Falange records demonstrate that there were explicit government orders to shutter the organization late in 1937 but that these orders were ineffective, since the government was once again trying to close down the Falange in April 1939.[79] Denise Urcelay-Maragnès claims that the lack of effective enforcement on the Falange was due to assistance from the chief of the national police.[80] On the Republican side, activists founded the Casa de la Cultura y Asistencia Social (House of Culture and Social Assistance) as a legal front in order to continue their work for the Spanish Republic.[81]

The Casa de la Cultura was just one of the methods by which Cuban antifascists worked around Decreto Presidencial No. 3411. Recalling that many in Cuba flouted restrictions and aided the volunteer recruitment effort, Nicolau González described an operational antifascist network of supportive participants across the island. Hotel employees in Havana, "who were

linked to the Party by militancy or sympathy, or, simply, by being supporters of the Spanish Republican government," attended to volunteers from
other towns and provinces staying in the capital prior to their departure.
Two pawnshops in the city with Spanish Republican owners clothed the
volunteers, offering the recruitment commission a discount on prices.
Communists and sympathizers employed by the Cuban secretary of state
took great risks providing passports and other necessary documentation to
Cuban volunteers without official consent and in violation of the presidential decree. Prior to departure, a small committee of doctors examined the
recruits, and, Nicolau González boasted, not one volunteer examined and
approved for combat by the Cuban doctors received any objection from medical officials of the International Brigades upon arrival in Spain. The party
opened a travel agency to handle the voyages of the volunteers and cut down
on the cost of their trips; the agency "saved us fifteen percent on the price
of the tickets," the director of recruitment stated, "and, upon completion of
this mission, remained active operated by the Party for several years."[82]
Such centralized support of recruits at each step of the process was vital in
the quick, coordinated mobilization of hundreds of Cubans to perform the
extraordinary act of crossing the Atlantic to fight in the war in Spain.

Not just volunteers but the recruitment effort itself crossed borders and
oceans. In December 1937, Nicolau González set off on a multinational journey that would take him, prior to his arrival in Spain, to the United States
and France to meet with Communists. In New York City, he remembered,
he visited the Club Cubano Julio Antonio Mella—an important site of Cuban
exile activity—at the request of the U.S. Communist Party (CPUSA), where
he gave a talk detailing pro-Republican work in Cuba.[83] The CPUSA played
a vital role in the recruitment and support of Cuban volunteers from New
York. In 1935 the Comintern had determined that the U.S. party should
oversee and assist the parties of Caribbean nations, and until 1946, Cuban
Communists pledged allegiance to CPUSA general secretary Earl Browder,
at a time when the U.S. party exerted substantial control over the Cuban
party.[84] The U.S. Communist representative most recognizable to Cubans
at the time was African American leader James W. Ford.[85] Called an "old
friend of Cuba and the Cubans" by *Mediodía*, Ford helped to recruit Cuban
volunteers in New York City and to promote the cause of the Spanish Republic on the island.[86] He was an important point of contact between U.S.
and Cuban activists—a Communist link in the transnational antifascist
network—during the Spanish Civil War. Nicolau González continued on

after his stop in New York: first to visit French Communists; then on to Barcelona, where he visited another Club Cubano Julio Antonio Mella; and finally to the front, where he brought an "encouraging message from the distant homeland" to Cuban volunteers.[87]

The Clubs Mella in New York City and Barcelona served as important nodes in the Cuban antifascist network. The New York club was a hub of organizing efforts for Cuban political exiles in the United States. Founded in Washington Heights by Cuban activists exiled for their participation in the anti-Machado struggle and named for their martyred hero, the club became a center of antifascist activism and recruitment during the Spanish Civil War. Italian American volunteer John Tisa, who documented his friendships with many Cubans during the Spanish conflict, recalled that prior to his departure, he had been "directed uptown to the headquarters of the Julio Mella Club, a left-wing organization comprising mainly Cubans, many of whom were refugees from the Batista dictatorship. At this club I met others like myself, with passports, listening to briefings and impatiently eager to leave for Spain."[88] Along with many other Hispanic and Hispanic American organizations in the city that made up the Sociedades Hispanas Confederadas de Ayuda a España (Confederated Hispanic Societies of Aid to Spain), the Cuban club lived the Spanish conflict "with palpable immediacy," in the words of James D. Fernández.[89] The painting by U.S. artist Henry Glintenkamp titled *Club Julio A. Mella (Cuban Workers' Club)* (1937) depicts a multiracial crowd of men and women eating, drinking, smoking, reading, and talking. A famous pro-Republican poster above the head of the painting's central figure visually marks the vibrant connection between the Cuban club and the Spanish Republic in 1937.[90]

As Nicolau González's transnational journey demonstrated, Cuban volunteers in Spain could visit another Club Mella in Barcelona. On its walls hung portraits of Mella and Torriente, as shown in a photograph published in *Mediodía*.[91] Like its counterpart in New York, the Catalan Club Mella was a place of transnational identities and exchanges. Tisa called it "a busy center for visiting North and South Americans, for those on temporary leave and looking for something to do, and for those passing through on their way to the States."[92] The club was also a location for political and military discussions, where, Tisa recalled, "we sat around and talked with some of the members about the course of the war, world developments, and the bold and tireless activities of many Cubans in various units of the army."[93] The Catalan Club Mella institutionalized characteristics of the Cuban struggle on Spanish soil: activists' transnational identities and exchanges, ideological and political debate, evaluation of the progress of the fight, glorification of Cuban combat volunteers, and celebration of martyrs.

Volunteering in Spain: The Cuban Experience as Continuity of Struggle

The large initial group of Cuban volunteers who left from New York joined the U.S. Abraham Lincoln Battalion, the common name for the 17th Battalion of the XV International Brigade (which would come to be known as the Abraham Lincoln Brigade). The 17th Battalion was a unit "composed of men from every State of the Union, Cuba and South America."[94] The XV International Brigade was "the genuine representation of the Popular Front of the world," inclusive of "Britishers, Americans, Canadians, Cubans, Argentines, Catalans, Spaniards: men of all races and colors, men of 26 nations," according to one account, and "plucky U.S., British, Cuban and Canuck lads" as per another.[95] Each of the descriptions from Anglo and Anglo-American perspectives placed some degree of emphasis on Cubans, indicating the conspicuousness of their relative overrepresentation. A celebratory description of the XV International Brigade—published in Madrid in 1938 and titled *The Book of the XV Brigade*—highlighted the diversity of the Abraham Lincoln Battalion and acknowledged the presence in its ranks of Latin Americans more broadly.[96]

Whereas the Abraham Lincoln Battalion was celebrated for its diversity of nationality, race, and ethnicity, Cuban volunteers were notable in particular for their diversity of political aims and ideologies. In the 1930s, activists fighting for a New Cuba were politically and ideologically diverse—they were anti-strongman fighters, anti-imperialists, Cuban nationalists, pan-Americanists, pan-Africanists, reformers, labor unionists, anarchists, socialists, Communists, and Trotskyists, among others. In light of the Communist influence over the international recruitment, Tisa observed that some of the Cubans were Communists, and some "had Marxist sympathies," but others "were just against Batista for his cruelties and let it go at that." They "loved to sing anti-Batista and revolutionary songs and did so at the club [Mella] in Harlem, on the ocean in time with the gentle sway of the ship, and in Spain at the training bases," Tisa remembered. "Each Cuban had his own blood-curdling story of life in Cuba under the fierce dictatorship, and each was going to Spain on a personal mission to fight fascism, for to them the defeat of Hitler, Mussolini, and Franco would be their vengeance on their own dictator, Batista."[97] A close friend of many Cuban volunteers during the Spanish conflict, Tisa encapsulated the idea of antifascism as continuity of the Cuban struggle.

English-language publications making observations about Cuban volunteers picked up this Cuban narrative of continuity from the island's domestic fight to the conflict in Spain. They did so in part because of Tisa's editorial role, which allowed him to publicize his knowledge of the Cuban volunteers.[98] *The Book of the XV Brigade* noted that Cubans were "exiled from their native island, escaping the terror groups of Batista." The book made concrete the continuity between the two struggles by asserting that both were antifascist. "Inspired by a hatred of tyranny," it stated of the Cuban volunteers, "realising how Batista had turned Cuba into a hell of Fascist terror, they were determined to come to grips with International Fascism whose disciple Batista is."[99] The periodical of the English-speaking members of the International Brigades, the *Volunteer for Liberty*, drew the same connection in February 1938: "Many Cubans have given their lives and many more will continue to sacrifice themselves fighting with the Loyal Spanish people against the forces of fascism that would want to enslave a free people. With fascism driven out of Spain once and for all, the Cubans know that it will mean the gathering of forces to destroy fascism in the rest of the world. A victory for the Republic would be a death blow to Batista's fascist aspirations. The Cuban people, too, are waiting to strike for freedom."[100]

Tisa and other observers had picked up on the multiple ways in which Cubans connected their fight against Batista with their fight against Franco. One method was to symbolically commemorate their domestic fight in the foreign one. An example was the Clubs Mella, which celebrated the martyred activist by being centers of Cuban antifascist organizing in New York and Barcelona. Another example was what was known as "the Cuban Section" of the U.S. Abraham Lincoln Battalion. The members of this unit, which left from New York early in January 1937, chose to name it the "Centuria Antonio Guiteras," for the martyred Joven Cuba leader killed by Batista's forces shortly after the March 1935 general strike.[101] The Club Mella was the birthplace of the Centuria; the unit "consisted of young men who belonged to the 'Julio Mella' Cuban Club of New York City," stated a 1938 article in the *Volunteer for Liberty*.[102] Cuban exiles of various political backgrounds had gathered at the Club Mella in New York on 8 May 1936 to commemorate the one-year anniversary of Guiteras's death.[103] When the Spanish conflict began several months later, politically diverse Cubans gathered there again and organized the military unit that would further commemorate Guiteras by fighting for the Spanish Republic in his name. And one of their central inspirations for transferring their activism into antifascism and the fight to defend the Spanish Republic was Torriente, whose name and picture would be similarly publicized, commemorated, and adopted by multiple other Cuban antifascist organizations. Torriente, Guiteras, and Mella served as the Cuban Section's three central martyrs, from whom they gained inspiration and strength, and with whom they memorialized the Cuban struggle as they fought in Spain.

The symbolism of the Centuria's three martyrs helps to explain the development of antifascism among Cuban political activists—particularly those who became combat volunteers. Encompassed within international Communism and a U.S.-dominated battalion, the Centuria needed elements of Cuban identity, nationalism, anti-imperialism, and the political and ideological diversity characteristic of the fight back home to assert itself as a continuation of the island's domestic struggle. The Centuria served as a location of a particularly Cuban antifascism even amid the internationalist and Spanish conflict. Mella, Guiteras, and Torriente symbolized and reinforced the elements of antifascism that were authentically Cuban.

Mella was not only a central figure of the origination of the anti-Machado and anti-imperialist struggles in Cuba during the 1920s and 1930s but also a vital link from earlier eras through his collaboration with leftists and nationalists of the previous generation. He embodied the continuity of Cuba's domestic struggle and its political diversity. Mella was a founding member of the PCC and had clashed with Communist authorities for being too individualistic and for engaging in activism parallel to—and therefore detracting from—the party agenda. He had strong Communist credentials as well as a complicated relationship with the party, and he wrestled with the challenge of making internationalist Communism work for Cuban domestic problems. Additionally, as discussed in the introduction, he was an originator of Cuban antifascism, which he connected to his anti-Machado and anti-imperialist work. For these reasons, he was the Centuria Guiteras's first symbolic martyr.

The Centuria's second symbolic martyr was Guiteras. Guiteras represented the militant branch of the fallen Grau administration and his subsequent organization, Joven Cuba. He and his revolutionary anti-imperialist and Cuban nationalist organization were mistrusted and derided by leftist internationalists, such as anarchists and the Communist Party; by fellow anti-imperialists, such as members of the Liga Anti-Imperialista de Cuba; and by political moderates. That which made him a focus of critique may also have been what made him an attractive symbol for Cuban antifascism, especially when combat volunteers integrated into a U.S. battalion organized by the Communist Party. He was authentically Cuban in his aims, which were backed by many loyal followers; he embodied an ideal Cuban revolutionary masculinity, to which many male activists aspired; he did not shy away from violence, as his activist methodology was based on a belief that ends justified means; he was a committed anti-imperialist but no close friend of the Communists; and he combined various ideological currents into one activist group. His death further served to bridge factionalist gaps: many, like Torriente, who disagreed with Guiteras in life were able to commemorate him after his death as a legendary hero and a true "man of the revolution," even as they recalled his "imprudent excesses and serious errors."[104] The essay in which Torriente, neither a Joven Cuba nor a Communist Party member, analyzed and celebrated Guiteras was published by local branches of both organizations in Mexico City.[105] Around the same time, the event at the Club Mella in New York celebrating Guiteras on the first anniversary of his death brought together members of Joven Cuba, ORCA, the Auténticos, the Communist Party, and others. As a martyr, Guiteras had "the power to convene all the Cuban revolutionary sectors represented in the exile" in New York, wrote Ana Suárez Díaz.[106] That unity was necessary to continue advocating for a New Cuba, and it would be bolstered when it was reconceived as antifascism. Like Guiteras himself, Cuban antifascism came to be politically diverse, a camp in which many different goals, beliefs, organizations, and people mixed and stood side by side, but which always remained recognizably Cuban.

The final symbolic martyr for the Centuria Guiteras was Torriente, whose example served as a catalyst for Cubans to make a connection between their domestic fight and the defense of the Republic in Spain. Torriente was not the only Cuban stuck in exile in 1936, feeling bored and burning to step back into revolutionary waters. He showed his fellow Cuban exiles—and activists on the island—a compelling path forward, and his writings established a substantial foundation for the construction of Cuban antifascism vis-à-vis Spain as the continuation of that fight. The members of the Centuria Guiteras, in Suárez Díaz's words, were a group of exiles "who instead of returning to Cuba, chose to transfer to a new stage of political struggle: the Spanish people's war against fascism."[107] They followed Torriente to Spain, though they arrived a few weeks too late to see him alive. Thereafter, however, they carried with them his image, name, and memory as one of their martyrs for the cause.

Rodolfo de Armas, organizer and leader of the Centuria Guiteras, was like Torriente in that he died fighting for the Republic and received similar attention from Cubans and others after his death.[108] If Pablo, by way of his inspiration, was a posthumous leader of the first Cuban volunteer contingent from New York, Rodolfo was its actual commander. Of all the Cubans killed in the Spanish conflict, the international press singled out these two for special remembrance; for example, the *Volunteer for Liberty*, in a list of those killed from many nations, picked Pablo and Rodolfo as the notable dead of Cuba.[109]

Rodolfo de Armas became an activist on the island in 1927 at the University of Havana and later as a member of Guiteras's Joven Cuba, which culminated in a leadership role at the university during the March 1935 general strike.[110] While in exile in the United States, he was a founding member of ORCA's Philadelphia delegation, as well as a participant in the Club José Martí and ORCA in New York City.[111] De Armas was only in his mid-twenties when he volunteered, and yet he was clearly already admired by many as an effective leader. The *Volunteer for Liberty* noted that in Spain, "the energetic Cuban student leader" stood at the head of a large number of "youthful antifascist Cubans," acting as "the leading spirit in the organization of the 'Centurie [sic] Guiteras' Column" that "played such an honorable role on the Spanish antifascist front."[112] Another account noted that Rodolfo "became the cynosure of admiring eyes" in the small village where the Americans had their training headquarters, "as he strolled during the paseo with a young Villanueva girl who had consented to become his wife."[113] Tisa remembered: "When he spoke, one felt that one was in the presence of a powerful tractor in motion. He wasted no words, and one moved fast under his command. Always serious and in a hurry, he seemed intolerant and angry, until one got to know him; then one understood his vigor, his short temper, and his anxiety that everything be done quickly and perfectly. To his friends he was no mystery; he was considered to be one of the gentlest of human beings, as well as the most advanced Marxist of all the Cubans." Despite his ideological convictions, the young leader united his politically diverse brethren in the Centuria Guiteras. "By the magnetism of his personality and the soundness of his reasoning," Tisa recalled, he "was able to pull together in common bond the various political shades among these antifascist Cubans."[114] Rodolfo de Armas, remembered for his powerful voice, his romantic success, his effective leadership, and his ideological sophistication—in other words, his revolutionary manhood—was the quintessential male Cuban political activist.

This beloved Cuban fell during the Battle of Jarama in February 1937, not long after his arrival in Spain.[115] The story of his death was repeated again and again in both Spanish- and English-language written accounts and circulated orally; CPUSA leader James W. Ford stated that a North American had recounted to him the details of the event.[116] A tank exploded into flames as approximately 450 Cuban, Irish, U.S., and Canadian volunteers "were advancing against a well-entrenched enemy."[117] Cuban and Irish units had gone out ahead of other members of the Abraham Lincoln Battalion to engage the Nationalists. "The Cuban section advanced, led by their charismatic leader, Rudolfo [sic] de Armas, who raised a clenched fist high in the air and signaled his men forward. Hit in the leg, he stooped to check the wound when he was hit again in the head and jaw. He was probably dead before he hit the ground."[118] In another telling, the Cuban leader had just helped an injured soldier when he was shot: "After rescuing a wounded comrade he continued the advance, and beckoned the others to follow" just before being hit. He was the first among many, this account noted: "The losses of the Cuban section were heavy."[119] Tisa also gave an account decades later with more personal details, indicating that he was one of the closest eyewitnesses to the death. "I was alongside him, about twenty feet to his right," he remembered, "and felt secure under his leadership." As he looked at Rodolfo, "a bullet struck him in the right leg, and when he stooped to grip his leg with his hands, shouting obscenities toward the fascists, two more bullets hit him, one in the head and the other in the jaw." Tisa's account is poignant, that of a friend: "Instinctively, I ran to him, oblivious of whistling bullets, but I was too late. I stood over him in sadness and uncertainty, and in sudden loneliness, for the one person I had looked upon as indestructible, the one I had admired, lay dead."[120]

Ford, too, became emotional as he recounted the death for *Mediodía*. Pulling out a handsome photograph of the young leader, Ford commented: "Look, all heroism, youth, and fortitude. It seems incredible that he has died." Perhaps caught up in the image and the moment, Ford exaggerated somewhat the details of the death: "The heroic boy, even though the blood flowed copiously, continued his march over the hill. But eventually he could not anymore. He tried to tie a handkerchief to control bleeding. In that moment he was the target of another bullet, but this time it was necessarily deadly as it had pierced his jugular." Concluding his account, Ford honored the Cuban leader and all the Cubans killed in Spain by comparing them to Mella.[121] It is clear from Ford's telling, Tisa's remembrance, and other accounts that de Armas's fellow volunteers greatly admired him and his capacity for leadership. Of the numerous Cubans who died during the Battle of Jarama, his death was the one told and retold, suggesting that he possessed a charisma that made him especially notable. Of course it was probably this charisma that placed him in a leadership role in the first place, but in death, his legacy became a particular form of political currency. As Ford's comparison to Mella makes clear, Rodolfo de Armas was transformed into a martyr. His Cuban identity and history in the domestic fight made him a martyr not only for the Spanish Republic but also for Cuba. Thus, he served in death as he had in life—as a point of continuity between the struggles of Spain and Cuba—and in death, he received international attention for the role he had played.

Another Cuban volunteer to receive substantial attention upon his death in battle was Alberto Sánchez Menéndez, a man in his early twenties of stern and brooding countenance. Sánchez Menéndez had been a close collaborator of Guiteras's after beginning his political engagement as a student activist in the anti-Machado struggle when he was fifteen years old. He helped lead the March 1935 general strike, after which he went into exile in Central America, then Mexico, and finally Spain in March 1936. He was already there, then, when the Spanish Civil War began, and he joined the fight in defense of the Republic immediately upon its initiation, becoming a commander of the Fifth Regiment—a unit of the regular Republican forces formed by the Partido Comunista de España (Spanish Communist Party, or PCE). A member of the Spanish party, Sánchez Menéndez was trusted by its Central Committee, a representative of which sought his assessment of the first Cuban volunteers to arrive from the island.[122] *Facetas de Actualidad Española* notified readers on the island that "the young Cuban whose career in the Popular Army of the Spanish Republic had been so brilliant" had died in July 1937 in the Battle of Brunete.[123] "Alongside the blood of Pablo de la Torriente, Rodolfo de Armas, and so many other Cubans the blood of the Cuban youth remains in the Spanish countryside," read the caption of a photograph of the late Cuban, "fertilizing the NEW SPAIN that is being forged."[124] A commemorative poem by Chilean poet Pablo Neruda stated that out of the young Cuban volunteer's body flowed "our blood," and "in the soil of Brunete his body remains as a flag."[125]

In these types of imaginings, Cuban volunteers killed in the conflict permanently connected the struggle for a New Cuba with the struggle for a New Spain. The example of these martyrs would serve to inspire more Cuban volunteers to travel to Spain and more Cuban activists to continue in the domestic fight. In the Cuban revolutionary saying vocalized by Torriente and Roa, even after death, they were useful.

The Blood of These Children . . .
   Runs through Our Veins

   The Cuban Campaign to Aid Republican Children

   ·

Teté Casuso learned from a newspaper of her husband's death in Spain. Her partner in love, life, intellect, and activism, Pablo had died nobly, fighting fascism for Spain and Cuba. He was a hero, a martyr—he would have been proud of this end—but he was gone. As a martyr, he might continue to serve the struggle, but he would not continue to be her husband. She had lost the great love of her life, and she was only in her mid-twenties. They had had no children, and as she confronted Pablo's sudden absence in her life, their never-born child added painful volume to the hollow. She was torn from her present and also her potential future families, a devastating blow. She suffered this deeply personal loss in addition to all the many political disappointments she, Pablo, and their *compañeros* had already borne. Given that political work together had been so fundamental to Pablo and Teté's union, it is unsurprising that it was to political work that Casuso turned following Torriente's death. Activism was the natural choice for Teté to occupy herself during her mourning.

   The first task that occurred to her was to publish Pablo's writing from Spain, but he had sent his work to Jaime Bofill in New York, and she could not immediately acquire it.[1] "While waiting for his chronicles to be sent to me from New York," she wrote, "I determined to do something to help the unhappy people for whose liberty Pablo had given his life."[2] She founded the Asociación de Auxilio al Niño del Pueblo Español (Association of Aid to the Child of the Spanish People, or AANPE) in Havana in February 1937, with help from the "generous initiative of a group of enthusiastic people," including such notables as Fernando Ortiz, Emilio Roig de Leuchsenring, and Roberto Agramonte, who lent their names and prestige to the cause. The tone of Teté's memoir, dull with grief following Pablo's death, brightens momentarily as she expresses her pride in the AANPE. Its membership grew to 300,000, she boasted, "with a delegation in every town on the island, and the amount of assistance we gave to the Spanish people was enormous." She felt particularly proud of the "frequent boatloads of food" sent to Spain and of the Casa-Escuela Pueblo de Cuba (People of Cuba Residential School) established and run by the association in the Catalan town of Sitges, which housed children orphaned or otherwise displaced by the war.

Furthermore, the AANPE was "the only organization for Spanish aid not banned by Batista," according to Teté's recollection.[3] In fact, other groups continued solidarity work for the Spanish Republic after the Cuban government issued Decreto Presidencial No. 3411 (the decree of neutrality) in December 1937. It is safe to say, however, that the AANPE was one of and perhaps even the most prominent. The association "firmly rejected" the suggestion that it supported foreign hostilities; its members were pacifists, its leaders affirmed the same month the neutrality decree was issued, who helped civilians, not belligerents.[4] The following March, AANPE leader Ismael Cuevas addressed confusion that had followed the issuance of the decree and clarified that the association was still legal due to its nonpartisan and humanitarian nature.[5] Jorge Domingo Cuadriello comments that "its closure would have been a scandal," hinting at both its perceived status as a moderate and neutral entity and its widespread popularity.[6]

Cuba's AANPE was in part a product of the transnational "child-saving movement." This movement, organized by largely middle-class Progressives during the late nineteenth and early twentieth centuries, sought to protect and remove children from unhealthy and unsafe circumstances, such as households of alcoholics or those beset by extreme poverty. Though much of the sentiment and language of the AANPE echoed those of Progressive child-saving efforts, Cuban humanitarian activists facing the prospect of assisting Spanish children during the war dealt with a substantially different set of considerations. The fact that the children in question were living in a war zone gave the effort an intensity of drama and urgency that day-to-day social work endeavors generally did not inspire. AANPE leader Francisco Domenech pleaded with Cubans to recognize that while it was true that many Cuban children lacked resources and protection, they at least did not live in a fascist war zone. According to Domenech, it was rational and sensible to address first that which was "most urgent and immediate, the greater danger, the deepest disaster."[7] The problem to be addressed in the association's case was not an insidious familial or societal ill, such as alcoholism or poverty, but a specific military and political enemy: fascism. Though the AANPE claimed to be a nonpartisan humanitarian organization, it was solidly antifascist and aided Republican children. The idea that there existed such a thing as "Republican children" exposed the difference war introduced into the act of child saving. In keeping with the Cuban and transnational political climates, the AANPE and its supporters viewed the children they helped as political allies rather than simply helpless children. A politicized understanding of children as partisan actors meant that they could not be viewed as passive recipients of aid, as the children benefiting from traditional Progressive child saving generally would have been. Instead, these children's identities melded with the cause. For one, they symbolized the special relationship imagined between Spain and Cuba. In contrast to an attempt to help lower-class people by predominantly middle-class social workers (often criticized for expressing fear, pity, and condescension toward those they aided), Cubans perceived Spanish children and families in need during the war as kin—as equals who would do the same when roles were reversed, such as when Spaniards aided Cubans after a hurricane. Furthermore, children—and the endangered Spanish children in particular—symbolized the future. As children and allies, then, Spanish children were innocent victims whose plight illustrated the extreme brutality of fascism; activists-soldiers in miniature, who demonstrated the same loyalty and courage as adults; and transcendent symbols of antifascist hope for a better world.[8]

This Cuban antifascist imagining of Spanish children echoed a different transnational movement, one that was very much opposed to the type of middle-class effort exemplified by Progressive child saving: anarchism.[9] Anarchism played an influential role in Cuba during the late nineteenth and early twentieth centuries. Its cultural and educational influences are those most evident in the AANPE, which did not adopt anarchist politics. Kirwin R. Shaffer has extensively analyzed the cultural and educational program anarchists directed at working-class children, women, men, and families on the island from 1898 through the mid-1920s, when the Machado regime's brutal repression of anarchists drove underground those who had not been killed or deported. By that time, however, anarchism and its proponents had greatly influenced Cuba's working class in multiple provinces, not only through anarchist schools and cultural activities but also through activists such as Julio Antonio Mella, who received direct mentorship from anarchists.[10] Despite the fact that repression as well as Communist ascent had diminished the influence of anarchists on the island by the 1930s, many of the tenets of their philosophy retained strong resonance in the Cuban imagination—especially the Cuban revolutionary imagination—during the 1930s and beyond.[11] The AANPE vision of saving Spanish children, though constructed within an organization that was socioeconomically and ideologically diverse, reflects this anarchist influence.

For example, both Spanish women taking up arms in the defense of the Republic and radical views within the island's pro-Republican alliance challenged the demure sensibilities of moderate antifascists, and the impact of this challenge was evident in AANPE rhetoric. Anarchists envisioned a special multifaceted role for the anarchist woman in achieving political, societal, and cultural goals and in moving humanity forward: she was the noble woman, the revolutionary mother, and a potential heroine. She had to hold herself to anarchist standards in life, love, and work; raise and educate her children according to anarchist principles; and engage in the anarchist struggle when needed.[12] Cuban antifascists in the AANPE imagined a similar figure when they envisioned the female antifascist, though they shrouded her role as a militant activist in the trappings of more traditionally feminine ideals. In both cases, propagandizing the mistreatment of women and children not only symbolized the ills that anarchist-antifascist progress was to overcome but also suggested the roles the mistreated could play in advancing such progress. Metaphorically speaking, the idea was that the canaries in the coal mine should join the coal miners' union—that those most susceptible to society's ills should be protected but also simultaneously stand and fight. The plight of women and children was meant to inspire change; at the same time, women and children were active in the struggle on their own behalf. Women's and children's activism was particularly significant because children *were* the future, and their revolutionary mothers were responsible for shaping that future.[13] These ideas were anarchist and also present in the Cuban campaign to aid Spanish children.

Both literally and metaphorically, the history of the Cuban campaign to aid Spanish children is a family history. Actual families were destroyed by death and separation: children were orphaned or sent away, and adults were killed, hospitalized, or at the battlefront. The destruction of these families was caused by a civil war, a war of brother against brother within the nation. Cubans lamented this war of Spaniard against Spaniard but also framed it as a generational interpretation—New Spain versus Old Spain—in such a way that symbolic patricide was viewed as a positive. In addition to waging a war of New Cuba against Old Cuba, Cubans had fought their own fratricidal or patricidal war of independence against Spain several decades prior. The language Cuban antifascists used to characterize their position vis-à-vis the Spanish Republic, therefore, constantly grappled with relationships defined in familial terms. This tendency was especially highlighted in the case of the Cuban campaign to aid Spanish children, in which metaphoric and literal descriptions of family relations frequently existed side by side, and political agendas and personal affairs intertwined.

Such was the case with Teté Casuso. Initiated in the wake of her husband's death in Spain, the AANPE grew out of her painful experience of the familial consequences of activist choices. Teté transferred her energy from personal grief to political organizing. Her poems offer a glimpse into her inner turmoil and the motivation for her shift in focus following Pablo's death. Her horror at her individual tragedy and Spain's national tragedy intertwine in these works, written in 1937 and 1938, and the devotion of the author and her organization to the cause of children becomes particularly poignant. The poems exemplify the way in which fluidity between the personal and the political can inspire transnational solidarity, facilitate continuity of commitment, and strengthen activist resilience. Teté had already been an activist alongside Pablo for years by the time he died in Spain. His death could have marked an endpoint to her engagement, just as the defeat of the 1933 Cuban Revolution by Batista's rise and repression could have several years before. Like Pablo, and in fact *through* Pablo after his death, Teté transferred her energy from the Cuban struggle to the defense of the Spanish Republic. In Teté's mind, no effort seemed better suited to the goal of a better future than caring for the vulnerable children of activists in the global antifascist struggle, and especially of Cubans' "kin" in Spain, the people for whom Pablo had died.[14]

The first of her two poems, "Lullaby without Child," describes a haunting scene in which a woman sits sewing children's clothes and sings a lullaby to a child who is not there. "Who holds my child in arms such that I cannot reach him?" she asks, then declares, "Life took my dream, and the child has not arrived." It seems probable that these lines express the emotions Teté felt in the wake of Pablo's death upon the realization that a dream perhaps once close at hand was now impossible forever. In the poem, the narrator decides to transfer her maternal feeling from the lost child to all motherless children across the globe, "the children without cradle." The narrator struggles, shedding "some tears singing to the child who did not arrive and a song of the future breaking my heart!" Yet she is determined. "My lullaby has no child," she laments, but proclaims: "For the earth and for the children, my love has come to sing."[15]

The second poem switches perspective, from that of the childless mother to that of the orphan. "Christmas of the Motherless Child" begins with a joyful voice addressing "my mama, so pretty!" The child wants to decorate "the Christmas tree of my memories" and begs his mother: "Take my joys from that forest of stories and let us sprinkle the whole tree with colorful globes, reds, blues, greens, the color of happiness!" Yet something is not right, as the title has forewarned. The child's memory is a forest of stories, and he is trying to remember. "Bring all my childhood," he implores his mother—only his mother is not there. He must search for the right memory, the right story or dream in which to find her. While he searches, a new voice exclaims, "But you are sad, child of the stories!" This second narrator addresses the motherless child as the poem concludes, telling him, "Come to my heart." Only in the second narrator's heart will the child recover his memories and his absent mother—there, his mother will return from a dream. There are at least three ways to interpret the poem's message and its personal resonance for Teté. It is possible, especially given the poem's emphasis on Christmas, that she intended the voice of the second narrator to be that of Jesus Christ. "I am this night," he states, promising to resurrect the child's mother in his heart. A few lines earlier, the poem reminds the reader of another story, the story of "that star that went one night to parade across the skies." Alternately or additionally, perhaps Teté imagined herself as this second narrator, in keeping with the motherless child–childless mother relationship she established in the first poem. In her heart, she believed, the orphan could find maternal love, a metaphorical rather than metaphysical resurrection of his lost mother.[16] A provocative line in Teté's memoir suggests that a third interpretation could be based on her identification with the motherless child. Her parents were alive, but in reference to her young age relative to that of Pablo at the time of his death, Teté commented that it "made me more than a widow: I was an orphan."[17] He was not only her husband but also a father figure.

An ideologically moderate Cuban nationalist of an elite background, with pride in her own Spanish ancestry, Casuso set the tone for an organization that claimed to be a nonpartisan charity, motivated by transnational Hispanic solidarity and universal human sympathy, yet acted nonetheless as one of the most effective pro-Republican organizations in Cuba. As a formidable veteran of the Cuban struggle and a former political exile, and having already lost her husband for the cause of the Republic, Teté had unquestionable activist credibility. Her station in life, her own moderate views, and the deeply personal pathos she brought to the cause of children in Spain gave her substantial philanthropic credibility as well. Under her direction, the AANPE would strike a balance between activism and charity that was both ambiguous and effective. It became a central vehicle for moderate antifascism in Cuba and drew widespread popular support, recruiting men, women, and children from across the island and Cuban communities abroad. Moderate antifascism derived its significance in large part from its popularity and its diversity. Its supporters represented a wide range of ages and backgrounds, not only those passionately devoted to the cause of the Spanish Republic but also uncertain moderates and people without political or ideological affiliation. In order to maintain this diversity of supporters, the AANPE held to its claim of being a strictly nonpartisan charitable organization, raising monetary and material aid for all Spanish children affected by the war. The message succeeded in being picked up by other outlets on the island, such as the *Mediodía* article that described the organization as being "composed of numerous humanitarian people, devoid of any political partisanship, inspired exclusively on the idea of doing good."[18] However, the association's bulletin, *¡Ayuda!*, and its archived organizational records leave no doubt that the AANPE was in fact firmly and even militantly pro-Republican.[19] Its organizational culture included significant leftist undertones. An examination of its messaging, finances, and accomplishments reveals tensions between activism and charity, and between the Spanish Republican cause and the various Cubans who offered their support for Spanish children.

Campaign Messaging

The Cuban campaign to aid Spanish children was part of a larger effort focused on children during the war, coordinated in Paris and with adherents in many countries.[20] However, from the beginning of its messaging efforts, the AANPE's Comité Directivo (Directing Committee) asserted that the well-being of Spanish children besieged by war was a specifically Cuban concern. Seeking validation of its cause in the very essence of Cuban-ness, the committee quoted José Martí. "Martí said it," it wrote. "'Children are the hope of the world.' With these grave and profound words, we implore the people of Martí: Save the children of Spain! Save the hope of the world!"[21] The same words from the Cuban patriot also appeared on the association's letterhead.[22] AANPE leaders expressed what they believed was self-evident: that their mission to save the children was not *only* a Cuban concern. Indeed, voices of the association argued repeatedly that their mission was both a Christian and a universal one. Thus, they cast three wide nets in efforts to recruit supporters and raise funds: universal human obligation to charity, Christian imperative, and a special relationship with Spain.

First, the association put forward a broad call to save children based on the universal human obligation to charity, emphasizing the plight of Spanish children with intense emotion, suggesting both genuine empathy and a fund-raiser's knack for wielding pathos. In a typical example, one editorial in *¡Ayuda!* described life for children in war-torn Spain as one in which they "learned to flee before they learned to walk, to scream before they learned to smile, to cover their eyes and faces with their tiny, trembling hands before they looked at the sky of their country torn by foreign shrapnel, not yet able to distinguish between the stars and the death that falls, also illuminating the night."[23] Descriptions characterized by dramatic language and strong sentiment—often accompanied by arresting images of tragedy, including children's corpses—rallied readers to donate their money and energy to a cause presented as universally compelling.

If simple human pathos proved insufficient, *¡Ayuda!* articles offered the pragmatic addendum that children represented the future of humanity, and therefore their protection constituted a biological, existential necessity of the species. To shield and rescue the children of war-torn Spain was to save "the flower of life," "the conscience of future humanity," and even "hope incarnate."[24] This language indicated not only the vital role of children in sustaining the human race biologically but also the child's symbolic role as the spiritual and emotional essence of humanity's progress. One typically dramatic statement read: "In the enormous pupils of the Spanish orphan is now glimpsed the radiant dawn of the world."[25] The primary goal of these exhortations was to motivate volunteers and donors with an assertion that people should feel obliged to help. The phrase "save the conscience of future humanity," for example, formed part of the text on one bulletin cover— accompanying an image of a crying toddler flanked by falling bombs—that concluded: "to abstain is to be guilty of indifference."[26] All good men, stated another *¡Ayuda!* article more explicitly, are obliged to construct a defense of the Spanish children's destiny.[27] An AANPE-produced advertising poster read: "We are sure to find in every child, every mother, every generous person a member of the Association who guarantees his moral solidarity to the cause of those thousands of innocent creatures."[28]

At the heart of the association's argument of universal human appeal, however, was a pro-Republican stance. As one poem in the AANPE bulletin put it, "Children are happiness / they are the dawn of the future / and they die assassinated / by Spain's traitors."[29] In another example, an illustration showed improvements in children's health under the Republic, and subsequent negative consequences of the "fascist movement."[30] Association voices called Nationalists persons "who revile the sacred principles of democracy" and "have attacked and violated the will of a people," yet in the same few lines of text assured readers that the AANPE "undertakes a highly humanitarian work free of any partisanship."[31] The universal human appeal of saving children from violent aggressors might be nonpartisan, but the association's view on the identity of the violent aggressors was not.

In its second broad appeal, the AANPE emphasized its mission as a Christian imperative and, in doing so, revealed its position relative to the Republicans and Nationalists. Cubans of Christian faith were confronted with a set of powerful Nationalist narratives mobilizing Christian rhetoric: that the Republicans were anti-church and irreligious, were godless Communists, represented a Jewish and/or Masonic conspiracy against Christianity, and destroyed churches and murdered priests. How, then, were Cubans to make the pro-Republican cause a Christian one, particularly in relation to children?

Voices of the AANPE asserted an understanding of Christ and Christianity as fundamentally pacifist. This rhetoric indicted Nationalists at news of bombed population centers, such as Guernica (April 1937), in which innocent civilians—including children—were killed and maimed. Georgina Martínez—identified as a member of the association's provincial delegation of Camagüey—introduced this Christian perspective in July 1937. "The children of Spain are the pain of the world" and the "remorse of Humanity traitorous to Christ," she stated emphatically. Christ was not, she argued, present in the bombs dropped on cities, far from any legitimate military target. He could not be found among "the worst human instincts and ambitions." It was "sacrilegious," "profane," and "inexcusable" to murder people—especially children—while "invoking God's protection and benediction," Martínez wrote.[32] Teté echoed these themes. Elaborating her vision for a "victorious peace" desired by "Friends of the Spanish People," she defined such a peace as "justice and the right to work and live and love." Thinking perhaps of the state of Cuba subdued under Batista, she argued that peace could not be a ruthless triumph or a violent dominance; rather, it must be a constructive peace of brotherly love, a "Christian peace." Christ was not in the sinister bombers flying over Spain but rather "with the children" or even "fighting in the trenches against the barbarous invaders," Teté believed.[33]

As this image of Christ suggests, the AANPE mobilized a concept of Christianity as not only pacifist but also active in justice seeking and self-defense, and it did so from a position of self-defined antifascism. It was a

Francoist paradox, wrote intellectual José Antonio Portuondo, to say that they were fighting for family, religion, and fatherland but in fact to be "creating a generation without any idea of family, religion, or fatherland." The young scholar imagined a Christianity that would not "demand of the poor submission to the powerful, resignation to his miserable state," and would not expect from the rich "charity, which is a supplementary virtue," and "leave tangled, forgotten in the gold altars and vestments, drowned in the fumes of votive incense, the higher and more urgent duty of Justice." Christianity must not "sanctify fascist despotism and barbarism" but rather "save every man" from the current "hell" in Spain, and move the country toward "the universal peace of tomorrow and the future brotherhood of men," creating a "new world of Love and of Justice." Of what would such justice consist? Portuondo offered a vivid scene set in the Spanish countryside to reconcile a Christian vision of justice with the undeniable radicalism of some on the Republican side. Recounting the reception of revolutionary poet Rafael Alberti by a group of humble folk in Andalucia, Portuondo wrote that after the poet's declaration of "irreligious and libertarian propaganda," the peasants "saw him off affectionately," saying, "'Well, Don Rafaé, may God accompany you in this Communism.'"[34] Here, Portuondo met the Nationalist rhetoric head-on by melding the radicalism Nationalists abhorred with an authentic Spanish Christianity. In a similar spirit, Asela Jiménez—widow of prominent Cuban intellectual and activist Rubén Martínez Villena, who died of tuberculosis in 1934—defended Republican violence as "sacred" rage against injustice, and self-defense against attacks "by foreign assassins," reminding readers that the "ire of Jesus of Nazareth was divine when, clutching the lash, he threw the merchants out of the temple."[35] She predicted that the Spanish people would "turn into a new Jesus and throw the merchants out of Spain."[36] In these more active, even aggressive visions of a Christian response to the Spanish conflict, AANPE writers abandoned the pretense of nonpartisanship and at times even set aside the specific cause of Spanish children, crossing the line between children's charity and pro-Republican activist organization.

Even as their militant antifascism peeked through, AANPE leaders grounded themselves in Christianity and positioned the organization as a peace-seeking Christian charity, meeting Nationalist propaganda head-on and painting themselves as moderates in their ongoing attempt to appeal to the widest possible variety of Cubans. Their tactic involved continual deradicalization of the Republicans' popular image. In one article for ¡Ayuda!, for example, Tomás Blanco claimed that the "natural impulse of the human heart and social obligation" to defend innocent children "finds stimulus and support as much in that which is most mystical in Christianity as in that which is most materialistic in Marxism." Also, he positioned the instinct among "the biological necessities of the species."[37] Equating Christianity and Marxism did not only suggest "biological necessities," of course; it challenged accusations of Republicans as godless Communists and suggested provocatively that Marxism might be compatible not only with Spanish-ness but also with Spanish Catholicism, an idea that was anathema to Nationalists. This association tactic radicalized the Nationalist position. When AANPE volunteers seeking clothing for Spanish children were rebuffed by one store owner who, they remembered, "dared to tell us that 'his religion did not permit him to donate clothing to children in loyalist territory,'" they labeled him a "fanatic." What, they asked with indignation, could possibly be the religion of this fanatic?[38] To close the door on charitable volunteers seeking clothing for children could not be defended from behind a veil of Christianity, the volunteers suggested. Forget about accusations of Republican Communism, this argument demanded; the heartless Nationalists were the real zealots and radicals.

As their third wide net cast for participation, leaders of the Cuban campaign to aid Spanish children asserted that there existed between Spain and its former colonies a special relationship of historical, cultural, and familial ties. This special relationship, they argued, required people in Spanish American nations generally and in Cuba especially to assist Spaniards. From their shared history, AANPE voices selected examples of fraternity and cooperation. In an article titled "Debt of Love and Gratitude," for example, Portuondo claimed that Spain had supported Cuba in the aftermath of several natural disasters, such as the hurricane of 1926, and provided assistance to victims of Machado's dictatorship.[39] Others referenced a shared Hispanic pantheon. Authors of various nationalities (Venezuelan, Spanish, Cuban) writing for the association's bulletin invoked Bolívar and Cervantes, identifying their cause with great men from a shared history.[40]

Even Cuba's independence struggle against Spain provided a historical context from which to craft solidarity between the two nations, though authors arguing for Cuban support of the Spanish Republic had to distinguish between the Spain Cubans fought against and the one they should fight for. They asserted that the same "bad" Spain victimized both Spanish Republicans and Cubans: "When Cuba remembers its past, it evokes a militarism in the pay of a colonizing tyranny, and knows that the *miliciano* has been a victim as has been the *guajiro* [Cuban peasant] in turn," wrote Cuban feminist Berta Arocena.[41] Portuondo reminded Cuban readers of the colonial-era divide between "defenders, Creoles and Spaniards, of Spanish absolutism" on the one hand, and Martí and the people on the other.[42] Spaniards addressing pro-Republican Cubans supported this concept of kinship between Cuba and the "good" Spain, associated with the Republic, as distinguished from an imperialist and oppressive Spain, associated with the Nationalists. Consuelo Carmona de Gordón Ordas, wife of Spanish Republican official and future president of the republic in exile Félix Gordón Ordas, addressed Cubans over the radio: "Your great José Martí is ours also, of the good Spaniards, who have always been his brothers."[43] Surely Cubans would be motivated to help Martí's brothers.

Genealogical metaphors abounded in the Cuban campaign to aid Spanish children, the most direct possible expression of the sense of historical, cultural, and familial solidarity at the heart of the special-relationship argument. Writers from both Spain and Cuba portrayed the relationship between Spain and Spanish America as either one of mother and children or one of siblings. Spain was "the mother of this world of ours."[44] The countries of Spanish America were Cuba's "sister lands," and together these lands were "daughters" of Spain.[45] Mexico was the "sister Aztec republic" and a "fraternal republic," and Venezuela a "sister republic."[46] Cuba was to Spain a "brother in race and in history."[47] Some authors asserted that the peoples of Cuba, Spanish America, and Spain were all one and the same.[48] "That which is Spanish is very much ours," wrote ¡Ayuda! editor-historian Gustavo Fabal. "We live so close, with such parallels, that it is impossible to resist."[49] Not only were the countries of Spanish America metaphorical family members of Spain, but Spanish Americans were, in innumerable cases, literally family members of Spaniards, and sometimes born in Spain themselves.[50]

Young Armando Martínez, a Cuban schoolboy chosen to greet Spanish child refugees, melded these familial themes in the remarks he made when the ship *Mexique* stopped in Havana harbor on its way to Mexico. Addressing his "Spanish brothers," Armando assured them that Cuban children—united with them by "multiple ties of confraternity that are not chains which could be broken"—sympathized with their pain. He tried to comfort the refugees on their voyage to Mexico by reminding them that they were going to live in a "brother country," a country of their race, blood, and language.[51] Armando used this theme to try to calm the fears of Spanish children on their way to exile, and association members used it more broadly to engage Cubans in assisting their Spanish "kin." The special-relationship argument was one of the most frequently emphasized themes in the AANPE's message to Cubans—as well as within Cuban antifascism generally. Just as Cuban members of the association emphasized their country's special relationship with Spain to inspire support, so, too, did Spaniards. Consuelo Carmona de Gordón Ordas included in her radio address a plea along the same lines: We need help from all nations, she stated, but especially from those who "come from the same trunk as we do and speak the same language." Think of your children, Gordón Ordas pleaded, and then help ours.[52]

Universal human imperative, Christian calling, and solidarity built around shared historical, cultural, and familial ties all helped to inspire and energize Cuban aid to presumably *all* Spanish children. Yet the AANPE stood with the Spanish Republic and aided children in Republican-held territories and those fleeing as the Nationalists advanced. How, then, could these three components of the association's messaging—helping Spanish children because of universal, Christian, and cultural responsibilities—function within its poorly hidden mission of aiding the Spanish Republic? Surely Cubans supportive of the Nationalists would see the AANPE as the pro-Republican organization it was and abstain from contributing, but what about the politically moderate and the apolitically uncertain? When encompassing rhetoric collided with instances of pro-Republican word and deed, the association was in danger of losing support. Therefore, to bolster its messaging, association voices defended the organization as a nonpartisan charity with widespread popular support. Repeatedly reassuring would-be supporters that the AANPE did not discriminate against Spanish children based on their parents' political affiliation and that the organization had been endorsed widely by the Cuban general public, association representatives spoke to those who, confused or repulsed by the Spanish Civil War, might turn away unless reassured. A note addressed to a hypothetical member of this target audience read as follows:

> Perhaps you are not a political man, perhaps you have not wanted to raise, in regard to the Spanish conflict, the question of responsibility or guilt, perhaps you, as a man, have felt shaken to your core with pity at the horror of this war, without passing judgment. Well then, friend, you can help to make the Spanish war less hard, you can serve peace in the midst of the contest's horror, helping the Association of Aid to the Child of the Spanish People, which only wishes to save the defenseless children of Spain from orphanage and misery. Send us your donation in clothing or cash.[53]

Adults divide themselves up with political and ideological "isms," writers for the AANPE bulletin argued, but children are not ideological and should not be divided like adults into fascists and Communists, Catholics and Protestants.[54] Teté—never a Communist Party member and already on her way to becoming anticommunist—followed an emotional portrait of Spanish war orphans with bitter sarcasm: "These are the 'red children,' the terrible children, 'the children who have learned to rob and murder and rape.'"[55] Teté responded to Nationalist accusations that the Republic represented a Communist takeover of Spain with terrible consequences. If the children developed political partisanship, she claimed, it was due to the horrors of war, "the natural result of the moment in which they have lived." She continued: "And—red phobia—a great number of children are with the Republican Party. And one who raises his fist [levanta el brazo] does so because he wishes to," she wrote. Surely before the split of July 1936 "these children neither raised a fist nor knew of politics. But neither did they know the sinister sound of the Italian 'Capronis' and of the German 'Junkers,'" Teté concluded, referring to the military aircraft of Franco's Fascist and Nazi backers.[56] If children were politicized, it was only because of their exposure to violence—but this fact was irrelevant to the association's work. As Portuondo put it, beyond any "racial, party, or religious limitation," the AANPE wanted "only to save the children, for Love, from Hatred."[57] Association leaders walked a careful line between charity and partisan activism. As a charity, the association was more likely to garner a higher level of participation, but as dedicated pro-Republicans, its activist leaders were unwilling to abandon their commitment. They worked to master a subtle blend of the two that would not only aid children but also draw moderates and the undecided—through their support of charity—to the cause of the Republic, ultimately advancing moderate antifascism in Cuba.

Part of the message AANPE members crafted to garner widespread popularity was to claim that they already had widespread popularity, an organizing tactic intended to foster a sense of momentum and inclusion. They took pains to demonstrate that the people of Cuba supported the association's work on behalf of Spanish children in order to encourage more Cubans to do so. This seemingly circular methodology was in fact critical to building solidarity around their cause. By emphasizing the extent of their support, they conveyed excitement and crafted a sense of community for both supporters and would-be supporters. No one in Cuban society could "remain indifferent to the tragedy" or "avoid a generous impulse toward the victims," stated an advertising poster, and AANPE leaders had "the conviction to interpret the general sentiment."[58] The association addressed a collective desire "in the bosom of Cuban society" and had the privilege of being the organization that would "channel this enthusiasm and convert it into a magnificent reality."[59] On the one hand, AANPE writers wanted to give the impression of spontaneous support by all of Cuba, yet on the other hand, they understood that effective organizing always requires more than supportive sentiments. Association organizers asserted that supporters would be joining a large crowd going in the right direction. On the back cover of their first bulletin—accompanied by a dramatic image of a weeping toddler superimposed over photographs of bombed-out buildings—the association called on "all who desire and feel that this voice of Cuba should reach a Spain that is hurting and suffering, in need of all our support and cooperation. HELP US!"[60]

In order to convince Cubans of its widespread popularity, the AANPE highlighted three elements of participation. First, it emphasized the activities of children on its behalf. Its bulletin included a special "Children's Page," a devoted space for children to express their thoughts and feelings regarding the events in Spain and to show off their accomplishments for the cause. In July 1937, the bulletin published a letter in which Berta Rodríguez Barco, age eight, wrote that she wanted to help her little brothers and sisters in Spain, so she was sending the entirety of her savings, forty cents.[61] In March 1938, the bulletin featured a letter written by a Mexican boy in which he pledged solidarity with the war victims of Republican Spain and told Cuban children that in Mexico, children did not eat sweets because the Spaniards were suffering. "I ask of you, the Cuban children, to help the children of Spain," he wrote.[62] In May 1938, ¡Ayuda! published a poem written by a Spanish orphan living in Mexico praising Mexican president Lázaro Cárdenas for welcoming the children from "sister Spain" to his country and treating them like Mexico's own.[63] In addition to pieces written by children, the Children's Page featured the work of the AANPE's children's committees, subgroups composed of boys and girls who appear, from photographs, to have had at least a small degree of racial diversity.[64] The Children's Page featured appeals for aid and transcripts of radio addresses from officers of the children's committees, noting in two cases the officers' ages as nine and ten. One boy had told radio listeners that when the AANPE was established, he "felt a great desire to join the work of these *compañeros* who were to help my comrades the little Spanish children." Since the association was an organization of grown-ups, he noted, he and his friends started their own group to support the effort, which later became a children's committee.

Featured during the AANPE radio hour and published in its bulletin, José Alvarez had clearly earned inclusion from the grown-ups.[65] The Children's Page continued throughout the bulletin's existence, indicating that the association was just as eager to show off children's participation as children were to participate.[66]

Similarly, Teté emphasized the role of youth in the Havana reception of Spanish children on their way to refuge in Mexico. In addition to Armando Martínez's addressing of the Spanish child refugees, this "poor boy" from the José Miguel Gómez School also gave the shirt off his own back to a Spanish boy who needed one, Teté claimed, demonstrating the extent of Cuban generosity. Another of Casuso's anecdotes made an interesting comparison between Spanish war orphans on the ship and the "little black children of the bay," who improvised a show for them. It was, she wrote, a "greeting from our own ragged and hungry children[,] . . . full of creole sympathy and the generous heart of Cuba," to the children from Spain, "these hungry children without shoes, almost as naked as they, whom the horror of war . . . pushed to our generous land."[67] In this statement, Teté implicitly raised but left unanswered the question of why these black children, children who were "our own" and represented the "heart of Cuba," were not similarly recipients of the AANPE's generosity.

Second, the association highlighted participation by mothers—and women more generally, who were declared maternal regardless of their actual parental status. "Two hundred thousand children stretch from Madrid their imploring little hands! What Cuban woman, what mother, what pious heart will deny their gathering [concurso]?" asked journalist Félix Pita Rodríguez in a letter from Paris, where the AANPE had sent him to report about efforts on behalf of Spanish children.[68] An autumn 1937 editorial titled "Message from the Association to Women" cited the season as a call to action. Noting that even in Cuba's warm and pleasant climate, mothers changed their children's wardrobes from summer to winter clothing, it reminded readers that in Spain, children would be ravaged not only by war but also by the bitter cold of winter, and stated: "It is now, Cuban mothers, when our feminine sensibility feels most overwhelmed by the abandonment and the poverty of the unhappy creatures." Every woman could make coats for the poor Spanish children, the article offered—none need shoulder the guilt of a Spanish child frozen to death. The sad smile of the Spanish mother from afar would be the Cuban mother's reward.[69] On the bulletin's very next page, the call to Cuban women for clothing took a harsher tone. A poem aimed at mobilizing women titled "Words to My *Compañera*" admonished the reader: "YOU, WHO ARE ALSO A MOTHER, TELL ME, WHAT HAVE YOU DONE, COMRADE?" Your place is in the rearguard, the poem told women: Sew something for the loyalists; knit a coat.[70] Clearly, some in the AANPE saw the traditionally female activity of sewing as not only an important avenue of contribution but also an obligation based on gender. Similarly, voices of the association mobilized an assumed maternal imperative, alongside imagined universal, Christian, and Hispanic imperatives, in the attempts to recruit women. "And you, Creole mother, representative of the universal woman, who gives birth with love and pain," essayist Luis Felipe Rodríguez reminded the reader, your child is a brother of the child who dies in Spain.[71] "Woman reader," pleaded feminist, political activist, and author Mariblanca Sabas Alomá, "I who have never forgotten the Cuban child, in the name of the Cuban child, I ask you to help the Spanish child."[72]

Third, in addition to emphasizing women's and children's participation, representatives of the AANPE claimed that it had the support of all of Cuban society and that it represented "the collective effort of groups and individuals regardless of nationality, race or party. Everyone must come to our ranks, the rich and the poor; intellectuals, workers and students; the elderly and children." Those who could not afford to contribute financially could stand in solidarity, stated the Comité Directivo, "which is a great contribution."[73] In solidarity were "all the people of Cuba, women, men and children, black and white, Spanish, Hebrew, Cubans," claimed Teté.[74] All the provinces of the island contributed, the Comité Directivo noted in July 1937: New regional and local subcommittees were establishing themselves, making the association's efforts truly national.[75] Qualitative assessments showed diverse people and groups offering donations and volunteering their time to serve the AANPE.[76] The clearest validation for the claim of diversity, however, was quantitative, coming from financial data detailing contributions large and small from people and groups all over Cuba and abroad.

Campaign Finances

For most of its existence, the AANPE recorded and published detailed accounts of its sources of income, going so far as to record the five cents someone found once in an empty jug in the association's office.[77] Organizational records also indicate that, at least at first, AANPE leaders penned handwritten thank-you notes to individual donors and those who organized group collections; such notes dated May–November 1937 expressed gratitude for donations ranging from $0.80 to $178.00.[78] This meticulousness in financial record keeping allows for quantitative analysis that provides another view of the association—particularly regarding its claim of widespread popular support.

The AANPE raised more than $18,800 during the nineteen months for which financial data are available.[79] Fund-raising success grew quickly during the first few months, with an average income of $13.51 per day from mid-March 1937 through the end of July, which more than doubled to an average daily income of $29.17 between August and December 1937.[80] The rapidity with which financial support poured in may confirm that there was a collective desire and enthusiasm to help the Spanish children. It may also indicate preexisting activist organizing networks at play, such as those which Casuso had from her days as a student organizer. During 1938, the daily average income ranged from a low of $22.77 for the month of June to an extraordinary $147.71 for December, by far the AANPE's best month. The organization gained income using a variety of methods: it collected membership dues and subscription fees; sold copies of ¡Ayuda!, bonds, stamps, postcards, fans, and buttons; held ticketed events; received funds raised by its delegations and children's committees across the island and during radio drives; and enjoyed numerous donations sent in without direct solicitation by organizations, groups, businesses, families, and individuals.

A graphic representation (graph 4.1) of available monthly income and expense data (no records were located for January–March 1938) illustrates several points related to AANPE finances. Income maintained relative stability from month to month compared to expenditures, which varied much more widely. The notable exception is December 1938, when income spiked dramatically, but that month was extraordinary for a number of specific reasons, which we will discuss further. Overall, income generally increased in 1937 and declined in 1938. Expense data display two different types of spending. Day-to-day association expenditures account for the gradual slope of slow increase over time, whereas spikes show large shipments of monetary and material aid to Europe. Aside from these discreet expenditure events, income exceeded expenses, suggesting that the association was thrifty in terms of its administrative costs.

What does the income pattern visible in graph 4.1 indicate about the popularity of the AANPE? To break down income into two categories is illuminating. Centralized fund-raising consisted of money collected directly by AANPE leaders or participants: membership dues and subscription collection, and

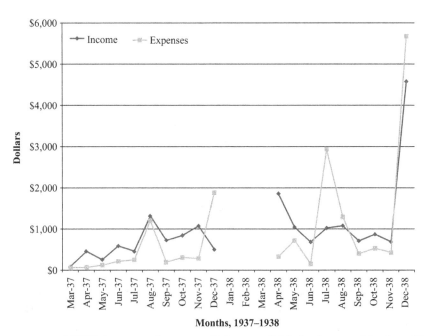

GRAPH 4.1 AANPE income and expenses (data unavailable for January–March 1938)

bond, stamp, postcard, fan, button, bulletin, and ticket sales. Grassroots fund-raising consisted of money contributed without direct sale or solicitation in person or in writing: contributions sent into AANPE headquarters by regional delegations and children's committees; organization, group, business, family, and individual donations; and money pledged during association radio broadcasts. Getting people to pay dues and buy items in one-on-one interactions required systematic work by core AANPE leaders or participants in Havana. Such income represented the hard work of a relatively small, central group of the association's most dedicated activists. In contrast, donations made by radio listeners, organizations, groups, businesses, families, individuals, and AANPE adherents self-organized in various regions of the country—grassroots contributions—may be interpreted as supporting association leaders' claims of spontaneous, widespread support by Cubans.

Using April 1937 as a starting point, graph 4.2 compares centralized and grassroots income at three-month intervals, though complete data are unavailable for January 1938.[81] The graph illustrates trends over the course of the association's existence.

Starting off slightly greater than grassroots income, centralized income dipped between April and July 1937, then grew strongly and steadily. That

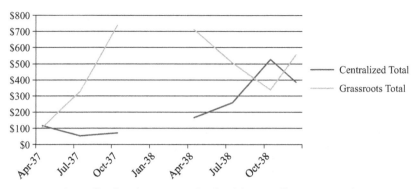

GRAPH 4.2 Centralized and grassroots fund-raising, April 1937–December 1938 (data unavailable for January–March 1938)

leaders built up their fund-raising structures and capacity over time, maintaining contacts while cultivating new ones, likely explains this trend in centralized income. In contrast, grassroots income grew sharply during the first year and plummeted during the second in a curve similar to that of overall income (graph 4.1), excluding the extraordinary month of December 1938. Similarities between grassroots and overall income suggest that grassroots income drove fund-raising; indeed, for much of the AANPE's existence, grassroots income figures were higher than those for centralized income.

What does the steep decrease in grassroots income during 1938 indicate? One hypothesis is that donors became disheartened by bad news from the Spanish front as Nationalist forces gained momentum and Republicans lost ground. To test the theory, we must account for the surge in income in December 1938. The fact that association leaders were instrumental in the organization of a massive reception for Fernando de los Ríos, the Spanish Republic's ambassador to the United States, at Havana's Polar Stadium that month (discussed later in this chapter) explains the notable decrease in forms of centralized fund-raising other than event income: with all the work they did for the stadium event, AANPE activists had little time for other efforts. Meanwhile, excitement surrounding the ambassador's visit boosted both spirits and donations. Though the reversal in trends for centralized and grassroots income in December 1938 might appear to challenge the theory of an inverse relationship between demoralization and grassroots support, in fact, it does not. The stadium event that month was unique in the association's history, and it accounts for the recovery of grassroots support precisely because it rallied supporters weary of Republican losses.

Total income is one way to measure popular grassroots support; qualitative information about donations is another. Information recorded for each donation beyond the monetary amount is not standardized in AANPE records: sometimes just a person's name was noted; other times title, family, location, institution, and/or dedication information was included. The portrait of giving observed in sample months October 1937 and 1938 exemplifies the diversity typical of contributors, showing a combination of *donativos* (donations from single individuals or families) and *colectas* (collections) from a variety of donors of different ages, genders, relationship status, and geographic origin.[82] The AANPE seems to have been particularly eager to highlight donations by women and children, a practice unsurprising given its messaging. The diverse geographic origins of donations were also a point of pride for the association, a point illustrated by a handwritten list of donations that noted the province of each donor: twelve from Oriente, ten from Camagüey, eight from Santa Clara, three from Havana, and two each from Matanzas and Pinar del Río.[83] The archival record as a whole shows that collaboration came not only from every part of the island but also from locations abroad, such as Kingston, Jamaica; San Juan, Puerto Rico; Santo Domingo, Dominican Republic; Port-au-Prince, Haiti; Tampa, Florida; and New York City.

Other donation records offer further clues about the diversity of participants in various regards: occupation, collaborative effort, personal motivation, and racial identification. In May 1937, the AANPE received $20.00 from the fishermen of the Sociedad de Marineros Pescadores de Batabano (Society of Fishermen Mariners of Batabano) on the Caribbean coast south of Havana; in September 1937, "la señora Ana Rodríguez y Serrano" and "la señorita Chana García y Hernández" collected $7.00 in the neighborhood of Luyanó in Havana; in October 1937, the sister of Cuban combat volunteer Angel Rufo, "who fell in Jarama assassinated by fascism" while fighting with the Centuria Guiteras, along with her late brother's friends, collected $4.60; and in November 1937, the association welcomed an institutional donation of $5.00 from the Club Atenas (Athens Club), the most eminent traditional black society in Cuba.[84] In addition to that of its adherent regional delegations and children's committees across the island, the AANPE enjoyed support from labor unions, businesses, publications, Masonic lodges, and other groups. Their donations to the association not only gave strong credibility to the claim that widespread and diverse popular support for its work existed among Cubans but, more importantly, allowed for impressive accomplishments on the part of the association.

Campaign Accomplishments

The AANPE's first major act after its founding was coordination of the reception of the ship *Mexique*. The Cuban government did not allow the ship to land, in keeping with its policy of neutrality, but Cubans either met the ship in the water and boarded it or lined the shore to welcome the young Spaniards and send them on to their new home. The association used support for the reception as evidence of its grassroots character: a single call from the AANPE, the Comité Directivo declared, mobilized "all of society represented in its parties, associations, unions, and individually" for the reception. In turn, the committee stated, the experience of coming face to face with the war's young victims had reinforced public desire to assist them.[85] The association used its bulletin to bring even more Cubans face to face with the young refugees on the page.

In an article titled "With the Children Who Voyaged on the *Mexique*," Casuso expressed her own and others' reaction to meeting the Spanish children, depicting a scene of tenderness, sorrow, and hope. The eyes of Casuso's friend Ramiro Valdés Daussá—a man "hardened in tough fights" in Cuba's revolutionary struggle—filled with tears as he held the tiny hands of Pepa Henares. A child named María Luisa Corzo gave Avelino Rodríguez— the president of the Círculo Español Socialista (Spanish Socialist Circle), who had fought for the Republic—the only property she had, a photograph of her family. Casuso described a peaceful scene of Corzo's family seated by a lake with swans, then quoted the photograph's inscription written by the girl's mother: "My little girl, do not forget me." The family in the photograph no longer existed, Teté told readers. The girl's father died fighting alongside La Pasionaria (Dolores Ibárruri), and her mother was in the hospital. That the child would give away this photograph to one of the Cubans required no commentary, Casuso stated, offering some nonetheless: "A child who gives away the last thing left to her in the world as a token of gratitude gives us a piece of her heart." After narrating a number of similarly dramatic vignettes and touching on all of the central themes of the association's message, Casuso concluded by emphasizing the momentous importance of the *Mexique* reception for AANPE organizing. Here were the people of all races and nationalities, she claimed, neither loyal (Republican) nor rebel (Nationalist). "It was the unanimous gesture of the multitude that congregated to see them pass through, and to say to them that here, in Cuba, we love them, we empathize with them, with them we know suffering." As the ship departed, sailing out past El Morro at the entrance of Havana's harbor, Teté envisioned Spaniards and Cubans "in a salute that is now neither communist nor socialist because it has become the salute against fascism, the salute of world democracy."[86] In these statements, the president of the AANPE encapsulated the complexity of balancing the organization's unifying, nonpartisan ideal and the reality of its strong commitment to antifascism.

AANPE leaders' next task was collecting winter clothing for children in Spain, an effort they dubbed the Ropero Invernal del Niño Español (Spanish Child's Winter Clothing Drive). The association received individual, family, *colecta*, and organizational donations and held a fund-raiser at the Prado Cinema during the autumn of 1937 to support this effort. Organizational donors included the association's Hebrew Committee and several regional delegations, socialist groups, labor unions, a women's organization, and the radio program *Diario Español del Aire*. One highlighted individual donor was Dr. Luis Álvarez Tavío, an AANPE leader, a former military medical officer, and a member of the Communist-led commission organized to send Cuban combat volunteers to Spain. The majority of funds raised went immediately to purchase clothing and sewing supplies.[87]

While monetary donations came from various sources, women especially were asked to contribute their time and effort as volunteers.[88] The AANPE's Women's Committee took on leadership of the drive and organized volunteers to sew and collect clothing.[89] An *¡Ayuda!* reporter visited the AANPE offices one evening late in November 1937 to provide bulletin readers with a view of volunteers at work. At ten thirty at night, the atmosphere in the room was feverish and agitated, the author reported, but the Ropero volunteers felt happy and proud to be engaged in such important work. In addition to volunteer work at this central office, distinct AANPE delegations throughout the island sewed and collected clothing. The delegation of Santiago de Cuba, for example, had sent 858 coats (*piezas de abrigo*) up to that point. Other organizations supportive of the Spanish Republic conducted clothing drives of their own and brought in the items collected. These donations demonstrate coordinated collaboration within Cuba's antifascist network. Many women volunteered to sew in their homes, while others directed the purchasing of supplies. María Prieto's Dressmaking Academy devoted entire days to the Ropero. Clothing stores owned by Spaniards contributed, as did "several establishments of Hebrews," but reception among the majority of clothing stores had been negative. The aforementioned store owner who claimed that "his religion did not permit him to donate clothing to children in loyalist territory" may have believed the Republic to be anti-Catholic. It is certainly also possible that he simply hit upon the first excuse that would keep him from having to give away his merchandise, a proposition likely unattractive to many retailers without strong partisan motivation. Overcoming the difficulty of requesting goods, money, or volunteer effort was a central AANPE activity. The *¡Ayuda!* reporter visiting the clothing drive sought to convey the industrious commitment of its volunteers and the good feeling in the room to inspire new participation and contributions. Evoking revolutionary feminine heroism in language that echoed Cuban anarchist rhetoric, he envisioned a Spanish boy dressed in a suit sewn with care by the "noble women of Cuba," and the child's father finding solace amid the devastation of war in this act of solidarity by his Cuban sisters. The clothing drive would elevate the "moral prestige" of the Cuban people, the reporter assured readers, before "another indomitably heroic people"—those of Spain.[90] Indeed, the first Ropero enjoyed considerable success: by December, the association reported having sent five enormous crates containing five thousand children's coats to the consul of the Spanish Republic in France.[91]

Through much of 1938, the principal goal toward which the AANPE labored was the establishment of its residential school for refugee children, the Casa-Escuela Pueblo de Cuba, in the Catalan town of Sitges.[92] The association enjoyed widespread support for this effort from political, social, cultural, nationalist, worker, women's, black, Jewish, Spanish, and Masonic organizations, which "offer[ed] their generous and cordial hand to help save the life and soul of 100 Spanish children" (see table 4.1).[93]

The political and social diversity represented in this list of organizations early in 1938 previewed the type of alliance antifascism would inspire as it became mainstream in Cuba that same year. The association highlighted, in particular, Masonic contributions, gratefully acknowledging a pledge by the Supreme Council of the Grand Lodge of the Island of Cuba to support the Casa-Escuela's creation. "With this gesture that enhances it and honors us," the AANPE stated, "Cuban Masonry says loudly that it does not forget the duty of human solidarity which the Masonic tradition obliges."[94] In addition to this strong institutional support, many Cuban and Spanish individuals worked toward the creation of the residential school.[95] While a group of Cubans fought alongside Republican forces, Berta Arocena wrote, once again betraying the association's partisan stance, the "little Cuban house" symbolized the "honorable rearguard" of the Cuban people.[96]

In May 1938, the AANPE announced that black Cuban educator Rosa Pastora Leclerc would travel to Spain to become the director of the Casa-

TABLE 4.1 Initial contributors to the AANPE Casa-Escuela

Asociación de Obreros Manuales	Resp. Logia "Antonio de la Piedra"
Asociación Unión Revolucionaria	Resp. Logia "Fe Masónica"
Centre Català	Resp. Logia "Hijos de la Fe Masónica" (Sagua)
Comité Estudiantil 28 de Enero	Resp. Logia "Los Apóstoles"
Comité Femenino Hebreo	Resp. Logia "Pí y Margall"
Gran Logia Isla de Cuba de Ciego de Avila	Resp. Logia "Progreso" (Santa Clara)
Gran Logia Obreros de Morón	Sindicato de Obreros de Cervecerías
Hermandad de los Jóvenes Cubanos	Sindicato de Panaderos de la Habana
Nueva Agrupación de Jóvenes del Pueblo	Sociedad Naturista "Vida"
Organización Auténtica	Sociedad Unión de Vendedores de la Habana
Partido Agrario Nacional	Unión de Empleados de Cafés
Partido Revolucionario Cubano	Unión Nacional de Mujeres

Escuela.[97] Symbolic herself, Rosa was the "personification of Cuban teaching" and "knew as her own the sacrifice and the pain of the Spanish people."[98] The Casa-Escuela opened its doors that May. An editorial described the "happy and luminous morning" when a cable arrived from Spain announcing the "anxiously awaited news," and encouraged further donations to fund the work of educating the children.[99] Another article took the form of a conversation between Pastora Leclerc and a student, in which the director teaches the young Spaniard about her distant island home. The article describes a tender scene between teacher and student sitting by the sea, where high above, fluttering in the breeze, are "the flag of Martí" and "the tricolor flag with which Spain gloriously opens its new history."[100] In July of that year, at the International Conference to Aid the Spanish Children in Paris, Pastora Leclerc delivered an impassioned address, and the AANPE was "jubilant with healthy satisfaction" at the participation of its distinguished delegate in a world event of such importance.[101] Thus, the Cuban teacher succeeded in connecting Cuba to Spain and to the transnational antifascist network.

Though the school would operate under her leadership for less than a year before a Nationalist military advance would send Pastora Leclerc out of Spain, Cubans felt great pride in this direct care they were able to provide to a small number of Spanish children. A photograph published in October 1938 showed a visit to the school by members of the "Cuban Club Julio Antonio Mella in Barcelona, who overwhelmed the surprised and joyful children of the residence with Cuban songs and rhythms."[102] With grim optimism in December 1938, the AANPE continued its attempt to rally support for the school with statements and samples of schoolwork from the children there. Ten-year-old Rafael González wrote with appreciation that Cubans "bring us food, clothing," and "they sacrifice for us." Twelve-year-old Enrique Orejón wrote that he and his fellow students were "very content and grateful for the help of Cuba and other nations," especially the Cuban *campesinos* (peasants), "who work cheerfully to send us everything we need so that we will be healthy and strong." He looked forward to being a man and to the future, when peace would reign and Spain and all the other nations would be free.[103] Though such gratitude and optimism surely warmed some Cuban hearts, the reality of looming Republican defeat was sobering. Pastora Leclerc urged Cubans to turn their attention to aiding child refugees in Barcelona, whose numbers she estimated to be in the hundreds of thousands, and told readers that the children of the Casa-Escuela had stated that they did not wish to be evacuated to France but instead wanted to go to Cuba.[104] Her words surely evoked both pride and sorrow in Cubans who had devoted themselves to aiding the children of Spain, yet it was beyond their capacity to fulfill the children's request.

Over the same few months in autumn 1938, the AANPE continued with an aid project it *could* accomplish: a second clothing drive. As cold weather in Spain approached once again, the association called for a renewed effort to collect winter clothes, expressing the hope that the Ropero of 1938 would outdo that of 1937. A published thank-you note written by two Spanish children in gratitude for past donated clothing was meant to inspire new commitment.[105] Men should contribute their money, the association indicated, while women should donate their time—sewing in their homes or with other volunteers at the offices, where sewing machines and materials were available. "If you have already made a donation," the bulletin stated, "repeat it, because wartime necessities also reproduce themselves continuously."[106] In her radio address, Señora Gordón Ordas praised clothing-drive volunteers, expressing gratitude to the women who worked day and night—women with "the soul of mothers of children they have never even met."[107] As the deepest part of winter 1939 coincided with Republican despair, AANPE board member María Josefa Bolaños called on "the conscience of the Cuban woman" to save the children of the Spanish mother, "because the blood of these children is blood that runs through our veins."[108]

The drive achieved greater success in 1938 than it had in 1937. During autumn 1938 it raised $3,108.15. Some of the money went to organizing benefits, but financial records show that these expenses were well worth it—

for example, the AANPE spent just $208.38 on a large gathering in Hatuey Park at the beginning of September, and the event raised more than half of the total fund-raising income for autumn 1938. That the Ropero spent the majority of its funds on sewing supplies and other expenses related to its central mission contributed greatly to its success.[109] In October, an exhibit displayed thousands of coats at the Casa de la Cultura.[110] In November, that year's first shipment to Europe included 7,326 coats, the "fecund result of two months of work," as well as food, clothing, and supplies.[111] In January 1939, the second shipment included 4,700 pieces of clothing (*piezas de ropa*) and assorted provisions.[112] Toward the end of January, the association sent almost all of its remaining funds—$130.00—to the Committee for Spanish Children in Paris for "urgent aid to evacuated children." Meanwhile, its delegations from Guantánamo and Santiago de Cuba sent shipments of clothing and other supplies independently.[113] Published photographs of the delegation from Camagüey show a large group of women and girls posed with sewing machines and needles and thread, and a room full of children's clothing piled, draped, and hung on every surface.[114]

In the end, the second Ropero sent well over twelve thousand pieces of clothing, along with food and other helpful items, expanding significantly on the successes of the first. With their effort, Cubans combated an enemy that stretched the definition of *fascist* for one association writer: "Winter was feudalism congealing battalions during the French Revolution, was Tsarist when sinking the revolutionaries in Siberia, and today is fascist when he tortures with his black sword the child of Spain and his enlightened people."[115] Leonor Pérez Almeida—a Cuban student leader of "fighting spirit and very agile mentality," stationed in Barcelona while working for the Consejo Nacional de la Infancia Evacuada (National Council of Evacuated Children)—recounted witnessing an emotional scene in the Ministerio de Instrucción Pública (Ministry of Public Instruction) that emphasized the Ropero efforts: "Upon opening the boxes of clothing," she wrote, a Spanish man hardened by the war was unable to hold back tears as he took "in his callused hands the tiny, delicate clothes made with so much love and conscientiousness by the hands of Cuban women."[116] This image, suggestive of a transatlantic Spanish Cuban family striving and suffering together, surely evoked emotion in Cuban readers.

The AANPE's final large accomplishment was the organization of the massive gathering in the Polar Stadium on 18 December 1938 to hear Fernando de los Ríos—the Spanish Republic's ambassador—speak. This event occurred when Republican defeat in Spain was already apparent, yet it was by all accounts a rousing success. The AANPE called it "one of the most extraordinary mass events Cuba has witnessed throughout its republican life," stating that eighty thousand people attended and publishing photographs showing the stadium packed with an enormous crowd.[117] The event was vital at a moment when grassroots energy—and financial support—had dropped. It raised spirits and, as previously noted, significant funds.

In his introduction, leftist intellectual and political activist Juan Marinello[118]—addressing the "representatives of the Spanish, Mexican, and Chinese republics" in attendance—noted that upon entering the stadium, he had witnessed "the worker arm in arm with the intellectual, the peasant in the company of the student, the man with the woman and the white with the black." A multitude was present in the stadium, and many more clustered around radios to hear the ambassador's voice. Marinello evoked broad solidarity and popular support, seeking to reenergize Cuban antifascists. His oration combined leftist vision with *hispanismo* or *hispanidad* in a manner common to Cuban antifascism vis-à-vis Spain. To inspire Cubans, Marinello drew a link between Don Fernando and José Martí, reiterating the common theme of a "bad" Spain, represented by colonialism and Franco, and a "good" Spain, embodied in the Republican ambassador and Cuba's anticolonial struggle.[119] He reinforced this connection with the example of his late friend, Pablo de la Torriente Brau. Pablo died for Spain, which was the same as dying for Cuba, Marinello said. Pablo had been proud to have learned to read using the texts of Martí, and it was Martí who taught him that "the obligation of a man was to be where he was needed most." Thus, it was Martí who sent Pablo to Spain, Marinello suggested, and Spain inspired in him a vision of a marvelous new dawn. The Spanish children for whom the AANPE organized Don Fernando's visit would live this glorious future, he concluded to a prolonged ovation.[120] The connection drawn between Pablo's sacrifice and the work of the AANPE surely must have pleased Teté, who would remain fond of Marinello even as her anticommunist beliefs solidified and he became affiliated with the Communist Party.

Similarly, Fernando de los Ríos emphasized the special relationship between Spain and Cuba. He called his Cuban listeners "a substantial element of an eternal Spain that lives in you." He pointed out their shared language and history. The Spanish ambassador also highlighted the strength of international solidarity with the Spanish Republic and of transnational antifascism. Like Marinello, he made salutations to the Mexican and Chinese representatives present. He stated that the Republic's situation was an issue of "universal" relevance and concern, and he noted majority popular support in multiple countries. At various times throughout history, he claimed, Spain had inspired Germans, the British, and the Chinese, serving as an example and as "the only hope of the world." Therefore, he argued, the shared struggle for the Spanish Republic "in this hour of moral semi-darkness" was a defense for the future of all humanity.[121]

In support of the claim of international solidarity and transnational antifascism, the AANPE published many of the telegrams received in support of the event and read even more aloud in the stadium. Messages of support came from Ciudad Trujillo (Santo Domingo), Dominican Republic; from a union in Buenos Aires, Argentina; and from the Círculo Cubano de Tampa (Tampa Cuban Circle) and the Centro Español de Tampa (Tampa Spanish Center) in Tampa, Florida. Fifteen solidarity telegrams from across Cuba came from groups such as the Santa Clara Provincial Assembly and the Palma Soriano Committee of the Communist Party, the Cayo Hueso neighborhood branch of the ABC, the Eastern Regional Anarchist Federation in Palma Soriano, an Isabela de Sagua chapter of the youth-oriented black Cuban group Jóvenes del Pueblo (Youth of the People), and the Santa Clara Provincial Assembly of the Organización Auténtica (a splinter group of the Partido Revolucionario Cubano—Auténtico), as well as from individuals.[122] This outpouring of support, as financial analysis shows, produced a dramatic final boost of income before Republican defeat, allowing the AANPE to continue serving its cause during the final months of the war.

Teté's Journey

In the wake of her personal tragedy, Teté summoned a remarkable burst of energy, as demonstrated by her hard work and tangible results on behalf of the AANPE. The association she founded organized diverse Cubans to provide substantial assistance to children affected by the Spanish Civil War and simultaneously built Cuban solidarity with the Spanish Republic. Rather than becoming defeated by her husband's death in Spain, she did indeed "do something to help the unhappy people for whose liberty Pablo had given his life." Though her creative energy and commitment in the aftermath of her tragedy produced these remarkable results, long-term resilience proved to be more challenging. "For seven months I worked hard building up this organization, speaking over the air and at meetings, visiting villages all over the island, helping to get out our monthly publication, soliciting co-operation through magazine and newspaper articles," she wrote. Then, in early 1938, she stepped down from her role as AANPE president and escaped once again into exile, leaving for Mexico to work on publishing Pablo's Spanish chronicles.[123] "I went for three months," she wrote of her trip, "and stayed for almost two years."[124] Her activist impulse had not been extinguished forever, but for the time being, Teté's energy had run out. Her flight to Mexico did not, however, break the thread of continuity in her political activism and that of her late husband, which lived on in the organization she had created. Pablo was celebrated posthumously when several of the AANPE children's committees across the island took his name. In February 1939, *¡Ayuda!* published a photograph of one of those committees in Santiago de Cuba, noting that it was the third such group to take Torriente's name "with just pride." It was a name, the caption stated, that "due to his noble life, and his heroic death, is a worthy medallion, and a faithful shelter to the effort of these children." Torriente's blood was not spilled in vain, the comment concluded in the bleak winter of Republican defeat, for it "lights by fires of daybreak this dawn of humanity."[125]

5 Cuba Can Be Proud of Her Sons

Transnational Work by Cuban Antifascists

. . . .

Transnational identities and experiences were common among Cuban anti-fascists. Those who had not been born abroad and those who were not the children of immigrants, nor migrants themselves, nevertheless lived in a postcolonial and neocolonial country shaped by the historical legacy of Spain and the presence of the United States. Cuba was flooded with foreign capital, owners, managers, and workers. Cubans encountered foreign people, languages, businesses, goods, and ideas on the island and abroad. Those who did leave the island found refuge and possibility in countries such as the United States, Spain, and Mexico when conditions at home became bleak politically or economically, or whenever individuals and families sought a new start. Cubans' transnational movements were frequently circular: they left and returned repeatedly. In the process, Cubans became bi- or multilingual; connected with people of other nationalities, establishing and joining transnational networks; picked up cultural competency in foreign lands; and, in some cases, compared other political, economic, and social systems to their own. The encounter with the foreign at home and abroad shaped Cubans' transnational identities. Their transnational outlook also fundamentally shaped their experiences, inclusive of popular politics. Transnational movement, networks, and solidarity proved critical for the strength of Cuban antifascism as a continuation of the fight for a New Cuba.

In addition to migration and the colonial condition, internationalist political ideologies and groups led to transnationalism for some Cubans. For others, racial or ethnic identification and a sense of membership in a diaspora or connection to an ancestral home was a point of access to transnationalism. Institutionalized fraternal loyalty created points of contact across borders and oceans for members of multinational societies and orders. A general sense of connectedness provided by the ever-increasing capability of global travel and communication enhanced people's ability to foster transnational identities and have transnational experiences. Representing multiple sources of Cuban transnationalism, Cuban volunteers in Spain, antifascist Cubans of African descent, and Cuban Masonic antifascists show

how transnational identities and experiences, networks and solidarities, facilitated the continuation of struggle for a New Cuba through antifascism.

"We Could Not Do Much in Cuba or in U.S.A.":
Transnationalism and Cuban Volunteers

In a July 1937 *Mediodía* interview with Alberto Moré Tabío titled "Cuba puede estar orgullosa de sus hijos" (Cuba can be proud of her sons), African American Communist leader James W. Ford celebrated the notable actions and achievements of Cuban volunteers on foreign soil. The Centuria Guiteras, he stated, was one of the most important units of the U.S. Abraham Lincoln Battalion. Cubans who had never been soldiers advanced against the armies of Germany and Italy, forcing the enemy to retreat. Cuban volunteer Alejandro "Cheo" Anceaume, who had lost an eye, joked with Ford about the glass replacement, demonstrating to the North American "the extent to which the Cuban can maintain his sense of humor." Besides their good humor, Cubans brought their good music to Spain. Ford commented: "The Creole music brings a note of color in the middle of horrible war. The Cubans have a magnificent pianist Arsenio Brunet, a violinist Gustavo Rodríguez, and lack neither a maracas player nor a master of the bongo." Other notable Cuban talents being put to use in Spain included those in medicine—"a loyal representative of the Cuban intelligentsia caring for wounded Americans and Cubans on the front"—and baseball—a player who "put his craft, with all his heart, in the service of the Spanish people and of world democracy" as a grenade launcher.[1] Also important was the Cubans' good cheer; Ford claimed they "always [brought] the note of happiness to the trenches." Ford celebrated, in Moré Tabío's words, "the boys who, from New York and Havana, embarked for Spain demonstrating that on our island there are many men—very many—who do not recognize borders when it comes to defending a noble and just cause."[2]

In this celebratory account, Ford focused on volunteer characteristics that he identified specifically as Cuban. That their identities were transnational also affected Cubans' experiences as volunteers in Spain, putting them in a unique position relative to many other international volunteers: they served as translators, could blend in among Spaniards, and could fall back on their foreignness when it was advantageous to do so. Those chameleonlike qualities took root in the Cuban antifascist imagination: the Spanish and Cuban fights could be blended, compared, or distinguished at will. Thus, transnational identities also informed Cubans' sense of themselves as carrying out a continuity of their domestic struggle for a New Cuba in the foreign conflict.

Cubans understood the language of the conflict. For all of the unity and solidarity the International Brigades represented, it was impossible to overlook the practical problems created by foreign volunteer participation. As one 1938 article in the 35th Division periodical *Reconquista* put it, people from the little villages close to the International Brigades base "stared in amazement at the strange men who spoke unintelligible languages." Not only did they speak different languages than that of their host nation, but they spoke different languages from one another. Language, the article noted, was "a very difficult barrier to cross," particularly on the field of battle.[3] The work of the pro-Republican fighters in Spain thus suffered from the same affliction as the biblical builders of the Tower of Babel. The difficulties of communication between people of different tongues were amplified under the stressful, chaotic, and often terrifying conditions of war. All Cubans spoke Spanish, and some also spoke English, allowing them to communicate with Spaniards and international volunteers from multiple countries.

Sharing a common language with their hosts—and especially bilingualism—gave Cubans an enhanced opportunity to contribute to the antifascist cause. Recognizing that basic Spanish comprehension could make the difference between life and death, leaders in the International Brigades made Spanish instruction part of their larger educational program. "Culture militias" offered daily Spanish classes meant to teach international volunteers military vocabulary, common phrases, and basic grammar. Bridging the language gap was important for practical, ideological, and political reasons. As foreign volunteers developed their Spanish-language skills, an article in *Reconquista* celebrating the culture militias noted that the "comrades of different nationalities found in our manner of speaking the formidable bond of unity that was lacking for their work."[4] In other words, being able to speak to one another was a foundation of solidarity. Facilitating this language ability was a helpful role some Cubans could play in Spain. Bilingual Cubans could teach Spanish to volunteers from the United States, Canada, Great Britain, Ireland, and elsewhere. For example, Cuban Oscar Soler tutored U.S. nurse Fredericka Martin, his coworker at the Villa Paz military hospital in Saelices. Soler called himself Martin's "Spanish professor," and in a letter to her after the conflict ended, he prodded her to keep practicing: "Since I suppose you will not have forgotten it, I want, when you reply to me, that you do so in Spanish."[5]

Soler also worked as a translator in the military hospital during the conflict, exemplifying another important function served by bilingual Cubans. Despite their language instruction, many English-speaking volunteers still struggled to understand and to be understood. U.S. volunteer John Tisa recounted one such episode in his memoir. He recalled the story of a volunteer from New York serving as quartermaster for his battalion who called in an order for food. "His diction as yet was far from perfect and he was misunderstood." Instead of the request for *jamón*, or ham, which he thought he was making, an "order was placed for a hundred pounds of *jabón*—soap." Fortunately, someone in Madrid thought the order sounded odd and called back to check. "A Cuban got on the line," Tisa concluded, "and thanks to him we ate ham."[6] Spaniards, Cubans, and U.S. volunteers may have had a good chuckle over this misunderstanding, but it is representative of a serious problem that plagued the international forces and of how the transnational identities of Cuban volunteers equipped them to play the critical role of translating during the conflict.

English-language observations and remembrances of the Cubans often made note of the importance of bilingualism. In the village of Villanueva de la Jara, where a training headquarters was located, the men of the Centuria Guiteras impressed their U.S. counterparts when they "quickly established rapport with the villagers through a shared language."[7] U.S. volunteers had a more difficult time fitting in. "Language, at first, was a barrier, but it was surmounted with the aid of the Cuban volunteers, who never tired of helping," remembered Tisa.[8] Cubans, stated another U.S. volunteer, deserved credit for winning "the villagers' goodwill." They "acted as interpreters for the other volunteers. They were a very amiable group—personable and *simpatico* in the truest Spanish sense. With the Americans they were warmly welcomed and invited to dine in village homes."[9] These accounts of the Cubans' ability to meld into Spanish communities illustrate the importance of their role as intermediaries for other foreign volunteers.

The so-called Spanish Battalion (originally the 24th, later renumbered the 59th) of the XV International Brigade was another site in which Cuban volunteers were able to integrate relatively seamlessly with their Spanish hosts. The battalion consisted primarily of Spaniards, but alongside them were "other sons of Spain, those who feel palpitating in their soul the desire for complete freedom. CUBA," *Reconquista* noted. "The sensibility of the moral values of the beautiful Antillean country is among us." There were Greek, Polish, and U.S. volunteers in the "group of courageous fighters," the article stated, but Spaniards and Cubans made up its bulk. The men of multiple different nationalities spoke the same language, the article claimed: the language of liberty. In reality, however, they did not all speak the same language. The Spanish Battalion may have been "authentically Spanish [o]f soul and of sentiments," as the article claimed, but in fact, it was a cultural and linguistic jumble—just like the rest of the International Brigades. Therefore, the Cubans' ability to integrate with the Spaniards in the unit contributed to the positive feelings of the Iberian hosts toward their Caribbean brethren.[10]

Recognizing this special position of the Cubans and other Spanish Americans based on shared language and culture, the Republicans welcomed them into the regular Spanish armed forces as well as the International Brigades. Cuban Communist recruitment coordinator Ramón Nicolau González recalled that the leaders of the PCE conceived of placing willing Spanish American volunteers in the regular Spanish army. Nicolau González remembered that Cubans felt "overwhelming joy" at this invitation. Soldier placement was based on "positive factors such as the identity of language and other characteristics common to Spaniards and natives of their former colonies."[11] This invitation to integration was the clearest example that Cuban volunteers could choose when to blend in with the Spaniards.

When Cubans passed as Spaniards, it gave them a way to circumvent the non-intervention policies that made getting to Spain difficult for many foreign volunteers. For example, Cuban medical volunteer Pía Mastellari Maecha, companion of Dr. Luis Díaz Soto, another Cuban volunteer in Spain, pretended to be Spanish in order to enter the country. "For my trip to Spain a Spanish woman's passport was facilitated for me," she reported in a letter from Barcelona in March 1938, requesting assistance from the Spanish Communist Party in orchestrating a similar arrangement for her trip home. Like many other Cubans of her era, Pía had a complex transnational identity. Her father was Italian, and she was born in Mexico. She moved to Cuba with her family when she was a child and became a citizen as an adult. For her trip to Spain, she became "María García," a Spanish woman, and entered the country without incident.[12] Her relatively easy entrance into the country would not have been possible had she not been a native Spanish speaker, an advantage that Cuban volunteers enjoyed over those volunteers who did not share a language and culture with Spain.

On the other hand, Cubans could fall back on their foreignness in situations in which being Spanish would put them at a disadvantage, such as at the end of the conflict. Foreign volunteers began to head home en masse late in 1938, as Nationalist victory loomed. Many of those who did not make it out in time ended up in French concentration camps with Spanish refugees, while other international combatants were imprisoned in Spain. Back home on the island, activists petitioned the Cuban government to assist in bringing home the Cuban volunteers. One such petition appeared in November 1938, produced at an enormous assembly held by Cuban Communists in Havana's Polar Stadium and "signed" by the "80,000 attendees of the rally." These attendees requested official action by the Cuban government to liberate Cubans imprisoned by Spanish fascists.[13]

Due to such intervention of foreign activists and governments, as well as to their citizenship status, international volunteers had a relatively easier time than Spaniards arranging for transport to other countries. Fleeing Spanish refugees sought new homes for an unknown length of time; relocating them, therefore, was complicated. Cuban citizens, on the other hand, might not have been able to resume their lives in exile but could generally return to the island relatively easily, especially since Batista had made significant moves toward an antifascist position by the time international volunteers were leaving Spain.[14] Soler's marriage to a Spanish woman illustrates this disparity. In June 1939, Soler found himself in the Camp de Gurs in the Aquitaine region of southwestern France.[15] He wrote to his friend and student Fredericka Martin with sarcasm: "You know already that I am a *guest* of the French government and that they take very good care of me." At that time, he still had hope that he would travel to the United States, where he had lived before the war. By August, though, he was in Havana. He did not get his first choice of locations, and his life in Cuba was very hard.[16] At least, however, he was out of harm's way; his Spanish wife was stuck in a concentration camp in France.[17] He had hoped his friends in the United States would help raise money to bring her to Cuba. Then the Cuban Department of State had stated that the government would have her on a ship to the island by the end of August.[18] However, she was still in the camp two months later. The Cuban government, he had come to believe, was working to arrange for U.S. ships to take Cubans stuck in France to the United States and then to Cuba. Although his wife might be included in this group, it would probably take a long time, and "nothing effective" had yet been done. Winter approached, he lamented, and his wife was "in a very cold region of France" and was probably not equipped to deal with the cold.[19] The record of Soler's concerns ends here, and the reader is left to wonder if he and his Spanish wife were ever reunited. Their story illustrates the relative ease with which Soler, with his transnational identity, was able to escape the

French concentration camps relative to his Spanish wife, who languished there.

Some of the preceding examples show glimpses of the role of Communist Parties in the experiences of Cuban volunteers: in getting them to Spain, assisting them while there, and trying to get them home. International Communism provided experienced organizers, material resources, and an established network that greatly aided the recruitment of volunteers from multiple nations to fight for the Spanish Republic. The goals of this recruitment were internationalist; its mechanisms were transnational. The transnationalism of the Communist effort interfaced with the transnationalism of the Cuban volunteers, the two connected by particular individuals, places, and campaigns. In considering the transnational identities and experiences of Cuban volunteers in Spain, it is necessary both to uncover the influence of Communist organizing and to recognize Cuban transnationalism as distinct and separate from that organizing, even when the two are intertwined.

Volunteer recruitment in New York City following Torriente's death is one example of Communist organizing and Cuban transnationalism as distinct and separate yet intertwined. Torriente left for Spain before the Comintern call for foreign participation and the inauguration of the International Brigades, and he identified his decision to defend the Spanish Republic with his commitment to revolutionary change in Cuba, tying the two together with specifics of shared history and culture. Other Cubans followed Torriente's revolutionary example. Although some of the Cubans who followed his path were Communist Party members, others were unaffiliated Marxists, other leftists, members of Cuban political groups, or general antifascists. The pool of Torriente-inspired New York Cubans gathered at the Club Julio Antonio Mella. The Club Mella and the Communists shared many interpersonal and organizational connections, as exemplified by Cuban Communist leader and Club Mella representative Leonardo Fernández Sánchez, who had collaborated with Mella and later worked on the LAI publication *Masas* with Torriente, Roa, Marinello, and other Cuban anticolonial activists. Fernández Sánchez became a political and intellectual actor of central importance in the Cuban exile community in New York.[20] That he was both a Communist leader and a prominent Cuban activist positioned Fernández Sánchez to connect the Comintern call for volunteers with Cuban antifascists eager to follow in Torriente's footsteps. His leadership of the Club Mella provided the venue for Communist recruitment of Cuban volunteers for the International Brigades. Yet Communist recruitment at the

Club Mella succeeded in large part due to a strong sense of solidarity with the Spanish Republican cause among New York's Cubans, who had no political affiliation with Communism.[21] The club remained a diverse and authentically Cuban space, one of multifaceted transnational connection, even as it hosted a specifically Communist project.

The occasion of the first group of volunteers being sent from the island to serve the Spanish Republic was another moment in which the Communist Party and Cuban popular politics intersected within antifascism. In response to the call for trained fighters, Cuban Communist recruiter Nicolau González organized a group of experienced military men—those who had fought on the side of the revolution in Cuba in 1933 and remained loyal to it. The makeup of this group was particularly significant due to the fraught nature of the relationship of the military to both the people and the government in Spain and Cuba. Its military identity infused Cuba's first group of volunteers to leave from the island with meaning. They left for Spain on 15 April 1937, several months after the first Cuban group from the United States. Although they had been officials of the Cuban armed forces, the director of recruitment noted, they had "clean records," and numerous assessments made of the volunteers celebrated their antifascist credentials.[22] Their political histories served as foundations for their antifascism. Andrés González Lanuza, a forty-four-year-old captain, interpreted his involvement in Joven Cuba as antifascist, writing that he had "taken an active part in the Cuban revolution against fascism." Another member of the group— "Don" Julio Valdés Cofiño—had served in the Cuban military for thirteen years and had taken part in all the antireactionary fights on the island, according to his personnel file. All the Cubans in the group, according to correspondence between an official of the 11th Division of the Republican forces and the PCE Central Committee, had been "persecuted for their fight against Yankee imperialism." These facts were offered as proof to Spanish Communist officials of the Cuban volunteers' worthiness, "although they did not belong to the C[ommunist] P[arty] of Cuba," demonstrating the way in which the Cuban domestic struggle intertwined with Communist antifascist efforts.[23] Communists in Spain deemed non-Communist military Cubans with loyalty to and experience in anti-imperialist and antidictatorial struggles worthy, even those who were members of groups on the island that were not always on good terms with the PCC, such as Joven Cuba. In a similar vein, the Volunteer for Liberty commented that it was "not long since the Army and Navy were fighting on the side of revolution" in Cuba, and that "many men have come over from both branches and brought useful experience and training into Spain."[24] These volunteers' credentials were considered "antifascist," in that the PCE deemed Cuba's prior struggle as one against fascism. For the Spaniards, categorizing the Cuban struggle in this way allowed them to accept particularly useful volunteers, ones who had formal training and fighting experience and spoke Spanish. For the Cubans, this categorization acknowledged a continuity between the Cuban fight and antifascism, the importance of which was central and vital to the journeys of many Cuban volunteers.

Dr. Eduardo Odio Pérez embodied the continuity between the Cuban and Spanish struggles. He exemplified the ways in which prior experience in domestic activism and exile led some Cubans to volunteer for the Spanish Republic, and how transnational identity and experience shaped their antifascist trajectories. Odio Pérez was born in Santiago de Cuba in 1893 to a family one source called "petit-bourgeois."[25] Like many Cubans of his era, Eduardo lived a transnational life, frequently moving across national borders from an early age; unlike many, however, he ended up highly educated and employed in a relatively elite public post. He attended primary school in Santiago de Cuba and secondary school in Far Rockaway, New York, then pursued medical training at the University of Havana, Loyola University (1917), and Chicago Memorial Hospital, earning his medical degree.[26] From 1933 to 1935, Odio Pérez led the Disinfection and Sanitation Health Department in Havana.[27]

In addition to being a medical doctor and public employee, Odio Pérez was a committed political activist. He fought against Machado's regime, became a member of the Central Committee of Cuba's Partido Agrario Nacional (National Agrarian Party, or PAN), stood before trial courts in Havana in 1929 and 1930, spent time in jail, and went into political exile in 1930 and again in 1932.[28] In February 1930, he participated in an effort to organize his profession against Machado as part of a group of doctors who protested a planned homage to the strongman. The celebratory event divided the Federación Médica Cubana (Cuban Medical Federation), with some members supporting it and others vehemently opposed. Odio Pérez was one of the leaders of the latter group, helping to organize a protest against the federation when the homage went on as planned.[29] An editorial in the New York City Spanish-language periodical *Gráfico* (Graphic) on 15 February 1930 concluded that although the tribute event would take place despite the protest, the Cuban people would know that "honorable doctors" did not support it.[30] In May 1932, the secret police foiled a plot by "Dr. Eduardo Odio, revolutionary by profession," and others to stage an armed expedition from Honduras to Cuba. The group planned to land in Pinar del Río and join forces with troops led by General Mario García Menocal against Machado, an article in *La prensa* (The press) of San Antonio, Texas, reported on 9 June 1932. According to the article, members of the failed uprising, including Colonel Carlos Mendieta, were imprisoned on the Isle of Pines, the large island off the southern coast of Cuba. Menocal and Mendieta—the most prominent leaders of this wing of the resistance to Machado—had just been released the previous January from their imprisonment following the Río Verde uprising of August 1931.[31] A few years later, rebel-leader-turned-puppet-president Mendieta would be among those Dr. Odio Pérez—and many other Cuban activists—protested.

With a wife and three children, Dr. Odio Pérez found himself in exile again in 1935, this time in New York City. Odio Pérez recalled in 1968 that this exile was in response to his participation in the "struggle against the Machado Government."[32] In fact, he was exiled because of his involvement in the March 1935 strike.[33] For many Cuban activists, the fight against Batista was a continuation of the fight against Machado; this sense might explain Odio Pérez's statement that he was exiled in 1935 for fighting against Machado. Alternately, perhaps, he chose to reference the fight at which he and his *compañeros* had succeeded rather than the more ambiguous one. Nevertheless, the doctor continued his activism in exile.

Eduardo remembered attending May Day celebrations in New York City in the spring of 1935, which means he must have left Cuba soon after the March strike.[34] In October 1935, identified in his capacity as a representative of the Partido Agrario, the doctor spoke at a city meeting of Cuban exiles and their supporters against the "government of Caffery-Batista-Mendieta," a triumvirate of U.S. ambassador, military strongman, and puppet president identified as "traitorous to Cuban nationalism and an instrument of Yankee imperialism." The doctor argued that the "lands of the *guajiro*" had been "robbed by the North American companies." Members of Joven Cuba, the Auténticos, ORCA, and Puerto Rican political activists attended the meeting, held at a dancehall at 146th Street and Broadway. U.S. writer Carleton Beals sent a supportive telegram to the meeting calling for a triumph of revolution in Cuba before Christmas. Odio Pérez spoke alongside at least two other future Spanish Civil War volunteers from Cuba: Pablo de la Torriente Brau and Communist leader Joaquín Ordoqui.[35] During his time in New York, the doctor also became a member of the Club Julio Antonio Mella.[36] Like many of his fellow political exiles from Cuba, Odio Pérez continued the domestic struggle during his time in New York, and this continuity led him to antifascism.

It was likely through his involvement in the Club Mella that Odio Pérez became involved in supporting the Spanish Republic. He remembered attending a rally at Madison Square Garden, which featured an exhibition of ambulances to be donated to the Republicans. This became a moment of inspiration for him.[37] The gathering the Cuban doctor recalled was likely the New York reception for Spanish Republican ambassador Fernando de los Ríos, which took place on 4 January 1937. The *New York Times* reported that approximately sixteen thousand people attended the gathering organized by the "United Spanish Societies, an organization of fraternal and benevolent groups in the Spanish colonies of the metropolitan area." The American Medical Bureau (AMB) presented four ambulances "to the Spanish Leftist government," AMB members pushing two of the vehicles into the giant hall to rousing applause.[38] "I could appreciate it was a serious and strong organization," Odio Pérez noted, which inspired him to volunteer with the first AMB contingent to leave for Spain.[39] The group left for Europe twelve days later, on 16 January.[40]

Explaining his arrival at antifascism, Odio Pérez cited his "political awareness" and "humanitarianism" as motives for his choice to travel to Spain. Also, he stated explicitly the connection he saw between the Cuban struggle and the Spanish one: "We could not do much in Cuba or in U.S.A., helping to win the war in Spain, it was much easi[e]r [than] to knock down Machado."[41] This quotation appears in the same 1968 document in which the doctor names Machado where chronology would indicate he meant Batista. For many activists of the period, fighting against Machado had been the defining struggle of their lives. Odio Pérez suggested that it would be easier to defeat Franco's still-young military uprising in Spain than to oust Batista's already substantially entrenched military takeover in Cuba. Using Franco as a proxy for Batista in this way would become a Cuban tradition with significant longevity.

Sons of America, of Spain, and of Africa:
Black Cuban Antifascism and the Spanish Civil War

Cubans of African descent had the same transnational identity as their compatriots of other ancestries, but they had the additional transnational framework of pan-Africanism. Chapter 2 introduced how Cuban antifascists concerned with the defense of Ethiopia projected that fight onto Spain; this section discusses how the black Cuban antifascist embrace of the defense of the Spanish Republic was another exploration of Cuban transnationalism, one that brought into tension multiple identities among Cubans of African descent.

As they had in the case of Ethiopia, black Cuban antifascists viewed the conflict in Spain as an anticolonial struggle and identified with it by imagining themselves as fellow anticolonial fighters. Even though Spain was itself a European power, it was still in danger of falling to others far more powerful. Spanish collaborators of foreign fascists would "bring about the dismemberment of their country, imposing on the lands of Spain servitude to foreign powers," stated José Luciano Franco in February 1937, having turned his attention from the declarations of Emperor Selassie to Universal Panorama, a recurrent column on world events that appeared in Nicolás Guillén's periodical *Mediodía* as well as in the black activist publication *Adelante*. If fascism triumphed, he argued, Spain would become "a mere Italo-German colony."[42]

The question of colonization brought with it familiar claims of civilization and barbarity. Black Cuban antifascists praised the Republicans for their forces of "popular militias that have made safe the best of the intelligentsia of the country, in order to take the immortal and civilizing soul of Spain today away from the dangers of the fierce and exterminating fighting." By protecting the intelligentsia, Republicans promoted the antifascist version of civilization: cultural and social progress. In contrast to Republican civilization and progress, José Luciano Franco emphasized the brutality of fascist violence in Spain, calling Spanish Nationalists "hordes" and accusing them of committing "horrors" and "barbarous deeds." Fascists' ferocious acts reminded Cubans, he noted, of the "tragic repressions" of the Spanish colonial era on the island, such as those committed by the infamous Valeriano Weyler during the Cuban War of Independence.[43] This comparison referenced a common Cuban antifascist argument about Spain: that the Spanish Nationalists represented the Old Spain that colonized Cuba—Weyler's Spain—whereas Republican triumph would herald the permanence of a New Spain characterized by progress.

While criticizing fascist violence, black Cuban antifascists praised violence in defense of the Republic as necessary and progressive. *Adelante*'s administrator, Mariano Salas Aranda, made a direct comparison between new Republican Spain's struggle in the 1930s and that of Cuba for independence beginning in 1868. The achievement of liberty and rights resulted from revolution, he wrote. Discussing historical examples of important revolutions, Salas Aranda emphasized that these struggles were characterized by necessary violence and cost nations "the blood of their sons." Indeed,

Cuban independence would not have been achieved if not for the armed movement of 1868. Like Cuba, *Adelante*'s administrator argued, the Spanish people "must necessarily give their contribution of blood," for only then would the results last: "The conquests of the revolution obtained will be sealed with blood and imperishable."[44] This optimistic assessment of triumph and permanence glossed over many complexities and disappointments in the history of revolutionary change but nevertheless demonstrated Salas Aranda's attempt to place the Spanish conflict in a global context of justified armed struggle—in Cuba and elsewhere—throughout time.

When Salas Aranda conflated the powerful forces of old, colonizing Spain with fascism, he contrasted them with democracy, his desired goal. The Spanish Nationalists—the forces of the monarchy, military, landowners, and clergy in Spain—represented domestic fascism and allied themselves with foreign fascists. Hitler and Mussolini sought to seize Spain "in their eagerness to 'fascistize' the world," he wrote in April 1938, just as German and Italian leaders had already become the "owners of the defenseless peoples of Austria and Ethiopia." Francisco Franco and his "henchmen" committed treason when they "took up the dangerous adventure of overthrowing the legitimate government of Spain, counting on the help of such powerful friends" from abroad, Salas Aranda argued. He believed that the price exacted by foreign fascists for this help would be paid in Spanish territory and that the lack of intervention by world democracies such as France and England made them in large part culpable for the transaction. Despite his frustration with these democracies, Salas Aranda nevertheless expressed optimism, writing that despite the danger of fascism, "we have hope that democracy will come out victorious in this titanic struggle." Even if powerful democratic countries did not come to Spain's aid, democracy was still at work. Without the "men of all parts and of all races" who fought for the Republic, it would have succumbed to fascism already. Antifascist aid would need to grow a hundredfold to defeat fascism in Spain and be sustained in all parts of the world—including the Americas, where people "suffered constantly the despotism and oppression of bloody and cruel tyrants" who resembled fascists. To establish true democracy against fascism, Salas Aranda exhorted Latin Americans to follow the example of revolutionary Mexico. The alternative would be Latin American fascism.[45]

Salas Aranda outlined a typical moderate Cuban antifascist argument in his conflation of Spanish Nationalism with old, colonizing Spain and with the foreign fascisms of Italy and Germany; his condemnation of powerful world democracies such as France and England; his embrace of "true" democracy as the antidote to fascism; his admonishment of the Americas to beware the fascist threat posed by their own authoritarian rulers; and his celebration of Mexico as a counterexample. Aside from his explicit mention of men "of all races" in the ranks of antifascists in Spain, there is nothing in the *Adelante* administrator's statement of his argument that hints at a race-based antifascism. Whereas the defense of Ethiopia had elicited frequent direct references to race and African diasporic solidarity among black Cubans, the Spanish conflict led some black Cuban antifascists to these more general arguments, shared with racially diverse antifascists based on understandings of Cuban transnationalism.

In contrast, other black Cuban antifascists emphatically foregrounded in their antifascism the importance of their identity as people of African descent. Addressing the Second International Writers' Congress in July 1937, mixed-race Cuban poet and political activist Nicolás Guillén said: "I come as a black man." Guillén foresaw the importance of black antifascists in achieving a brighter future in which men would be "without colors, without wars, without prejudices and without races." He told his audience: "I am here to remind you that the pariah status of the black is his strongest human engine, the force that projects him towards a broader, more universal and more just horizon, towards the horizon for which all honorable men of the world are fighting." Fascism attacked the most exploited people, Guillén argued, because their "utility as slaves" necessitated the impediment of their elevation. No one made a better antifascist than the black man, Guillén stated, because he knows that fascism "is fueled by race hatred and the division of men into inferior and superior beings, and that he, the black, is assigned to the lower place."[46] Racial segregation imposed by fascism would destroy Cuba, Guillén asserted in an argument to the writers' congress that echoed Cuban nationalist conceptions of a mixed-race or raceless *cubanidad*.[47] Together, black and white Cubans made up the nation of Cuba, and to divide them would destroy the nation, according to Guillén.[48] Black Cuban antifascism needed to resist such division, he believed. A month before the writers' congress, Guillén had debated in the pages of *Mediodía* a Cuban sociologist who had argued for racial segregation in education on the island; the poet compared such arguments to fascism.[49]

To Guillén, Basilio Cueria—the mixed-race Cuban baseball player, former Harlem resident, and Spanish Civil War volunteer—embodied the antifascist dedication of Cubans of color. Guillén and African American poet and journalist Langston Hughes wrote profiles of Cueria in *Mediodía* in December 1937 and the *Afro-American* in February 1938, respectively. Cueria, who served as captain of a machine gun company for the Republican army, was born in Marianao near Havana and had a transnational genealogy. His father was white, from Asturias in Spain, and his mother was a black Cuban. Seizing on this identity, Guillén asserted that Cueria's desire to fight fascism derived from his lineage on both sides: from Asturias, "the fierce impetus, the hard resilience, the unbroken tenacity," and from Africa, "the tempest of the spirit that crushed slavery and that finally explodes in search of a revolutionary way for its ascent." Cueria's *piel mestiza* (mixed skin) was for Guillén "a symbol of union before an enemy common to the workers of all races." In this way, Guillén's vision of Cueria made him representative of both a nationalist Cuban identity—mixed-race or raceless *cubanidad*—and an internationalist political identity (as a worker). Both "our people" and people all over the world, Guillén told Cuban readers, suffered persecution, "economic anguish," and "terrible inequality." Asked by Guillén his reason for traveling to Spain to fight, Cueria focused on transnational class solidarity, citing his shared "condition as a man of the people" with Spaniards. Hughes emphasized the role Cueria's race played in making the Cuban volunteer an antifascist. "We can't let the Fascists put it over on us. They'd put all the worst old prejudices back in to force and probably even introduce new ones, like Hitler and his Aryanism in Germany," Cueria told Hughes. Guillén's report did not mention Cueria expressing any sense that his racial identity played a specific role in his decision to become an antifascist, but it did note how Cueria's Cuban identity influenced his role as a volunteer in Spain. He recounted a meeting with the Spanish general José Miaja in which the general asked Cueria about his origin and expressed satisfaction that Cubans "come voluntarily to Spain to fight for liberty." Hughes referenced the cultural connections between Spain and Cuba, noting that Spain was particularly hospitable to Cubans due to a shared language, and that Cubans of color seeking homes away from the island had often chosen to live in Spain rather than the United States, "where they might run into difficulties on the basis of complexion."[50]

Guillén gave a different example of the special relationship Cubans of color had to Spain when he stated in his first speech to the writers' congress: "I can tell you that [in Cuba,] the black lives the tragedy of Republican Spain because he knows that this moment we go through is only one episode in the struggle . . . between the democratic forces . . . and the conservative classes that already enslaved him once and that have to enslave always."[51] In his second speech to the congress, he asked: "How is [the black Cuban] not going to feel in the depths of his tragedy the tragedy of the Spanish people? He feels it, and shares with the white of the people the same ardors of liberation and struggle that move all oppressed people of the world, with no race other than the human."[52] In this interpretation, Cubans of African descent were supporters of the Republican cause because the fight was against Old Spain, which had been the enslaver of black Cubans during the colonial period, and because they transformed their experience of exploitation into empathy with the exploited Spanish people. To illustrate the exploitation, Guillén quoted a ten-year-old boy he met in Madrid: "Here we are all poor; here there is no one who has a thousand *pesetas*; here we all work, and to win[,] the fascists would have to kill us all." The Cuban author described the boy as half-naked and having lost his father and two siblings in the war.[53] Black Cuban antifascists felt cross-racial, transnational solidarity with this ragged boy and other exploited people of the Spanish Republican cause based on an understanding of their suffering, regardless of race, he asserted.

Guillén connected the motivation driving black Cuban antifascism in the Spanish conflict to Hispanic as well as black Cuban identity. In his poem about the Spanish conflict, "España: Poema en cuatro angustias y una esperanza" (Spain: Poem in four anguishes and one hope), Guillén expressed how he, a multiracial black Cuban—American, Spanish, and African—found himself drawn to the Spanish conflict. Addressing Spain directly, the poem's narrator—with his "curly head" and "brown body"—identifies himself: "I, son of America, son of you and of Africa, slave yesterday of white overseers, owners of angry whips; today slave of red Yankees, sugary and voracious." Amid a vivid imagining of the war, this narrator says to Spain: "I, son of America, I run to you, I die for you."[54] Guillén told the audience in his second speech at the writers' congress that "the Cuban black is also Spanish." He maintained that the black Cuban, "along with the infamous marks of the servant[,] received and assimilated the elements of that culture," and he had a "Spanish soul."[55] The type of tension exhibited in this argument between diasporic and nationalist identities is typical of members of diasporas, and the black Cuban poet was no exception. For Guillén, the assertion of a mixed-race identity was literal due to his ancestry. That he extended the claim to all Cubans of African descent, however, defined his concept of mixed race as being broader than genealogy. Those at work on the campaign to aid Republican children knew the power of shared blood to motivate Cuban antifascism; Guillén sought to include Cubans of color in this sense of solidarity.

Guillén also asserted that all Cubans, not just black Cubans, experienced oppression and should therefore support the people of Spain. He argued that black Cubans faced exploitation on the island because of racial prejudice and because all Cubans suffered for political reasons. He believed that fascism existed on the island in the forms of oligarchic economic control, military dictatorship, circumscribed liberty, and a lack of democracy. Guillén's own loyalty to the Spanish Republic came from his identity not only as a black man and a man with Spanish heritage but also specifically as a Cuban: "because my country is also struggling against fascism, represented by a minority that enslaves and exploits, a minority that has the same quality as that which took up arms against the legitimate government of Spain." Cuba faced a situation in which "the will of one man dominates over the others," and it was "true that there is a dictatorship of the military and fascist type, that stifles free expression of thought and that kills the weakest attempt at democratic restoration," he wrote. Guillén expressed conviction about antifascist solidarity as not only universal among oppressed peoples but also based on the specific historical relationship between the island and its former colonial master. Calling Cuba a "child of Spain," he asserted that "the whole Cuban people are at the side of Republican, democratic Spain because they know that both have identical enemies, identical destinies and identical heroic solutions."[56]

Cubans of African descent strengthened transnational antifascism by combining their commitments to the global antifascist and anticolonial struggles, the emancipatory politics of the black diaspora, and Cuban nationalism and the domestic struggle. Some asserted their equal place in the fight by deemphasizing their racial identity; others claimed a special place in antifascism based on the particularly severe oppression faced by blacks everywhere. In both cases, their Cuban identities intersected with their transnational ones; they were children of Cuba and proud Cuban antifascists.

Intemperate Campaigns against Very Respectable Entities: Cuban Freemasons as Antifascists

Defending the democratically elected Republican government of Spain was also the concern of Cuba's Masonic antifascists. In 1936 there were between 183 and 195 Masonic lodges and as many as 16,500 Masons in Cuba.[57] The fraternal order had considerable influence on the island, with more than 130 years of history, including a prominent role in the Cuban wars of independence and a long tradition of Cuban Masons networking across national borders with their brothers in Europe and the Americas. Though Cuban Masons as a group did not have a unified position on the issue of the Spanish conflict, a strong current of antifascism existed within the institution. At the most basic level, Masons had powerful collective motivation to support the Spanish Republic: the virulent anti-Masonic ideology of the Nationalists. As one eminent historian of modern Europe put it, Francisco Franco blamed Masons for Spain's problems just "as Hitler blamed Jews for those of Germany."[58] Fascism in Spain, then, posed an existential threat to Freemasonry, and on this foundation, antifascist Cuban Masons built a multifaceted Masonic antifascism.

The Spaniards who sought to topple the Republic despised Masons. Nationalists engaged in an active anti-Masonic campaign during the war, building on centuries of persecution and repression of Freemasonry in Europe. Over the course of centuries, Masons challenged secular rulers they deemed tyrannical, scaring first monarchs and later authoritarian governments, while virulent anticlericalism within Freemasonry drew the wrath of the Catholic Church. Both Catholic and Protestant states prohibited Masonic activity during the eighteenth century, based on fear of revolutionary plots, and Pope Clement XII issued the first papal encyclical against Freemasonry, "In Eminenti," in April 1738.[59] Anti-Masonic feeling in Spain persisted throughout the nineteenth century, intertwining with anti-Semitism and anti-British sentiment. Arguing against Spain's nascent liberal movement and its values of freedom, equality, and the rights of man, conservatives in favor of monarchal and church rule used fabulous stories depicting Freemasonry as a legion of evil and sacrilegious men who were enemies of God plotting to destroy the world. Pope Leo XIII asserted in April 1884 that Freemasonry "revived the contumacious spirit of the demon,"[60] and twentieth-century authoritarian governments—both left and right—used anti-Masonic arguments. Beginning in 1917, Soviets banned Freemasonry, invoking anti-Semitic fear and antibourgeois sentiment in the process. In Fascist Italy and Nazi Germany, officials conflated Masons, Communists, and Jewish people, imagining a single enemy.[61] Spanish Nationalists feared Freemasonry for both political and religious reasons. They found liberalism and anticlericalism abhorrent and considered them threats to the ideals of a traditionalist, Catholic Church–guided Spain. From the conservative Catholic perspective, the dangerous faults of Freemasonry included secrecy, paganism, blasphemy, and revolutionary tendencies. In 1937 an anonymous Spanish author speculated about the identity of Freemasonry's leadership with evident bias: "A man? A people? A devil? The Jews? The Protestants? The anarchists?"[62] Whatever secrets Freemasonry hid, Spanish Nationalists were certain it was composed of their enemies.

Spanish Masons believed in the Spain of the Second Republic.[63] Fascism and Nazism, Spanish Masons asserted, destroyed liberty; halted human progress; and represented oppression, barbarism, and race hatred. Masons endeavored to foster "tolerance, moral dignity, contempt for the prejudices born of ignorance, devotion, and selflessness for the good of all."[64] The 1930s saw such pro-Masonic arguments crescendo in cacophony with anti-Masonic rhetoric as the Republican government defended itself from those who imagined themselves battling for Christian civilization against Judeo-Masonic Communism.[65] The same divide existed in Cuba. A series of three anonymous pro-Nationalist essays published on the island in 1937, for example, denounced the "gold of the French Jews and the Russian Bolsheviks," which had bought the loyalty of Spaniards trying to sell Spain to "perverse and bloody communists."[66] Spain was theirs, the essays reminded Cubans, Spain's "children in America."[67] Republicans wanted to give their country to Russia, the author warned. They wanted "to turn us into Jews and Masons."[68]

Cuban Masons would not be passive bystanders to the conflict in Spain. Just weeks after fighting began, Spanish-born Cesáreo González Naredo, director of leading Havana Masonic periodical *Mundo Masónico* (Masonic world), urged his Cuban readers to become informed about the conflict in "the motherland."[69] Taking an antifascist stand in August 1936, González Naredo outlined the central tenets of Cuban Masonic antifascism. He called on Cuba's lodges to "awaken from their slumber and channel public and Masonic opinion to follow the paths of justice, freedom, and democracy that are in imminent danger of being lost for many years" to "despots, dictators, and exploiters." The elected Republican government of Spain was just and legal, he argued; the rebels could have waited for an electorally sanctioned opportunity to gain power and enact change, but they instead chose treason, oppression, fanaticism, and dictatorship. Masonic values dictated a need to defend freedom and democracy in Spain, ultimately demanding a triumph over fascism, which threatened the institution of Freemasonry itself. González Naredo directed his Cuban readers to look to other examples in other lands for an idea of what "this criminal fascist movement" in Spain would do to Masons. In Italy, lodges were burned and Masons persecuted, exiled, and murdered. Germany and Portugal provided further examples of what would happen to Spanish Masons at the victory of enemies bent on destroying them. And Russia, suffering under a "fascist-proletarian dictatorship," González Naredo wrote, demonstrated that Freemasonry "drowns" without freedom. It was not his intention to disturb or offend his Masonic brothers, he insisted. In keeping with Masonic ideals, he encouraged readers to open lodges to rational debate, free from politicking and personal attacks. By insisting that he did not mean to offend, González Naredo hinted at potential dissent existing within the brotherhood. He argued that in carefully considering both sides of the conflict, Cuban Masons would come "to understand the danger to our institution if fascism triumphs in Spain" and take action to defend Spain's liberty with all their moral and material force. "Masons," *Mundo Masónico*'s director implored, "you know your duty."[70]

Antifascist Cuban Masons would return repeatedly to the themes outlined in González Naredo's early editorial as they mounted their defense of the Spanish Republic. The *Mundo Masónico* director had invoked the Masonic tradition of political involvement and proclaimed its necessity, while balancing his assertions with a stated commitment to rational debate, the plurality of opinions, and respect for dissent. In this, he affirmed Masonic politics as pro-democratic, antidictatorship, anticommunist, and antifascist. He also presented three central components of Masons' pro-Republican stance: the political, philosophical, and self-defense arguments. While setting these parameters for Cuban Masonic antifascism, González Naredo took for granted that this antifascism would be transnational. The fraternal institutional connections of Freemasonry and Masons' conceptions of themselves as part of a collectivity that spanned the globe meant that fascist attacks on Masons anywhere needed to be countered by Masons everywhere. Masons were brothers in transnational antifascism, he asserted.

The Masonic political argument for the Spanish Republic—asserted by Spanish Masons and picked up on the island—resonated with two domestic political goals of vital importance to many Cubans: democracy and sovereignty. The people of Spain had elected their government democratically, the Supreme Council of Spain emphasized to Cuban Masons late in 1936, and the Spanish Republic was, therefore, not only desirable but also legally constituted and "a government of maximum legitimacy." It was, the Spanish Supreme Council wrote, "a democratic republic with great aims of social progress."[71] It was a Masonic principle, wrote leaders of Cuba's Grand Lodge in September 1937, that governmental transfer of power should occur without violence and follow democratic norms.[72] González Naredo opined: Freemasonry respects the legally constituted governments of countries in which it operates, leading the majority of Masons to "understand perfectly the reason Freemasonry should be on the side of the legitimately constituted government of the Spanish Republic."[73] That the Spanish Republic was legitimate was sufficient reason for no Mason to oppose it, argued another writer in an anonymous editorial.[74] In these ways, antifascist Cuban Masons sought to sidestep partisanship by imploring their brothers to support the Republic not because of political loyalties but because of Masonic principles. Unspoken, but surely present in their minds, was the undemocratic nature of their own government.

Beyond being antidemocratic, the revolt was "a bloody treason," and its leader, Franco, was a traitor.[75] The rebellion invited into Spain foreigners who threatened the country's sovereignty, warned multiple Cuban Masons. These "Moors and foreigners" or "the Moorish, Italian, and German hordes" fought with the Nationalists against the Republican forces.[76] Using the term *Nationalist* to describe Franco and his supporters was absurd, Cuban Masons asserted, because so-called Nationalist forces were made up of regiments and divisions of the German and Italian armies.[77] Indeed, the ideology of fascism itself was a foreign import, argued a prominent Mason in Spain in a speech published in Cuba in March 1937.[78] In January 1938, Cuban anarchist and Mason Antonio Penichet combined arguments regarding fascism as a foreign ideology and the Nationalists as foreign forces, claiming that "fascism has nothing in common with Spain, much less with the Spanish people." Fascism had invited North Africans, Italians, Germans, and Portuguese into Spain and paid them "to manage the apparatus of death." This "human debris," Penichet wrote, shared nothing spiritually with Spaniards.[79] The "odious foreign invaders" sought to extract minerals and other resources from Spain for their imperialist wars and to enslave the Spanish people.[80] The Spanish people rose up against those who would enslave them.[81] The foreigners considered their mission "a business of the colonial type," and the Spanish people, fighting for their independence, would "die before they would become slaves of foreigners."[82] Fascism represented "stupid racisms" and "imperialist greed."[83] In one particularly colorful iteration written by González Naredo, imperialism hovered "like a ghost over the white head of the noble Spanish matron."[84] These Masonic antifascist statements employed concepts and rhetoric that were ubiquitous in Cuban antifascism as well as antifascism more broadly, and that resonated with Cuban domestic concerns.

Making a case for the Republic as a democracy caused antifascists to confront non-intervention by the European democracies and the United

States. Although Masons praised these nations for their hospitality toward Freemasonry, they, like other antifascists, believed that the Non-Intervention Agreement was a cowardly betrayal of democratic values that ultimately aided fascism. "The absurd policy of panic followed by the European 'democracies' frightened by the madness of those two lunatic drivers of Italy and Germany" marched the world toward the abyss, wrote *Mundo Masónico*'s correspondent in Spain, who went by the pseudonym Bolívar.[85] France, England, the United States, and all other democracies had become pale, silent, and trembling, in the descriptive language of another Masonic writer.[86] They treated the legal government and the traitors equally, which many observers condemned, including Masons.[87] The democratic countries were being duped by the fascist states, they argued, because fascists were indeed breaking their commitment and intervening in Spain. Without foreign fascist aid, Bolívar asserted in August 1936, it was "absolutely unquestionable" that Franco's forces would have already lost.[88] Italians and Germans occupied parts of the country, he wrote in February 1937. Spain was being colonized by foreigners and would serve as a testing ground for Hitler and Mussolini to plan future attacks.[89] As one European Mason asserted presciently in a speech printed in Cuba in March 1937, the Spanish conflict was transforming into a world war.[90] Masons warned that tacit accommodation of fascist leaders' involvement in Spain by the democracies actually jeopardized democracy and sovereignty in Spain and across the globe.[91]

Like other antifascists, Cuban Masons saw the hand of fascism reaching across Europe, from Portugal to Turkey, and to Ethiopia, China, and the Western Hemisphere. In January 1938, Cuban Masons reacted in horror to news from South America that, following the 1937 coup d'état of Getúlio Vargas, in which the Brazilian leader abrogated constitutional government, all Masonic lodges in the country had been closed, and their archives ransacked, by Vargas's "strong" government. The Masonic press reported that "that which was the great Republic of Brazil today converted into a totalitarian fascist state." They took liberty with their definition of fascism—as did many antifascists in the Americas—but remained consistent in opposition to anti-Masonic strongman rule. They saw Vargas's actions as dictatorial, and therefore placed him among "our secular enemies."[92] His coup in 1937 convinced Cuban Masons that fascism had arrived in the Americas. By supporting the Spanish Republic as politically legitimate and desirable, they hoped to fight back against the global tide and protect democracy and sovereignty in Spain and promote them at home.

The Masons' philosophical argument for the Spanish Republic had two parts: religious and secular. The religious argument followed the Masonic tradition of anticlericalism, asserting that the Spanish Catholic Church aided Franco in committing the sins of fascism against the country and its people, and that true Christians, including Masons, must support the Republic. As a group, Masons were anticlerical but not atheistic. Those Cuban Masons who professed their faith in God and Jesus Christ nevertheless condemned the Vatican, the Catholic Church of Spain, the clergy, and "religious fanaticism."[93] One Mason from Ciego de Avila expressed his belief in God, not men, stating, "The Pope of Rome himself is no more Catholic than I." To be Catholic was to believe in a supreme being, he wrote, not in priests.[94] When the church in Spain controlled not only Catholicism but also government and society before the Republic, the Spanish people became subservient to the clergy. "The proclamation of the Republic was a happy awakening," and the Republican government "strove to instruct the people and free them of the clerical yoke."[95] Fascists sought to reverse these positive changes, Masons argued, favoring traditional church rule over true Christianity, "the best known and most tender preaching." The Church of Spain, in conflict with principles of true Christianity, they believed, favored fascist power over legitimate government. Quoting a prominent Spanish Catholic, a Masonic author from Santa Clara asserted that Christians should not tolerate God's name being used to attack a legitimately constituted state.[96] Editors of *Mundo Masónico* published a piece by leading Spanish religious figures (whom the editors called the "Good Catholics") condemning fascism similarly. As Catholic priests, the men wrote, they had decided in such grave times to speak out to their brothers in the faith. Quoting statements by church officials, including papal bulls, they argued that rebellion against legitimate government authority violated Catholic principle. "No political party identifies itself with Catholicism, and fascism in its most fundamental aspects is in conflict with it," they wrote.[97]

Imprinting their antifascism with their own conception of Christianity, Cuban Masons asserted that fascists were spiritually suspect. They were "men without souls," argued one brother from Morón. They uprooted the seed of brotherly love planted by Jesus and replaced it with a seed of hatred against those with different opinions or beliefs, he wrote.[98] In contrast, Masons pictured themselves as martyrs in a role parallel to that of ancient Christian martyrs, dying "for the cause of liberty, of honor, and of justice." In an "Anecdote from the Spanish Civil War," an anonymous author described the martyrdom of a Masonic brother named Victor Abeal, who had been an engineer in Ferrol, Galicia. Brother Abeal, like many other Masons in his region, the author wrote, was arrested and condemned to be executed. His captors offered liberty in exchange for a renunciation of Freemasonry and a "conversion" to Christianity. These events had nothing to do with Jesus Christ or his doctrines, the author stated. Abeal refused the proposed "conversion" and was assassinated by the bullets of "the eternal inquisitors of Spain."[99] To be a Mason in Nationalist territory in Spain, Cuban Masons warned, was "to have a signed death sentence."[100] Within the religious argument, then, they previewed the self-defense argument.

In one notable instance, the Masonic religious argument veered off in an unexpected political direction. A parable published shortly after a period of intense fighting in Teruel provocatively mixed Christianity and leftist politics.[101] In May 1938, "God Is Justice" by Father Hugo Moreno—a Spanish Republican priest from Andalusia, who used the pseudonym Juan García Morales, Presbyterian—imagined that falling bombs had awakened the thirteenth-century Lovers of Teruel, Don Diego Martínez de Marcilla and Doña Isabel de Segura.[102] Confused and terrified, Don Diego feared the final judgment. Judgment would take place in Spain, the story's anonymous narrator said, because that which the psalm predicted was fulfilled: "The poor have occupied today the chairs of the rich; the poor have driven from Spain those who, proud, had them under their yoke. Today the poor lead in Loyalist Spain." The kings, emperors, nobles, rich men, and rentiers once had power in Spain, among them Don Diego, the narrator said. "You remedied all with charity and abandoned the enormous problem of justice, and the finger of Providence has condemned you. You have filled your mouths, as the prophet says, speaking God's name and not carrying God in your heart." Don Diego wondered if the narrator were an angel or Jesus. "I am a red," the narrator responded. Rather than buying a spot in heaven with charity, he said, "I believed that the poor should have for their work all the amenities enjoyed by the rich." Jesus of Nazareth, God of the laborer and the destitute, directed the poor fighters. Don Diego, haughty, could not understand the narrator's message. He felt love but failed to understand justice, and so he and his lover returned to the eternal sleep of death, not having comprehended the truth—that Labor would triumph over Capital because Labor was on the side of justice, and justice was God.[103] Moreno equated Christian and leftist values in a defense of the Spanish Republic, a socialist position that unapologetically mixed the religious and the secular. By publishing the parable, Cuban Masons indicated that their principles and values overlapped with socialism to some extent. That there was room in Cuban Freemasonry for celebrating "a red"—or, for that matter, room for anarchist Antonio Penichet—was indicative of the fraternity's political diversity and its values and principles celebrating such diversity.

The secular part of the Masonic philosophical argument for the Spanish Republic stated that the Spanish Republic represented and practiced Masonic values and principles and that fascism contradicted all such values and principles, therefore requiring Masons to support the Republic. Freemasonry aligned itself with "those who defend the rights of man and the liberties of the people in the motherland," wrote González Naredo.[104] Accordingly, Masons argued, they supported the "persons of liberal character" who made up the Republican government, individuals of esteemed and respectable "republican-liberal-socialist lineage."[105] Masons also valued reason, and they argued that the Republic represented this value. Republicans displaced Nationalists from power by the force of reason, they stated, and Nationalists sought to reclaim it through the reason of force. "Fascism does not believe in anything but its own force," asserted Penichet.[106] Like other antifascists, Masons saw themselves as fighting for civilization against a savage fascism. They read, for example, Spanish Masons' portrayal of Franco's rebellion as "the most abominable crime against civilization" and the Republicans' fight as one of "civilization against barbarity."[107] Spanish Masons asserted that "on our side are reason, justice, and rights, while the insurrection represents despotism, injustice, and barbarity."[108] To his fellow Cubans, Penichet claimed that fascism's military tactics—bombing cities and killing people with poison gas—would cause civilization to "disappear."[109] In addition to physical structures and population centers, civilization "ought to consist of the functioning of social institutions that serve the greatest good for the largest number of individuals," argued Cuban Mason Alfredo Padrón. These should include freedom, housing, clothing, insurance for illness and old age, improved and more accessible public schools, prolongation of life, and maximization of happiness, "not only for the privileged but also for those who have lived until now at the margins."[110]

Clearly, Masons shared some political ground with leftists. Masons presented ideas about the equality of men, a positive role for socialism or social democracy, and a conception of justice for the poor and the people generally. Some imagined the triumph of the poor over the rich, brotherly love as an end to prejudice, and even Christian values shared by "a red." Within Masonic antifascism, there were individuals who held beliefs corresponding with a wide range of ideologies. Cuban Freemasonry, however, officially articulated a policy of anticommunism. Even where their values overlapped with leftist ideologies—or where anticommunism was moderate—antifascist Masons made a distinction between Spanish Republicanism and leftist radicalism, dispelling claims that the Republic was controlled by Communists or anarchists. The Republican government was democratic and diverse, they asserted.[111] Many Masons, even some who felt favorably toward socialism, condemned the Communist Party and Moscow nearly as fervently as they condemned the ideologies of Rome and Berlin.[112] Cuban Mason A. Pereira Alves characterized both the Left and the Right as foreign, writing that leftists would substitute the "despotism of a Lenin" for the "democracy of a Simón Bolívar," while those on the right would exchange the "ideology of José Martí" with that of Hitler. "We are Americans," he stated. "These exotic ideas are daughters of Old World despotism, and must be rejected outright."[113] Both were equally dictatorial: "One brings dictatorship from above, and the other, dictatorship from below; Freemasonry repudiates all dictatorships" and is persecuted by all autocracies.[114] In "Germany, Italy, Portugal, Rumania, Brazil, Russia, and other countries that suffer the boot of tyranny," González Naredo decried, "Freemasonry has been destroyed and annihilated."[115] Anticommunism as well as antifascism brought Masons back to the self-defense argument.

Masons' most salient antifascist claim was self-defense, though they used ardent pro-Republican arguments based on ideological and philosophical principles forcefully and often. Cuban Masons received accounts of indignities and atrocities perpetrated by fascists against their brethren in Spain.[116] Fascists committed these terrible acts in every nation in which they came to power, Masons claimed. Franco said and did all the same anti-Masonic things as did his contemporaries in other places, and if Franco and his allies triumphed against the Republic in Spain, Spanish Freemasonry would perish and anti-Masonic forces would count another victory in their global quest to destroy the fraternal order worldwide. "Where fascism prevails," summarized Penichet, "Freemasonry cannot survive."[117] Masonic antifascism, therefore, was a necessity.

Antifascist consensus did not exist within Cuban Freemasonry, and when erudite pleas couched in political and philosophical values failed to convince their brethren, Masons supportive of the Spanish Republic resorted to emphasizing existential threat. The Supreme Council of Cuba unanimously approved a motion in November 1936 condemning persecution of Spanish Freemasonry by Nationalists. Forces in favor of "exclusive and despotic systems," the council stated, tried to destroy Freemasonry."[118] "Great exploiters of humanity," wrote González Naredo several months later, have always fought against Freemasonry because it is synonymous with "liberty, democracy, justice and reason."[119] A concise summary of the Cuban Masonic position on the Spanish Civil War, anonymously authored and published in March 1937 and following points concerning government legitimacy, Masonic values, and the "liberal character" of the Republic's leaders, concluded: "Fourth *and foremost* is that on the part of the government, Freemasonry has suffered no persecution." On the contrary, Republicans loved and respected Freemasonry "because, among other things, almost all of these great men identified are Masons." Having asserted a correspondence between Masonic and Republican values, antifascist Masons went further in the self-defense argument: not only were Republican principles Masonic principles, but Republican principals were Masons. Masons were safe with the Spanish Republican government because they ran it.[120]

The threat of fascism was close at hand in Cuba. Like he had done in Ethiopia and Spain, Mussolini was sending agents to Latin America to advise sympathetic governments, Penichet warned.[121] Proponents of the Spanish Nationalists made their opinions known on the island. An incident of anti-Masonic propaganda by Franco supporters that took place late in 1937 illustrates the existence of such attacks on the island as well as the power Masons had to activate their networks in self-defense. For many months, the Comité Nacionalista Español (Spanish Nationalist Committee) had contracted with radio station CMCD of Havana for broadcast time, and in November, the committee cast aspersions on Freemasonry over the airwaves. The Masonic response was swift and effective. Cuba's grand master wrote to the station's administrators, thanking radio staff for their "rapid intervention" in response to the broadcast of "concepts unfavorable to this Institution."[122] One of the administrators told the grand master that he was "honored to count [him]self" among the island's Masons and passed along a copy of the letter he had sent to the Spanish Nationalist Committee.[123] Careful to take a nonpartisan tone toward the Nationalist group, the administrator praised the "excellent relations that unite us" with its directors, "persons of our highest regard." However, he wrote, the prestige of the station had been jeopardized by "intemperate campaigns, in language outside the rules to which we are accustomed, against very respectable entities." The attack had offended national pride, he asserted, because Masonic lodges represented the "best and most valiant nucleus" of the movement for Cuban independence. Aggression toward Freemasonry, therefore, was an affront to Cuba's honor. Regretfully, the station administrator said, he was forced to terminate the committee's contract with the station.[124] The Nationalists had been delivering their message over Cuban airwaves for months, surely to the dismay of all Cuban antifascists, but when they attacked Freemasonry, they were quickly silenced. Masonic self-defense, then, was an antifascist tool more powerful than many.

Antifascist Masons claimed self-defense when other arguments failed to convince their brethren. A short letter to the editor of *Mundo Masónico*, in which a Mason from Cienfuegos condemned the magazine's "leftist campaign" and requested termination of his subscription, sparked the reiteration of the Masonic antifascist position vis-à-vis dissenters in March 1938. The letter's author thought the magazine preached Communism, despite its many iterations of anticommunism. He acknowledged political diversity among Masons but argued, "If Freemasonry adopts Communism as its creed, it would cease to be Masonic." Communism, he wrote, destroyed society and civilization and "all the conquests Christianity has made for the good of humanity."[125] The publication's response forcibly stated the overarching message of Cuban Masonic antifascism. "Distinguished sir," editor Mary Nieves wrote, "This publication does not maintain partisan tendencies; it only shows the enemies of the Masons in order to warn the honorable brothers. If a situation analogous to that of Spain were to develop here," she continued with sarcasm, "surely you would not dare tell those good Christian gentlemen that you are Mason."[126] Individualizing antifascism in such a visceral way—suggesting to a Mason that his own life would be in danger under fascism—was a vital recruiting tactic because of existing dissent among the Masonic ranks. On the one hand, while leftist groups suffered plenty of infighting within the antifascist movement, radical leftists were at least not also fascists. Some Masons, on the other hand, were, much to the public consternation of their antifascist brothers. Though antifascists saw right-wing Masons as oxymoronic and disgraceful, they tried to reach them. The degree to which Freemasonry valued diversity of political opinion, however, handicapped antifascist organizing within the order, which made the self-defense argument a vital method of reasoning. Reports of assassinations carried it beyond an institutional existential threat to each individual Mason. "This is not a question of politics of the right or left, or of races or much less religion," pleaded an anonymous author on behalf of endangered Spanish Masons. "It is a proven fact and unfortunately true that many of our brothers in those valleys have been killed for the mere crime of being Masons."[127] Antifascists begged their fellow Masons to set aside all political and philosophical opinion and consider the issue of life and death among their brothers.

The self-defense argument transitioned into a plea for charity, reminiscent of a similar claim of nonpartisanship in the Cuban campaign to aid Spanish children (AANPE). "Masons in Spain are undergoing active, bloody, merciless persecution; our bounden duty is to run to their aid, support them morally and materially, no matter the political ideology," urged the director of *Mundo Masónico*.[128] "What has Cuban Freemasonry done," asked an anonymous author, "for its brothers persecuted, killed, injured and exiled[?]"[129] Freemasonry on the island was already deeply committed to charitable fund-raising and giving, both in providing for members, members' widows, and families during difficult times, and in sponsoring efforts that benefited Cuban society more broadly, such as building medical facilities and providing poor schoolchildren with shoes. Charitable aid was fundamental to Freemasonry. In fact, helping one another and providing for the needy were among Masons' cited reasons for supporting the Spanish Republic, which they saw as sharing their belief in these values.[130] Masonic charitable efforts to aid Spain were a given.

To inspire generosity while raising funds for war victims in Spain, Cuban Masons used graphic depictions of suffering, such as images of destroyed buildings, wounded civilians, and corpses, including those of children. A full-page notice that included a handful of such images appeared in *Mundo Masónico* in September 1937. It stated, "Spanish Freemasonry awaits our help," and informed readers that the Spanish Republican Circle, one of the Spanish antifascist organizations on the island, "requests assistance for the victims of the war." The notice urged Cuban Masons to put themselves in the place of their Spanish brethren, to consider the Spaniards' tragic situation "a personal issue."[131] Cuban Masons also used the example of aid given by their Masonic brethren from other countries to motivate giving on the island. In March 1938, Jewish and Turkish-born Marco Pitchón—Cuba's Masonic president of the Commission on Foreign Relations—reported on the efforts of European Masons to mitigate "the sufferings of the victims in this tragic struggle, especially of our brothers, who have suffered doubly for being Masons."[132] Fragmentary evidence shows instances of successful Masonic fund-raising. In September 1938, for example, Masons in Pinar del Río resolved to distribute a flyer inviting all lodges, in their first sessions following receipt of the request, to take special collections "destined to aid Spanish Masons."[133] And in March 1939, Cuban Masons reported having raised $620.35 in a collection for the Grand Lodge of Spain.[134]

Additionally, Masons strongly supported the Cuban campaign to aid Spanish children, a commitment to helping war victims beyond Freemasonry. At the Masons' annual meeting of 1938, they resolved to take a special collection during that session to send to the Grand Lodge to aid Spanish children, and they pledged a monthly donation during the coming year.[135] Cuban Freemasonry as a whole gave to the cause of the Spanish children, and individual lodges in locations around the island donated separately, demonstrating support for the cause among various groups of Masons beyond a centralized institutional agenda.[136] Masons proved a particularly important constituency within the campaign to aid Spanish children. In May 1938, in response to notably generous Masonic support of the Casa-Escuela Pueblo de Cuba in Sitges, leaders of the campaign praised Cuban Freemasonry for its commitment to "the obligation of human solidarity which the Masonic tradition requires."[137]

Like that of the AANPE, Masonic antifascism was moderate and tried to claim a nonpartisan stance during the Spanish conflict. Dissent and tension remained, however, within the institution of Freemasonry. In November 1938, after an uncharacteristic three-month break in publishing *Mundo Masónico*, director González Naredo proclaimed in an exultant headline triumph for the periodical in the Grand Lodge's determination that "one cannot be an acting Fascist and a Mason at the same time." The article explained that a Mason had been successfully expelled from his lodge for professing himself an enthusiastic member of the Falange. The brother had "accepted and practiced the doctrines of an institution" fundamentally opposed to the Masonic principles of liberty, equality, and fraternity, and with a program calling for "the destruction and persecution of Freemasonry and of Masons in the whole universe." Many other Cuban lodges, González Naredo noted approvingly, were readying to cleanse themselves of traitors such as these. Even more encouraging to the author behind *Mundo Masónico's* long-standing commitment to antifascism were the voices of official Freemasonry he cited as publicly supporting the expulsion. He listed and quoted esteemed Cuban Masons espousing antifascist views, noting that such opinions were glorious "for this humble magazine that just a short time ago seemed to be alone and abandoned to its own fate."[138] More than two years prior, the director had felt certain that his Masonic brethren knew their duty in the face of fascism. Cuban Freemasonry's stance over the course of the

Spanish conflict, however, had proved often contradictory. Political diversity within the order had allowed for multiple Masonic antifascist voices, but it had also allowed in their opponents. A struggle took place, and *Mundo Masónico*'s adamant antifascist position came out on top in the end. By November 1938, however, there was not much left to be done for the Spanish Republic beyond ameliorating the suffering of those fleeing Nationalist advance. Progress at home in Cuba, however, was closer at hand, as antifascism steadily went mainstream.

Transnational Cuban Antifascism

Identities and experiences shaped by physical movement, diasporic identification, and institutional links across borders and oceans by Cuban volunteers in Spain, Cubans of African descent, and Cuban Freemasonry demonstrate some of the ways in which Cuban antifascism was transnational. Each group of Cuban antifascists had its own method of solidarity—the strength of Cuban antifascism generally depended on many such solidarities. In turn, antifascism strengthened the various groups that embraced it. The result was both a continuity of efforts for a New Cuba and significant, substantial antifascist contributions by Cubans. For valiant personal sacrifice, for noble and passionate commitment, for principled stands, and for generous aid, Cuba could indeed be proud of her sons and daughters.

6 Factionalism, Solidarity, Unity

The Antifascism of the Cuban Left

• •

The internationalist Left was an additional contributing factor to the transnational character of Cuban antifascism. Cuban anarchists, socialists, Trotskyists, and Communists each viewed their movements as transnational, and each belonged to transnational networks of individuals and organizations adherent to their ideologies. These political identities had much in common and much that distinguished them. Tension and shared purpose, conflict and collaboration, characterized the antifascism of the Cuban Left. The intraleft factionalism of the era—contentious and often violent divides over such questions as the nature of the Russian Revolution, the role of the Soviet Union and of the state in general, the character of Joseph Stalin and his approach ("Stalinism"), and whether or not a social revolution was necessary to win the war in Spain—was apparent, but so, too, were unity and solidarity. Though limited and imperfect, unity and solidarity were notable not only among the leftist internationalist groups but also between these ideological cohorts and Cuban domestic political actors. The Spanish Civil War reenergized leftists and reconnected them in many cases with their fellow Cubans. The conflict caused each leftist group on the island to reckon with its existence, role, values, and aims. Each committed to antifascism and each used antifascism to sustain and grow its activism. Leftists played vital roles in the antifascist movement on the island and helped connect the Cuban movement across borders and oceans to the broader transnational struggle.

Anarchists and Socialists

As the Spanish conflict built during the years of the Second Republic, Spanish anarchists engaged in ongoing battles both ideologically and in the streets. They wielded substantial power among the Spanish working class and had done so long before the establishment of international Communism centered in the Soviet Union. Though internationalist and anti-statist in their ideology, Spanish anarchists identified deeply with their particular regions of Spain and integrated into the cultures, societies, and politics of a nation in tumult. Scholars view Spain as the classic example of triumphant anarchism, whereas Cuban anarchism has received comparatively little scholarly attention despite its deep history and influence on the island. Indeed, one debate in the small literature on Cuban anarchism questions whether it was simply a derivative of Spanish anarchism, brought across the ocean and maintained on the island primarily by Spaniards. In fact, Cuba's most prominent anarchists were native born, and Cuban anarchist participation in the island's fights for independence, popular politics, society, and culture localized their internationalist philosophy in Cuban realities. They addressed anticolonialism and national identity, health and education, women's and family issues, justice and equality for diverse Cubans, and especially militant labor organizing. In so doing, they fostered an anarchism that was genuinely Cuban. Simultaneously, by building solidarity with Spanish anarchist immigrants on the island, they constructed network links that stretched across the Atlantic and facilitated collaboration. During the period of harsh repression and brutal attacks on anarchists that began under Machado and continued once Batista came to power, many Cuban anarchist individuals and whole families fled to Spain. By the 1930s, Cuban anarchism had left an indelible mark of its influence in multiple arenas of Cuban life; had built strong connections across borders and oceans with other anarchists, especially in Spain; and had been diminished by unrelenting state violence and the growing influence of Cuban Communism. As antifascism began to grow in Cuba, anarchism on the island was in a weakened condition, but its proponents were tenacious and its legacy apparent.[1]

Following the violent defeat of the March 1935 general strike, Cuban anarchism was in dire disarray. Individuals hid, groups dissolved, and the movement moved underground. Anarchists functioned clandestinely.[2] The Spanish conflict, however, reinvigorated Cuban anarchism. In September 1936, the island's foremost anarchist organization, the Federación de Grupos Anarquistas de Cuba (Cuban Federation of Anarchist Groups, or FGAC), initiated the publication of a bulletin focused on Spain, *Boletín Información y Propaganda* (Information and propaganda bulletin). The publication reproduced news items from Barcelona's anarchist periodicals, annotated with the views of anarchists on the island.[3] Publicizing the war from the anarchist perspective served to inspire solidarity and motivate organizing, and ultimately to build and strengthen the anarchist antifascist network, both domestic and transnational. As events in Spain inspired anarchists, their groups reemerged or formed anew: fifteen months into the war, there were at least seven anarchist groups in Havana, with others in Marianao, Pinar del Rio, Camagüey, Santiago de Cuba, and other locations. In addition to geographic diversity, rejuvenated anarchism on the island boasted diversity in age among participants: there were five youth groups in Havana, and six more across the island. These groups worked together in underground efforts to aid the anarchist cause in Spain, such as fundraising for the Spanish anarchist Confederación Nacional del Trabajo (National Confederation of Labor, or CNT), Spain's most formidable anarchist organization.[4]

Clandestine operation negatively affected the groups' effectiveness, so Cuban anarchists formed a front group, the Centro Federalista Español (Spanish Federalist Center, or CFE), and legally registered it with both the Cuban provincial government and the Spanish embassy.[5] The CFE was officially established as a cultural organization in July 1937. Its founding bylaws promised to unite members for the purpose of "human betterment" by providing a library, legal assistance, and medical aid. The CFE bylaws stated that the organization would "support and cooperate with any entity that is akin to our ideology," without specifically identifying anarchism. On letterhead far more formal in appearance than that of most Cuban anarchist publications, CFE vice secretary of correspondence Jesús Diéguez wrote to a Spanish colleague in January 1938 explaining that the center was "an antifascist organization made up of revolutionary workers" united by the ideal of a federalist Spain.[6] In relation to the Cuban government, however, its demure front as a nonaffiliated cultural organization allowed the CFE to function successfully within the law, despite the fact that leaders of the organization—including Domingo Alonso, Manuel González, Francisco Pena, and Antonio Penichet—were known anarchists.[7] The leadership was Cuban, but like-minded exiles fleeing Spain—such as notable anarchist Miguel González Inestal and Republican politician Eduardo Ortega y Gasset—integrated as they arrived in Cuba, reinforcing transatlantic antifascist links.[8]

Cuban anarchists understood one cause of fascism to be reactionary nationalism against ever greater transnational connection. Prominent anarchist intellectual Adrián del Valle, a Spanish-born longtime resident of Cuba, observed that many powerful and rapid boats, trains, buses, and planes crossed nations, borders, and seas. Telegrams and cables transmitted daily word of each country's events. The radio broadcast news instantly, and the press commented on everything. Edited books continually distributed important information in multiple languages. Frequent international conferences brought together people and ideas from multiple countries. Multi-national organizations and agreements addressed political, economic, social, scientific, literary, and cultural topics. The 1930s were an era of progress in these ways, del Valle asserted. Ultimately, the "triumphal march toward fraternity and human solidarity would end the nationalisms and racisms that divide humanity into aggressive hordes," the eminent anarchist predicted.[9] At present, however, a terrible backlash occurred, a response in the form of narrow and xenophobic nationalism. In the place of transnational solidarity—"the manifestation of the noble sentiment of human fraternity," in del Valle's words—fascism bred feelings that were "anti-human, aggressive, brutal, [and] full of hatreds," reinforcing borders at the expense of connection.[10]

Fascism's brand of nationalism seemed extreme to many antifascists, but anarchists decried nationalism generally, claiming that fascism was a natural outgrowth of nationalism and capitalism. Capitalist nationalism was "the wet nurse of the Fascist," wrote anarchist youth of the Federación de Juventudes Libertarias de Cuba (Federation of Cuban Libertarian Youth, or FJLC).[11] Thus, fascism could emerge from democracies and even revolutionary governments.[12] Historically, many anarchists had chosen to support Cuban nationalism when it was revolutionary and anti-imperialist, such as during the wars of independence; not all, however, saw recent Cuban history in a similar light. Writing about events many of their fellow antifascists celebrated, anarchist youth of the FJLC asserted that in the island's Revolution of 1933, "jingoistic nationalism" had triumphed with "bloody bayonets," destroying all human goodness.[13] Likewise in Spain, the Republic had not overthrown the state, and therefore it served fascism. The cases of Cuba in 1933 and the Spanish Republic demonstrated that a revolutionary government and a democratic government, respectively, had the potential to birth fascism, anarchists pointed out. Democracy was a means to an end. It could lead to true revolution, but if it did not overthrow capitalism, the state, and the church, then it served fascism, they believed. Fascism was a toxin produced by a rotting system, and it could not be expelled without overthrowing the system entirely. Full anarchist revolution was the only cure, and without it, fascism would always remain, whether boldface or lurking in the shadows.[14]

Fascism in Spain moved away from modernity and progress toward all the worst elements of Spanish history, asserted anarchists. In addition to nationalism and capitalism, causes of fascism included the Spanish monarchy, the military, and clericalism: "ferocity, authority, evil, ignorance."[15]

Fascists threatened modern civilization in Spain as they did in Italy and Germany, and sought to return the country to the era of the Spanish Inquisition, when the clergy oversaw execution by burning. They used barbaric violence, assassinating women and children. Spanish fascists were not only executioners but also enslavers, just as Spaniards of past centuries had been.[16] In the anarchist conception, they posed an existential threat to the Spanish people. Choosing brute force over reason, justice, honor, liberty, science, and art, Spanish fascists would "destroy Iberia with the shameless help of the most abominable monsters on earth: Mussolini and Hitler," Cuban anarchists proclaimed.[17]

Though Spain was their primary foreign focus, anarchists on the island warned of fascism in other countries as well. Prominent anarchist Antonio Penichet was active in the antifascist campaign in defense of Ethiopia in 1935 and 1936. Cuban anarchist youth railed against the "tortures, prisons, murders by starvation, harassment, and a whole range of evils" that fascism brought to Italy, Germany, Portugal, and many other countries.[18] They compared the governments of neighboring Santo Domingo and Haiti to fascist regimes. Dominican strongman Rafael Trujillo ordered his "army of beasts" to assassinate Haitian workers, anarchists recounted, referring to the October 1937 massacre by Dominican soldiers of Haitians and Haitian descendants living along the border between the two countries. The "tyrant of Haiti," Sténio Vincent, was complicit in the bloodshed, anarchist youth asserted, and both Trujillo and Vincent were an affront to the Americas and an embarrassment to the world. Distant China was "invaded by the bestial typhoon of Japanese fascism," and Romania, in "the clutches of fascism," committed terrible acts against racial minorities.[19] Cuban anarchists used such foreign examples to inspire fervent antifascism in the Cuban people, rousing them to fight the menace abroad and at home.

Cuban fascism was also a serious threat, Cuban anarchists warned. Fascism on the island came in part from resident foreign fascism, both its dispatched agents and local adherents. Representatives of foreign fascism on the island engaged in conspiracy against the country and its people, anarchists warned.[20] The far more ominous threat, however, was homegrown fascism. Dictatorship, neocolonialism, the military, capitalism, and clericalism led to violence, execution, enslavement, repression, and regression on the island.[21] Anarchists asserted that the Batista government was the central source of domestic fascism. Albeit from behind the cover of anonymity, anarchists were more direct in calling Batista a fascist than many of their antifascist counterparts. They considered Batista's regime to be "an eminently reactionary government" that subjugated the Cuban people to "criminal repression" and "fascist repression."[22] He sought to "fascistize" the people of Cuba.[23] Antifascists working to fight fascism abroad were subjected to "barbarous attacks" and an "avalanche of fascist savagery" in the form of arrests and organization closures, causing anarchists to ask, "Are we in Germany? What is happening in Cuba?"[24] The constitutional army carried out the dictatorship's fascist directives, as when military personnel arrested a worker, detained him illegally, and tortured him, anarchists claimed. They shut down a union radio transmission, brutally beating the broadcast's producers. Anarchists considered such events representative of Cuban fascism's barbarism, and the frequency of these events demonstrated its dominance.[25] Anarchists warned about an "oligarchy" in Cuba made up of "repressive and obscurantist" forces on the island—"the magnates of industry, of the bank, of commerce, and crafty Jesuitism, creole and foreign"— keeping the people subjugated with "insolent arrogance."[26] In order to impose a fascist regime in Cuba, anarchists claimed, the government established militarism in the name of order, and the clergy joined in, mobilizing its "regressive forces" as it had in Italy in a "pact with the cannibal Mussolini."[27] In publishing such assertions, anarchists attempted to counteract the influence of another source of fascism they perceived on the island: the media. The mainstream press in Cuba was "blatantly fascist" and printed "slanderous fabrications" in its "eagerness to favor the fascist scoundrel," they alleged.[28] It was up to them, anarchists believed, to inform the Cuban public about the truth of fascism and antifascism at home and abroad.

To anarchists, Batista, his military, the oligarchy, financial interests, the church, and the media were the most obvious fascists in Cuba. The fighters in the Cuban Revolution of 1933 were not safe from anarchist criticism either, however, especially not those who held any kind of political position afterward. Despite being "men of good will," Cuba's revolutionary politicians had become ineffective and corrupted, going astray once they attained power, only pretending to liberate Cuban workers.[29] Effective revolutionary leadership, anarchists chastised, would require the "force of tenacious work" and "fecund sacrifices." It would not happen "in the comfortable armchairs of your little Party offices," they told politicians. To anarchists, such Cuban revolutionary parties were little better than fascists.[30]

Taking those in Cuba whom anarchists considered fascist together with those they considered fascist-like or potentially fascist assembled the full range of forces anarchists saw as obstructing a New Cuba and a better world. Fighting domestic fascism, therefore, was a continuation of the same fight in which the island's anarchists had always engaged. They simply saw fascism as more serious and urgent, and as bringing their fight to a new level. Whether foreign or domestic, fascism was a catastrophic threat to Cuba and Cubans. In one particularly colorful description, anarchists transformed fascism from a mere toxin to a fatal parasite, an "apocalyptic monster" that was "slowly but surely infiltrating the entrails of the Cuban People." They posited that if the fearsome creature were not stopped, it would devour the population from the inside out. In another iteration, they imagined fascism as a flood that would submerge the island "in the darkest shadows of horror and misery, never before known." Without constant vigilance and resistance, the island would "drown in the black abyss," and Cubans would be enslaved like other "peoples under the death grip of Fascism."[31]

Anarchists sought to strengthen themselves in the fight against fascism through collaboration. One axis of their alliance was on the island with other antifascists, though they struggled to create strong partnerships with Communists and Cuban nationalists; the other was transnational cooperation with fellow anarchists, especially those in Spain. The scarce availability of anarchist documents may skew our view of the extent of the effort that went into these two avenues of collaboration. References to anarchist individuals and groups in the records of other antifascist organizations and campaigns attest to their participation in the whole. Anarchist-specific documentation, however, emphasizes communication with Spanish anarchists and often highlights criticism of other Cuban activists.

Domestically, anarchists collaborated extensively with the Ateneo Socialista Español (Spanish Socialist Athenaeum, or ASE), an organization founded on the island in August 1935 primarily by resident Spanish socialists. During the years of the Spanish conflict, socialists, Trotskyists, and some whose only political designation was antifascist worked together within the ASE.[32] Anarchists felt tension between seeking solidarity and unity with other antifascists and advancing their specific vision and goals for antifascism. For many Cubans observing the Spanish conflict, "antifascist" was interchangeable with "pro-Republican," but anarchists did not idealize the Republic; rather, they understood themselves to be fighting for a much broader, longer-term goal than the preservation of an elected government. Following the lead of their brethren in the CNT, Cuban anarchists attempted to strike a balance between challenging other antifascists and collaborating with them against the fascist threat.[33] Knowing that they were not strong enough to stand alone against fascists, they conceded that an alliance was necessary, if uncomfortable.[34] Defending against fascism would require a coalition made up of "our libertarian comrades," "sympathizers and friends" of anarchism, and "all liberal men."[35] This course of action challenged those committed to true anarchist revolution, but under such extreme circumstances, they believed democracy might "serve as an anti-reactionary force." Such pragmatism did not mean abandoning principle, however: although they would not attack democracy for the time being, neither would they endorse it. And when the revolution arrived, they would "clear the field" in the final fight of all those not fully committed to anarchism.[36]

Transnationally, Cuban anarchists made an energetic and persistent effort to build solidarity with their Spanish brethren, and their interest in developing a relationship was mutual. The war provided an opportunity and an impetus to connect. The FGAC proposed a propaganda tour of the island by CNT representatives residing in New York City as one means to connect transnationally. Cuban anarchists hoped the visitors would explain the Spanish Revolution and its significance to assembled Cuban anarchists, socialists, and other antifascists, yet they impressed upon their Spanish comrades the importance of proper advance preparations. The political and economic situation was poor, and careful planning would be necessary to ensure an effective and safe visit.[37] Building and maintaining antifascist networks required attention and care, especially under conditions of severe repression.

Less risky than Spanish anarchists touring the island was their correspondence with Cuban anarchists. Transatlantic anarchist correspondence did face serious challenges. Materials had to travel between Cuba and Spain along disjointed routes that included stopovers in Paris and often required transmission via an individual, possibly Spanish, named David Alonso in Langeloth, Pennsylvania.[38] Writers cautioned each other to use safe mailing addresses and gave instructions for covert transmission.[39] Yet such correspondence proved vital to strengthening the antifascist network. Spanish anarchists wrote to representatives from Cuba's FGAC, CFE, and ASE. Collaboration between anarchists and the ASE paralleled the revolutionary alliance in Spain between the CNT and the socialist Unión General de Trabajadores (General Union of Workers, or UGT).[40] Thus, the antifascist network that connected Spanish and Cuban anarchists included significant socialist threads. Indeed, one important goal of the transatlantic correspondence was to work against factionalism within the antifascist movement.

During 1937 and 1938, as the formation of the revolutionary alliance between the CNT and the UGT took place, letters traveling between Cuba and Spain demonstrated their mutual commitment to unity and solidarity.[41]

Transatlantic correspondence between Spanish and Cuban anarchists had inherent value, as the communication buoyed anarchists on both sides of the Atlantic. Cubans showed their eagerness to support Spanish antifascism; Spaniards deeply appreciated the Cubans' "devotion to our cause."[42] In December 1937, a representative of the Federación Anarquista Ibérica (Iberian Anarchist Federation, or FAI) wrote to the FGAC, calling them "comrades of maximum reliability" and "true compatriots," seeking to foster "the most effective relationships with the Cuban movement."[43] In February 1938, a representative of the FGAC wrote to the CNT and the FAI, hoping "to establish relationships that allow us to see firsthand the true characteristics of the events taking place [in Spain]" and shared his desire to inform Spanish anarchists about the work of the movement in Cuba.[44] In April, the CNT and the FAI conveyed their gratitude for the Cuban correspondence.[45] Solidarity across borders meant a lot to anarchists under siege in Spain. They expressed "the satisfaction it produces in us to know that in distant lands there are comrades who are deeply concerned with our struggle."[46] They wrote to the FGAC: "We are excited about the level of understanding that motivates you and that you have a clear vision of our fight."[47] Since the Cuban anarchists viewed the Spanish fight and theirs as one and the same, the feeling was mutual. Beyond being vital for the fight against fascism, solidarity moved anarchists closer to their ultimate goal: a better world.[48]

Trotskyists

Like other Cuban leftists, Trotskyists suffered nearly catastrophic defeat in the general strike of March 1935. In fact, in the estimation of some historical accounts, both sympathetic and hostile, Cuban Trotskyism ended with the strike's failure.[49] A fatal combination of government repression, Communist opposition, internal ideological disagreements, and membership attrition into Joven Cuba and the Auténticos (by even some of its top leaders, such as Sandalio Junco) dissipated the Partido Bolchevique Leninista (Bolshevik-Leninist Party, or PBL) established in September 1933.[50] Casting doubt on this narrative, however, a contemporary observer from the radical student movement places the PBL demise in the middle of 1937.[51] Indeed, in 1936, the PBL published the inaugural issue of *Noticiero Bolchevique*, in which the first item concerned "the National Political Situation" and the second covered "the Spanish Revolution," and in which Cuban Trotskyists called Batista's dictatorship "a fascist demagogy."[52] Not only did the PBL exist sufficiently at this time to issue a periodical, but it was ready with biting commentary on domestic politics and engagement with the struggle in Spain. Antifascism sheds light on the disconnect between the assumed disappearance of Cuban Trotskyism in 1935 or 1937 and the establishment of the Trotskyist Partido Obrero Revolucionario (Revolutionary Worker Party, or POR) in 1940, which would go on to play a role in Cuban politics for over two decades. Trotskyism's influence in Cuba outpaced its membership, doggedly maintaining a place in the ideological milieu and, to varying degrees, in organized labor—especially in Guantánamo—into the 1960s.[53] As did other leftist groups on the island, Trotskyists regrouped and gained strength from the antifascist struggle during the late 1930s, and this regeneration positioned them to continue their fight for their ideology as well as a New Cuba.

As in other cases of Cuban activism, Trotskyism's tenacious if perilous survival after the disaster of March 1935 owed much to antifascism. While most of the other principal leaders of the PBL defected to Joven Cuba or the Auténtico—which were themselves antifascist—during the mid-1930s, leading Cuban Trotskyist and antifascist Juan Ramón Brea Landestoy remained committed to the cause, though he did so mostly from political exile. Along with Junco, Brea had been a central figure of the Oposición Comunista de Cuba before the founding of the PBL in 1933. After the collapse of the Grau government in January 1934, he went into exile with his partner, Englishwoman Mary Low, who was also a Trotskyist activist. When the Spanish conflict began, the couple traveled to Barcelona and got caught up in the Spanish Revolution. Brea traveled to battlefronts to fight and work as a reporter for publications of the Partido Obrero de Unificación Marxista (Workers' Party of Marxist Unification, or POUM), while Low served as an English-language reporter for the POUM radio station and publication. The couple would go on to narrate their experiences of the revolution in the *Red Spanish Notebook*, released with a preface by C. L. R. James in London in 1937. Other Cuban Trotskyists who went to Spain and fought against the Spanish Nationalists included members of the PBL who were deported from Cuba in 1934; union leader Edelmiro Blanco, who was killed in action early in the conflict; and a "group of Cuban Trotskyists which had fought valiantly," acknowledged on multiple occasions by POUM leader Juan Andrade.[54]

Cuban Trotskyists often criticized Spain's elite democratic Republicans and the Communists—or "Stalinists," as the Trotskyists called them, as a derogatory term for the particular character of Soviet Communism under Stalin's leadership—for their alliance with the Republican "bourgeoisie." In turn, Trotskyists were vehemently despised by Communists, despite sharing elements of communist ideology. In Barcelona, Brea was twice harassed by Communist security forces in late 1936 and was denied protection by the POUM, for reasons that are contested in the historical record. These incidents caused Brea and Low to leave Spain in late 1936 or early 1937.[55] Factionalism in Spain existed within and among groups. Not only was there dramatic tension within communism between Communists and Trotskyists, but there were problems within Spanish Trotskyism. During the Spanish conflict, members of the PBL across the ocean in Cuba appear to have been largely unaware of the disunity shaking Spanish Trotskyism. Instead, they "followed a broad Trotskyist perspective" and, having dramatically lost membership to Cuban nationalist groups, collaborated in Cuban antifascism within the ASE alongside anarchists and socialists.[56]

Unlike these distant observers, Brea, who experienced the war up close, was critical of Comintern policy in the fight against fascism but also sharply criticized the POUM, the CNT, and the FAI. These parties understood Stalinism for what it was, he believed, and should not have been surprised by Communist misdeeds.[57] Furthermore, the anarchists and anarcho-syndicalists "threw away the power when it fell into their hands because their principles were against taking it." Dismissive of other ideologies, Brea believed that fascism had to be met with communism if it was to be defeated; he argued for what he called a "Common Front," an alliance of the proletariat.[58] Unity was important to Brea, but it did not preclude criticism of one's own group, the "bourgeoisie" broadly defined, non-communist leftists unwilling to hold power, or Stalinist Communists who were wont to attack other leftists and ally with elites.

Communists

From the struggle against Machado to their alliance with Batista beginning in 1938, Cuban Communists repeatedly alienated other leftists and Cuban nationalists. Yet as part of antifascism on the island, Communists wielded substantial authority and influence. Consensus in the historical scholarship is that during 1935–40, the Communist Party failed to establish its coveted Popular Front in Cuba, having been undercut by the remaining influence of other leftists and rebuffed by most of the power holders in domestic politics, and therefore pursued its controversial marriage of convenience with Batista.[59] Yet within the context of antifascism, Communists interfaced day to day with various leftist and Cuban nationalist antifascist activists. The party publicized the plight of Ethiopia; sent diverse Cuban volunteers to Spain; and spent time and resources working on antifascist propaganda, organizing, and fund-raising. Despite serious distrust from other leftists and Cuban nationalists, the party earned a new level of respect and authority in Cuban popular politics through its efforts in the antifascist movement and especially the defense of the Spanish Republic. It attained within the antifascist context the collaborations with diverse Cuban activists and parties that it could not achieve in the domestic political arena. There may not have been a general Popular Front in Cuban politics, but there was an antifascist Popular Front in Cuba.

To acknowledge Communist collaboration in an antifascist Popular Front is not to assert that Communists were solely or even primarily responsible for the formation of this coalition movement; in fact, many factions were working for antifascist solidarity and unity. Cuban antifascism offered Communists an opportunity to connect the dictates of the Comintern to a genuinely popular domestic effort. Cuban Communists faced an uphill battle to overcome the lasting effects of the Comintern's Third Period, during which they had considered all moderate reformers and other leftists to be "social fascists," such as when they called Trotskyists "allies of fascism" in 1936, even after the Third Period had ended.[60] Many Cubans remembered such accusations bitterly, but during the second half of the 1930s, Cuban Communists attempted to define fascism in such a way as to build broad antifascist solidarity that could heal old political wounds. As did other antifascists on the island, Communists had an inclusive conception of fascism that encompassed not only Italian Fascists and German Nazis but also multiple forces in Spain and Latin America, such as monarchs and dictators, feudal nobility and large landholders, the church, the military, and capitalist and imperialist interests. Defining fascism so loosely aligned the international Communist position with the general tenor of Cuban antifascism. Within the antifascist arena, Communists met with a range of other Cubans committed to fighting a shared enemy at home and abroad.

Communists, like other Cuban antifascists, feared both foreign and domestic sources of fascism on the island. They believed that dictatorial regimes in Latin America, including their own prior to 1938, were fertile ground for penetration by foreign fascist agents from Germany, Italy, Japan, and Spain.[61] An illustration on the cover of *Mediodía* in March 1937 by political cartoonist José Cecilio Hernández Cárdenas, a black Cuban leftist known as "Her-Car," depicted the leaders of Germany, Italy, and Japan with leering faces pulling the island in a tug-of-war with Uncle Sam.[62] Though the cartoon overstated the level of interest foreign fascist leaders had in possessing Cuba in 1937, it did clearly illustrate Cubans' fear of the geopolitical threat of foreign fascism on the island, as well as the ambiguous role the United States played. A more concrete threat than Germany, Italy, or Japan was Spanish fascism, which could come from pro-Nationalist agents operating in Cuba. Communist leader Joaquín Ordoqui described the insolence of a Nationalist representative who demanded that Cuba's Spanish centers fly the monarchic flag rather than the Republican tricolor, threatening to "excommunicate from Spain" the members of any center that did not comply. The Spanish Falange in Cuba was "completely dominated by foreign fascism," Ordoqui asserted.[63] Cuban Communists called it "the center of the reactionary conspiracy against Cuba and against the people," an organization "in which are grouped the most rotten representatives of fascism, domestic and foreign, and especially the henchmen of Franco, fierce executioner of the heroic Spanish people."[64] They believed that the Falange was one of the greatest fascist threats on the island.

Domestic fascism was also an imminent threat. The island's "fascistoid" reactionaries threatened Cubans, warned Francisco Calderio, secretary general of the National Committee of the PCC, better known as Blas Roca.[65] Roca believed that individuals on the island guilty of supporting fascism included "figures holding high offices of state or high positions in society."[66] Communists targeted more specifically those who were or served capitalists, imperialists, sugar industrialists and other large landowners, large Spanish merchants, and large business owners.[67] Although no Cuban political parties officially adopted the title "fascist," Roca asserted, the rightwing ABC Society and the Conservative Party of Mario García Menocal were reactionaries and enemies of the Cuban people.[68]

Cuban Communist critics also went after individuals. One political figure who drew Communist criticism despite being a pro-Republican antifascist was Eduardo "Eddy" Chibás, an anticommunist politician and activist in, among other efforts, the Cuban campaign to aid Spanish children. Regardless of his idealistic claims, Roca wrote, Chibás worked only to protect his father's vast fortune, earned from abusively renting houses to workers in Havana and Santiago de Cuba. Communists insisted that politicians like Chibás, who looked out only for themselves, were "reactionaries and fascists."[69] Short of Cuba's dictator himself, the individual most vehemently excoriated by Communists as a fascist was José Ignacio "Pepín" Rivero y Alonso, director of the conservative newspaper *Diario de la Marina* and son of its formidable Spanish-born publisher, Don Nicolás Rivero. Generally unpopular among leftists for his views and those of his paper, Pepín Rivero garnered especially vitriolic attention from Cuban Communists, who portrayed him as an archetypal representative of evil. "The caudillo Pepín's forces" (las fuerzas que acaudilla 'Pepín') became Cuban Communist shorthand for all fascist and fascist-like individuals and groups on the island.[70] They claimed he was "decorated by the governments of Hitler, Mussolini, and Franco."[71] By attacking both of these men, Communists staked out a radical antifascism but perhaps alienated some antifascists. Eddy and Pepín stood for the public debate in Cuba over the Spanish conflict. In a column in *Bohemia* titled "¿Qué opina usted sobre la guerra de España?" (What do you think about the Spanish war?), Chibás expounded on his pro-Republican stance, while Rivero wrote the column "Impresiones" (Impressions) in his *Diario de la Marina* to promote the Nationalists. The resultant public dialogue influenced many Cubans in relation to the conflict.[72] That Communists attacked both voices distanced them from an important public arena of antifascist debate.

Unsurprisingly, the single individual Cuban figure most associated with fascism by Communists early in the Spanish conflict was Batista. During the first few years of Cuban antifascism, Communists considered Batista to be the worst of the reactionaries and fascists on the island. In 1936 they called his power a military dictatorship, claimed he would turn the Cuban public into his puppet as he had the Cuban president, and asserted that he had "robbed the people of the human right to freedom of thought."[73] Batista committed "acts of terror" against Cuba and commanded "fascist hordes of the military dictatorship" to attack supporters of the Spanish Republic.[74] In all these ways, Batista was equivalent to Franco. In Spain, the people had "achieved a legitimate electoral victory that ensured their improvement," Communists claimed, but reactionaries had rejected this triumph of democracy. Just as power holders had in Cuba following the Revolution of 1933, traditionalists in Spain, following the election of the Republican government, found "a military officer willing to impose by blood and fire all the injustices that for centuries have been maintained in Spain."[75]

The perceived connection between fascism in Spain and Cuba grew out of lengthy historical connection. Communists were among the Cuban antifascists who compared the suffering of Cubans during colonial times—under the despotic rule of Miguel Tacón during the mid-nineteenth century and the vicious treatment of Valeriano Weyler during the final Cuban War of Independence—to that of Spaniards at the hands of Nationalists. They viewed Nationalists as the "successors" of Tacón and Weyler.[76] The comparison with Weyler had a particularly chilling resonance. His brutal policy of *reconcentración* during the war of independence turned municipalities on the island into concentration camps, in which hundreds of thousands of Cuban civilians suffered and died from malnourishment and disease. Communists told their fellow Cubans that Franco, Mussolini, and Hitler sought to do in Europe what Weyler had done in Cuba—in other words, Spanish colonialism was a forerunner of fascism. Reactionary forces had for centuries "sucked the blood" of the Spanish people and "subjected under their heel the peoples of Latin America." Spanish Nationalists and Communists disagreed about which forces threatened Spain. Nationalists asserted the existence of an "antipatria" composed of liberals, socialists, communists, Freemasons, and Jews.[77] Communists conceived of the forces of Old Spain— monarchists, clerics, feudal lords, and capitalists—joining with fascists in a traitorous "anti-Spanish" bloc that threatened the democratically elected Republican government and the Spanish people. The Nationalists were this bloc, and they fought for the "violent overthrow of the democratic regime won in long years of arduous struggle by the Spanish people." In its place, they sought to build a system like those of fascist Germany, Italy, and Portugal, a system to dominate and enslave Spanish peasants, workers, small business owners, and intellectuals.[78]

By portraying the Nationalists as the forces of Old Spain and therefore Spanish colonialism, Cuban Communists highlighted the relevance of the Spanish Civil War to their compatriots in the same manner as did many other Cuban antifascists. Their publications included passionate discussions of antifascist efforts in Ethiopia, European countries, and China, yet the volume of material devoted to the Spanish conflict was overwhelming, dwarfing the other locations of concern. Cuban Communists had—as did others in the movement—a conception of Spanish exceptionalism within antifascism. For example, Ordoqui stated in a speech in 1938 that Spain was different from the nations succumbing to fascism at the time. He claimed that Hitler, Mussolini, and Neville Chamberlain wished to resolve quickly the issue of Spain, as they had those of Austria and Czechoslovakia, "but the unity and bravery of the Spanish people has shown them that this is not so easy to achieve."[79] The Cuban might not have expressed his opinions about the superiority of the Spaniards so freely if he had found himself face to face with his Austrian or Czech comrades, but a feeling of pride in Cuba's Spanish heritage—or a sense that his audience would have such a feeling—prompted Ordoqui's seeming slight and lapse in universal solidarity.

Cuban antifascists beginning with Pablo de la Torriente Brau viewed Spain as an example for Cuba. Leftist intellectual and political activist Juan Marinello, who had been a good friend of Torriente's, made the argument that shared history and ties between Spain and Spanish America meant that Spain provided an ideal antifascist model for Cubans. After visiting Spain in September 1937, Marinello expressed joy as both a revolutionary and a Cuban. Revolutionary Spain was coming to fruition, he believed, and it would produce "prodigious works" and serve as an antifascist example for the world. If Spain was an example to revolutionaries the world over, he asserted, then, in a sense, Cuba was as well, because the Spaniards who achieved worthy revolutionary accomplishments were "people of our blood, of our psychological modes, of our historic rhythm." Echoing the common metaphor, Marinello called Spain "Mother, because now we do wish to be loyal children of her universal force."[80]

Similar in potential for revolutionary triumph, Spain and Cuba could also suffer parallel defeats by fascism. There was an external threat from Germany and Italy, and an internal threat from the forces of Old Spain and Old Cuba, which were intertwined, according to Communists. Fascist victory in Spain would lead to fascist victory in Cuba, and fascist victory in Cuba would combine all its worst elements from Europe: regressive politics and social policy, extremist capitalism, an overly powerful clergy, and rampant bigotry. In multiple statements—several of them by Roca—Cuban Communists imagined a portrait of Cuban fascism. All revolutionary and progressive political parties would be banned, as would all popular organizations, including those for women, black Cubans, professionals, youth, and peasants. Cuba's constitution would be destroyed, and progressive social laws would be reversed. The press would be censored. Unions would be made illegal, wages would go down, work hours and rents would go up, benefits would be abolished, monopolies would form with impunity, and cheap labor would be imported from abroad. The church would reverse the nationalization of schools on the island, reimposing Catholic education. Cuba's "citizen equality proclaimed in the Constitution" would be destroyed, and Cubans would be persecuted for their race or religion—even Catholics, perhaps, if fascism came to the island from Germany. There would be an antiblack campaign with the resuscitation of the Ku Klux Klan, and the reimposition of segregation in jobs, schools, and public places. The fascist campaign of racial and religious intolerance would go far beyond segregation to genocide: "a campaign of assassinating blacks, en masse, in the same way as in Germany are conducted assassinations en masse of Jews," Roca claimed. Fascists would perpetrate "the murders of spiritualists, Masons and Catholics and all the religious who oppose their evil, anti-human ends," he warned. With this encompassing vision of the dangers of fascism in Cuba, Communists worked to rouse Cuban antifascist energy against a threat to "the foundations of our nation," a force that imperiled "the very existence of the Republic and national independence."[81] Fascism, they warned, would destroy Cuba's politics, economy, society, and culture.

As a counterexample to the horrors of a country that succumbed to fascism, Cuban Communists offered descriptions of the Soviet Union. In Russia, a Communist poster stated, "there will never be fascism because Bolshevism prevented it with its victorious fight."[82] Addressing a Cuban audience, African American Communist leader James W. Ford outlined the argument that the Soviet Union was the opposite of fascism on every count: people there had a right to work, to an education, and to security; there was no unemployment, and the profits of work were distributed among the workers; there was no prejudice or division based on nationality, ethnicity, race, or religion; farmers lived well in the countryside; and a great culture, with many innovations, had developed. It was, Ford asserted to an audience of Cubans who had no personal experience of the distant Communist country, utopia.[83] As "the bastion of freedom, progress and civilization of the peoples of the world," Cuban Communists asserted, the Soviet Union drew the ire of fascists who wished to destroy it.[84] In places fascism threatened, such as Spain, Communists would fight back.[85] For example, the Central Committee of the PCC cited a statement by Stalin, declaring, "The fight in Spain is not a private matter of the Spaniards."[86] In this view, fascism must be stopped, and Communism established. Some, such as Ford and Roca, envisioned the establishment of "the Soviet Cuba." Tying the idea to antifascism and the fight for a New Cuba, they proposed a gradual approach. "Our Party works so that in time Socialist Cuba can be established, but the popular triumph of tomorrow is not yet socialism," stated Roca. "The popular success we anticipate tonight is only that of the liberated and democratic Cuba."[87] Ford encouraged Cubans to imagine all the wealth stolen from the island by imperialism instead being invested in the Cuban people. The way to achieve these goals was through Communism, "the Party of the unity of all the Cuban people."[88] Communist-led antifascism could translate into a Communist-led New Cuba.

Yet it was by no means clear during the latter half of the 1930s that the PCC was "the Party of the unity of all the Cuban people," or that the distant and foreign Soviet Union should serve as a model for the island. In most instances of Cuban antifascist fervor for foreign fights, there existed at least some historical and cultural connection. The strongest case was that of Spain, which so many Cubans interpreted as their own fight. Pan-African symbolism lent Ethiopia an equal status among Cubans of African descent, and anticolonial sentiment drew others into solidarity with the Ethiopians. Small populations of Chinese, Germans, Italians, and Jews linked the island in modest but meaningful ways to the antifascist struggles of people across the world. Transnational antifascism flourished along such extant connections. Such ties did not exist, however, between Cuba and the Soviet Union during the 1930s. Migration did not link the two countries.[89] The only connection between the two was the presence since 1925 of the Cuban Communist Party, and the only way Cubans were likely to learn about the USSR and Communism in a positive light was through the PCC. Anti-Soviet and anti-Communist rhetoric and action came from multiple sources, including fascists, moderates, and critical leftists. Cubans debated the roles of the USSR and Communism in Spain. Some aligned with Spanish Nationalist rhetoric, while others attacked Communist actions in the conflict from a non-Communist leftist position. Some non-Communists embraced the Communist role, positioning themselves as sympathizers or fellow travelers.

Assertion of a leadership role in Cuban antifascism and support for the Spanish Republic proved to be an important organizing strategy for the PCC, which helped grow its membership and influence on the island. Though Cuban antifascism was not spontaneous—many people and groups worked hard to build and strengthen it—the movement was organic and multifaceted. Diverse Cubans understood antifascism as relevant to them. Cuban Communists' participation in this widely popular cause gave them an opportunity to effectively tout the benefits of the Soviet Union, the Comintern, and the system of interconnected national parties by relating them to genuine Cuban antifascist interests. Their transnational structure operated as a valuable antifascist network, one enhanced by considerable resources. They asserted Communism as the "guarantee of triumph in the antifascist and anti-imperialist fight."[90] They wanted antifascism to draw in new Cuban members: "Help conquer fascism!" exclaimed a PCC recruitment advertisement.[91] Through antifascism, Communists sought to increase their influence and leadership in the island's political landscape and to advance the Communist vision for a New Cuba. They touted an antifascist Popular

Front of "the worker, peasant, professional, and woman" that would defeat fascism, triumph in Cuba and Spain, and prevent a new world war.[92] Yet even their prominence in organizing volunteers to fight for the Spanish Republic did not guarantee Communists the political ascent they desired. As Cuba's antifascist Popular Front emerged, the Communists' 1938 partnership with Batista would complicate the politics of antifascism considerably.

Building Unity in Cuban Antifascism

In the devastating wake of the failed general strike in March 1935, there was a brief period in which many different groups—even the Communists and Trotskyists—joined together to rally support for jailed strikers and political prisoners held following Batista's repression.[93] The moment was short lived, but it showed the potential for solidarity built around specific demands or campaigns. A compelling enough action or cause could bring together disparate and even hostile organizations. In 1937, when the *Mexique* brought Spanish refugee children on their way to Mexico into Havana Harbor, the Reception Committee for the ship represented a unity that was highly improbable given the political factionalism of the day. When the leaders of the AANPE called the reception "all of society represented in its parties, associations, unions, and individually," they did not exaggerate.[94] In addition to members of the AANPE, the Reception Committee included thirty-two organizations. Of these, eighteen were labor unions and other worker organizations. The rest represented a tremendous diversity of Cuban politics, including the Auténticos, the PAN, Communists, socialists, Spanish centers, and organizations of women and Cubans of African descent.[95] As antifascism grew on the island, so, too, did cautious collaboration of this nature over otherwise contentious divides.

In 1935, Cuban Communists began attempting to build a broad coalition against dictatorship, imperialism, and fascism, drawing on the Popular Front directive from the Comintern. This new direction stood in stark contrast to their previous, Third Period policy of considering all non-Communist reformers and radicals to be "social fascists." They called on Cuban nationalist parties specifically to support the defense of Ethiopia: "Now more than ever the P.R.C., Joven Cuba, and all anti-imperialist parties must respond to the Communist Party's calls for the coordination of the Popular Front."[96] Once the conflict in Spain began, the PCC touted the Popular Front government there as the body that would lead the Spanish people to victory: "Cuban people, friend of freedom and democracy, come with us in support of the heroic Spanish people," Cuban Communists urged; "come with us to support the Popular Front government."[97] During the years of the Spanish Civil War, Cuban Communists repeatedly recommended organizing a Popular Front on the island to triumph over reactionaries abroad and at home.[98] Unity would conquer fascism, they urged, and the PCC was leading the way, "working ardently" toward bringing together the island's factious political groups into "sacred union" and embracing Communists and non-Communists alike.[99] Broadly, the Communists' effort to negotiate with other parties and groups—such as the Auténticos and Joven Cuba—was a failure, due in part to bitterness toward the PCC for past transgressions in domestic politics, such as the party's deal with Machado in 1933.[100] However, many of those approached by the Communists were or soon became antifascists. Though the Communists did not succeed in leading it quite the way they had hoped, a coalition was formed around Cuban antifascism. From here, an antifascist Popular Front grew and became more mainstream over time.

The non-Communist Left—anarchists, socialists, and Trotskyists—took part in the antifascist Popular Front, too, though they were at least as bitter at the PCC as were the Cuban nationalists. Even as they joined in antifascist unity, division remained a serious problem of the Left. From the perspective of the anarchist FGAC, before the government issued Decreto Presidencial No. 3411 in October 1937, making many antifascist groups illegal, antifascism of Cuba's internationalist Left was divided into two sets of organizations. On one side, Cuba's Frente Democrático Español (Spanish Democratic Front, or FDE) consisted of four organizations.[101] Of those, three were Spanish centers—Centre Català, Círculo Republicano Español, and Izquierda Republicana Española—which anarchists assessed as being "elements of the Spanish high and low bourgeoisie."[102] The fourth organization in the FDE was the Círculo Español Socialista (Spanish Socialist Circle, or CES), which, according to the FGAC, was controlled by the Communist Party.[103] The Círculo Español Socialista, established in Havana in December 1933, professed to be of the "Socialist-Marxist School."[104] Its leaders corresponded with the Partido Socialista Obrero Español (Spanish Socialist Worker Party, or PSOE), and once the Spanish conflict began, the CES raised funds for the PSOE as well.[105]

Members of the organizations in the Frente Democrático Español called themselves leftists, anarchists stated, but they defended a bourgeois, democratic, Republican Spain rather than a truly revolutionary one. In opposition to the FDE, anarchists collaborated with other non-Communist leftists on the island. These leftists included "a group of workers sympathetic to

[Francisco] Largo Caballero"—leader of the left-most faction of the PSOE—and "some other sincere antifascists" who made up the Ateneo Socialista Español. An FGAC representative wrote to a Spanish counterpart: "They asked for our collaboration and we gave it to them."[106] Some anarchist militants joined the organization and worked within it, alongside "elements of the Bolshevik-Leninist Party (Trotskyists)."[107] With this cooperation, the FGAC representative claimed, the Frente grew jealous of the Ateneo's growing membership and prestige and wanted to eliminate it. According to him, the Communist-led group disrupted meetings, tussled over property, and interfered in ASE radio airtime. He concluded that these "so-called antifascists" used any means, even betrayal, to attack anarchists and their leftist allies.[108] Just like in Spain, antifascism in Cuba was a site of occasional fragile unity, beset by persistent and sometimes violent factionalism.

The narrative of leftist factionalism during antifascism, especially in Spain, is so notorious and entrenched in both scholarship and historical memory that observers can lose sight of a centrally important truth: however much they were attacking each other, however much they had divergent visions of the future, antifascists were united by the powerful force with which they all moved together against fascism. A shared purpose brought together various people and groups and created a momentum that could transcend the pragmatic, calculating, and cynical machinations of various leaders. Both those who had to fight fascism in a life-or-death scenario and those who identified with the struggle from afar embraced antifascism as a mass movement. Many of the people so inspired cared little about the ideological or political goals and positions of groups, even in those cases in which they were members of the groups themselves. It is important to keep this antifascist mass of inspired, largely anonymous people in mind when considering the movement's impact. The power of vibrant antifascism was staggering, even though there were significant losses and divisions within the transnational movement.

Like transnational antifascism of the 1930s, Cuban history of the period has an entrenched narrative of disunity. In June 1938, a unified antifascist organization formed in Havana that defies this common narrative of political factionalism in 1930s Cuban history. The Asociación Nacional de Ayuda al Pueblo Español (National Association of Aid to the Spanish People, or ANAPE, not to be confused with the AANPE) brought together a surprising collection of Cuban political groups and individuals.[109] The official Partido Revolucionario Cubano—Auténtico of Grau was one part, as was the splinter group Organización Auténtica, led by Carlos Prío Socarrás. The smaller but persistent Partido Agrario Nacional was also there. Side by side stood perpetual leftist adversaries the Communist front group Partido Unión Revolucionaria (Revolutionary Union Party, or PUR) and the anarchist front group Centro Federalista Español, the latter with its ally the antifascist leftist conglomerate Ateneo Socialista Español. The presence of organized labor was strong: affiliated unions were the bus drivers (Sindicato de Ómnibus Aliados), chauffeurs (Sindicato de Choferes Particulares), metalworkers (Sindicato Metalúrgico), construction workers (Sindicato del Ramo de Construcciones), graphic artists (Unión Sindical de Artes Gráficas), needleworkers (Sindicato de la Aguja), brewers (Sindicato de Cerveceros), confectioners (Sindicato de la Galleta y Conservas), culinary workers (Sindicato Gastronómico), tobacco workers (Unión de Dependientes del Ramo del Tabaco), cigar rollers (Sindicato de Torcedores), cigar makers (Unión de Cigarreros), and cigarette makers (Unión de Obreros de Cigarrerías). The Federación de Trabajadores de la Provincia de la Habana (Federation of Workers of the Province of Havana)—a group representing 130 unions composed of 90,000 workers, formed in a unity congress in March 1938—also took part. Cuban students were represented in the antifascist organization by the Federación Estudiantil Universitaria (University Student Federation, or FEU) and the Comité Conjunto de Estudiantes de Segunda Enseñanza (Joint Committee of Secondary School Students). Black Cubans were represented by the Federación de Sociedades de Color (Federation of Societies of Color), the Hermandad de Jóvenes Cubanos (Brotherhood of Cuban Youth), and Jóvenes del Pueblo (Youth of the People). The Masonic lodges Minerva and Pi y Margall were also affiliated. The activist beneficent organizations Casa de Cultura y Asistencia Social (House of Culture and Social Assistance) and Asociación Nacional Protectora del Preso (National Prisoner Protection Association) took part. Groups specific to the Spanish Civil War—the AANPE, the Veteranos del Ejercito Popular Español (Veterans of the Spanish Popular Army), and Combatientes Cubanos (Cuban Combatants)—were affiliated. Institutions made up of Spaniards living in Cuba and their Cuban allies—including the Centre Català and the Unión Democrática de Hijos de Galicia (Democratic Union of Sons of Galicia)—embodied transnational solidarity within the association.[110]

All of these organizations joined the ANAPE, which immediately succeeded in delivering aid to Republican Spain. Its monthly donation totals steadily increased: $1,270 in July, $1,529 in August, $1,985 in September, $2,472 in October, and $3,085 in November of 1938. The association invested in goods sent to Spain, such as sugar, condensed milk, coffee, tobacco products, soap, and toothpaste. An additional $7,343 came in through bond sales, which the association turned directly over to the Spanish embassy. Additionally, the ANAPE encouraged, publicized, and sometimes coordinated the donations of groups all over the island.[111] In the summer of 1938, Salvador García Agüero—an "eloquent voice of Democracy" in the words of *¡Ayuda!*—served as delegate of the ANAPE at an international peace conference, strengthening transnational antifascist links.[112]

Operational records make clear that there was heavy Communist influence in the ANAPE and a concerted effort on the part of the Communists to maximize control of this antifascist Popular Front. However, records also show earnest attempts at building diversity in the antifascist coalition. An undated list of contact information for members of the ANAPE executive committee, held and annotated by the PCC, reveals the party's interest in keeping track of insiders in the organization. On the list of twenty-two organizations, half of the group representatives' names were marked with the letter *P* to indicate that they were members of the party. Given this designation were not only representatives of some of the labor unions but also those of the FEU, two black Cuban youth groups, and the Asociación Protectora del Preso. Francisco Mayobre of the Casa de la Cultura was not marked as a Communist on the list, but he was, along with his Casa colleague José Otero, among those who remained in the organization after many non-Communists withdrew in ideological disagreement in August 1940.[113]

Communist behavior such as keeping tabs on which individuals in the organization were Communists has contributed to the sense that antifascist efforts such as the ANAPE were primarily Communist projects.[114] Certainly, the PCC was trying to corral antifascist enthusiasm and activism to build up its strength and influence. In Cuba, however, there is no question that while Communists functioned significantly, they were only one part of a much larger and more diverse antifascist movement. Communists were famously hardworking, relentlessly strategic, excellent propagandists, and meticulous record keepers; each of these attributes has contributed to their strong representation in the historiography of Cuban antifascism, not to mention the boost they got in the history books following the 1959 Cuban Revolution. Though not intended to understate their importance in the movement, a corrective to this overrepresentation is necessary in order to see the full richness of Cuban antifascism and to understand the role it played in Cuban politics.

Conclusion

What Was Cuban Antifascism *For*?

On 10 December 1938, Cuban antifascists met at the Masonic Grand Lodge of the Island of Cuba in Havana to renovate the Asociación Nacional de Ayuda al Pueblo Español half a year after its establishment in June. The presidency of the association passed from one leader to another. The outgoing president was Communist labor leader of the Sindicato de Torcedores and former Julio Antonio Mella *compañero* José López Rodríguez.[1] The incoming president was formidable Masonic official Dr. Augusto Rodríguez Miranda, who had previously lent his gravitas to the Communist front group Partido Unión Revolucionaria.[2] At the meeting, the association recorded a new Presidium of Honor—a long and remarkable group of notable people—which represented both the continuity of and shift in Cuban antifascism during the latter half of 1938. The officially sanctioned national organization brought together long-standing antifascists and prestigious new participants, whose presence signified the movement's arrival to the mainstream.[3]

Antonio Penichet—secretary of the Masonic Lodge Minerva, anarchist, and ubiquitous fiery antifascist—served on the Presidium of Honor side by side with Freemasonry's highest official on the island, Gonzalo García Pedroso—grand master of the Grand Lodge.[4] Pedroso was a moderate whose antifascist stance developed out of Masonic principles and the urgency of Masonic self-defense against Spanish Nationalists.[5] Cuban Freemasonry's public stance against fascists participating in the brotherhood on the island—trumpeted triumphantly in *Mundo Masonico*—had been made just a month prior, in November 1938.[6]

A range of powerful political figures joined together in the presidium as they never had in Cuba's formal political arena. Auténtico leaders Grau and Prio stood alongside the Communists they rebuffed elsewhere, including Blas Roca, Lazaro Peña, and Carlos Rafael Rodríguez. Three sitting members of Congress participated: Liberal senator Lucilo de la Peña, and Representatives Ramón León Rentería and José Antonio Pascual. At least two members of the presidium would go on to become Batista's cabinet ministers:

future subsecretary of government Evangelina de la Llera de Sánchez Govín, and future minister of communications Pablo Carrera Justiz.[7]

Intellectuals dominated the presidium more so than politicians. Writers, journalists, and educators made up approximately 75 percent of the forty-person board, many of them prominent individuals, such as *Bohemia* director Miguel Angel Quevedo and Spanish novelist Mercedes Pinto. Those associated with the University of Havana were Ramón Miyar, its secretary general, and Professors Roberto Agramonte, Vicentina Antuña, Alfonso Bernal del Riego, Manuel Bisbé, José Elías Entralgo, Salvador Massip, and Emma Pérez. Prominent Communist intellectuals and committed antifascists Nicolás Guillén and Juan Marinello also served.[8] In the tradition of his late friend Pablo de la Torriente Brau, Marinello served alongside his partner, teacher María Josefa Vidaurreta. Another notable couple was feminist Berta Arocena, an activist in the Cuban campaign to aid Spanish children, and her husband, Guillermo Martínez Marquez, a member of the Grupo Minorista—a reformist, anti-imperialist group of activist intellectuals formed in 1923.[9]

Women held a prominent place in the presidium, although they were a minority. Interestingly, the eleven women on the board were the first eleven members listed in the published announcement, making the group look at first glance like a women's organization. The very first woman listed embodied the monumental shift that had taken place in Cuban antifascism by December 1938: that from a popular underground movement of resistance to an officially sanctioned national ethos. The first person listed on the Presidium of Honor of the Asociación Nacional de Ayuda al Pueblo Español was none other than Señora Leonor Montes de Laredo Bru, First Lady of the Republic of Cuba.[10]

By the end of 1938, then, Cuban antifascism as a concept and a movement had come out from behind any remaining veil of pseudoneutrality, emerged from the underground, taken on a new cadre of members of the reigning political elite, and brought together a group of influential individuals who were incompatible with one another elsewhere in the political arena. The variety of popular organizations represented by the membership of the ANAPE stood as a foundation for the star power of the First Lady of the Republic of Cuba, three sitting members of Congress, Grau and Prio, and the newly ascendant Communist leadership. Countless activists, most of them anonymous, had built and fostered the popularity and diversity of Cuba's antifascist movement. Their efforts over several years made the ANAPE's stature and representational span possible, but the ability of

Cuban antifascists to step fully and finally into legality and the mainstream in 1938 depended on the consent of a single man: Batista.

Batista, Antifascist?

In the midst of Cuban antifascism and support for the Spanish Republic, Batista did an about-face. Having firmly established strongman governance beginning in 1934 by using the military to impose order on the island with violent repression, Batista turned his attention to reform.[11] As a member of the British embassy observed, the colonel "attained a dominant position by his work to establish order throughout the island[,] and this brusque transition from the role of Military Governor to that of advanced social reformer has taken people by surprise."[12] Despite the shock, Batista represented his overall goal as consistent. First he had to restore order, but even as he did so, he claimed that he retained his own beliefs and aspirations from the revolutionary moment of 1933. Batista stated, "Many want to forget that I am the chief of a constructive social revolution, and see me as a mere watchdog of public order. My idea of order is that of an architect rather than that of a police man."[13] Subsequent history would demonstrate that the Cuban strongman was cynical in this endeavor and believed in democracy only when it served his interests, but for the time being, Batista's "populist turn" raised hopes and manifested itself in several tangible ways. He initiated a period of reforms that included pro-labor policies and wealth redistribution in the form of social programs. He moved toward the free and fair elections of a constituent assembly and of a president, which he worked to win himself.[14] Toward that end, he courted various political groups and parties on the island, including two organizations long opposed to him: Grau's Auténticos and the PCC. He made no progress with the former but found success in building an alliance with the Communists. It was, in the words of Samuel Farber, "a rather amazing turn of events."[15]

An antifascist turn accompanied Batista's populist turn—unsurprisingly, given antifascism's popularity on the island and increasing stature in geopolitics. It may be true that the strongman "never changed ideology because he never had an ideology," in the words of José A. Tabares del Real, but he was savvy and knew to place himself in a popular current.[16] Batista's embrace of antifascism resulted from international and domestic pressures. During the Spanish Civil War, Cuba remained neutral alongside the United States, adhering to the Non-Intervention Agreement. Cuban antifascists sharply criticized non-intervention, a policy that left the Spanish Republicans pummeled by Italian and German war materiel without equivalent assistance on the other side, and that resulted in what was perceived by antifascists in Cuba as an unequal enforcement of Decreto Presidencial No. 3411, the government's neutrality decree. Meanwhile, Mexico, under the leadership of Lázaro Cárdenas, took a stand unique in the Americas of antifascist strength throughout the Spanish Civil War; only the Soviet Union was similarly committed in its official position of support for the Spanish Republic.[17] Batista was comfortable diverging from Mexico early in the conflict, but as antifascist momentum grew, he began to draw closer to the country Cuban antifascists called a "sister Aztec republic."[18] The Mexican government had angered the United States by appropriating oil properties in March 1938, after which it sought stronger ties with Cuba, courting Batista by awarding him the Aztec Order of the Eagle in December 1938.[19] In February 1939, the Cuban leader traveled to Mexico City, met with President Cárdenas, and addressed the Mexican Congress. Deepening the alliance between Cuba and Mexico created a balancing act for the Cuban strongman. In 1938 and 1939, the administration of U.S. president Franklin Delano Roosevelt held a wary view of Mexico and a fear that Mexican socialism and nationalization might spread to Cuba.[20] However, antifascism brought together many countries as World War II approached. Although alliance did not erase tensions, antifascism did allow Batista to cultivate important relationships with other countries, such as Mexico and the United States.

Batista's movement toward antifascist cooperation played out at the national scale as well. The strongman had a shrewd understanding of popular politics in Cuba. Having helped to overthrow a previous government, Batista was determined to avoid the same fate. He knew that if he was to retain power for the long term, he needed to present himself as a reformer, legitimize his political power, and win over the *clases populares*—that is, he needed to present the road to a New Cuba. He could not choose a path of ever greater repression, because the Cuban people would not allow it. The early years of the decade had raised popular expectations, but real change had not come. Despite the peace Batista's crackdown had achieved, there remained many reasons for discontent: poor labor conditions, high unemployment and underemployment, and low standards of living for both the working and middle classes. A bad sugar crop and other economic problems, including reductions in public employees' salaries, increased tumult beginning in late 1937. In the face of popular unrest, Cuban elites pushed Batista for forceful law and order, and U.S. officials wanted to move him toward democratic governance while avoiding instability and leftist power (they often conflated the two). Though he owed much to both the island's elites and the United States, Batista did not let their agendas solely determine his actions. He understood intimately that the pressure of continued activism for a New Cuba could not be contained indefinitely. He knew he would have to deal with the *clases populares*, with labor and students, and with the left and the middle class, and he knew he would have to do so very carefully. As Batista courted the Cuban people, with so many of them engaged in antifascism and support for the Spanish Republic, he moved closer to those causes as well.

The notable extent to which Batista's unexpected and remarkable alliance with the Cuban Communist Party in 1938 was steeped in antifascism has received insufficient attention. Generally, the collaboration is viewed at the national scale and understood within the Cuban national political arena—or, in the words of Frank Argote-Freyre, "the spider web of Cuban politics."[21] This view emphasizes established political parties and leaders, power brokering, negotiations, corruption, factionalism, cunning, and even brutality. It is widely accepted that "Cuban politics was not for the meek," as Argote-Freyre puts it.[22] There are familiar themes in discussions of the national politics of 1938, 1939, and 1940: the failure of the Communists to form an alliance with the Auténticos, the intensity of personal rivalry between Grau and Batista, the failure of Batista to form an alliance with the Auténticos, and Batista's unexpected embrace of the Communists. To the Communist-Batista alliance, the term *strange bedfellows* applies, and the accepted analysis is that the partnership was a doggedly pragmatic, calculated marriage of necessity. The Communists needed Batista; Batista needed the Communists. Each put ideology and political beliefs aside. The alliance posed obvious problems for both, but they made some well-crafted rhetorical flourishes in an attempt to soothe the fears of their constituencies and ignored the criticism as best they could. Then Cuba formed a constitutional assembly, democratically elected Batista as president, and promulgated a new, highly progressive constitution, all of which were surprising developments. So goes the narrative that does not consider antifascism.

In 1938, 1939, and 1940, the Cuban political arena was transnational. Popular politics engaged with the ideals, excitement, and momentum of antifascism and, in particular, the cause of the Spanish Republic. The popularity of this movement on the island would have been significant regardless of the formal political climate, but as Batista shifted his stance, it became particularly influential. Popular politics were important in Cuba during the late 1930s in part because Batista cared about being elected and gaining political legitimacy—and popular politics in Cuba at this time were intertwined with antifascism. As the world's most powerful democracies— including France, Great Britain, and later the United States—joined the antifascist cause, Batista was for a time able to align national, transnational, and international political arenas with the help of Cuba's widespread grassroots antifascist movement and facilitation by the Cuban Communist Party.

A series of concrete advances for the Cuban Communist Party signaled the establishment of the alliance with Batista. In 1937 Batista allowed the party to form a front group, the Partido Unión Revolucionaria. With mediation by Mexican diplomat Octavio Reyes Spíndola, Batista began meeting with party leaders Roca and Ordoqui—both ardent, active antifascists— early the next year. In May 1938, the Communists secured permission to begin publishing a legal periodical, *Noticias de Hoy* (Today's news). Details of a formal alliance were worked out during July 1938, and legalization of the PCC, which had been illegal since 1935, was announced in September. As a result, Communist Party leaders were allowed to campaign for office. The party secured permission to organize labor legally and founded the Confederación de Trabajadores de Cuba (Cuban Confederation of Workers, or CTC) early in 1939. In exchange for all these concessions from Batista, Cuban Communists turned toward reformism and collaboration, and pledged their energetic, militant, and visible support on the page and in the streets. At the end of the decade, their commitment meant that approximately 24,000 PCC members and 350,000 ideologically and politically diverse workers unified in the CTC could be wielded by Communist leadership for the strongman's benefit.[23]

The Communists gained legal status and a respite from persecution in exchange for delivering a working-class constituency to Batista. The alliance with the strongman indicated that they had something important to offer him.[24] Communist publications from the period suggest that the Communists negotiated with Batista with a sense of confidence in their political heft. They praised the colonel's "democratic steps" and his "democratic and popular orientation," and stated that the alliance signaled the Cuban people's desire "to unite against fascism, for democracy, for better living conditions, for the development of our economy, for the consolidation of our independence"—a succinct summary of the idea that antifascism and the fight for a New Cuba were one and the same.[25] Yet simultaneously, the Communists sought to hold Batista accountable. With its "thousands of militants," the PCC demanded from the strongman "the culmination of that which is started" and "the realization of all his promises."[26] Batista, stated an editorial in *Mediodía*, "proclaims the legality of the Communist Party not as a concession but as a right."[27] According to U.S. chargé d'affaires Albert Nufer during the period of Communist-Batista alliance, the party had "growing strength and prestige"; at its helm were capable and energetic men, "some of the best political brains of the country," gifted and inspiring leaders, excellent orators; and its members maintained strict discipline.[28] The Communists could produce results. They were able "to steal the show in any public rally, in contrast to the poor attendance by members of the other loosely organized political groups," Nufer believed.[29] Cuban Communists could rally Cubans for the colonel, literally and figuratively, and they knew their strength. They saw their efforts as responsible for "the extension, in the popular masses, of the positive position regarding Batista," and in return they expected "the growth of the authority of our Party, which is already a national political factor of prime importance."[30]

With the influence they wielded, the Communists hoped to have a positive impact on Batista himself—that is, to move him to the left. In December 1938, the official Comintern periodical noted that both Cuba's sugar oligarchs and the Francoist and Falangist forces on the island were becoming increasingly hostile to the strongman.[31] The acolytes of Hitler and Mussolini in Cuba, noted an editorial in *Mediodía*, declared that they would combat Batista's legalization of the Communist Party. Under the pretext of combating Communism, the editorial argued, reactionaries disobeyed the law—and, by doing so, they threatened peace. Batista apparently agreed. "Those who provoke war," he stated, "will find us ready to defend peace."[32] This editorial positioned the Cuban Communists as legitimate law-abiding keepers of the peace, allied with Batista against domestic reactionaries and foreign fascists.

In summary, Batista began to adopt antifascist positions for at least three reasons. First, his new allies, the Communists, were militant antifascists, and they asserted clearly their expectation that with their guidance, he would take an antifascist as well as a democratic turn. Second, international factors were at play. Cuba drew closer to antifascist Mexico as Cárdenas courted Batista. As the United States under the Roosevelt administration began its fight against fascism, it became strategic for the Cuban leader to follow suit and thus create political space for confrontations and demands in other areas. Third, Batista was seeking political legitimacy through reforms and attempts to build his popularity; thus, he needed to woo the *clases populares*, and one way to do so was to join a large number of Cubans in their ardent antifascism. His government assumed progressively more radical antifascist positions manifested in both words and actions. The increasingly grim and polarized international situation reinforced Batista's evolution toward antifascism and brought him closer to the Communists, the United States, Mexico, the Spanish Republicans, and Cuban antifascists.[33]

Cuban Communists' incongruous yet fervent embrace of FDR in 1938 and 1939 made Batista's allegiance with both entities easier. This stance was likely influenced in part by the Cuban Communists' relationship with CPUSA leader Earl Browder, who had adopted a mostly favorable view of the U.S. president beginning in 1935.[34] As Batista sought cooperation with the U.S. administration, the island's Communists viewed the development positively. After a trip to the United States in October–November 1938, the colonel's return to Havana was met with a government-organized rally attended by three thousand Communists, "who, waving red flags and holding clenched fists in the air, chanted, 'Democracy! Democracy!'"[35] Commenting on the colonel's trip, U.S. Communist leader Ford told Cubans it was "an example of how democratic cooperation can be supported."[36] Roca, echoing Browder's position on the U.S. president, called FDR a "great democrat."[37] Roca expressed his hope that "a strengthening of democracy in Cuba, a strengthening of the democratic steps of Colonel Batista," and "a greater cooperation between the people of Cuba and the United States against this worldwide threat which is Nazism" would come out of the U.S. president's meeting with the Cuban leader. The Cuban Communist leader stated in November 1938 that Cuban Communists wished to tell the democratic government of Mr. Roosevelt that they were ready to fight the Nazis.[38] Indeed, a conference of American Communist Parties in New York City in July 1939—attended by Roca and representatives from the United States, Mexico, Venezuela, Chile, and Canada—produced a manifesto outlining Communist antifascism in the hemisphere, in which Latin American Communists pledged antifascist cooperation not only with Anglo-Americans but also with the Roosevelt government specifically. Their collective goal was "finding improved methods for cooperation among all democratic forces in our hemisphere for struggle against aggression by the fascist powers and for the defense of peace and the freedom of our peoples."[39]

During the period from the legalization of the PCC and Batista's trip to the United States in autumn 1938 through Cuba's official entrance into the Allied Forces in 1941, Batista was able to work with both the Cuban Communist Party and the Roosevelt administration. Ties between these improbable allies were created in large part by antifascism. Over this period, antifascism expanded from a popular transnational movement to a global geopolitical position. Batista adopted it both because it was widespread on the island and because of its newly ascendant position internationally.[40]

The beginning of the alliance between Batista and the PCC coincided with the end of the fight for the Spanish Republic. As the Cuban Communists gained full legality in September 1938, the Communist-led International Brigades were pulling out of Spain, and the Republican defeat approached. Over the first few months of 1939, Franco's Nationalists swept through remaining Republican-held territories and achieved their final victory. Meanwhile, the newly legalized Cuban Communists looked ahead to the looming threat of world war and related changing antifascist circumstances to their ongoing domestic struggle. They left behind their prior condemnations of Yankee imperialism and Batista's fascism, and moved toward the moderate, mainstream, officially sanctioned antifascist collaboration that would become Cuba's position among the Allied Forces during World War II.[41]

Defeat in Spain

As Cuban Communists moved toward an antifascist alliance with those they formerly considered imperialists and fascists, other Cuban antifascists reacted to the Republican defeat in varying ways. Some organizations attended to practical concerns, while others dealt with ideological, political, or emotional questions and needs. Some shut down, some changed course, and some kept a steady eye on the future. A new organization, the Comite Pro-Repatriacion de Cubanos en Francia (Committee for Repatriation of Cubans in France), attended to an immediate logistical concern: trying to return Cuban volunteers to the island following "the invasion of Catalonia."[42] Cuban antifascists were proud to have contributed volunteers to the Republican cause—men and women whom they viewed as brave and heroic. The Cubans in Spain had earned the respect and admiration of the Spanish people, and many had become martyrs for the Republic. Now, however, those who were alive languished in French concentration camps, and it was the duty of Cuban antifascists to bring them home. In April 1939, the Comité Pro-Repatriación implored Cubans—always "by the side of Republican Spain"—to bring their antifascist countrymen back to the island. It would be, the committee stated, "in addition to fulfilling a patriotic and human duty, a way to help the Spanish Republic" by alleviating one small part of its responsibilities during a time of great need.[43] It was a way to continue to aid the cause, even as the cause was lost. It was continuity in the face of defeat.

Cuban Freemasonry also addressed a practical question as the Spanish Republic fell, but it was a question of a very different nature. In the spring of 1939, some Masonic leaders on the island were concerned with easing conflict within the brotherhood. The war in Spain had led to a war within the island's lodges; they hoped the war's end abroad would similarly relieve the situation at home. In March 1939, as Nationalist victory came to fruition, Octavio S. Martínez—the president of the Cuban Masonic Commission of Foreign Relations—concluded a report of international news with a comment on Spain. His commentary was addressed to the grand master and the Masonic leadership body and published in the Masons' official annual report. Though the situation in Europe was ever more "bleak and saddening," he wrote, there arrived from Spain "a ray of light." In that country, "the land to which we are so closely linked by blood and language; the land whose pains we feel like our own," a discussion of peace had begun, Martínez stated. After so much bloodshed and horror, he hoped a "real and stable peace" would be "reborn," not only to "appease the spirits there" but also to "calm those here in our temples." Martínez believed Masonic principles dictated "that we admit no more difference than merit and demerit; that we reject no one for his beliefs and opinions; that we do not accommodate debates of religion or politics." He asserted that such disagreements acted as "small infernos in which—painful as it is to confess—the Brotherhood and Tolerance have suffered grave losses."[44]

Martínez's comments, made just five months after Cuba's highest Masonic leaders declared Freemasonry and fascism fundamentally incompatible, represented a wholly different point of view than that of antifascist Masons. Though certainly not an endorsement of European fascism, Martínez turned away from Cuban Masonic antifascism and favored the fight ending with Nationalist triumph over a commitment to pro-Republicanism. Whereas committed antifascist Cuban Masons equated Hitler, Mussolini, and Franco with one another, Martínez's conclusion showed a willingness to accept Franco in exchange for peace. The Masonic values of openness to debate and of political and ideological plurality meant accepting more ambiguity than what the antifascists among Freemasonry's ranks tolerated. Perhaps also some leaders within Cuban Freemasonry simply became resigned to inevitable defeat. Even at this minimum, however, the conciliatory stance set them apart from other Cuban antifascists who remained loyal to the cause. And the Franco regime would pose a challenge to Martínez's position. The short time following the end of the war provided respite, Juan José Morales Ruiz writes, but then "the permanent combat against the enemies of Spain . . . the Judeo-Masonic-Communist-separatist conspiracy" from whom Nationalists believed they protected traditional Spain, resumed.[45] In other words, Masonic self-defense against fascism remained relevant, even as some Cuban Masons sought reconciliation.

Activists' antifascist commitment in the Cuban campaign to aid Spanish children did not waver, but their ability to provide meaningful aid evaporated. Spanish ambassador Fernando de los Ríos's December 1938 visit to Havana and his speech to tens of thousands of people in the Polar Stadium consolidated the prestige of the Asociación de Auxilio al Niño del Pueblo Español, wrote its president, Ramiro Valdés Daussá, and demonstrated the seriousness of the association's work. In appreciation of this work, Daussá wrote in January 1939, prominent U.S. groups supportive of the Spanish Republic had put at the AANPE's disposal a ship to bring food and supplies to Barcelona. One more time, he directed readers, the people of Cuba must mobilize all the individuals and groups supportive of Spain to send coffee, sugar, and other supplies to their "Spanish brothers."[46] Aid could not keep up with the need, and by early 1939, need was expanding rapidly. Just fifteen days after Daussá published his impassioned plea, Barcelona fell to Nationalist forces.

The AANPE published a cable from the Paris Office Internationale pour l'Enfance (International Office for the Children) in February 1939: "Our Delegation receives report names all assistance organizations Barcelona QUOTES hundreds refugee children little ones mothers arms arrive Barcelona after evacuation Reus Valls Tarragona STOP Urgent all Committees begin campaigns support organizations to supply provisions clothing refuge offensives innocent victims AIDENFANT."[47] Describing the plight of children in Spanish war zones, which had never required exaggeration, now acquired a tone of desperation. Starvation threatened 300,000 infants and 3 million children, a notice published by the association stated. Telegrams from Paris sounded Spain's SOS to "the civilized world."[48] The call for help did not so much change in the face of Republican defeat as it increased in both urgency and futility. The AANPE bulletin ¡Ayuda! focused on the "Tragic Exodus"— the evacuation of Catalonia—and emphasized the plight of child refugees.[49] As the Republic fell and hundreds of thousands fled, AANPE activists expressed with rage and tenderness the increased drama and severity of the Spanish children's condition. The reality of the day in Spain was "cannibalistic, lacking all military and political decency, lacking all virility," stated an editorial. Conditions in Spain destroyed and negated fraternal feeling, a sense of community, and every good quality of human nature. Trapped in this gruesome reality, the poor innocent children were in dire need of assistance.[50]

Despite this continued need early in 1939, the AANPE was coming to an end as an organization. The final issue of ¡Ayuda! (published in April 1939) represented Cuban activists' desire to celebrate what they had been able to achieve, their need to restate their values, their call for a continuation of charitable effort, and, ultimately, their helplessness. A timeline listed all the aid the AANPE had donated, but its mere existence as an exercise in taking stock betrayed that an endpoint had arrived despite calls for continuity.[51] Other articles tried to give a sense of strength, reaffirming the place of the Cuban campaign for Spanish children in the global antifascist movement. One described the work of the Office Internationale pour l'Enfance and stressed the international quality of the effort to aid Spanish children, acknowledging efforts by the peoples of Argentina, Australia, Belgium, Canada, Chile, Cuba, Egypt, England, France, Holland, Norway, Sweden, Switzerland, the United States, and Uruguay.[52] In other words, the Cubans could find comfort in having achieved good works for the children of Republican Spain in the good company of people from many lands. Another article reiterated a familiar plea to the women of Cuba and beyond who were central to the effort on behalf of Spanish children, attempting to boost their morale and contributions.[53]

On the final page of the final issue of ¡Ayuda!, a brief message included a pledge to continue the association's work. It stated that the organization needed to sustain its effort as long as there were Spanish children in need, urging that "we cannot abandon them." No pen could describe the misery and fear felt by Spanish children refugees in French concentration camps. Now more than ever they need help, ¡Ayuda! writers concluded. Peppered with emphasized phrases, the article sought to leave readers of the last issue with a renewed sense of urgency.[54] For good measure, the magazine's back cover featured no images, just a restatement of the final article's most salient points, alone on the page, in nearly all uppercase letters: "400,000 Spanish children, women, and men are refugees in the concentration camps of France. Hunger and cold are decimating those guiltless victims. The concentration camps are inhospitable. (They do not have shelters.) The Association of Aid to the Children of the Spanish People asks for help for these refugees. Now more than ever, people of Cuba, help them!"[55] With these impassioned lines, ¡Ayuda! ended after ten issues spanning twenty-two months of publication. The Asociación de Auxilio al Niño del Pueblo Español was shutting down.

One year later, in April 1940, Valdés Daussá notified the Office Internationale pour l'Enfance that the AANPE had abandoned its organizational headquarters the previous November and had since been operating out of the home of Rosa Pastora Leclerc, former director of the Casa-Escuela Pueblo de Cuba in Sitges. He informed the Paris organization that the association was liquidating its assets and sent a final donation of all its remaining funds, $979.27. Valdés Daussá made a few small requests regarding the money, including directing $25.00 to a French concentration camp for the mother of former Casa-Escuela resident Francisco Pelayo. The remainder was to serve as "our final donation to the Spanish refugee children in France."[56] The next day, the AANPE president wrote to Francisco Pelayo's mother in the Cahartre-Evre-Loir camp, informing her of the money sent in her name. "With true sorrow," he wrote, "we wish to express that we have terminated all the work of this Association."[57] Thus, defeat of the Spanish Republic brought Cuban antifascists' efforts to aid the Republic's children to an end.

As some Masons abandoned the antifascist position and the AANPE closed down, Cuban anarchists rallied to continue the fight. In the wake of the Nationalist victory in Spain, they initiated the publication of a new periodical, *Rumbos Nuevos: Órgano Libertario* (New directions: Libertarian publication), with a mission "to maintain upright the banner of the ideals of social liberty and social justice, object and purpose of the libertarian philosophy."[58] The publication took a full inventory of the recent tragedy and present threat, and called for moving forward and continuing the fight. Various anarchist authors argued that Spain fell because of "the conjunction of declared enemies and delinquent friends," the aggression of fascists, and "the complacency of the so-called democrats," the "limping democracies." Reactionary forces grew unimpeded, which was both "truly discouraging for those of us who hold libertarian ideals" and seriously dangerous for all nations, including democratic ones.[59] The fence that divided the democratic and fascist sides, Cuban anarchists reminded readers of *Rumbos Nuevos*, was not as large as many believed.[60] The "intransigent nationalism" that became Fascism, Nazism, and Falangism in Italy, Germany, and Spain, respectively, also infected the democracies.[61] Fascists sought to dominate the entire globe, including all of Latin America, ushering in "a new Middle Age, with all its obscurantism, intransigence, persecutions, and atrocious fights."[62] Democracies, republics, and Communists all failed to impede the march of fascism, as evidenced by defeat in Spain. Anarchists accused Republican leaders of colluding with Stalinists, hindering progress in the struggle, and betraying "the best antifascists"—anarchists.[63] From these disappointments, anarchists gleaned a lesson applicable to their own situation on the island: "Not all who sell themselves as friends of the people are in reality; not all who shout revolution are sincere revolutionaries."[64] Yet they strived to continue the fight, even with a degree of anarchist optimism: if conditions were getting bad enough for everyone to see, perhaps more people would begin to fight.

All libertarians must join together with all workers and "men of progress" in unity for the ongoing struggle against fascism, authors in *Rumbos Nuevos* asserted.[65] True unity was the key—a message Cuban anarchists understood as paramount.[66] Unified revolution was the only means by which to prevent the impending clash between totalitarian nations such as Germany, Italy, and Japan and the "so-called democratic nations, led by England and France." Through revolution, anarchist antifascists envisioned themselves leading humanity away from all-consuming conflict toward a new world. They would give society "a truly human organization." Though they advanced this optimistic vision for a brighter future, their assessment of the present and hope for the realization of their ideals remained grim. Unfortunately, the peoples of many nations did not seem prepared for so momentous a revolution, Adrián del Valle wrote in May 1939. Before achieving a better world, he concluded, "we must first pass through the horrors of a world war."[67]

World War II

Supporters of the republic in the Spanish Civil War were among the first in the United States to publicly recognize the threat of fascism. Activists from this era were famously dubbed "premature antifascists" and suspected of being dangerous leftist radicals. This designation would come back to haunt them in the form of harassment and discrimination by the U.S. government, most notably during McCarthyism, the strident hunt for alleged Communists carried out by Senator Joseph McCarthy in 1950–54. However, upon U.S. entry into World War II following the Japanese attack on Pearl Harbor in December 1941, antifascism suddenly became politically supported and socially acceptable. In other words, because prior antifascist efforts such as supporting Spain were considered fringe positions, antifascism "matured" only when the U.S. government became antifascist. Cuban antifascism also changed over time, but the process was distinct from that in the United

States. In both cases, part of the transformation was due to official government acceptance. However, as a result of its vibrant recent history of political revolution and especially its close connection to Spain, Cuban antifascism did not transition from premature to mature; long widely popular, it transitioned from illegal to legal, from underground to prominent and even elite. Cuban antifascism before 1938 had enjoyed significant successes despite domestic repression and international indifference. The movement's tenacity during the 1930s laid the groundwork for its official debut during World War II.

As World War II approached and Batista moved toward antifascism, the Cuban government intensified its actions against the threat of foreign fascism on the island. Batista had been cracking down on the Falange for several years—at least officially—but early efforts by the Cuban government against this Spanish organization had proven ineffective. In conjunction with the government censure of groups on the left, Cuban officials targeted overt Francoists as early as December 1937; Decreto Presidencial No. 3411, clearly issued with the Spanish Civil War in mind, made illegal any group formed with the aim of providing moral or material aid for military conflicts in foreign countries. Antifascist groups complained consistently that the decree, like the Non-Intervention Agreement with which it was meant to comply, unfairly penalized the Left while allowing fascists to continue their activities. Potential leftist bias aside, the archival record suggests that enforcement of the decree did not put an end to the activities of the Falange as an organization. The Cuban government ordered the Falange to close indefinitely in December 1937 in compliance with the new law; in April 1939, it issued the organization a citation, once again ordering it to dissolve "for having violated with its conduct the oft cited Presidential Decree No. 3411."[68]

In 1939, 1940, and 1941, the Cuban government took further actions against Spanish Nationalists. In a blow to Franco supporters, it did not fully establish formal relations with the new Spanish government in 1939, putting in place only a chargé d'affaires rather than an ambassador. Early in 1940, it shuttered the suspect right-wing organization Auxilio Social (Social Assistance) on the island, after deeming it a threat "against the stability of the Republic." After Batista's inauguration as president in October 1940, the Cuban government's antifascist stance hardened and intensified. In January 1941, the Cuban Senate, with the approval of the minister of state, expelled the Spanish consul general in Cuba, Genaro Riestra, for his allegiance to the Falange. Over the next few years, another Spanish consul, the inspector general of the Falange Exterior, and the head of the Falange in

Cuba were also expelled. In 1941 a *tribunal de urgencia* (provisional court) charged the directors of various groups—including the Falange, which had defied government orders to disband in December 1937 and April 1939—with endangering the stability of the country. Though the tribunal absolved nearly all of the accused individuals, their organizations were legally dissolved. Other men found to have collaborated with Axis powers were jailed or deported, and pro-fascist publications were discontinued under pressure or forcibly closed. In the context of World War II, many viewed the Falange as the Axis powers' "secret army in the Americas" and therefore a threat of the utmost urgency.[69]

Following Pearl Harbor, Cuba declared war against the Axis powers. As a result, the Cuban government established diplomatic relations with the Soviet Union and cut ties with the Vichy government. In September 1944, the island would be the first Latin American nation to recognize the provisional republican government of France. Upon entering World War II on the side of the Allies, Cuba instituted obligatory military service. Copying its powerful northern neighbor, it interned foreign nationals from Axis countries without proven antifascist credentials in camps on the Isle of Pines. At the time, Cuba was home to 777 Japanese, 1,330 Italians, and 3,484 Germans. Cuban officials justified the internment of foreign nationals considered suspicious based on the discovery of Axis spies in Cuba, namely Nazi Heinz August Lüning and some Spaniards.[70]

As the government interned foreign nationals, domestic Jewish and German antifascists organized against Nazism in Cuba. In May 1939, the Comité Central de las Organizaciones Hebreas de Cuba (Central Committee of Cuban Hebrew Organizations) warned the Cuban general public about the threat posed by a "few isolated outbreaks of anti-Semitic ideas in our country," including a radio program and a morning newspaper that had begun campaigns against Jewish immigration to the island. Quick to uphold the principle of freedom of thought and acknowledge Cuba's need for a "policy of national protection," the committee couched its plea in terms meant to appeal to Cuban nationalism. Applying to one race or religion the "most derogatory adjectives that the dictionary can contain," the committee argued, "violates the Cuban principles of brotherhood." Cuba had one race and one nationality: Cuban. Equal within it were "white and black, Chinese and Spanish, Hebrew and Catholic." All were children of Cuba.[71] Like antifascists before them, Jewish Cubans concerned about anti-Semitism infecting the island tried to connect with other Cubans by invoking nationalist sentiments and values. Like others, they warned their fellow Cubans that fascism posed a direct threat on the island, not just in Europe.

In April 1943, a group of men and women led by German artist Gert Caden founded the Comité Alemán Antifascista (German Antifascist Committee) in Havana. Like many antifascist organizations before it, the Comité claimed to be an organization without "any sense of partisan politics," inclusive of diverse individuals, and "based in democratic ideals." Among its aims were to assist the Allies against the Axis powers "alongside Batista, Roosevelt, Churchill, Stalin, and Chiang Kai-shek," as well as the United Nations; to give "moral and material aid to the global German anti-Nazi movement"; to fight for a free Germany and Europe; to combat "Fifth Column-ism," referring to an organized enemy within, in this case, the work of fascists in Cuba; to promote antifascist propaganda in German and Spanish; to foster national and international solidarity in order to defend liberty; and "to combat unconditionally anti-Semitism wherever this vile and stupid weapon of fascism manifests itself."[72] Like their black Cuban and Hispanic Cuban counterparts during the Italian invasion of Ethiopia and the Spanish Civil War, antifascist German Cubans saw fascism during World War II as a threat to the world, to their distant homeland, and to the island of Cuba and its most fundamental values.

Long-standing Cuban antifascist organizations—including some Masonic lodges and anarchist organizations—sustained their antifascism during World War II in part by providing assistance to Spanish Republican refugees fleeing Europe and arriving in the Americas. Mexico famously received the largest number of these Spaniards, but Cuba took in a substantial number as well, as is detailed in Jorge Domingo Cuadriello's *El exilio republicano español en Cuba* (2009).[73] The transnational relationships and networks that had formed and been strengthened during antifascist efforts on behalf of the Republic served this migration fleeing Franco. In turn, Spanish antifascists joined Cuban antifascist efforts and organizations.

Antifascist veteran organizations formed on the island in 1940, 1942, and 1944, founded by Cubans who had fought against fascism on the battlefields of Spain.[74] The Asociación Cultural de Ex-Combatientes Antifascistas (Cultural Association of Antifascist Ex-Combatants), founded in June 1940 and headed by veterans Julio Constantino Cabarrocas (sometimes written Cavarrocas) and Alberto Monteagudo Seoane, organized veterans and antifascist young people regardless of sex or race, as well as Spanish Republican refugees. The organization's bylaws made a strong commitment to political diversity, but several of the identifiable members listed in the association's file were anarchists, and it seems as though the majority of the group may have had this political orientation.[75] The Formación de Excombatientes Antifascistas (Squad of Antifascist Ex-Combatants) was founded in October 1942 and headed by veterans Norberto Hernández Nodal and Mario Alvarez Izquierdo. The large majority of members were Cuban veterans of the Republican forces, and they stated the group's mission as "exclusively antifascist."[76] They welcomed other veterans—Cubans and those from the rest of the Americas—to join their organization, along with any antifascist properly recommended by two veterans or two active members of a recognized antifascist organization in Cuba. They took as their mission the "development of a collective war morale," the "establishment of a national economy adequate for the development of the war plan," struggle against "the fifth column" of fascists in Cuba, and raising funds "by all licit means" to support "the Democratic Cause."[77] In November 1942, twenty-six members of the group gathered to vote on officers.[78] Some of those listed as having attended were among the anarchist members who were previously or concurrently part of the Asociación Cultural de Ex-Combatientes Antifascistas, and some were Communist Party members—a remarkable combination for the time and a testament to the real if imperfect opportunities for unity in Cuban antifascism. The inclusion of members of the Asociación Cultural de Ex-Combatientes Antifascistas (founded in 1940) in the Formación de Excombatientes Antifascistas (founded in 1942) indicates that the former may have split or dissolved; likewise, members of these two organizations showed up again in the rosters of the Asociación de Ex-Combatientes Anti-Fascistas Revolucionarios (Association of Revolutionary Antifascist Ex-Combatants), founded in September 1944. Intended to bring together both Cuban veterans and Spanish refugees, the new organization borrowed language directly from the bylaws of the earlier two groups.[79] In June 1946, members elected as president Gustavo Rodríguez Malagamba, anarchist member of both of the previous groups. For vice president, they elected Norberto Hernández Nodal. Hernández Nodal reported being a member of the Communist Party in 1937, served as president of the Formación de Excombatientes Antifascistas in 1942, and would go on to die in the anti-Batista attack on the Cuban presidential palace in March 1957.[80]

While these veteran associations seem to have been dominated by anarchists and Communists, the broader Cuban antifascist movement was increasingly diverse during the late 1930s and early 1940s. Founded in the summer of 1941, Cuba's Frente Nacional Antifascista (National Antifascist

TABLE C.1 Frente Nacional Antifascista Comité Gestor

Dr. Gustavo Aldereguía	Dr. Ramón Miyar
José Luis Amigo	Dr. Benjamin Muñoz Ginarte
Dr. Alfredo Antonetti	Dr. Alfredo Nogueira
Dr. Manuel Bisbé	Alfredo Padrón
María Josefa Bolaños	Lázaro Peña
Eduardo Cañas	Antonio Penichet
Dr. Pablo Carrera Jústiz	Dr. José M. Pérez Lamy
Dr. José Guadalupe Castellanos	Hermenegildo Portuondo
Carlos Fernández Cabrera	José Antonio Portuondo
Edith García Buchaca	Ramón León Rentería
Dr. Ramón García Pujol	Dr. Carlos Rafael Rodríguez
Dr. Angel Alberto Giraudy	Dr. Emilio Roig de Leuchsenring
Eloy González	Comandante Bernardo Sandó
Dr. José Angel González Rubiera	Dra. Clara Luz Sifontes
Dr. Luis Grau Agüero	Ing. Gustavo Urrutia
Nicolás Guillén	Dr. Manuel Antonio Varona
Dr. Alejandro Ibarra	Dr. Alejandro Vergara
Francisco Malpica	Luis Gómez Wangüemert
Dr. Juan Marinello Vidaurreta	Dr. Ricardo Zamanillo

Note: Frente Nacional Anti-Fascista letterhead, Frente Nacional Anti-Nazi Fascista, expediente 10624, legajo 354, RA-ANC. The organization changed its name to Frente Nacional Antifascista by February 1943.

Front) was representative of the "broad democratic sectors of Cuban society" against fascism, in the words of Domingo Cuadriello.[81] The Comité Gestor (Managing Committee) counted among its members a formidable who's who of influential Cubans—politicians, intellectuals, labor and student activists, feminists, doctors, lawyers, and veterans of the war of independence, both black and white, male and female, and representative of diverse political persuasions, parties, and connections (see table C.1). Many of those members were committed antifascists prior to 1939; the presence of others indicated further movement in Cuban antifascism's progression into the political mainstream on the island.

The Frente Nacional Antifascista's mission was "to fight in an organized manner against the political tendencies called Nazism, Fascism, and Falangism, to defend democracy and manage support for all peoples fighting against Nazi-Fascism." The organization sought to provide economic, military, and moral aid to antifascist causes, and to fight the fascist threat in Cuba and alongside the Allies against the Axis powers, confronting fascism any place on earth.[82] The Frente Nacional Antifascista's position was both distinct from and an evolution of the defiant, militant, underground Cuban antifascism of just a few years prior, and represented the transformation that had taken place starting with the Asociación Nacional de Ayuda al Pueblo Español. Rather than a domestic and transnational grassroots antifascism, the stance of the Frente Nacional Antifascista was an official, geopolitical, and international antifascism as Cuba engaged in World War II alongside some of the world's most powerful democracies. This outcome was an important development for Cuban antifascism, but what about in the struggle for a New Cuba?

What Was Cuban Antifascism *For*?

Equal to Cuban antifascism's stance *against* fascism, both foreign and domestic, was its position *for* a New Cuba. That goal contained a multitude of hopes and plans, which were different for a Mason than for a Communist, for a Cuban nationalist than for a pan-Africanist, for an anarchist worker than for a university student. Every Cuban antifascist, however, encompassed his or her idea of what a New Cuba would be within his or her own definition of antifascism. Thus, antifascism served as a vehicle for the continuity of Cuban activism following the defeat of the March 1935 general strike. This continuity meant that Cuban popular politics retained vitality—and even momentum—during a period that otherwise appeared to be a lengthy, defeated lull. And as followers of multiple political tendencies sought a New Cuba, the vibrancy of antifascism on the island guided them away from the authoritarian and even fascist-inspired ideologies that gained traction in other Latin American countries at the time.[83] Cuban antifascists sought an end to strongman governance and U.S. neocolonialism, economic and social progress, and some form of democracy and/or revolution. Their popular activism pushed Batista to proclaim himself in favor of a New Cuba. When strongman Batista wanted to become democratically elected President Batista and needed to court the *clases populares*, antifascism provided an avenue for him to travel toward his aim.

Batista's populist turn was steeped in antifascism. The colonel sought political legitimacy by cultivating popularity on the island and friendlier relationships with Mexico and the United States. He embraced antifascism toward the end of the Spanish Civil War, seeking both an alliance with Mexico and the support of Cubans engaged in antifascist popular politics. As World War II approached, antifascism was changing significantly, and new pressure from the United States conflated Batista's political legitimacy and antifascism. Arguably, however, it was the *clases populares* and their politics that had the greatest impact on the colonel's actions. In addition to promising reforms, Batista could win the adherence of many Cubans by promoting antifascism—the latter was easy relative to the former, which required substantial money, time, and effort. Batista said he was an antifascist and preached the values and aims of antifascism to the United States, Mexico, the world, and the Cuban people. Mainstream antifascism succeeded in bringing together Cuban political actors who did not otherwise see eye to eye, even Batista. In this context of antifascist collaboration, cooperation in the broader political arena—though undeniably imperfect—achieved great steps toward a New Cuba.

Batista's populist turn, his increasingly reformist stance, his embrace of the Communists, his election as president and the election of the constituent assembly, and the promulgation of Cuba's 1940 constitution paralleled the transformation of Cuban antifascism from a widely popular but underground movement into an ascendant and official stance endorsed by many of the island's most respected leaders. The accepted narrative that the Communists constituted Batista's conduit for support from the *clases populares* need not be abandoned but rather expanded in light of the inclusion of antifascism. Antifascism lubricated the Communist-Batista alliance, helped Communists bring Cubans to Batista, and operated outside this single relationship, connecting Batista directly to Cubans in a way that helped make him, in the words of the British embassy, "a social leader, that is to say, a leader of the masses" who had significant popular support.[84]

Antifascism also provided a context for the extraordinary constituent assembly convened in 1939, in which representatives of a broad spectrum of Cuban politics—many vehemently opposed to one another—served. The type of trans-partisan collaboration present in the antifascist conglomerates operating in Cuba beginning in 1938 was apparent in the constituent assembly—for example, in the productive if highly contentious debate between Auténticos and Communists.[85] Given the overlap in participation by groups and individuals in late Cuban antifascism and in the constituent assembly, a strong influence of antifascism on the assembly is probable. This politically diverse assembly, operating in the context of antifascism, produced "a remarkably progressive constitution," in the words of Louis A. Pérez Jr.[86] Cuba's 1940 constitution included new rights and regulations, such as universal suffrage, social welfare programs, and worker-friendly labor laws, and legitimated Cuba's post–Platt Amendment sovereignty.[87] It was, in fact, reminiscent of the Spanish Republic's 1931 constitution.[88] The new constitution was indeed remarkable, but if the strength and momentum of Cuba's antifascist movement, as well as the ways in which the movement carried forward the various ideals of a New Cuba, are taken into consideration, it was not particularly surprising. It was informed in process and content by antifascism and Cubans' relationship to the Spanish Republic, a conglomeration of domestic and international influences, and the culmination of sustained activist continuity through victories and defeats. Robert Whitney summarizes the arc of 1933 to 1940: "Intense social mobilization, revolution, and finally defeat provided a foundation for a new form of authoritarian rule after 1937 and eventually for Cuba's transition to a constitutional democracy in 1940."[89] Antifascism as a continuation of the fight for a New Cuba is one powerful explanation for this otherwise surprising "eventually."

Cuba had transformed since the Machado era. Activists forced substantial change during and just after the 1933 uprising, but violent reversals in 1934 and 1935 seemed to have crushed advances, leaving only defeat, disappointment, and disillusionment. Rather than a lifeless period from 1935 to the end of the decade, however, there was antifascism. Activists stayed engaged in, connected with, and committed to the fight for a New Cuba throughout these years, even as they concerned themselves with fascism. By the time the 1940 constitution was put in place, followed by Batista's election to the presidency, Cuba had become more democratic and progressive.[90] This New Cuba was not solid and stable, as the violent 1940s and 1950s on the island would attest. It was, however, codified in deeply significant and longed-for achievements: constitutional legitimacy, progressive reforms, judicial sovereignty, and free and fair elections. Despite political, social, and ideological difficulties going forward, constitutional principles served as guides to debate and action and were "interpreted in potentially radical ways."[91] This official codification of constitutional principles made the promulgation of the new constitution in 1940 a great culmination and arguably the most significant event in Cuba's history since the inauguration of the Republic in 1902.[92] Though still highly imperfect, Cuba was indeed new. And this New Cuba did not spring forth from a political desert—the current of change had never dried up.

Postscript

Memory and Forgetting: Activist Continuity in the Cuban Revolution and Beyond

∙∙

As Cuban revolutionary forces neared their triumph over Fulgencio Batista late in 1958, a U.S. foreign relations officer sat in a Havana nightclub. The island was in tumult, but the dictatorship was still in place, and Wayne Smith could feel the emotional energy around him, the excited tension and fearful nerves of Cubans contemplating imminent but still uncertain victory. Pro-rebel club patrons were hopeful but unsure of how much they could risk celebrating without suffering consequences. Suddenly, a tipsy man unable to contain himself leapt to his feet and began loudly singing a revolutionary song of the Spanish Republic: "Down with the tyrant, down with the dictator!" Fear gripped the club, patrons bracing themselves for Batista henchmen to appear. Waiters silenced the man quickly, then went from person to person around the club assuring everyone that the man's song did not reference the leader of Cuba but rather Franco of Spain. No authorities interfered. Batista's forces either were not present, Smith concluded, or believed the waiters' explanation.[1]

On the eve of the Cuban Revolution, two decades after the Spanish Civil War's end, Cubans brandished revolutionary Spain as an ideal and conflated Franco and Batista. As they did with Cuba's previous revolutionary and anti-imperialist struggles, the Cuban revolutionaries of the 1950s idealized and used the Spanish Republic and its defense as inspiration—as the collective version of a martyr. Many participants and observers of these two historical events—the Spanish Civil War and the Cuban Revolution—made the connection. Alistair Hennessy was particularly succinct in a 1982 essay: The war in Spain was the great revolutionary failure of the first half of the twentieth century, he asserted, and the Cuban Revolution was the great revolutionary triumph of the second. It is significant, he argued, that two such intertwined countries "provided the touchstone for revolutionary enthusiasm on a world-wide scale."[2] A 1974 Soviet celebration of the International Brigades made similar assertions. "Inspired by the heroic example of Spain, the Cuban people carried on the cause of the Spanish revolution," the Soviet work stated. "Cuba was the first of the Spanish-speaking countries to have a victorious socialist revolution." Fidel Castro's *Granma* expeditionary participants received military training from Spanish Civil War veteran Alberto Bayo, the Spanish conflict had an impact on "the political consciousness of the young Ernesto Che Guevara," and the symbols and slogans from "the heroic battle of Madrid" were highly significant for "revolutionary Cuba's confidence in victory during the days of the Bay of Pigs." The Soviet text concluded by stating that Cubans were "greatly indebted to the heroic struggle of the Spanish people."[3] In 1970, U.S. nurse and Spanish Civil War veteran Fredericka Martin wrote to her old Cuban friend Dr. Eduardo Odio Pérez and mused that he must be so much happier than he had been in their younger days, "having seen so many of your dreams come true for your homeland and to have been able to help with the process."[4]

Continuity of activism to a revolutionary end, however, did not mean that every revolutionary activist's dreams came true. Vehement Batista opponent, antifascist activist, and Spanish Civil War widow Teté Casuso reengaged with activism during the 1950s only to be bitterly disappointed. The same was true for many of her *compañeros* from the Generation of the Thirties during and especially after the triumph of the Cuban Revolution, particularly those who were, like Casuso, anticommunist. Batista's 1952 coup d'état followed twelve years of democracy beset by corruption and the political violence that came to be known as *gangsterismo* in Cuba. Especially following the end of World War II, when wartime prosperity ended and "the economic foundation for political stability disappeared," as Whitney put it, politics in Cuba became increasingly tumultuous and cynical.[5] The Auténticos governed the country from 1944 to 1952 "with reckless abandon . . . before an incredulous national audience," in the words of Pérez.[6] A prominent student leader in the Revolution of 1933 and an eloquent antifascist, Eduardo Chibás stepped forward to challenge the Auténticos, forming the Partido del Pueblo Cubano—Ortodoxo (Cuban People's Party—Orthodox, or PPC-O), commonly known as the Ortodoxos. Claiming to carry forward the lost ideals of the Generation of the Thirties, Chibás and the Ortodoxos—among them the young lawyer Fidel Castro—thoroughly discredited the Auténtico administration and revived the struggle for a New Cuba. New hopes, however, were dashed with Chibás's suicide in 1951. The next year, Batista retook power. The coup succeeded flawlessly, not only because of the skill and savvy of its leaders but also because the Cuban people were so disillusioned with the Auténtico government and demoralized by Chibás's death that resistance was weak. Neither the discredited Auténticos nor the leaderless Ortodoxos could respond effectively, and a broad swath of the Cuban people were generally indifferent.[7] Also, the coup took place in the international context of hardening Cold War ideologies and the Latin American context of a dramatic turn away from the brief democratic opening that had accompanied antifascism during and just after World War II.[8] Domestic, transnational, and international pressures once again aligned, this time pushing Batista toward dictatorship.

Following the antifascist tradition, Teté compared the Cuban strongman to Franco. She wrote that like the Spanish dictator, Batista in 1952 "set himself up as Chief of State—despite the fact that the deposed government of [Auténtico president Carlos] Prío [Socarrás] had been an absolutely democratic one."[9] Teté was not indifferent; she was outraged, but she was also tired. She had fought Machado and rejoiced in the victories of 1933. She was devastated as Batista came to power the first time, but then maintained her activism by fleeing into exile in New York, organizing against Batista and fascism. Her greatest personal loss was in the antifascist fight—the love of her life killed on the battlefields of Spain, the country they called "the motherland"—but it was antifascism, too, that inspired in her the resilience to keep fighting as a widow. Left without the children of her husband for whom she had hoped, she created a formidable and effective organization to aid the children of Republican Spain. When her own stamina faltered after months of intense and demanding work and she left for Mexico, the organization she had built carried on, achieving great works of antifascism and bringing together diverse Cubans committed to a New Cuba.

For Casuso, the period from the end of the Spanish Civil War in 1939 to the mid-1950s constituted a lengthy era of sadness and discouragement. From her perspective, the activists of her generation existed in a vacuum, in "the quiet of exhaustion and forgetfulness," in "a demoralized, conservative state of mind."[10] She felt haunted by "the ghosts of dead friends," such as Professor Ramiro Valdés Daussá, the former leader of the AANPE, who was murdered in 1940 in an act of political violence by a group of "student gangsters."[11] Teté lived in Mexico during the 1950s, having lost all will for political activism. Then, in the summer of 1956, she read in a newspaper that a group of Cubans had been imprisoned in Mexico after being caught preparing for an expedition to overthrow Batista. They had been trained by former Spanish Republican Army captain Bayo, whom Teté described as "a pleasant, harmless man in his sixties." Upon reading about the would-be revolutionaries, she "smiled bitterly." She had little hope for these young prisoners, but their "illusions, so remote from reality," touched her, and she decided she wanted to meet them.

Aware of the weight of her activist identity in Cuban political history, she recounted her reception: "Fidel began calling over his comrades and introducing them to me. Most of them knew of me and my past, largely through Pablo's writings or from what they had heard about us. Fidel was moved by my visit. . . . He said he felt deeply honored that I, with all I symbolized in Cuba, had come to see them."[12] What did Teté Casuso symbolize in Cuba? A revolutionary past, but one she distinguished with some degree of disappointment from the revolutionary future brewing in 1956. Beyond Fidel and his closest associates, the men in that Mexican prison were "much humbler and cruder" than the activists of her youth, she believed. "Their language was coarse, and from the things they said I thought some of them irresponsible." Nevertheless, Casuso's encounter with Castro and his men set her life on a new course.[13] She would go on to become, for a time, a close friend and personal caretaker of the revolutionary leader.

Describing her state of mind at the beginning of her friendship with Castro, Casuso spoke with the wisdom of an experienced activist: "For revolutions, enthusiasm is essential, and this I did not have." She was cautious, weathered by past disappointments and traumas. Of Castro, she commented, "I had known so many like him whose dreams had been shattered by life's realities." Of his revolutionary exuberance, she wrote, "I could not easily surrender to his ardor and confidence—I had seen too much of that. I would not lightly accept a 'messiah,' a 'savior of Cuba.' I had known many people of high quality to compare him with, and enough of low quality to be on my guard. And I was in a discouraged frame of mind. Knowing my people's mood, and the spirit of irresponsibility to which it had abandoned itself, I was unable to believe in it once more and to hope for a resurgence of heroism at the signal of another would-be liberator."[14] Continuing activist efforts was not easy or straightforward. Repeated defeats and personal losses at home and abroad turned many away from politics altogether; it was only her close contact with Castro that brought Teté back from her apolitical existence. The young revolutionary organized her. He asked her to describe the compatriots and experiences of her political youth, and then worked to rekindle her enthusiasm for the struggle. He did not pressure her for a commitment to his cause during their first private conversation. She admitted that she "was eager to be convinced by him," though she expressed a great deal of skepticism about the chances Castro and his "naïve" companions had for success, and "felt a kind of pity" for him regarding his "confidence and firm conviction." She compared him to an "irresponsible, irrepressible child." Nevertheless, Castro was a skilled organizer who recognized Teté as someone he could commit to the struggle. She recalled that "during that long conversation I began to have a feeling of esteem for him and sympathy for his cause. My past appeared to join with his present and with Cuba's future." Castro's implied promise of continuity from the fight of her youth to his own resonated with her: "Even before he left, I had already more or less decided to help him all I could." Castro returned the next day, and this time he asked if he might store "a few things in her home"—a few things turned out to be seven carloads of weaponry. He proceeded, she recalled, to "take possession of my house." She had cast her lot with the revolutionaries.[15]

Storing weapons for the Cuban revolutionaries led Teté to time in a Mexican jail, but she was undeterred. She continued to help them in Mexico, losing her lease and many of her possessions in the process. When, on New Year's Day 1959, she got the news of Batista's flight from Cuba, her reaction was shaped once again by her revolutionary past: "I felt only a kind of sad emptiness. Nothing seemed to affect me any more. I was accustomed to winning and losing, to rising and falling unexpectedly."[16] Winning and losing, rising and falling—these were the constants in Cuba's revolutionary waters. Activists and organizations had to find ways to keep going. A great deal of Teté's pessimism came from the ascent of the Communists, most of whom she detested. She was particularly disappointed in her late husband's friend Raúl Roa, who had been "an irreconcilable enemy of the Communist Party," in her words, prior to becoming a Communist.[17] And indeed, despite her early—albeit cautious—enthusiasm for and devotion to Castro, Teté would break publicly with the Cuban Revolution in October 1960. Both the nature of the revolution and the intensity of her denunciation shaped the rest of her life, which she spent like many other anti-Castro exiles in the United States. In *Cuba and Castro*, her memoir published in 1961, her own emotions and memories are crowded by the acrimony surrounding Castro and the revolution. In a book of 250 pages, for example, just one paragraph is devoted to the AANPE, Teté's greatest and proudest activist achievement. In this way, Casuso—or her book editor—performed an act of antifascist erasure to make more room for discussion of Castro and the Cuban Revolution. Official Cuban narratives of Cuban antifascism have also minimized Teté. For example, the official celebratory book-length account of Cuba's defense of the Spanish Republic, published in 1981, does not erase her name from a reprint of a piece written by her husband, Pablo de la Torriente Brau, but neither does it mention her in its discussions of the AANPE, focusing instead on her colleague Rosa Pastora Leclerc, who remained devoted to the revolution.[18] Much more recently, an essay on the AANPE in a book on the Spanish Civil War in Cuban society, published in Cuba in 2010, includes Teté's name in a few lists of leaders but completely neglects to discuss her role or contribution as founding president of the organization.[19] Teté Casuso, who symbolized a revolutionary past to Fidel Castro in 1956, has been largely erased from Cuban history.

Not just Casuso but all of the Cubans involved in 1930s antifascism symbolized a revolutionary past to the activists of the 1950s, and as the Cuban Communists became increasingly powerful and influential in the months and years following the triumph of the revolution, so, too, did the Communist narrative of antifascism. The symbolic revolutionary past of antifascism was potent, but it was not static due to the reality that many of the 1930s activists were still alive and vibrant; this fact meant that the symbolism had to be managed carefully. One method was a formal assessment of Cuban Spanish Civil War veterans, which took place during the first few years following the revolution.[20] The Cuban Communist Party played a substantial role in the effort. Incomplete and disorganized, the records of the assessment comprise a fascinating and sometimes chilling portrait of Cuban revolutionary historical memory of 1930s antifascism. Investigators recorded information on a card for each known veteran. Some cards had only the person's name; some included a small head shot; and some gave further information about the person, including some combination of service in Spain, trajectory since 1939, current place of residence, current employment, or current political engagement. Some provided revolutionary commentary on the individual in question. Mario Alvarez Izquierdo, for example, one of the leaders of the Formación de Excombatientes Antifascistas, was listed as a secretary general of the port workers' union, a "Mujalista" (a term indicating either a follower of anticommunist labor leader Eusebio Mujal or simply slander by Communist opponents),[21] and, as of 1963, an exile. The card about Manuel Rivero Setien, member of the Asociación de Ex-Combatientes Anti-Fascistas Revolutionarios, stated that he had been a bad combatant in Spain, a representative to the House for the Auténticos in Cuba, and a participant "in all the shamelessness of that epoch," and that he had fled to Miami. In other cases, the cards revealed a more dramatic end than exile. Hector Morales Muñoz was listed as "currently imprisoned," and Armentino Feria Pérez and Eufemio Fernández Ortega were listed as having been executed. Fernández Ortega's record stated: "Shot as a traitor, an agent of the C.I.A. in Cuba."[22] One document listed thirteen "traitors" among 167 veterans.[23] Other veterans received more favorable evaluations. About Casimiro Jiménez, for instance, the assessment read: "His performance in Spain was good. Currently he holds up well politically." Similarly, the report regarding Manasés Romero Salicrup stated: "His performance in Spain was good. He remains with the Revolution."[24]

The search failed to locate information about the majority of the veterans, but not for lack of effort. An undated report by veteran Federico Chao Rodríguez chronicles his travels through the provinces of Villa Clara and Havana seeking out "ex-combatants of the antifascist war of Spain." A member of the Communist Party of Cuba beginning in 1932, Chao Rodríguez tracked down his fellow veterans of the Spanish conflict for assessment. His report demonstrates the seriousness and limitations of the effort. In the province of Villa Clara, for example, Chao Rodríguez found only one volunteer who had died in combat, three who had died following the war—"excluding Rivero Setien, who died in Miami"—and three survivors. The note regarding the omission of Rivero Setien indicates an intentional erasure from the historical record of those Spanish Civil War veterans deemed unworthy by authorities. Indeed, his name is omitted from official lists of veterans in the two major Cuban books on the subject.[25] Chao Rodríguez's report describes the way in which the search for veterans was channeled by the Cuban Communist Party, ascendant in Cuba during the period in which the search took place. He sought out local Communist contacts, such as fellow long-standing Communist and veteran Manuel Corcho Díaz in Villa Clara, who coordinated the effort to find veterans in their area. Upon leaving the province, Chao Rodríguez noted that he had established "a close bond" with the local Central Committee. In the province of Havana, Chao Rodríguez reported that he did "a thorough job" of seeking information "at all levels" of the Cuban Communist Party.[26] Given that structuring the search around Communist contacts and organizations would likely result in finding more Communist veterans, Chao Rodríguez's efforts demonstrate one of the ways in which Communist ascent following the revolution began to shape an official Cuban narrative of 1930s antifascism.

The fact that Communist officials felt that such an assessment project was worth their time and resources during the first few years after the revolution is indicative of the value they placed on 1930s antifascism. The narrative that began to emerge from their efforts demonstrates the extent to which Communists came to shape historical memory. Anticommunist Teté Casuso, celebrated and then erased, is one example. Like Teté, living Spanish

Civil War veterans could be villains or heroes from the point of view of revolutionary leaders, or their role could be ambiguous. Manuel Cala Reyes, Rolando Masferrer, and Rafael Chao Santana exemplify, respectively, the ambiguous, villainous, and heroic position a veteran of the Spanish conflict could assume relative to the Cuban Revolution. Their respective treatment indicates the way in which the revolutionaries attempted to manage the symbolism and reality of the antifascist generation. The case of Universo Lípiz Rodríguez, discussed in the next section, illustrates the way some assessments could change over time.

Veteran Manuel Cala Reyes, also known as Niño Cala, was an ambiguous participant in the Cuban struggle of the 1950s as well as in the Spanish Civil War. A native of Santiago de Cuba, an agricultural worker, and an activist in the anti-Machado struggle, Cala was remembered alternately as "a professional revolutionary who did not agree with any government" and "an expert marksman with a notorious reputation as a gun-slinging gangster."[27] This combination of characteristics was common among politically involved individuals in Cuba during the 1940s and 1950s. Batista's forces killed Cala in Santiago de Cuba the morning after Castro led his attack on the Moncada military barracks in July 1953.[28] In a list of "Martyrs of the Moncada," published by the island's Revolutionary press, Cala is listed among the civilians killed.[29] Despite this historical distinction, his activism in the anti-Machado fight, and his service in the Spanish Civil War, Cala did not receive much attention from the Revolutionary government as a hero. An observer of the Moncada attack commented later that he "was old and exhausted. There was no need to kill him. He was not involved in anything."[30] This dismissive assessment suggests that perhaps Cala was not, in fact, an active rebel supporter but simply in the wrong place at the wrong time. Alternately, the 1930s historical record hints that he may have been downplayed on account of his being an unsavory character. While in Spain, Cala caught the attention of officials for possible sexual impropriety. Already in his late forties, he had become enamored of a fourteen-year-old Spanish girl and claimed to want to marry her. After a confrontation, a report recorded, "little Maria" denied having told Cala that she wanted to run away with him, and "when he tried to kiss her, she struggled and was embraced by force." As he was, in the report's highly euphemistic terms, "a fanatical and incurable romantic," officials proposed detention until repatriation.[31]

In 1968 a Cuban observer wrote to a friend who had served in Spain: "There were quite a few who fought for the Republic, came back to Cuba, and proceeded to fight for Batista." Among them was "the notorious Rolando

Masferrer," arguably Cuba's most infamous Spanish Civil War veteran.[32] Masferrer traveled at the age of eighteen to Spain, where he was shot in the leg and left with a limp. A Communist during the 1930s and early 1940s, he worked for the party newspaper *Noticias de Hoy* while studying for a law degree at the university, where he won a prestigious award for outstanding students. In 1945 he cofounded the newspaper *Tiempo en Cuba* (Cuban times), which, under his direction and after his expulsion from the Communist Party that year, was both anti-Franco and anticommunist.[33] *Tiempo en Cuba* criticized Batista prior to the 1952 coup and went on to become a journalistic voice supportive of his regime, contributing to the sense that Masferrer was politically inconsistent. Masferrer was involved in *gangsterismo* during the 1940s, a leader in the unsuccessful Cayo Confites expedition to oust Dominican dictator Rafael Trujillo in 1947 (in which Fidel Castro was also a participant), and a representative of the Province of Oriente elected in 1948. When Batista's coup succeeded, Masferrer took a group of his men—"including, curiously, the ex-colonel of the Spanish Republican Army Valentín González (Campesino)," according to Domingo Cuadriello—to the university "to take part in the armed defense of the constitutional system of the country." Once President Prío fled the country and Batista took over, however, Masferrer became a supporter of the new leader. In 1954 he was elected senator, representing Oriente Province.[34] Described as a "political gangster" and a "Batista henchmen," Masferrer was most notorious for his leadership of the brutal Tigres de Masferrer (Masferrer's Tigers), a "paramilitary gang known for its crimes" and commonly understood as Masferrer's private army of two thousand men.[35] There existed a longstanding animosity between Masferrer and Castro dating back to Castro's days as a university student in Havana.[36] The offices of *Tiempo en Cuba* were ransacked during the triumph of the revolution, and some claim that Castro was responsible for Masferrer's death by car bomb in Miami in 1975.[37] Hugh Thomas opines that Masferrer's trajectory made him "a man of great wasted talent."[38] Domingo Cuadriello concludes that Masferrer's life "constitutes a strange and contradictory case of intelligence, personal courage, and thuggery."[39] In any case, Masferrer certainly did not earn the rank of celebrated Spanish Civil War veteran in revolutionary Cuba. He, like Rivero Setien, was left off the official Cuban lists of veterans of the Spanish conflict.[40]

The Cuban revolutionary government did not hesitate to make Spanish Civil War veteran Rafael Chao Santana a hero, awarding him numerous medals of honor.[41] A native of Havana who was born in 1916 and worked as a dry cleaner, Chao Santana joined the Communist Party in Cuba in the 1920s.[42] In Spain, the Central Committee of the PCE assessed his conduct as good, disciplined, serious, and valiant. It also noted that he was well respected and referred to him as a "good communist."[43] After spending time in a concentration camp at the conclusion of the Spanish conflict, Chao Santana sailed to Cuba on the ship *Orduña* in May 1939, along with almost two hundred other returnees.[44] Chao Santana joined Castro's 26th of July Movement during the anti-Batista struggle of the 1950s. Having met Castro in Miami, he traveled to Mexico, voyaged on the *Granma*, and fought in the Sierra Maestra.[45] In these ways, Chao Santana embodied direct continuity between the 1930s antifascist generation and the 1950s revolutionary one. As a result, throughout his life he enjoyed the benefits of a positive assessment of his credentials by the Cuban state. For example, as a member of the Agrupación de Veteranos Internacionalistas Cubanos (Association of Cuban Internationalist Veterans), he was among those elderly Spanish Civil War volunteers honored with a trip to Spain in 1996 for a commemoration of Cuban participants.[46]

Cuban antifascism of the 1930s was valuable to the Cuban revolutionaries of the 1950s for a number of reasons. A Spanish Civil War veteran provided military training to the rebels, and Cuban combat veterans fought with them. The symbolism of the approval of antifascists such as Teté lent credibility to the cause, while an antifascist breaking with the revolution was a particularly notable betrayal. Two decades after the end of the Spanish conflict, Franco still served as a proxy for Batista in a tense Havana nightclub in 1958. Furthering the link following the revolution, the Soviet Union dispatched Spanish Communists who had graduated from Soviet military academies to Cuba to serve in the revolutionary armed forces.[47] The value of 1930s antifascism to the Cuban Revolution derived not only from the powerful idea of a continuity of activism across time but also from the sense of a continuity of activism across space. As the title of one Cuban book on Cuban support for the Spanish Republic put it, Cuban antifascism was a "glorious epoch of internationalism."[48] Cuban revolutionaries should learn from the antifascist struggle, stated another celebratory account published in Cuba in 1981, for their own fights to bring "the encouragement and committed support of our people to Vietnam, Angola, Ethiopia, Nicaragua, El Salvador, and other countries in Asia, Africa and Latin America."[49] Fighting in Spain had been an early example of Cuban activists crossing borders and oceans to fight for a better world.

Antifascism across Time and Space

Antifascism continues to cross borders and oceans today. Coincident with the passing away of the 1930s antifascist generation over the past few decades has been an ascent of many of the forces its members fought. Capitalism stands victorious over many previously asserted alternatives; corporations have taken the place of nation-states as principal exploiters of the resources of the earth's less powerful people and more vulnerable places; many strongman governments reign oppressively; right-wing fundamentalism makes itself apparent in different settings and contexts around the globe; and even fascism itself—"neo-fascism," with a nod to the earlier era— is on the rise, both at the grassroots level and in the form of political parties capable of winning in elections.

Far from forgetting antifascism, new generations of activists have continually, especially since the 1970s, reclaimed and remade antifascism again and again as anti–Far Right, antiauthoritarian, anticapitalist, antiracist, antimysogynist, antixenophobic, antihomophobic, pro-worker, and pro– building a better world, generally informed by "pan-socialist politics," in the words of Mark Bray. Antifascist nostalgia for the Spanish Civil War has been evident in more recent antifascist movements from time to time, such as in the formation of a network in France in 1992 named for the Spanish antifascist slogan ¡No Pasarán![50] Yet antifascist activism, or "Antifa," as it is often called, has consistently moved ahead, constantly evolving to tackle current threats and propose visions of progress in societies around the world. And despite continued ideological diversity within antifascism, many Antifa activists agree "that such ideological differences are usually subsumed in a more general strategic agreement on how to combat the common enemy," in Bray's assessment.[51] Bray's 2017 book, *Antifa: The Antifascist Handbook,* surveys the entire history of antifascism in Europe and Anglo– North America and discusses responses to the rise of such parties and political phenomena as Golden Dawn in Greece, neo-Nazism in Germany, Marine Le Pen's Front National in France, and the so-called alt-right in the United States. Connecting the history of antifascism to its present, Bray makes clear the strong continuity of activism that has fought fascism in its many forms across time and space.

Cuban antifascists who fought across time and space during the 1920s, 1930s, and 1940s nonetheless grounded their movement in a specific place with specific domestic issues: Cuba. Cuban antifascism was both transnational and deeply Cuban. In being Cuban, it was inherently connected to

Spain, and that connection—like global antifascism—has endured. At a February 2011 march commemorating the Battle of Jarama in Spain, march organizers asked a very elderly Spanish man who had fought for the Republic to say a few words as a veteran commemorating the struggle. Rather than talk about his memories of the Spanish Civil War, he took the opportunity to speak at length and with great intensity in support of the Cuban Revolution. In the audience, another man held aloft the tricolor flag of the Spanish Second Republic and wore an olive-green cap with a Cuban flag patch sewn on one side.[52] These men represented in 2011 the robust and lengthy tradition of Cuba's presence in the Spanish antifascist fight.

A Cuban death less than two years earlier, however, represented the equally present tradition of Cuban revolutionary ambiguity surrounding the historical memory of antifascism. In August 2009, obituaries in the Spanish and Cuban presses heralded the death of one of the last known Cuban veterans of the Spanish Civil War, Universo Lípiz Rodríguez, who died at the age of ninety-one in his hometown of Matanzas. Lípiz was the son of anarchist parents exiled from Cuba in 1932 by the Machado regime. His family moved to Barcelona, and when the war began, Universo was involved "in the early skirmishes with the rebels in the Plaza Catalunya" in July 1936. When Nationalists entered Barcelona, he "went with a group of anarchists to deal with them in the streets" and got shot in the knee. Spanish anarchist Buenaventura Durruti was a friend of the family, and after Universo's convalescence, he joined the anarchist Durruti Column to fight against the Nationalists in various fronts of the war. After Republican defeat in 1939, Lípiz spent time in French concentration camps, joined the French resistance, and was taken by the Gestapo and held in the German concentration camp at Dachau. Early in 1942 he and several companions were able to escape during a blackout, he claimed. After making it back to Spain, Lípiz was arrested and deported to Cuba late in 1942. While there, he took part in the fight against Batista during the 1950s and later the defense against the Bay of Pigs invasion. In October 2008, less than a year before his death, the veteran traveled to Spain as a guest of the Asociación de Amigos de las Brigadas Internacionales (Association of Friends of the International Brigades, or AABI), where he was honored with two medals as an internationalist combatant in the war and expressed the "pride and satisfaction of having defended an ideological position in which I still believe." Upon his death, his coffin was decorated with "the numerous awards received during his long life."[53]

Yet Universo Lípiz does not appear in the official Cuban lists of veterans of the Spanish conflict published in 1981 and 1990, or in other sources published on the island that account for the Cuban volunteers, even one that documents those in Catalonia specifically.[54] If the obituaries are accurate, Lípiz was a committed anarchist with an undeniable history of revolutionary activity in Cuba and internationally: anti-Machado, antifascist, anti-Batista, and anti-imperialist. Raúl Roa, 1930s activist and later devoted Communist within the Cuban revolutionary government, stated, "Lípiz is not a surname; it is a revolutionary institution."[55] It is probable that with this history, Lípiz would have been a complex figure politically for Cuban revolutionary officials. Archival records of the Cuban Communist Party concerning Spanish Civil War veterans make little mention of him, but given his activism, it is unlikely that he was unknown.[56] Due to other instances of intentional omissions from the official record on political grounds, there exists some suspicion. Indeed, one obituary author, referring to the idea that Lípiz might be unknown, stated provocatively: "There must be other explanation(s)."[57] With a biography published on the island in 2004, several articles in Cuban publications in the years following, and commemorative obituaries in both *Granma* and *Juventud Rebelde* upon his death in 2009, Lípiz received significant official recognition during his last years. Perhaps, then, the explanation is the passage of time: that publicly celebrating an anarchist veteran who was by all accounts highly intelligent and outspoken was deemed risky—or at least not useful—in revolutionary Cuba until he was a very elderly man.

Teté Casuso's 1994 obituary in Miami stated that she was survived by no one. She arrived in that city, where her parents were already living, in 1965 and remained for the rest of her life. She worked as an editor and a translator until being diagnosed with Alzheimer's disease in 1980, when she was about seventy years old.[58] For Teté, continuity of activism had too often meant living with ghosts, haunted by memories of the traumas of her past. Indeed, she herself became a memory used by a younger generation of activists seeking a New Cuba, one she believed betrayed her and her *compañeros* of the Generation of the Thirties. When, in turn, she broke with them, they erased her. And in their triumph, they took control of the historical memory of her entire generation and the vibrant activist movement of her youth: antifascism. The official narrative forgot much, as all histories do. In the end, Teté forgot, too. As the disease of forgetting ravaged her brain, it seems there were few left around her to help keep her memories alive. Despite a brave and impactful life, she both forgot and was forgotten. Here, we remember.

Notes

Abbreviations

AHP	Archivo Histórico Provincial, Albacete, Spain
CEDOBI	Centro de Documentación de las Brigadas Internacionales, Universidad de Castilla–La Mancha, Albacete, Spain
CNT-IISG	CNT (España) Archives, Internationaal Instituut voor Sociale Geschiedenis, Amsterdam, Netherlands
CSPDC-IISG	Cuba Social and Political Developments Collection, Internationaal Instituut voor Sociale Geschiedenis, Amsterdam, Netherlands
FE-ANC	Fondo Especial, Archivo Nacional de Cuba, Havana, Cuba
FPPCC-IHC	Fondo Primer Partido Comunista de Cuba, Instituto de Historia de Cuba, Havana, Cuba
FRUS	*Foreign Relations of the United States: The American Republics*
FSV-IHC	Fondo Salvador Vilaseca, Instituto de Historia de Cuba, Havana, Cuba
LAIP-LC	Latin American and Iberian Pamphlets, Library of Congress, Washington, D.C.
PSOE-AO-FPI	Partido Socialista Obrero Español, Archivos de Organizaciones, Fundación Pablo Iglesias, Madrid, Spain
RA-ANC	Registro de Asociaciones, Archivo Nacional de Cuba, Havana, Cuba
RGASPI	Russian Center for the Preservation and Study of Recent History, Moscow, Russia
RG-IHC	Registro General, Instituto de Historia de Cuba, Havana, Cuba

Introduction

1. Casuso, *Cuba and Castro*, 61.

2. Casuso, 78.

3. Pablo de la Torriente Brau, "Me voy a España," 10. This essay or unaddressed letter is also reprinted in *Cartas y crónicas de España*, 55–57. The editor of that volume, Víctor Casaus, suggests that it may have been a letter to Juan Marinello.

4. Pablo de la Torriente Brau, "La revolución española se refleja en Nueva York," 275. Emphasis added.

5. Sometimes Cubans used the term "antifascist" specifically; other times, they defined themselves as antifascists by declaring their opposition to broadly defined fascism.

6. I will use the capitalized "New Cuba" throughout the book to indicate this concept of the domestic struggle used by Cuban activists.

7. Pérez, *Cuba: Between Reform and Revolution*, 216; Whitney, *State and Revolution*, 140. See also Pérez-Stable, *Cuban Revolution*, 42; Córdova, *Clase trabajadora y movimiento sindical en Cuba*, 219; Hennessy, "Cuba," 102; Farber, *Revolution and Reaction*, 79–80; Tabares del Real, *La revolución del 30*, 315. Likewise, Hortensia Pichardo calls the strike "the end of this period," though she does go on immediately to note the revolutionary and anti-imperialist groups that continued fighting during "the advance of fascism in the world." Pichardo, *Documentos*, vol. 4, pt. 1, 3–4.

8. See, for example, Pérez, *Cuba: Between Reform and Revolution*, 217; Whitney, *State and Revolution*, 167–68; Farber, *Revolution and Reaction*, 82–83, 88. Accounts produced in post-revolutionary socialist Cuba reinforce the idea that the Communist Party was largely responsible for Cuban antifascism. See Bello and Pérez Díaz, *Cuba en España*; Instituto de Historia, *Cuba y la defensa*. López Civeira does acknowledge the participation of diverse antifascists but singles out the Communists and calls their role "outstanding." López Civeira, *Cuba entre 1899 y 1959*, 133. I will capitalize the term "Communist" when referring to international Communism headquartered in the Soviet Union and represented by the Communist International (Comintern) and national Communist Parties. I will use the term "communist" when referring to examples of communist ideology apart from international Communism; for example, Trotskyists were communist.

9. "Among the most influential international events in Cuba in those years, the proclamation of the Republic in Spain and the Civil War that followed it had a very special weight." López Civeira, *Cuba entre 1899 y 1959*, 132.

10. Payne, *History of Fascism*, 3.

11. On using empirically based comparative work to conceptualize fascism, see Mason, *Nazism, Fascism and the Working Class*, 323–31.

12. Doing so is a gargantuan task. One estimate puts the number of titles on fascism at 59,000 (compared to just 2,000 on antifascism), and Roger Griffin states that the greater the number of scholars addressing fascism, the greater the number of explanatory models. Seidman, *Antifascismos*, 21; Paxton, *Anatomy of Fascism*, 221; Griffin, *International Fascism*, 3, 12.

13. Two particularly useful summaries are Paxton, *Anatomy of Fascism*, 218, and Griffin, *International Fascism*, 14.

14. One historical exception to a gender norm otherwise understood as universal prior to the contemporary era is Eva "Evita" Perón, First Lady of Argentina; however, the question of whether or not Eva and her husband Juan Perón were fascists is hotly contested, so Evita's status as a gender exception depends on a broader debate about Argentine fascism.

15. Payne, *Fascism in Spain*, 27–28.

16. Payne, *Falange*.

17. Payne, *Fascism in Spain*, 51–96.

18. Payne, 90.

19. Payne, 151–78.

20. Payne, 44–46, 83, 98–100, 115, 123–24; Robinson, "Parties of the Right," 57, 65, 72–73.

21. Payne, *Fascism in Spain*, 184.

22. Payne, 207; Robinson, "Parties of the Right," 68.

23. Payne, *Fascism in Spain*, 187–200.

24. Payne, 236, 242–45; Pérez Montfort, *Hispanismo y falange*, 79.

25. The Mexican government sent weapons and ammunition to the Spanish Republic, provided official consent to Mexicans wishing to volunteer in Spain, and gave asylum to five hundred Spanish war orphans during the conflict. After Republican defeat, Mexico took in many Republican refugees and never recognized the Franco government, maintaining official diplomatic ties with the Republican government in exile until 1977. Baumann, *Los voluntarios latinoamericanos*, 22, 120.

26. Broué and Témime, *Revolution and the Civil War in Spain*, 31–42.

27. Pike, "Background to the Civil War," 5.

28. López Civeira, *Cuba entre 1899 y 1959*, 123.

29. Mella, "Machado: Mussolini Tropical," *Juventud* 2, no. 11 (March 1925): 6, reprinted in Cabrera, *Mella*, 169–70. See also Gronbeck-Tedesco, *Cuba, the United States, and Cultures*, 40; Carr, "'Across Seas and Borders,'" 233; Tabares del Real, *La revolución del 30*, 76.

30. Cuevas and Olivier, "Julio Antonio Mella," 129.

31. Ángel Augier, "Cómo era Julio Antonio Mella," *Bohemia* (23 and 30 January 1949), excerpted in Cairo, *Mella 100 años*, 1:207.

32. Domingo Cuadriello, *El exilio republicano*, 11.

33. Russell B. Porter, "Students Guiding Destinies of Cuba," *New York Times*, 15 September 1933; Suchlicki, *University Students*, 32. For another example of Cuban opinions on the Spanish Republic prior to the Spanish Civil War, see the special issue titled "Número Homenaje al Cuatro Aniversario de la República Española," *Bohemia* 27, no. 15 (14 April 1935).

34. This definition appeared in the LAI's periodical *Masas* (Masses, published 1934–35). J. A. Guerro, "El Trotskismo Criollo frente al Fascismo y la Guerra," *Masas* 1, no. 3 (July 1934): 7.

35. *¡Ayuda!* is discussed and cited extensively in chapter 4. *Facetas* and *Mediodía* appear periodically throughout the book. The former is available at the Library of Congress in Washington; copies of the latter had to be collected from multiple U.S. libraries and the Biblioteca Nacional José Martí in Havana.

36. "El Gobierno y el Congreso contra la Guerra la Intervención y el Fascismo," *Masas* 1, no. 4 (August 1934): 5. A photograph of a pre-Congress planning meeting held in Santiago shows a racially diverse group of men. "Un aspecto de la Conferencia . . . ," *Masas* 1, no. 3 (July 1934): 10.

37. "Resoluciones del Congreso contra la Guerra, la Intervención y el Fascismo," *Masas* 1, no. 4 (August 1934): 6–7, 20, 22–24; "Congreso Nacional contra la Guerra la Intervención y el Fascismo: A las Masas Populares de Cuba," *Masas* 1, no. 4 (August 1934): 12.

38. "Congreso Nacional contra la Guerra la Intervención y el Fascismo: A las Masas Populares de Cuba," *Masas* 1, no. 4 (August 1934): 12.

39. "Los Que Luchan Contra HITLER (Alemania Subterranea): Frente a la Muerte," trans. Carlos Rojas, *Masas* 1, no. 6 (October–November 1934): 20–21.

40. Federación Obrera de la Habana, *El Sindicado General*, 9–10; Mesa Ejecutiva de la Federación Obrera de la Habana, "A Todos los Trabajadores de la Provincia," 4.1, CSPDC-IISG; "Obrerismo Idealista," *Nuestra Palabra: Órgano del Sindicato General de Obreros de la Industria Fabril* 1, no. 2 (15 May 1934): 2.

41. Ticiano, "Lo Fundamental: Aplastemos al Fascismo," *Nuestra Palabra* 1, no. 3 (1 June 1934): 4.

42. "Como en la Alemania Hitleriana," *¡Tierra! Órgano de la F.G.A.C.* 1, no. 8 (10 April 1934): 2.

43. "Combatir el fascismo . . . ¡¡La consigna del momento!!," *Insurrexit: Órgano de la Juventud Libertaria de la Habana* 2, no. 1 (10 February 1935): 1.

44. For one example, see Federación de Grupos Anarquistas de Cuba, "Manifesto al Pueblo de Cuba," n.d., Ugo Fideli Papers, Internationaal Instituut voor Sociale Geschiedenis, Amsterdam, Netherlands.

45. "Comprimido," *Nuestra Palabra* 1, no. 8 (1 September 1934): 4.

46. "A Todos," *Nuestra Palabra* 1, no. 7 (15 August 1934): 1.

47. I will use the terms "black Cubans" and "Cubans of African descent" rather than the externally imposed term "Afro-Cuban." I will use the terms "black diaspora" and "African diaspora" to indicate a collectivity of all the disparate peoples of African descent around the world. During the period of this study, there existed a transnationally networked, politically engaged subset within the diaspora, inclusive of many notable intellectuals and activists, as discussed in chapter 2. Melina Pappademos points out that it is important to remember that the term "diaspora" is an invention of scholars and was not used by the historical actors considered in this study; they were more inclined to think in terms of "pan-Africanism," which is also discussed in chapter 2. Personal communication, 30 May 2018.

48. Finchelstein, *Transatlantic Fascism*; Schoonover, *Hitler's Man in Havana*; Hagemann, "Diffusion of German Nazism," 71–94; Gentile, "I Fasci Italiani All'Estero," 95–115; Bulmer-Thomas, *Political Economy of Central America*, 85–86.

49. Penichet, "¿Está actuando el Fascismo en Cuba?," *Mundo Masónico* 6, no. 66/67 (October/November 1937): 15.

50. Schoonover, *Hitler's Man in Havana*, 96.

51. Schoonover, esp. 110–11; Chase, *Falange*, esp. 106–19. It should be noted that Schoonover has substantially corrected Chase's contemporary antifascist account. Chase's perspective is useful because it conveys the high level of fear of foreign fascism present in the Americas at that time. For Cuban perspectives, see Gómez Álvarez, *U-Boats del III Reich en Cuba*; Leiva, *El fracas de Hitler en Cuba*.

52. Schoonover, *Hitler's Man in Havana*, 93–99.

53. Bowen, *Spaniards and Nazi Germany*, 5, 14, 33, 59; Payne, *Fascism in Spain*, 250. Leiva, *El fracas de Hitler en Cuba*, 43; Kulístikov, "América Latina en los planes estratégicos"; Chase, *Falange*, 3–9.

54. Bowen, *Spaniards and Nazi Germany*, 36.

55. Rein, "Francoist Spain and Latin America," 135.

56. Bowen, *Spaniards and Nazi Germany*, 55; Payne, *Fascism in Spain*, 288–89.

57. Bowen, *Spaniards and Nazi Germany*, 26; Naranjo Orovio, *Cuba, otro escenario*, 1.

58. Naranjo Orovio, *Cuba, otro escenario*, 28.

59. Domingo Cuadriello, *El exilio republicano*, 3–31; Rein, "Francoist Spain and Latin America," 125; Naranjo Orovio, *Cuba, otro escenario*, 1–58, 66. Domingo Cuadriello notes that there were other Spanish Nationalist or Spanish fascist groups operating in Cuba.

60. Schoonover, *Hitler's Man in Havana*, 34–35.

61. Chase, *Falange*; Robert Gale Woolbert, "Review: *Falange: The Axis Secret Army in the Americas*," *Foreign Affairs* 22, no. 2 (January 1944).

62. Rein, "Francoist Spain and Latin America," 139–40.

63. Urcelay-Maragnès, *La leyenda roja*, 156–58.

64. H. García, "Was There an Antifascist Culture?," 95. The Spanish anarchist periodical cited is *Orto* (September 1933).

65. For consideration of the interaction between international forces and domestic trends in Latin America, see Collier, "Labor Politics and Regime Change," and Drake, "International Crises and Popular Movements," both in Rock, *Latin America*. Drake examines how "external influences were refracted through different internal political prisms" (109).

66. H. García, "Transnational History," 563.

67. H. García, 564. García discusses the "transnational turn in anti-fascist studies" and cites an exciting new diversity of nation-based projects and those that push previously assumed chronological limits. A recent work geared toward a general audience not cited by García is Bray, *Antifa*.

68. For an excellent brief discussion of defining antifascism, see Copsey, Preface.

69. García et al., *Rethinking Antifascism*, 6; García, "Was There an Antifascist Culture?," 92, 99, 100–101; Fronczak, "Local People's Global Politics," 246.

70. García et al., *Rethinking Antifascism*, 4.

71. García et al., 6.

72. Pérez, *Cuba: Between Reform and Revolution*, 159–63.

73. Pike, "Making the Hispanic World Safe from Democracy," 307.

74. Pike, 307.

75. Rein, "Francoist Spain and Latin America," 118.

76. Stavans and Jaksić, *What Is* la hispanidad?, 55–57.

77. On the adoption of Martí by activists of the 1920s and 1930s, including Mella, see Rodríguez, "La idea de liberación nacional," 123–24.

78. Rodríguez, "La idea de liberación nacional," 144.

79. On Martí's thought and legacy, see Guerra, *Myth of José Martí*; Rodríguez, *De los dos Américas*, esp. chap. 1 on Latin American unity; Turton, *José Martí*; Kirk, *José Martí*. I am indebted to one of the anonymous readers for the University of North Carolina Press for emphasizing Martí's importance in the development of a Cuban conception of *hispanismo* or *hispanidad*.

80. Stavans and Jaksić, *What Is* la hispanidad?, 5; Finchelstein, *Transatlantic Fascism*, 147; Rein, "Francoist Spain and Latin America," 117–18, 120–21, 137; Naranjo Orovio, *Cuba, otro escenario*, 1–3. It is interesting to note that, under the direction

of Faupel, the Ibero-American Institute of Berlin celebrated the pan-Hispanist Día de la Raza during the Nazi era. Bowen, *Spaniards and Nazi Germany*, 51.

81. Rein, "Francoist Spain and Latin America," 123.

82. Pablo de la Torriente to Pepe Velazco, New York, 2 August 1936, in *Cartas y crónicas*, 47.

Chapter One

1. An exceptionally thorough treatment of the controversy can be found in Hatzky, *Julio Antonio Mella*, 330–54. See also Gronbeck-Tedesco, *Cuba, the United States, and Cultures*, 54; Carr, "Review"; Argote-Freyre, *Fulgencio Batista*, 38–39; Whitney, *State and Revolution*, 42; Arboleya, *Cuban Counterrevolution*, 15; Liss, *Roots of Revolution*, 91; Soto, *La revolución del 33*, 1:501–3; Beals, *Crime of Cuba*, 266–69.

2. Helpful biographical works on Mella include Carr, "Review"; Hatzky, *Julio Antonio Mella*; Cairo, *Mella 100 años*; Padrón, *Julio Antonio Mella*; González Carbajal, *Mella*; Soto, *La revolución del 33*, 1:459–514; Dumpierre, *Julio Antonio Mella*.

3. Hatzky, *Julio Antonio Mella*, 39–45.

4. Throughout this study, I use the term "*compañero*" in the same ways the historical actors did: as "friend," "partner," "comrade," and "fellow traveler." When it appears in a text directly quoted, I will leave it in Spanish so as to convey the proper possible breadth of meaning. Only "*camarada*" will I translate as "comrade."

5. Whitney, *State and Revolution*, 35.

6. López Civeira, *Cuba entre 1899 y 1959*, 58.

7. Beals, *Crime of Cuba*, 225.

8. López Civeira, *Cuba entre 1899 y 1959*, 60–61; Whitney, *State and Revolution*, 25, 40; Young, *Postcolonialism*, 117, 120; López Civeira, Loyola Vega, and Silva León, *Cuba y su historia*, 153–54; García Álvarez, "La consolidación," 132–36; Aguilar, *Cuba 1933*, 68–69.

9. Pérez, *Cuba: Between Reform and Revolution*, 175–79; López Civeira, *Cuba entre 1899 y 1959*, 53; Whitney, *State and Revolution*, 22–25, 28; García Álvarez, "La consolidación," 136–38; Collazo Pérez and del Toro González, "Primeras manifestaciones," 195–208; Soto, *La revolución del 33*, 1:91–97; Aguilar, *Cuba 1933*, 43–44; Suchlicki, *University Students*, 19; Roig de Leuchsenring, *Historia de la Enmienda Platt*, 216–19; Beals, *Crime of Cuba*, 225–32.

10. Pérez, *Cuba: Between Reform and Revolution*, 179.

11. In his 1933 observations, U.S. writer Carleton Beals argued that the Zayas administration "merely represented the culmination up to that time of governmental corruption." According to Beals, Zayas's predecessor, Conservative Mario García Menocal, was far worse. Beals, *Crime of Cuba*, 232–34. See also López Civeira, *Cuba entre 1899 y 1959*, 54; Collazo Pérez and del Toro González, "Primeras manifestaciones," 197, 208–11.

12. Pérez, *Cuba: Between Reform and Revolution*, 179–84; Whitney, *State and Revolution*, 25–31; Soto, *La revolución del 33*, 1:99–106; Tabares del Real, *La revolución del 30*, 68–75; Aguilar, *Cuba 1933*, 45–48.

13. For a Cuban definition of neocolonialism, see Tabares del Real, *La revolución del 30*, 21–22. For an in-depth Cuban description of neocolonialism on the island, see Cantón Navarro et al., *Historia de Cuba*. For a more general treatment of neocolonialism and imperialism, see Young, *Postcolonialism*, chaps. 3 and 4.

14. Pérez, *Cuba: Between Reform and Revolution*, 189. See also Roig de Leuchsenring, *Historia de la Enmienda Platt*.

15. Pérez, *Cuba: Between Reform and Revolution*, 191–92; López Civeira, *Cuba entre 1899 y 1959*, 64–65; Whitney, *State and Revolution*, 31–36; Collazo Pérez and del Toro González, "Primeras manifestaciones," 213–16; Soto, *La revolución del 33*, 1:143–60; Tabares del Real, *La revolución del 30*, 70.

16. Pérez, *Cuba: Between Reform and Revolution*, 192.

17. Pérez, 192–95; Whitney, *State and Revolution*, 38–39; Callaba Torres, "La alternativa," 240–53; Pérez, *Cuba under the Platt Amendment*, 257–62; Soto, *La revolución del 33*, 1:189–201. For a view that is negative and cynical about Machado from before his election, see Tabares del Real, *La revolución del 30*, 75–78, 83. Tabares del Real specifically critiques non-Marxist historians who claim that Machado had popular support initially.

18. Beals, *Crime of Cuba*, 235–37. López Civeira notes that the idea of a "good" period and a "bad" period of Machado's presidency has been much debated. López Civeira, *Cuba entre 1899 y 1959*, 74.

19. Pérez, *Cuba: Between Reform and Revolution*, 195–98; Pérez, *Cuba under the Platt Amendment*, 265–68.

20. Whitney, *State and Revolution*, 46.

21. Whitney, 57–58.

22. Aguilar, *Cuba 1933*, 91.

23. Pérez, *Cuba under the Platt Amendment*, 266.

24. Pérez, *Cuba: Between Reform and Revolution*, 184.

25. Hatzky, *Julio Antonio Mella*, 119–24; Shaffer, "Freedom Teaching"; Fernández, *Cuban Anarchism*, 53–54; Whitney, *State and Revolution*, 44–47; Collazo Pérez and del Toro González, "Primeras manifestaciones," 222–23; Liss, *Roots of Revolution*, 84–85; Soto, *La revolución del 33*, 1:106–28.

26. Hatzky, *Julio Antonio Mella*, 124–27, 156; Young, *Postcolonialism*, 195; Ruiz, *Cuba*, 122.

27. Whitney, *State and Revolution*, 37.

28. Pérez, *Cuba: Between Reform and Revolution*, 189–90; Whitney, *State and Revolution*, 47–52; Callaba Torres, "La alternativa," 274–77; Liss, *Roots of Revolution*, 87–89.

29. Whitney, *State and Revolution*, 58.

30. Whitney, 57; Pérez, *Cuba under the Platt Amendment*, 269; Suchlicki, *University Students*, 24–25.

31. Soto, *La revolución del 33*, 1:383–421. The end of this account of the power grab discusses a comparison between Machado and Mussolini.

32. Pérez, *Cuba: Between Reform and Revolution*, 196–98; López Civeira, *Cuba entre 1899 y 1959*, 86–90; Whitney, *State and Revolution*, 58–61; Pérez, *Cuba under the Platt Amendment*, 279–84; Aguilar, *Cuba 1933*, 98.

33. Pérez, *Cuba: Between Reform and Revolution*, 198–99; Aguilar, *Cuba 1933*, 92.

34. Pérez, *Cuba: Between Reform and Revolution*, 198–200; López Civeira, *Cuba entre 1899 y 1959*, 84, 92–94; Whitney, *State and Revolution*, 61–63; Soto, *La revolución del 33*, 2:1–23; Tabares del Real, *La revolución del 30*, 113, 121–22; Aguilar, *Cuba 1933*, 98–102.

35. The date of Teté and Pablo's marriage remains uncertain. A Miami obituary for Casuso claimed that they married when she was fifteen (which would have been in the mid-1920s). However, a 1935 letter by Torriente and a remembrance by his sister Zoe published in 2006 claim the date of the wedding to be 1930. Casuso's memoir from 1961 makes clear that Torriente released her from their first engagement on account of her young age and desire to get an education, and that they finally married when she was in her early twenties, probably in 1934. Maydel Santana, "Teresa Casuso, Maestra, Diplomática, Escritora, a los 82," *El Nuevo Herald*, Miami (30 July 1994): 4B; Pablo de la Torriente, New York, to Ricardo S. Freire, Mendoza, Argentina, 7 July 1935, in Suárez Díaz, *Escapé de Cuba*, 180; Zoe de la Torriente Brau, "Pablo," 21; Casuso, *Cuba and Castro*, 73.

36. Casuso, *Cuba and Castro*, 53–58. Deceptively titled, Casuso's memoir covers Cuban history and her life prior to her involvement in the Cuban Revolution of the 1950s (pp. 9–95). There is also a Spanish-language edition of the memoir that contains additional information.

37. López Sánchez, *Pablo*, 3; Díaz-Quiñones, "1898," 578; G. L. García, "I Am the Other," 40; García Passalacqua, "Dilemmas of Puerto Rican Intellectuals," 122–23; Mintz, "Review."

38. Zoe de la Torriente Brau, "Pablo," 15.

39. Torriente Brau, 13–15.

40. Casuso, *Cuba and Castro*, 53–58; Pablo de la Torriente, New York, to Freire, Mendoza, Argentina, 7 July 1935, in Suárez Díaz, *Escapé de Cuba*, 180.

41. Zoe de la Torriente Brau, "Pablo," 15–16.

42. Casuso, *Cuba and Castro*, 52.

43. López Civeira, *Cuba entre 1899 y 1959*, 94–95; Zoe de la Torriente Brau, "Pablo," 21–22; Whitney, *State and Revolution*, 67; Soto, *La revolución del 33*, 2:32–38; Tabares del Real, *La revolución del 30*, 122–23; Aguilar, *Cuba 1933*, 102–3; Suchlicki, *University Students*, 25–26; Casuso, *Cuba and Castro*, 53.

44. Casuso, *Cuba and Castro*, 53.

45. Casuso, 53; Zoe de la Torriente Brau, "Pablo," 19–22. Pablo gives a vivid and dramatic description of time with Trejo in the hospital prior to the student's death in a section titled "Junto a Rafael Trejo" in the essay "Las mujeres contra Machado." Pablo de la Torriente Brau, "Las mujeres contra Machado," 89–90.

46. Gronbeck-Tedesco, *Cuba, the United States, and Cultures*, 56–57; Whitney, *State and Revolution*, 67; Soto, *La revolución del 33*, 2:38–39; Aguilar, *Cuba 1933*, 102–4; Suchlicki, *University Students*, 26; Fernández, *La razón del 4 de septiembre*. It should not go unnoticed that the general strike of 200,000 Cuban workers in March 1930 garners far less attention in many historical accounts than does this protest of 100 Cuban students in September of the same year.

47. Pablo de la Torriente Brau, "¡Arriba muchachos!," 5–6. Ellipses in original.

48. Torriente, 6.

49. Pérez, *Cuba: Between Reform and Revolution*, 198–99; Aguilar, *Cuba 1933*, 106–7, 116.

50. Pérez, *Cuba: Between Reform and Revolution*, 201; López Civeira, *Cuba entre 1899 y 1959*, 96–97; Whitney, *State and Revolution*, 71–72; Pérez, *Cuba under the Platt Amendment*, 289; Aguilar, *Cuba 1933*, 111–13, 115; Fernández, *La razón del 4 de Septiembre*.

51. Whitney, *State and Revolution*, 87; Aguilar, *Cuba 1933*, 116; Suchlicki, *University Students*, 27. For a celebratory account of the AIE as well as a partial list of members, see Tabares del Real, *La revolución del 30*, 113. A detailed look at the organization, its members, and its acts by a participant can be found in González Carbajal, *El Ala Izquierda Estudiantil*.

52. Pérez, *Cuba: Between Reform and Revolution*, 201.

53. Roa, "Tiene la palabra," 39.

54. Ala Izquierda Estudiantil, "Manifiesto," 207. On the same theme, see also Roa, "Reacción versus Revolución," 71.

55. Roa, "Rafael Trejo," 40–44.

56. Torriente attributes this phrase to Mella. Pablo de la Torriente Brau, "Hasta después de muerto . . . ," 16.

57. For example, Mella, "Los universitarios contra el imperialismo yanqui," 174–75.

58. Casuso, *Cuba and Castro*, 52–53.

59. Zoe de la Torriente Brau, "Pablo," 20.

60. Pérez, *Cuba: Between Reform and Revolution*, 199; Whitney, *State and Revolution*, 82; Suchlicki, *University Students*, 30.

61. López Civeira, *Cuba entre 1899 y 1959*, 78, 82–83; Fernández, *Cuban Anarchism*, 53–57; Pérez, *Cuba under the Platt Amendment*, 264; Soto, *La revolución del 33*, 1:370.

62. Pérez, *Cuba: Between Reform and Revolution*, 199.

63. Casuso, *Cuba and Castro*, 58–59; Roa, "Presidio Modelo," 72–105.

64. Zoe de la Torriente Brau, "Pablo," 24. Zoe claims that Pablo helped found the club in 1932, but Teté writes that Pablo did not go into exile until 1933, and historian Ana Suárez Díaz dates the establishment of the club in the late 1920s. Casuso, *Cuba and Castro*, 59; Suárez Díaz, *Escapé de Cuba*, 23.

65. Pérez, *Cuba: Between Reform and Revolution*, 202; Whitney, *State and Revolution*, 95–96.

66. Casuso, *Cuba and Castro*, 59–60.

67. López Civeira, *Cuba entre 1899 y 1959*, 99–101; Whitney, *State and Revolution*, 81.

68. For an in-depth treatment of the mediations, see Ibarra Guitart, *Mediación del 33*.

69. On the ABC, see Pérez, *Cuba: Between Reform and Revolution*, 199–201; Pérez, *Structure of Cuban History*, 165–66; Domingo Cuadriello, "El ABC"; López Civeira, *Cuba entre 1899 y 1959*, 97–98; Whitney, *State and Revolution*, 84–86; Soto, *La revolución del 33*, 2:122–47; Farber, *Revolution and Reaction*, 52–59; Tabares del

Real, *La revolución del 30*, 100–109. Contemporary documents and accounts include ABC, *Doctrina del ABC*; ABC, *El ABC en la mediación*; Beals, *Crime of Cuba*, 308–20; Russell B. Porter, "Cuba's A.B.C. Maps Out Big Political Changes," *New York Times* (23 July 1933): XX4. Domingo Cuadriello points out that Marxist intellectuals who have claimed that the ABC was proto-fascist have not demonstrated with documents any links, open or secret, between the society and fascism, Nazism, or the Falange. He also lists a number of reasons the society does not fit into the traditional definition of a fascist organization and the ways in which it stood apart from anything that could be considered Cuban fascism, such as Falange activity and support for the Spanish Nationalists. Domingo Cuadriello, "El ABC," 87–88. I am indebted to one of the anonymous readers for the University of North Carolina Press for suggesting that I address the issue of whether or not the ABC was proto-fascist.

70. Pérez, *Cuba: Between Reform and Revolution*, 202–4; Whitney, *State and Revolution*, 83–91, 93. It is important to note here the ambivalence on the part of Cubans about President Franklin Delano Roosevelt in relation to U.S. imperialism. Many wanted to and indeed did believe that Roosevelt was well intentioned and that their struggle in 1933 was against the economic imperialism of Wall Street rather than the political imperialism of Washington. It is an important point of reference in discussion of Cuban antifascism in the late 1930s and early 1940s, in which Roosevelt's character would again prove ambiguous.

71. Whitney, *State and Revolution*, 82.

72. Pérez, *Cuba: Between Reform and Revolution*, 204; Whitney, *State and Revolution*, 97.

73. Garveyism refers to the transnational pan-Africanist movement led by Jamaican Marcus Garvey. It is discussed in chapter 2.

74. Whitney, *State and Revolution*, 99.

75. Pérez, *Cuba: Between Reform and Revolution*, 204; Whitney, *State and Revolution*, 97–100; Sims, "Cuba," 218; Suchlicki, *University Students*, 32–33.

76. Shaffer, *Anarchism and Counterculture Politics*, 230; Fernández, *Cuban Anarchism*, 58–59; Alexander, *Trotskyism*, 218.

77. Pérez, *Cuba: Between Reform and Revolution*, 205–6; López Civeira, *Cuba entre 1899 y 1959*, 102–3; Whitney, *State and Revolution*, 92–93, 100; Suchlicki, *University Students*, 33.

78. The Ambassador in Cuba (Welles) to the Secretary of State, Havana, 12 August 1933, 837.00/3650, *FRUS* V (1933), 358–59.

79. Casuso, *Cuba and Castro*, 59–61.

80. Pérez, *Cuba: Between Reform and Revolution*, 206–7; López Civeira, *Cuba entre 1899 y 1959*, 103–5; Whitney, *State and Revolution*, 100; Suchlicki, *University Students*, 33–34; Casuso, *Cuba and Castro*, 61–62.

81. The Ambassador in Cuba (Welles) to the Secretary of State, Havana, 15 August 1933, 837.00/3665, *FRUS* V (1933), 365–67.

82. Whitney, *State and Revolution*, 83.

83. Casuso, *Cuba and Castro*, 62.

84. Zoe de la Torriente Brau, "Pablo," 24–25.

85. Pérez, *Cuba: Between Reform and Revolution*, 207–9; López Civeira, *Cuba entre 1899 y 1959*, 105–6; Whitney, *State and Revolution*, 101.

86. Casuso, *Cuba and Castro*, 61–63.

87. Suchlicki asserts that "Batista's contact with Directorio leaders dated back to the anti-Machado struggle when he had served as stenographer during some of the student's [*sic*] trials." Suchlicki, *University Students*, 35. Suchlicki does not cite a source for this claim, but Casuso, who does not appear in his bibliography, supports it: "I recalled having seen Batista once before, during Machado's time, when civilians were tried by military tribunals. A very dear friend of Pablo's . . . was being tried, and after one of the hearings, his fiancée and I had approached that thin sergeant who was the court stenographer and who had from time to time thrown us a look of sympathy, and asked him if her fiancé was all right. Batista had reassured her, saying that he would probably not be condemned to death." Casuso, *Cuba and Castro*, 63. Batista's biographer takes the sergeant's connection with the anti-Machado opposition during his years as a stenographer further, asserting that Batista was a member of the ABC and that he collected information in the courts, which he then passed along to the revolutionary society and other anti-Machado activists. Argote-Freyre, *Fulgencio Batista*, 40–41.

88. Agrupación Revolucionaria de Cuba, "Proclama al Pueblo de Cuba," 6–9; the Ambassador in Cuba (Welles) to the Secretary of State, Havana, 5 September 1933, 837.00/3753, *FRUS* V (1933), 381–83.

89. The Ambassador in Cuba (Welles) to the Secretary of State, Havana, 5 September 1933, 837.00/3757, *FRUS* V (1933), 384.

90. Pérez, *Cuba: Between Reform and Revolution*, 209; López Civeira, *Cuba entre 1899 y 1959*, 106–7; Whitney, *State and Revolution*, 101–3; Suchlicki, *University Students*, 36.

91. Casuso, *Cuba and Castro*, 64.

92. López Civeira, *Cuba entre 1899 y 1959*, 108; Suchlicki, *University Students*, 36.

93. Casuso, *Cuba and Castro*, 62.

94. This law addressed long-standing tensions between Cubans and foreign laborers on the island, especially Spaniards, Jamaicans, and Haitians. Some activists, especially anarchists, decried the law as divisive of the working class.

95. López Civeira, *Cuba entre 1899 y 1959*, 108–9; Whitney, *State and Revolution*, 101, 103.

96. Whitney, *State and Revolution*, 104.

97. Casuso, *Cuba and Castro*, 64–65. Torriente also references these events in "We Are from Madrid," 238.

98. Pablo de la Torriente Brau, "Hasta después de muerto," 16–18.

99. López Civeira, *Cuba entre 1899 y 1959*, 109, 110; González Carbajal, *El Ala Izquierda Estudiantil*, 58, 85–86; Aguilar, *Cuba 1933*, 185.

100. Pérez, *Cuba: Between Reform and Revolution*, 210, 213–15; López Civeira, *Cuba entre 1899 y 1959*, 109–10, 112–14; Whitney, *State and Revolution*, 106.

101. Grant Watson of the British embassy quoted in Whitney, *State and Revolution*, 121.

102. Pérez, *Cuba: Between Reform and Revolution*, 215; Whitney, *State and Revolution*, 119–21; Farber, *Revolution and Reaction*, 45.

103. Whitney, *State and Revolution*, 124.

104. Casuso, *Cuba and Castro*, 70.

105. Casuso, 71.

106. Aguilar and Suchlicki state that the Grau administration granted university autonomy in October 1933, whereas Casuso's meeting at which autonomy was achieved was with Carlos Mendieta, who did not become president until January 1934. Aguilar, *Cuba 1933*, 174; Suchlicki, *University Students*, 37. Whitney notes: "All of the important reforms of the Grau regime were, in fact, implemented by future governments, including the repressive Mendieta-Batista regime of 1934–1935." Whitney, *State and Revolution*, 121.

107. Casuso, *Cuba and Castro*, 72.

108. Casuso, 72–73.

109. Casuso, 73.

110. Casuso, 73–74.

111. Whitney, *State and Revolution*, 124–31.

112. Pérez-Stable, *Cuban Revolution*, 42.

113. Whitney, *State and Revolution*, 124–27; Alexander, *History of Organized Labor*, 61–64.

114. Alexander, *History of Organized Labor*, 63–64.

115. Shaffer, *Anarchism and Counterculture Politics*, 230; Sims, "Cuba," 217.

116. See Partido Bolchevique Leninista, *Programa del Partido Bolchevique Leninista* and *Estatutos*.

117. Tennant, "Dissident Cuban Communism," chap. 5; Soler Martínez, "El Partido Bolchevique Leninista Cubano," 272–74, 289; Whitney, *State and Revolution*, 115; González Carbajal, *El Ala Izquierda Estudiantil*, 81; Alexander, *Trotskyism in Latin America*, 215–18; Comité Central del Partido Bolchevique Leninista, *A todos los Obreros y Campesinos. Al pueblo de Cuba*, 25 September 1933, número 136, legajo 1, FE-ANC, quoted and discussed in Soler Martínez, "El Partido Bolchevique Leninista Cubano," 271. For a critical analysis of the Trotskyist opposition, see Rojas Blaquier, *El Primer Partido Comunista*, 1:140–50, 206, 214–15, 218.

118. Cushion, *Hidden History of the Cuban Revolution*, 32–33; Tennant, "Dissident Cuban Communism," chap. 5; Alexander, *Trotskyism in Latin America*, 219.

119. Alexander, *Trotskyism in Latin America*, 219.

120. Casuso, *Cuba and Castro*, 74.

121. Whitney, *State and Revolution*, 131–32; Sims, "Cuba," 219–20; Tabares del Real, *La revolución del 30*, 307–11. For a number of useful primary sources on the general strike, see Pichardo, *Documentos*, vol. 4, pt. 1, 551–600. The total number of strikers is disputed; 500,000 is the high end of the estimate.

122. The controversy over factionalism, predictably, remains extant in the scholarship. One author claims the PCC issued the call for the strike; a second states that Joven Cuba and the PBL were at "the forefront" of the organizing, with the Trotskyists "among the most dedicated and determined of the opponents to the [Mendieta] regime"; and a third refutes both by claiming that the general strike "was largely a

spontaneous affair with no effective centralised leadership," which was undone by "concessions to the old traditions of anarcho-syndicalism and non-proletarian nationalism." Rojas Blaquier, *El Primer Partido Comunista*, 1:240; Alexander, *Trotskyism in Latin America*, 220–21; Tennant, "Dissident Cuban Communism," chap. 5. A contemporary observer asserted that the student movement issued the call for the strike and was the only tenuous "chain" holding the feuding "organizations of the proletariat" together. Aureliano Sánchez Arango, quoted in Farber, *Revolution and Reaction in Cuba*, 48–49.

123. Batista, quoted in Tabares del Real, *La revolución del 30*, 309.

124. Pérez, *Cuba: Between Reform and Revolution*, 216; Whitney, *State and Revolution*, 131–32; Alexander, *Trotskyism in Latin America*, 220–21.

125. Casuso, *Cuba and Castro*, 75–78; Zoe de la Torriente Brau, "Pablo," 27.

Chapter Two

1. Benito Mussolini, "La aurora de una nueva civilización," *Bohemia* 27, no. 8 (24 February 1935): 8–9, 66; "El cine del mundo," *Bohemia* 27, no. 9 (3 March 1935): 32–33.

2. "El estudiantado cubano Esta en pie," *Bohemia* 27, no. 9 (3 March 1935): front cover; "Del conflicto itálico-etiopico," *Bohemia* 27, no. 10 (10 March 1935): front cover.

3. "Editorial," *Bohemia* 27, no. 11/12 (24 March 1935): 33.

4. "Mundiales" and "Cine del Mundo," *Bohemia* 27, no. 11/12 (24 March 1935): 12, 30–31.

5. "Editorial: Europa en jaque," *Bohemia* 27, no. 13 (31 March 1935): 35.

6. "Número Homenaje al Cuatro Aniversario de la República Española," *Bohemia* 27, no. 15 (14 April 1935).

7. General studies of the Second Italo-Ethiopian War include Pankhurst, "Invasion, Occupation and Liberation," 219–49; Dugan and Lafore, *Days of Emperor and Clown*; Barker, *Civilizing Mission*.

8. Comité Distrital de la Habana del Partido Comunista de Cuba, "¡FUERA LAS MANOS DEL IMPERIALISMO ITALIANO DE ABISINIA!," September 1935, signatura 42, caja 1, FE-ANC; Comité Central del Partido Comunista de Cuba, "Defendamos al Pueblo Abisinio," 11 October 1935, signatura 53, caja 1, FE-ANC.

9. Jefferson Caffery was a U.S. diplomat who replaced Sumner Welles in December 1933. He was named "personal representative of the president" in order to avoid sending a formal ambassador to the Grau government. Whitney, *State and Revolution*, 119.

10. CC del PCC, "Defendamos al Pueblo Abisinio," 11 October 1935, signatura 53, caja 1, FE-ANC.

11. CC del PCC, "Defendamos al Pueblo Abisinio," 11 October 1935.

12. For varied comments on the Soviet stance, see Pankhurst, "Invasion, Occupation and Liberation," 238; Dugan and Lafore, *Days of Emperor*, 104, 117, 136, 271; Barker, *Civilizing Mission*, 136. After coming to power in 1916, Ethiopian leader Ras Tafari, the future Haile Selassie, recruited White Russian officers to train his troops.

Pankhurst, "Invasion, Occupation and Liberation," 210. Secretly, Hitler's Germany supplied Haile Selassie with a significant amount of war materiel during the Italo-Ethiopian conflict in an effort to keep Italy busy in an African war and out of Germany's way in Austria. Pankhurst, "Invasion, Occupation and Liberation," 226. Of course, both Ethiopia and the Soviet Union were far more complex than any group's ideology or symbolism would suggest.

13. CC del PCC, "Defendamos al Pueblo Abisinio," 11 October 1935.

14. Pappademos, *Black Political Activism*, 14.

15. Pappademos, 12.

16. Pappademos, 11–12.

17. Pérez, *Cuba: Between Reform and Revolution*, 168–69.

18. Pappademos, *Black Political Activism*, 12, 226–29; Montejo Arrechea, *Sociedades Negras*, 199–246; de la Fuente, *Nation for All*, 170–71.

19. Pappademos, *Black Political Activism*, 226.

20. Pappademos, 228–29.

21. Pappademos, 173.

22. De la Fuente, *Nation for All*, 201–2. Though the progressive agenda of these new clubs represented a significant shift from the modus operandi of the traditional black societies, there was great diversity of opinion among the new black Cuban activists, whose views ranged from middle-class conservative to revolutionary. See Arnedo-Gómez, "Debates on Racial Inequality," 711–35.

23. Serapio Páez Zamora, "La Misión Revolucionaria de la Juventud Negra," *Adelante* 2, no. 16 (September 1936): 8. For discussion of the continued work in the 1940s of this "member of the 1930s generation of Afro-Cuban activists," see Guridy, "From Solidarity to Cross-Fertilization," 37–38. On the periodical *Adelante*, see Montejo Arrechea, *Sociedades Negras*, 220. The periodical is available in the United States on microfilm.

24. As Frank Guridy notes, they were, in this respect, part of a broader shift in the African diaspora as a whole—a shift toward a working-class agenda and away from the middle-class "paradigm of racial improvement that had served as the dominant model of social and political organization since the nineteenth century." Guridy, "From Solidarity to Cross-Fertilization," 24.

25. "Primer Aniversario," *Adelante* 1, no. 12 (May 1936): 5.

26. Cohen, *Global Diasporas*, 37–38.

27. Cohen, 37; Kelley, "'This Ain't Ethiopia,'" 129; W. R. Scott, "Black Nationalism," 118. For example, Psalm 68:31 (King James Version) states: "Ethiopia shall soon stretch out her hands unto God."

28. Kelley, "'This Ain't Ethiopia,'" 129.

29. W. R. Scott, "Black Nationalism," 121.

30. "Cuba y Abisinia," *Adelante* 1, no. 6 (November 1935): 3. The omission of Liberia likely resulted from the sense that the African nation was "only nominally free," due to its original establishment as a colony of African Americans. W. R. Scott, *Sons of Sheba's Race*, 10.

31. Hughes, "Mussolini, Don't You 'Mess' with Me," 3. Hughes uses the English translation of the famous Spanish ¡No pasarán!, which was first used in an antifas-

cist context in Barcelona early in 1934. H. García, "Was There an Antifascist Culture?," 101.

32. Kelley, "'This Ain't Ethiopia,'" 123.

33. Cohen, *Global Diasporas*, 39; W. R. Scott, "Black Nationalism," 119–20.

34. W. R. Scott, "Black Nationalism," 122; Yates, *Mississippi to Madrid*, 92.

35. Yates, *Mississippi to Madrid*, 91.

36. Ferrer, *Freedom's Mirror*, 276.

37. Ferrer, 304–11.

38. Ferrer, 307–10.

39. Ferrer, 311.

40. Such distinctions regarding historical and cultural connections would gain significance for various Cuban actors as antifascism on the island moved from an Ethiopian to a Spanish Republican phase.

41. Ferrer, *Insurgent Cuba*.

42. See Miller, *Crucible of Empire*.

43. Ferrer, *Insurgent Cuba*.

44. José M. Saenz, "Menelik y Cuba," *Adelante* 1, no. 8 (January 1936): 17.

45. On Ellis, see Jacoby, *Strange Career of William Ellis*; Jacoby, "Between North and South," 210–39; Shinn, introduction, 7, 9, 16; Fisher-Thompson, "Ethiopia and U.S. Celebrate"; Pankhurst, "William H. Ellis."

46. Pedro Montenegro, "Hasta cuando dominados!" *Negro World*, 20 July 1929, 7, quoted in McLeod, "'Sin dejar de ser cubanos,'" 81.

47. McLeod, "'Sin dejar de ser cubanos,'" 84, 89–90.

48. Guridy, "'Enemies of the White Race,'" 122; Sullivan, "Radical Solidarities," 135.

49. McLeod, "'Sin dejar de ser cubanos,'" 82–84.

50. Lyrics reproduced in Bayor, *Columbia Documentary History of Race and Ethnicity*, 507–8. The song was composed in 1918 and named "National Anthem of Universal Negro Improvement Association and African Communities League." The name was changed to "Universal Ethiopian Anthem" in 1920.

51. Sullivan, "Radical Solidarities," 136; McLeod, "'Sin dejar de ser Cubanos,'" 83.

52. José L. Franco, "El Conflicto Italo-Abisinio," *Adelante* 1, no. 5 (October 1935): 8; Rojas Blaquier, "Nicolás."

53. Franco, "El Conflicto Italo-Abisinio," 8.

54. Guillén, "Soldados en Abisinia," 178–83.

55. "Cuba y Abisinia," 3.

56. Haile Selassie, "Appeal." Support for the League of Nations regarding its position in favor of Ethiopia, a member state, and its sanctions against Italy was a central defining characteristic of nations standing in solidarity with the besieged African country. The league, sanctions, and international supporters, however, all proved weak in the end and did little to slow Mussolini's conquest.

57. "Cuba y Abisinia," 3. Though it in no way contradicts concerns of exploitation by Italian invaders, it should be noted that under Haile Selassie, Ethiopia was actually in the process of abolishing its own internal chattel slavery in the early 1930s. Pankhurst, "Invasion, Occupation and Liberation," 210–11, 216. Indeed, Mussolini would celebrate Italian victory in Ethiopia as, in part, "the redemption of the miserable

which triumphs over the slavery of a thousand years." Speech given at Piazza Venezia, Rome, on 9 May 1936, quoted in Barker, *Civilizing Mission*, 288.

58. Alberto Arredondo, "El Negro en la Colonia," *Adelante* 1, no. 12 (May 1936): 15.

59. Liss, *Roots of Revolution*, 73–74.

60. José L. Franco, "El Conflicto Italo-Abisinio," 8. I am grateful to linguist Noelia Sánchez-Walker for providing me with an accurate translation of this phrase.

61. Arredondo, "El Negro en la Colonia," 15.

62. Historian A. J. Barker notes the development of the "civilizing mission" rhetoric from March 1934, when Mussolini proclaimed Italy's "territorial conquest" a "natural expansion," to three months later, when he declared it Italy's right and duty to civilize Ethiopia. Up to October 1935, "Mussolini's speeches followed a definite trend" in which the "brutal truth" was "camouflaged." Barker, *Civilizing Mission*, 66.

63. Tomás Borroto Mora, "Sintesis," *Adelante* 1, no. 6 (November 1935): 6. Ellipses in original.

64. Borroto Mora, 6.

65. Borroto Mora, 6. Barker notes that Pope Pius XI "was biased toward Fascism even before his ascension" and "found much to admire in the Fascist state." Barker, *Civilizing Mission*, 67.

66. Mariano Salas Aranda, "La Liga de las Naciones Frente a Etiopía," *Adelante* 1, no. 12 (May 1936): 4.

67. "Cuba y Abisinia," 3; Salas Aranda, "La Liga de las Naciones Frente a Etiopía," 4; Vicente Martínez, "La 'Barbarie' Abisinia," *Adelante* 1, no. 11 (April 1936): 15.

68. "Abisinia," *Adelante* 1, no. 9 (February 1936).

69. Lucas Pino, "Perillazos," *Mediodía* no. 55 (14 February 1938): 15.

70. Martínez, "La 'Barbarie' Abisinia," 15.

71. On alleged decapitation by Ethiopians, see Grip and Hart, "Use of Chemical Weapons," 1–2; Dugan and Lafore, *Days of Emperor*, 242; League of Nations, "Documentation Relating to the Dispute between Ethiopia and Italy," *Official Journal*, Annex 1605 (July 1936): 772–73.

72. Martínez, "La 'Barbarie' Abisinia," 15.

73. Martínez, 15.

74. Martínez, 15.

75. Selassie, "Appeal." Italy's relentless attack from the air on civilian centers and humanitarian targets with both bombs and mustard gas became notorious, though much of it was long denied by the Italian Ministry of Defense, which did not admit to the use of gas in Ethiopia until 1995. Pankhurst, "Invasion, Occupation and Liberation," 233–34. On doubt over the use of gas, see also Dugan and Lafore, *Days of Emperor*, 246.

76. Selassie, "Appeal."

77. Salas Aranda, "La Liga de las Naciones Frente a Etiopía," 4.

78. José L. Franco, "Al Comité 'Pro-Abisinia': El Drama Espantosa que ha Vivido un Pueblo," *Adelante* 2, no. 15 (August 1936): 14–15; no. 16 (September 1936): 10–11, 15; no. 17 (October 1936): 11, 16; and no. 18 (November 1936): 15–16.

79. The subject of Cuban antifascism vis-à-vis the fight in China will make a productive subject for future research. Kathleen López briefly addresses the subject several times in her book on Chinese Cubans. She notes that the Japanese occupation of China (1937–45) caused great hardships for the Chinese families whose relatives had migrated to Cuba. Also, she discusses Cuban Communist support for Chinese revolutionaries and the involvement of some leftist Chinese Cubans in anti-dictator, anti-imperialist, and antifascist struggles in Cuba. From the Chinese Cuban community's activism, she writes, "Support for the Chinese resistance against the Japanese occupation movement seeped into mainstream Cuban culture." López, *Chinese Cubans*, 207. See also pages 177, 198–200, 206–8.

80. Antonio Penichet, "Con los ojos sobre el mundo," *Adelante* 3, no. 29 (October 1937): 9.

81. Rubén Sinay, "Envio," *Adelante* 3, no. 29 (October 1937): 9.

82. Bronfman, *Measures of Equality*, 152–53. See also Kelley, "'Africa's Sons with Banner Red'" and "'This Ain't Ethiopia.'"

83. Kelley, "'This Ain't Ethiopia,'" 132.

84. W. R. Scott, *Sons of Sheba's Race*, 213.

85. Kelley states that the royal Ethiopian volunteer was Ras Imru, but Ras Imru was imprisoned in Italy beginning in December 1936, and the royal Ethiopian volunteer in Spain was his son. Barker, *Civilizing Mission*, 304–5.

86. Kelley, "'This Ain't Ethiopia,'" 139–40.

87. Jay N. Hill, "An Ethiope in Spain," *Crisis* (July 1937): 202; Nurhussein, "Ethiopia in the Verse," 431.

88. Kelley, "'This Ain't Ethiopia,'" 123–24.

Chapter Three

1. Pablo de la Torriente, New York, to Carlos Martínez, Miami Beach, 28 July 1936, in *Cartas y crónicas*, 45–46.

2. Casuso, *Cuba and Castro*, 77–78; Pablo de la Torriente, New York, to Aureliano Sánchez Arango, Mexico City, 13 January 1936, in *Cartas Cruzadas*, 2:23; José María Chacón y Calvo, unedited diary excerpt, 2 October 1936, quoted in *Cartas y crónicas*, 24.

3. Casuso, *Cuba and Castro*, 78.

4. Gronbeck-Tedesco, *Cuba, the United States, and Cultures*, 57–61; Suárez Díaz, *Escapé de Cuba*; Whitney, *State and Revolution*, 148.

5. Suárez Díaz, *Escapé de Cuba*, 208–12; Casuso, *Cuba and Castro*, 78.

6. Casuso, *Cuba and Castro*, 77–78.

7. Pablo de la Torriente, New York, to Carlos Martínez, Miami Beach, 28 July 1936, in *Cartas y crónicas*, 46.

8. Pablo de la Torriente, New York, to Pepe Velazco, Mexico City, 2 August 1936, in *Cartas y crónicas*, 47.

9. Pablo de la Torriente Brau, "Me voy a España," 12.

10. Torriente, 12.

11. Pablo de la Torriente, New York, to Carlos Martínez, Miami Beach, 28 July 1936, in *Cartas y crónicas*, 45–46.

12. Pablo de la Torriente Brau, "Me voy a España," 11. Torriente remembers the day of the Union Square rally as 30 July, but according to the *New York Times*, it took place on 31 July. "Spain Fascists Assailed: Union Square Meeting Backs Fight to Put Down Rebels," *New York Times*, 1 August 1936, 2.

13. Pablo de la Torriente Brau, "Me voy a España," 11–12. The *New York Times* estimated the number in attendence. "Spain Fascists Assailed," *New York Times*, 1 August 1936, 2.

14. Pablo de la Torriente Brau, "La revolución española se refleja en Nueva York," 274–75.

15. Pablo de la Torriente Brau, "Me voy a España," 12.

16. Pablo de la Torriente, New York, to Carlos Martínez, Miami Beach, 28 July 1936, in *Cartas y crónicas*, 46.

17. Pablo de la Torriente Brau, "Me voy a España," 11.

18. Torriente, 12.

19. Pablo de la Torriente, New York, to "Adolfo García," pseudonym for Raúl Roa, Havana, 10 August 1936, in *Cartas y crónicas*, 62.

20. Pablo de la Torriente Brau, "Me voy a España," 12–13.

21. Pablo de la Torriente, New York, to "Luis," pseudonym for Ramiro Valdés Daussá, Havana, 12 August 1936, in *Cartas y crónicas*, 66–67.

22. Pablo de la Torriente, New York, to Dr. Alfredo Sánchez Arango, Lawrenceburg, Ind., 6 August 1936, in *Cartas y crónicas*, 53; Pablo de la Torriente, New York, to "Adolfo García," pseudonym for Raúl Roa, Havana, 10 August 1936, in *Cartas y crónicas*, 62.

23. Pablo de la Torriente, New York, to "Luis," Havana, 4 August 1936, in *Cartas y crónicas*, 51–52; Pablo de la Torriente, New York, to "Adolfo García," Havana, 10 August 1936, in *Cartas y crónicas*, 62.

24. Pablo de la Torriente, New York, to Pepe Velazco, Mexico City, 2 August 1936, in *Cartas y crónicas*, 47. See also Pablo de la Torriente, New York, to Dr. Alfredo Sánchez Arango, Lawrenceburg, Ind., 6 August 1936, in *Cartas y crónicas*, 53–54.

25. Pablo de la Torriente, New York, to "Luis," Havana, 12 August 1936, in *Cartas y crónicas*, 67.

26. Pablo de la Torriente, New York, to "Luis," Havana, 4 August 1936, in *Cartas y crónicas*, 52.

27. Pablo de la Torriente, New York, to "Luis," Havana, 4 August 1936, in *Cartas y crónicas*, 52; Pablo de la Torriente, New York, to Dr. Alfredo Sánchez Arango, Lawrenceburg, Ind., 6 August 1936, in *Cartas y crónicas*, 54; Pablo de la Torriente, New York, to "Adolfo García," Havana, 10 August 1936, in *Cartas y crónicas*, 62.

28. Pablo de la Torriente, New York, to "Luis," Havana, 12 August 1936, in *Cartas y crónicas*, 66.

29. Pablo de la Torriente, New York, to "Adolfo García," Havana, 18 August 1936, in *Cartas y crónicas*, 69–70.

30. Pablo de la Torriente, New York, to Carlos Martínez, Miami Beach, 28 July 1936, in *Cartas y crónicas*, 45–46.

31. Casuso, *Cuba and Castro*, 79.

32. Pablo de la Torriente Brau, "Me voy a España," 13–14.

33. Pablo de la Torriente, New York, to Dr. Alfredo Sánchez Arango, Lawrence-burg, Ind., 6 August 1936, in *Cartas y crónicas*, 53–54.

34. Casuso, *Cuba and Castro*, 79.

35. Pablo de la Torriente, New York, to Gonzalo Mazas Garbayo, Havana, 2 August 1936, in *Cartas y crónicas*, 48.

36. Pablo de la Torriente, New York, to Raúl Roa, Miami Beach, 4 August 1936, in *Cartas y crónicas*, 49. Torriente's novel was published posthumously in 1940; a reprint of the novel was published in 2000.

37. Club Cubano Julio Antonio Mella, "GRAN VELADA Conmemorativa del Tercer Aniversario de la caída del tirano Machado," August 1936, Doc. 216, FSV-IHC.

38. Pablo de la Torriente, New York, to Raúl Roa, Miami Beach, 4 August 1936, in *Cartas y crónicas*, 49–50.

39. Pablo de la Torriente Brau, "Me voy a España," 13.

40. Pablo de la Torriente, New York, to "Adolfo García," Havana, 10 August 1936, in *Cartas y crónicas*, 61–62.

41. Roa, "Los últimos días," 333–34.

42. Pablo de la Torriente, New York, to Gonzalo Mazas Garbayo, Havana, 2 August 1936, in *Cartas y crónicas*, 48. For a brief summary and a concise selection of Torriente's writings during the months leading up to his departure, see Suárez Díaz, *Escapé de Cuba*, 521–48.

43. Suárez Díaz, *Escapé de Cuba*, 463, 523.

44. Suárez Díaz, 549. Bofill worked as Torriente's administrative assistant in New York during Pablo's time in Spain, translating articles when necessary and bringing them to the appropriate offices. Bofill would go on to follow his friend's lead, later traveling to the Spanish conflict and serving in the same post, political commissar of the brigade led by "El Campesino," Valentín González. According to later comments by Roa, all Torriente's letters from Spain published without an identified recipient were to Bofill. See editorial comment in footnote 23 in *Cartas y crónicas*, 78. Suárez Díaz attributes the same information to Carlos Montenegro. Suárez Díaz, *Escapé de Cuba*, 549.

45. Pablo de la Torriente, Madrid, to Jaime Bofill, New York, 25 September 1936, in *Peleando con los milicianos*, 17–18. See also Suárez Díaz, *Escapé de Cuba*, 549–51.

46. "Madrid's House of Culture," *Volunteer for Liberty* 1, no. 19 (18 October 1937): 3.

47. Zoe de la Torriente Brau, "Pablo," 29–30; Casuso, *Cuba and Castro*, 79; Pablo de la Torriente, Madrid, to Jaime Bofill, New York, 25 September 1936, in *Peleando con los milicianos*, 17–18.

48. Suárez Díaz, *Escapé de Cuba*, 555–56.

49. Zoe de la Torriente Brau, "Pablo," 30.

50. Pablo de la Torriente Brau, "En el parapeto," 222–37; Pablo de la Torriente, Madrid, to Jaime Bofill, New York, 10 October 1936, in *Cartas y crónicas*, 80–81.

51. Pablo de la Torriente Brau, "En el parapeto," 226–27.

52. Torriente, 227.

53. Torriente, 222–29. Here, Torriente greatly oversimplified the history of the Mexican bullet and showed his bias in favor of the revolutionary Mexico imagined by many during the presidency of Lázaro Cárdenas.

54. Torriente, 229.

55. Pablo de la Torriente Brau, "América frente al fascismo," 278–79.

56. Pablo de la Torriente, Madrid, to Jaime Bofill, New York, 21 November 1936, in *Cartas y crónicas*, 135–36.

57. Pablo de la Torriente, Madrid, to Jaime Bofill, New York, 21 November 1936, in *Cartas y crónicas*, 139–41.

58. The Inter-American Conference for the Maintenance of Peace, Buenos Aires, Argentina, December 1936, where representatives of the nations of the Western Hemisphere discussed the Spanish Civil War, fascist attacks on Ethiopia and China, and the potential for world war. Also, they adopted the "Declaration of Principles of Inter-American Solidarity and Cooperation."

59. Pablo de la Torriente, Madrid, to Jaime Bofill, New York, 13 December 1936, in *Cartas y crónicas*, 148–55.

60. Zoe de la Torriente Brau, "Pablo," 29–31; Roa, "Los últimos días," 336.

61. Casuso, *Cuba and Castro*, 79–80. See also Lino Novas Calvo, "El entierro de Pablo de la Torriente Brau," *Mediodía* no. 10 (25 February 1937): 9; "El cadaver de Pablo de la Torriente tendido en el Comité Ibero Americano de Barcelona," *Mediodía* no. 20 (5 June 1937): 14.

62. "Madrid's House of Culture," *Volunteer for Liberty* 1, no. 19 (18 October 1937): 3.

63. "Homenaje a Pablo de la Torriente," *Mediodía* no. 14 (5 April 1937): 7.

64. Emilio Ballagas, "A Pablo de la Torriente," *Mediodía* no. 14 (5 April 1937): 7; Gerardo del Valle, "Pablo de la Torriente Brau," *Facetas de Actualidad Española* 1, no. 3 (June 1937): 5.

65. Emilio Roig de Leuchsenring, "Por el Triunfo de la España, República de Trabajadores; contra la Barbarie Fascista," *Facetas de Actualidad Española* 1, no. 5 (August 1937): 4.

66. Mercedes Pinto de Rojo to Zoe de la Torriente Brau, 1941, in Rodríguez and Trujillo, *Papeles de familia*, 94.

67. Agrupación de Veteranos Internacionalistas Cubanos, "Grados militares alcanzados por los cubanos en los tres años de guerra," n.d., expediente 1/135, legajo Cuba, caja 63184, AHP.

68. Denise Urcelay-Maragnès, author of some of the only scholarly work on Cuban volunteers in the war, found records of 1,056 Cuban volunteers in 2009 and 1,067 by 2011. Urcelay-Maragnès, "Los voluntarios cubanos," 41; Urcelay-Maragnès, *La leyenda roja*, 82. Gerold Gino Baumann, an independent researcher who published a book on Latin American participation in the conflict (2009), found 840 Cuban volunteers. Baumann, *Los voluntarios latinoamericanos*, 34.

69. Ferrao, *Puertorriqueños en la Guerra Civil Española*.

70. Falcoff, Preface, x.

71. Falcoff, xi.

72. Baumann, *Los voluntarios latinoamericanos*, 21–27.

73. It is possible that the records of anarchists are simply less accessible or were lost or destroyed on the island, whereas Communist ones were preserved and are made available. Records available in other countries, however, follow the same pattern.

74. Editorial note in Instituto de Historia del Movimiento Comunista y de la Revolución Socialista de Cuba, *Cuba y la defensa*, 14. This length of engagement is "long-standing" given that the Cuban party was founded in 1925. Ramón Nicolau González remained active in Cuba following the revolution of 1959 and directed the team that produced the historical collection *Cuba y la defensa de la República Española* (Cuba and the defense of the Spanish Republic) for the party's Central Committee in 1981.

75. Nicolau González, quoted in Bello and Pérez Díaz, *Cuba en España*, 145.

76. "Nosotros y el Derecto de la Imparcialidad," *¡Ayuda!*, no. 3 (December 1937): 3; quoted in Naranjo Orovio, *Cuba, otro escenario*, 60.

77. Negdo. Asoc. Orden Pub. y Elecciones, Gobierno Provincial Habana, "Resolución," 3 January 1938, expediente 5189, legajo 214, RA-ANC. See also Naranjo Orovio, *Cuba, otro escenario*, 60.

78. Dictinio Gómez, Secretario de Actas del Círculo Español Socialista, to Comision Ejecutiva del Partido Socialista Obrero Valencia, 29 December 1937, Círculo Español Socialista, Correspondencia, 1934–37, AH-71-49, PSOE-CE, PSOE-AO-FPI.

79. Dr. Adelardo Valdés Astolfi to Sr. Jefe de la Policía Nacional, 21 December 1937, expediente 10768, legajo 357, RA-ANC; Joaquín Ochotorena, "Secretaria de Gobernación: Resolución," 21 April 1939, expediente 10768, legajo 357, RA-ANC.

80. Urcelay-Maragnès, *La leyenda roja*, 59–60. Based on documentation from Arch. Ministerio de Asuntos Exteriores, Madrid.

81. Urcelay-Maragnès, 60; Naranjo Orovio, *Cuba, otro escenario*, 60.

82. Nicolau González, "La organización y traslado," 9–10.

83. Nicolau González, 10–11.

84. Cuban Communists repudiated their allegiance to Browder at a National Assembly of the party in January 1946, following Soviet denunciation of the U.S. Communist leader. Alexander, *History of Organized Labor in Cuba*, 108–9; "Cuba Reds Pass Up 'Browderism' for Militant Campaign," *Chicago Daily Tribune*, 24 February 1946, 7.

85. Suárez Díaz, *Escapé de Cuba*, 22, 438–39, 450–51.

86. Alberto Moré Tabío, "Cuba puede estar orgullosa de sus hijos," *Mediodía*, no. 23 (6 July 1937): 10–11, 19.

87. Nicolau González, "La organización y traslado," 11–13.

88. Tisa, *Recalling the Good Fight*, 16.

89. Fernández, "Nueva York," 89.

90. Henry Glintenkamp, *Club Julio A. Mella (Cuban Workers' Club)* (1937), oil on canvas, owned by the Chrysler Museum of Art, Norfolk, Va.

91. "Actividades cubanas en España," *Mediodía*, no. 32 (7 September 1937): 11.

92. Tisa, diary entry, 30 October 1938, in *Recalling the Good Fight*, 188.

93. Tisa, diary entry, 4 September 1938, in *Recalling the Good Fight*, 163.

94. "Salud to all, from the XVth Brigade," *Volunteer for Liberty* 1, no. 27 (20 December 1937): 2.

95. John Gates, Commissar of War of the 15th Brigade, to the comrades of the Local Federation of the U.G.T., Barcelona, published as "Brigade Accepts Patronage of Local Federation of U.G.T.," in *Volunteer for Liberty* 2, no. 18 (23 April 1938): 2; "Bidding the International Good-Bye," *Volunteer for Liberty* 2, no. 35 (7 November 1938): 3.

96. Commissariat of War, *Book of the XV Brigade*.

97. Tisa, *Recalling the Good Fight*, 16.

98. Tisa was an editor for the *Volunteer for Liberty* and assisted in the production of *The Book of the XV Brigade*. He was also the unattributed author of *The Story of the Abraham Lincoln Battalion*, which is cited below.

99. Commissariat of War, *Book of the XV Brigade*.

100. "Cuban Volunteers in Spain," *Volunteer for Liberty* 2, no. 7 (28 February 1938): 5.

101. On Guiteras's death, see López Civeira, *Cuba entre 1899 y 1959*, 123–24; Cabrera, *Antonio Guiteras*, 52–54.

102. "Cuban Volunteers in Spain," 4.

103. Suárez Díaz, "La Centuria Guiteras."

104. Pablo de la Torriente Brau, "Hombres de la Revolución" (May 1936), reprinted in Suárez Díaz, *Escapé de Cuba*, 111–12, and discussed in Suárez Díaz, "La Centuria Guiteras."

105. Suárez Díaz, *Escapé de Cuba*, 111.

106. Suárez Díaz, "La Centuria Guiteras."

107. Suárez Díaz.

108. Lafita, *Rodolfo Ricardo Ramón de Armas y Soto*.

109. "A Year of the International Brigades," *Volunteer for Liberty* 1, no. 18 (11 October 1937): 2.

110. Suárez Díaz, "La Centuria Guiteras."

111. "Acta de Constitución de la Delegación de O.R.C.A. en Filadelfia," 8 August 1935, FSV-IHC, reprinted in Suárez Díaz, *Escapé de Cuba*, 236–38; Suárez Díaz, "La Centuria Guiteras."

112. "Cuban Volunteers in Spain," 4.

113. Eby, *Comrades and Commissars*, 38.

114. Tisa, *Recalling the Good Fight*, 16.

115. On Cubans in the Battle of Jarama, see Urcelay-Maragnès, *La leyenda roja*, 122–23.

116. Moré Tabío, "Cuba puede estar orgullosa," 10. The North American may very well have been Tisa.

117. Landis, *Abraham Lincoln Brigade*, 66.

118. Eby, *Comrades and Commissars*, 61.

119. Tisa (unattributed), *Story of the Abraham Lincoln Battalion*, 14.

120. Tisa, *Recalling the Good Fight*, 42.

121. Moré Tabío, "Cuba puede estar orgullosa," 10–11.

122. Comité Cental to Enrique Lister, 17 May 1937, file 601, subseries III, opis 6, fond 545: Records of the International Brigades, Comintern Archives, RGASPI; "Brigadista cubano Alberto Sánchez Méndez [sic]," No. 217, CEDOBI; Lafita, *Dos héroes*.

123. On Cubans in the Battle of Brunete, see Urcelay-Maragnès, *La leyenda roja*, 124–26.

124. "Los Héroes Caídos," *Facetas de Actualidad Española* 1, no. 5 (August 1937): 23. Emphasis in the original.

125. This poem is misquoted in Fernando Vera Jiménez, "Cubanos en la Guerra Civil española," 301. A lengthy excerpt from the poem appears in Olivares B., *Pablo Neruda*, 219.

Chapter Four

1. Cuban historian Ana Suárez Díaz notes that the friend Casuso referred to in her memoir here was Bofill, which is in keeping with his role as Torriente's assistant in New York during Torriente's time in Spain. Personal communication, 7 February 2012.

2. Casuso, *Cuba and Castro*, 80.

3. Casuso, 80. On the association's founding and for brief overviews of its work, see "Estatutos de la Asociación de Auxilio al Niño del Pueblo Español," February 1937, expediente 4948, legajo 209, RA-ANC, cited in Gutiérrez Coto, "Izquierda cubana y republicanismo español," 84; "De Organización: Como Crece Nuestra Asociación," *¡Ayuda! Órgano oficial de la asociación de auxilio al niño del pueblo español*, no. 1 (July 1937): 16; "Editorial: Saludo a la Colonia Escolar 'Pueblo de Cuba,'" *¡Ayuda!*, no. 6 (September 1938): 3; Ismael Cuevas, "Breve Memoria de la A.A.N.P.E.," *¡Ayuda!*, no. 8 (December 1938): 4; Domingo Cuadriello, *El exilio republicano*, 22, 580.

4. "Nosotros y el Derecto de la Imparcialidad," *¡Ayuda!*, no. 3 (December 1937): 3.

5. Ismael Cuevas, "Avances de nuestra Asociación," *¡Ayuda!*, no. 4 (February–March 1938): 22.

6. Domingo Cuadriello, *El exilio republicano*, 25.

7. Francisco Domenech, "El ejemplo de los niños muertos," *¡Ayuda!*, 2, no. 7 (October 1938): 6.

8. Family policy of the Franco regime following the war had some parallels to the child-saving movement, including the idea that children might need saving from their own (Republican) parents. In order to be remade into patriotic Catholic anticommunists, Spanish Republican children during the postwar period faced removal from the home, compulsory education, and forced moral renovation. Ryan, "Sins of the Father."

9. The Cuban public education system was built in the U.S. image following U.S. intervention in Cuba's war of independence. The system followed U.S. educational trends, which were tied to Progressive child-saving efforts by both shared beliefs and individual actors in common. In making their own schools, anarchists in Cuba

attempted to resist this U.S.-oriented, middle-class-directed education. Shaffer, "Freedom Teaching," 154–55.

10. Fernández, *Cuban Anarchism*, 53–54.

11. Shaffer, "Freedom Teaching," 153.

12. See, for example, "¡¡Mujeres!!," *Insurrexit* 2, no. 1 (10 February 1935): 3.

13. Shaffer, "Radical Muse," 131, 134–36, 152; Shaffer, "Freedom Teaching," 152, 161, 167, 178–80.

14. Casuso, *Cuba and Castro*, 80.

15. Casuso, "Nana sin Niño," *¡Ayuda!*, no. 3 (December 1937): 7.

16. Casuso, "Navidad del niño sin madre," *¡Ayuda!*, no. 8 (December 1938): 7.

17. Casuso, *Cuba and Castro*, 86.

18. "Una Gran Institución," *Mediodía*, no. 77 (18 July 1938): 6.

19. A full run of *¡Ayuda!* is available at the Biblioteca Nacional de España (BNE) in Madrid. Organizational records for the association can be found at the Instituto de Historia de Cuba (IHC) in Havana.

20. Davies, *Fleeing Franco*; Jiménez Trujillo, "Protection of Childhood"; Pons Prades, *Los niños republicanos*; Vinyes et al., *Los niños perdidos*; Legarreta, *Guernica Generation*. Chilean poet and educator Gabriela Mistral criticized Latin American governments other than Mexico's for being indifferent to the suffering of Spanish children during the conflict, stating, "Our America, blinded by political fanaticism, has crossed its arms." Kiddle, "Repúblicas Rojas," 101.

21. Comité Directivo, "Editorial: Asociación de Auxilio al Niño del Pueblo Español," *¡Ayuda!*, no. 1 (July 1937): 4.

22. Asociación de Auxilio al Niño del Pueblo Español letterhead, n.d., 28.3/82, RG-IHC.

23. "Nuestro Boletín," *¡Ayuda!*, no. 1 (July 1937): 3.

24. "Nosotros y el Derecto de la Imparcialidad," *¡Ayuda!*, no. 3 (December 1937): 3; "Sin hogar y hambrientos ¿Por qué he de morir?," *¡Ayuda!*, no. 2 (September/October 1937): front cover; Basilio Álvarez, "Palabas [*sic*] de Basilio Álvarez para 'Ayuda,'" *¡Ayuda!*, no. 5 (May 1938): 9.

25. José Antonio Portuondo, "La Infancia Española en la Guerra Civil," *¡Ayuda!*, no. 2 (September/October 1937): 10.

26. "Sin hogar y hambrientos ¿Por qué he de morir?," *¡Ayuda!*, no. 2 (September/October 1937): front cover.

27. Armando Martin, "Apuntes sobre el Destino y Ayuda al Niño Español," *¡Ayuda!*, no. 2 (September/October 1937): 5.

28. "Asociación de Auxilio al Niño del Pueblo Español: Llamamiento a Todos los Cubanos," n.d., 1/12:196/2.1/14, FPPCC-IHC.

29. "Palabras a mi Compañera," *¡Ayuda!*, no. 2 (September/October 1937): 9.

30. "Servicios de Higiene Infantil," *¡Ayuda!*, no. 5 (May 1938): 18.

31. "Asociación de Auxilio al Niño del Pueblo Español: Llamamiento a Todos los Cubanos," n.d., 1/12:196/2.1/14, FPPCC-IHC.

32. Georgina Martínez, "Niños de España: Dolor del mundo," *¡Ayuda!*, no. 1 (July 1937): 7.

33. Casuso, "Volverán las Canciones de Cuna a Escucharse," *¡Ayuda!*, no. 2 (September/October 1937): 7. On the AANPE view of religion as an avenue to future peace, see Rafael Suárez Solis, "La Educación del Hombre en el Terror," *¡Ayuda!*, no. 3 (December 1937): 5. A writer in multiple formats and contributor to numerous periodicals in Spain, Cuba, and other countries, Suárez Solis was born and raised in Asturias, Spain, and moved to Cuba in 1907, when he was in his mid-twenties.

34. José Antonio Portuondo, "La infancia Española en la Guerra Civil," *¡Ayuda!*, no. 2 (September/October 1937): 10.

35. Asela Jiménez, "No Pasarán," *¡Ayuda!*, no. 2 (September/October 1937): 12. See also Rojas Blaquier and Núñez Machín, *Asela mía*.

36. Jiménez, "No Pasarán," 12.

37. Tomás Blanco, "Un Llamado a la Conciencia Libre," *¡Ayuda!*, no. 3 (December 1937): 7. This brief article is directed specifically at Cubans, and there is no biographical information given about the author; therefore, it is only possible to surmise that he may have been the Puerto Rican writer Tomás Blanco (1896–1975).

38. G. F., "5.000 Piezas de abrigo enviadas a los Niños por nuestro Ropero," *¡Ayuda!*, no. 3 (December 1937): 19.

39. José Antonio Portuondo, "Deber de Amor y Gratitud," *¡Ayuda!*, no. 3 (December 1937): 4.

40. Ernesto Silva Tellería, "La tragedia de España está en sus niños," *¡Ayuda!*, no. 5 (May 1938): 4; Mercedes Pinto, "Repique de Resurrecciones," *¡Ayuda!*, no. 7 (October 1938): 17; Eddy Chibás, "Dellendá est Cartago!! Dellendá est Berlín!!," *¡Ayuda!*, no. 5 (May 1938): 6.

41. Berta Arocena, "Una Casita Sugeridora," *¡Ayuda!*, no. 4 (February/March 1938): 13.

42. Portuondo, "Deber de Amor y Gratitud," 4.

43. Consuelo Carmona de Gordón Ordas, "Defensa sin título del Niño Español," *¡Ayuda!*, no. 8 (December 1938): 17. On Cuban antifascist radio use, see Naranjo Orovio, *Cuba, otro escenario*, 63, 66.

44. Casuso, "Volverán las Canciones de Cuna a Escucharse," 16.

45. José Antonio Portuondo, article, *¡Ayuda!*, no. 4 (February/March 1938): 18.

46. "Notas Editoriales: Vida de la A.A.N.P.E.," *¡Ayuda!*, no. 4 (February/March de 1938): 21; Comité Directivo, "Editorial: Asociación de Auxilio al Niño del Pueblo Español," 4; Mercedes Pinto, "Repique de Resurrecciones," *¡Ayuda!*, no. 7 (October 1938): 17.

47. Guillermina Medrano, "Niños de España," *¡Ayuda!*, no. 6 (September 1938): 14.

48. Ernesto Silva Tellería, "La tragedia de España está en sus niños," *¡Ayuda!*, no. 5 (May 1938): 4.

49. Gustavo Fabal, "Ejemplo de Solidaridad," *¡Ayuda!*, no. 6 (September 1938): 24.

50. Despite the claim to Spanish kinship, such assertions did not indicate an exclusively white antifascism. As discussed in chapter 5, Cuban antifascists of color, including Nicolás Guillén, inserted themselves into the genealogical argument.

51. Armando Martínez, "Hermanos Españoles: Palabras del niño Armando Martínez, alumno de la Escuela 'José Miguel Gómez', que formó parte de la Comisión

Oficial que subió a bordo del 'Mexique', en representación de la niñez cubana," *¡Ayuda!*, no. 1 (July 1937): 6. There is a brief discussion of the significance of the *Mexique* stop in Havana harbor—though with some inaccuracy—in Kiddle, "Repúblicas Rojas," 102–3.

52. Consuelo Carmona de Gordón Ordas, "Defensa sin título del Niño Español," *¡Ayuda!*, no. 8 (December 1938): 27.

53. Advertisement, *¡Ayuda!*, no. 3 (December 1937): 20.

54. S. B. G., "A favor del Niño Español," *¡Ayuda!*, no. 5 (May 1938): 20; José Antonio Encinas, "Los Niños y la Guerra," *¡Ayuda!*, no. 7 (October 1938): 7.

55. Casuso, "Con los niños que iban en el 'Mexique,'" *¡Ayuda!*, no. 1 (July 1937): 13.

56. Casuso, 13.

57. Portuondo, "Deber de Amor y Gratitud," 4.

58. "Asociación de Auxilio al Niño del Pueblo Español: Llamamiento a Todos los Cubanos," n.d., 1/12:196/2.1/14, FPPCC-IHC.

59. Comité Directivo, "Editorial: Asociación de Auxilio al Niño del Pueblo Español," 4.

60. Back cover of *¡Ayuda!*, no. 1 (July 1937).

61. "2 Cartas de Niños," *¡Ayuda!*, no. 1 (July 1937): 6.

62. Jorge Kind, "Yo soy un niño mexicano," *¡Ayuda!*, no. 4 (February/March 1938): 18.

63. Francisco González Aramburu, "A Lázaro Cardenas," *¡Ayuda!*, no. 5 (May 1938): 11.

64. "Página Infantil," *¡Ayuda!*, no. 6 (September 1938): 22.

65. "Página Infantil," *¡Ayuda!*, no. 7 (October 1938): 20.

66. "Página Infantil," *¡Ayuda!*, no. 8 (December 1938): 22; "Comité Infantil 'Pablo de la Torriente,'" *¡Ayuda!*, no. 9 (January/February 1939): 20.

67. Casuso, "Con los niños que iban en el 'Mexique,'" 15.

68. Félix Pita Rodríguez, "Cartas de París: El comite internacional y los niños españoles," *¡Ayuda!* no. 1 (July 1937): 2, 22.

69. "Mensaje de la Asociación a las Mujeres," *¡Ayuda!*, no. 2 (September/October 1937): 8.

70. "Palabras a mi Compañera," *¡Ayuda!*, no. 2 (September/October 1937): 9.

71. Luis Felipe Rodríguez, "Ante el Niño Español," *¡Ayuda!*, no. 4 (February/March 1938): 10.

72. Mariblanca Sabas Alomá, "En nombre del niño cubano, ayudad al niño español," *¡Ayuda!*, no. 7 (October 1938): 5.

73. Comité Directivo, "Editorial: Asociación de Auxilio al Niño del Pueblo Español," 4.

74. Casuso, "Con los niños que iban en el 'Mexique,'" 13. It should be noted here that Casuso lists Jewish Cubans as if they were separate from Cubans—that is, by three differentiated categories: Spanish, Hebrew, and Cuban.

75. "De Organización: Como crece nuestra Asociación," *¡Ayuda!*, no. 1 (July 1937): 16–19.

76. "De Organización," 16–19; "Colectas y Actos realizados por la Asociación," *¡Ayuda!*, no. 1 (July 1937): 23; "Continúa Nuestra Organización Extendiéndose por

toda la Isla y hasta por el Extranjero," *¡Ayuda!*, no. 2 (September/October 1937): 18–22; "Prosigue el Desarrollo de Nuestra Asociación," *¡Ayuda!*, no. 3 (December 1937): 21–23; "Avances de nuestra Asociación," *¡Ayuda!*, no. 4 (February/March 1938): 22; Ismael Cuevas, "Breve Memoria de la A.A.N.P.E.," *¡Ayuda!*, no. 8 (December 1938): 4–6, 23, 27. The publication of messages received for Fernando de los Ríos's speech also demonstrated support from around Cuba and abroad. "Lista de telegramas de adhesión . . . ," *¡Ayuda!*, no. 9 (January/February 1939): 21.

77. "Finanzas: Ingresos del mes de octubre," *¡Ayuda!*, no. 8 (December 1938): 25; Carpeta 34.6/2005(1–103), Serie Asociación de Auxilio al Niño del Pueblo Español, Sección Otros Instituciones Nacionales, RG-IHC.

78. Carpeta 34.1/2005(1–24), Serie Asociación de Auxilio al Niño del Pueblo Español, Sección Otros Instituciones Nacionales, RG-IHC.

79. Unfortunately, the bulletin did not include comprehensive financial accounting for the months of January–March 1938, and no information on this period was found in archived organizational records.

80. The first calculation was based on figures from mid-March through July 1937 (137 days) and a fund-raising total of $1,850.91. The second calculation was based on figures from the beginning of August through December 1937 (153 days) and a fund-raising total of $4,463.50.

81. Omitted from centralized income totals here are the periodic influxes of ticket-sale cash; since ticketed fund-raising events took place at specific points in time sporadically throughout the association's existence, it does not make sense to include their contributions when seeking long-term trends.

82. "Finanzas: Ingresos 1937 Octubre," *¡Ayuda!*, no. 3 (December 1937): 25–26; "Finanzas: Ingresos del mes de octubre," *¡Ayuda!*, no. 8 (December 1938): 25–26. A partial accounting of AANPE finances is reproduced from the bulletin *¡Ayuda!* in Naranjo Orovio, *Cuba, otro escenario*, 235–82.

83. Documento 34.1/2005(9), Serie Asociación de Auxilio al Niño del Pueblo Español, Sección Otros Instituciones Nacionales, RG-IHC. One item is illegible.

84. Carpeta 34.6/2005(1–103), Serie Asociación de Auxilio al Niño del Pueblo Español, Sección Otros Instituciones Nacionales, RG-IHC.

85. Comité Directivo, "Editorial: Asociación de Auxilio al Niño del Pueblo Español," 4. For a list of the organizations that made up the Reception Committee, see "Comité de Recepción a los Niños Españoles Al Pueblo de Cuba," 1937, Doc. 12s168 1938, FSV-IHC.

86. Casuso, "Con los niños que iban en el 'Mexique,'" 12–13, 22.

87. "La Caja del Ropero del Invierno del Comité de Auxilio al Niño del Pueblo Español," *¡Ayuda!*, no. 4 (February/March 1938): 2, 27.

88. "Mensaje de la Asociación a las Mujeres," *¡Ayuda!*, no. 2 (September/October 1937): 8.

89. "24.000 Latas de Leche y 5.000 Piezas de Abrigo Enviadas a los Niños Españoles," *¡Ayuda!*, no. 3 (December 1937): 3.

90. G. F., "5.000 Piezas de abrigo enviadas a los Niños por nuestro Ropero," 18–19. The initials G. F. probably referenced Gustavo Fabal, one of the bulletin's editors.

91. "24.000 Latas de Leche y 5.000 Piezas de Abrigo Enviadas a los Niños Españoles," 3.

92. "La 'Casa Pueblo de Cuba' en Puigcerdá," *¡Ayuda!*, no. 3 (December 1937): 3, 27.

93. "La Comision Pro Casa Escuela en Puigcerdá," *¡Ayuda!*, no. 4 (February/March 1938): 3.

94. "Notas y Comentarios," *¡Ayuda!*, no. 5 (May 1938): 21.

95. "La Comision Pro Casa Escuela en Puigcerdá," 3.

96. Berta Arocena, "Una Casita Sugeridora," 13.

97. Fernando G. Campoamor, "Rosa Pastora Leclerc," *¡Ayuda!*, no. 5 (May 1938): 8. See also Alvarez Blanco, "Recuerdan en Sitges."

98. Guillermina Medrano, "Niños de España," *¡Ayuda!*, no. 6 (September 1938): 14–15.

99. "Editorial: Saludo a la Colonia Escolar 'Pueblo de Cuba,'" *¡Ayuda!*, no. 6 (September 1938): 3. The AANPE acknowledged that the Spanish Ministry of Public Instruction (Ministerio de Instrucción Pública) and other top-level functionaries of the Spanish Republican government assisted in the Casa-Escuela's establishment.

100. Angel Lázaro, "Rosa Pastora en Sitges," *¡Ayuda!*, no. 6 (September 1938): 9.

101. Introduction to Rosa Pastora Leclerc, "Los Niños de edad Escolar y las Colonias," *¡Ayuda!*, no. 6 (September 1938): 16–17.

102. "La visita a nuestra Colonia en Sitges, de un grupo de compañeros del Club cubano 'Julio Antonio Mella' . . . ," *¡Ayuda!*, no. 7 (October 1938): 17. For a brief discussion of the visit and more broadly of life at the Casa-Escuela, see Rosa Pastora Leclerc, "Violación de Correspondencia Cuba y la Infancia Española," *Noticias de Hoy* 1, no. 71 (5 August 1938): 2.

103. "Lo que piensan y lo que escriben los niños de la Colonia Pueblo de Cuba," *¡Ayuda!*, no. 8 (December 1938): 14–15.

104. Rosa Pastora Leclerc, "Rosa Pastora escribe," *¡Ayuda!*, no. 8 (December 1938): 10.

105. "El Ropero Invernal del Niño, realidad en marcha," *¡Ayuda!*, no. 6 (September 1938): 25.

106. Report, *¡Ayuda!* no. 8 (December 1938): 12.

107. Consuelo Carmona de Gordón Ordas, "Defensa sin título del Niño Español," *¡Ayuda!*, no. 8 (December 1938): 17.

108. María Josefa Bolaños, "Un llamado a la conciencia de la mujer cubana," *¡Ayuda!*, no. 9 (January/February 1939): 20.

109. "Balance del Ropero del Niño," *¡Ayuda!*, no. 7 (October 1938): 22–23; "Balance del Ropero de Invierno," *¡Ayuda!*, no. 9 (January/February 1939): 22–24.

110. Advertisement, *¡Ayuda!*, no. 7 (October 1938): 21.

111. Report, *¡Ayuda!*, no. 8 (December 1938): 12; "Nota del primer embarque del Ropero," *¡Ayuda!*, no. 8 (December 1938): 19. Items sent to Europe were 150 tins of sweets, 300 cans of condensed milk, 200 bars of guava paste, 5 ten-and-a-half-pound containers of cookies, 40 pairs of shoes, 720 stockings (60 dozen), 432 handkerchiefs

(36 dozen), 600 tubes of toothpaste, 900 bars of soap, 100 toys, and 50 care packages of school supplies, especially for the Casa-Escuela.

112. "El Segundo Embarque del Ropero del Niño," *¡Ayuda!*, no. 9 (January/February 1939): 4. Items sent were seventy-five boxes containing forty-eight cans of milk each, ten 120-pound boxes of soap, six crates of guava, and one box filled with sweets and other assorted goods.

113. "Balance del Ropero," *¡Ayuda!*, no. 10 (March/April 1939): 29–31.

114. "Un lote de vestidos y ropitas . . ." and "Comité de Damas del Ropero . . . ," *Facetas de Actualidad Española* 2, no. 8 (December 1938): 56–57.

115. Armando Martin Corsanego, "La Nieve y España," *¡Ayuda!*, no. 9 (January/February 1939): 6.

116. "LEONOR PEREZ ALMEIDA, líder estudiantil cubana," *¡Ayuda!*, no. 5 (May 1938): 13; Leonor Pérez Almeida, "Nuestro Deber Ante el Niño Español," *¡Ayuda!*, no. 7 (October 1938): 13.

117. "La Conferencia de Don Fernando de los Ríos," *¡Ayuda!*, no. 9 (January/February 1939): 3.

118. Cuban historian Ana Suárez Díaz calls Marinello prior to the late 1930s an "ideological communist" rather than a devoted Party Communist. He is, in her view, exemplary of the complicated nature of Cuban politics during the period and therefore difficult to label. Personal communication, 30 January 2019.

119. The same year, Emilio Roig de Leuchsenring published a book exploring Martí's connections to Spain, as well as his observations and opinions of the country and its people: Roig de Leuchsenring, *La España de Martí*. A piece by the author on the same subject appeared in *Mediodía*: Roig de Leuchsenring, "La España de Martí," *Mediodía* no. 77 (18 July 1938): 10, 32.

120. Juan Marinello, "Palabras de presentación de Don Fernando de los Ríos pronunciadas por Juan Marinello en el Stadium Polar," *¡Ayuda!*, no. 9 (January/February 1939): 12–13.

121. Fernando de los Ríos, "Discurso pronunciado por Don Fernando de los Ríos en el acto organizado por la A.A.N.P.E.," *¡Ayuda!*, no. 9 (January/February 1939): 14–15, 17, 19.

122. "Lista de telegramas de adhesión . . . ," *¡Ayuda!*, no. 9 (January/February 1939): 21.

123. Her effort resulted in Pablo de la Torriente Brau, *Peleando con los milicianos*.

124. Casuso, *Cuba and Castro*, 79–80.

125. Photograph caption in *¡Ayuda!*, no. 9 (January/February 1939): 20.

Chapter Five

1. Dr. Eduardo Odio Pérez and Basilio Cueria will be discussed later on in the chapter.

2. Alberto Moré Tabío, "Cuba puede estar orgullosa de sus hijos," *Mediodía*, no. 23 (6 July 1937): 10–11, 19.

3. "Nuestro idioma lazo de unión," *Reconquista* 1, no. 3 (20 October 1938): 35.

4. "2 años de Milicias de Cultura en las Brigadas Internacionales" and "Nuestro idioma lazo de unión," *Reconquista* 1, no. 3 (20 October 1938): 30, 35.

5. Oscar Soler to Fredericka Martin, 21 June 1939, folder 6, box 2, Fredericka Martin Papers, Abraham Lincoln Brigade Archive (ALBA 001), Tamiment Library, New York University, New York, New York.

6. Tisa, *Recalling the Good Fight*, 25.

7. Eby, *Comrades and Commissars*, 38.

8. Tisa, *Recalling the Good Fight*, 25.

9. Landis, *Abraham Lincoln Brigade*, 31.

10. "El Batallón Español," *Reconquista* 1, no. 3 (20 October 1938): 15.

11. Nicolau González, "La organización y traslado," 12.

12. "Solicitación de permiso (para el extranjero)," n.d., file 590, RGASPI; Ramón Nicolau, "Memorandum," 11 March 1938, file 590, RGASPI; Jefatura de Sanidad to Captain Antoon, 24 March 1938, file 590, RGASPI; Pía Mastellari Maecha to Camarada Minor, 24 March 1938, file 597, RGASPI; Mastellari Maecha, "El pueblo español se mantuvo," 105–8.

13. "Al Doctor Juan J. Remos, Honorable Señor Secretario de Estado; y al Gobierno de Cuba en pleno," 12 November 1938, 52–53, number 641, LAIP-LC.

14. Urcelay-Maragnès, *La leyenda roja*, 184–200.

15. On the Cuban experience in the French camps, and the Camp de Gurs in particular, see Urcelay-Maragnès, *La leyenda roja*, 202–13.

16. Soler to Martin, 21 June 1939; Soler to Martin, 11 August 1939; and Soler to Martin, 11 October 1939, folder 6, box 2, Fredericka Martin Papers, ALBA 001.

17. Martin to Odio Pérez, 31 October 1968, folder 5, box 2, Fredericka Martin Papers, ALBA 001.

18. Soler to Martin, 11 August 1939, folder 6, box 2, Fredericka Martin Papers, ALBA 001.

19. Soler to Martin, 11 October 1939, folder 6, box 2, Fredericka Martin Papers, ALBA 001.

20. Hatzky, *Julio Antonio Mella*, 181; Suárez Díaz, "La Centuria Guiteras"; Suárez Díaz, *Escapé de Cuba*, 188–89, 263, 316, 322, 332, 562.

21. Fernández, "Nueva York," 88, 90; Suárez Díaz, "La Centuria Guiteras"; Tisa, *Recalling the Good Fight*, 16.

22. Nicolau González, "La organización y traslado," 9. International Brigades documentation corroborates his memory of the group, showing that these volunteers, processed on 17 May 1937, were former military men involved in radical politics on the island.

23. Andrés González Lanuza, "Biografía Militar," 17 May 1937, file 594, RGASPI; "Don Julio Valdés Cofiño," n.d., file 603, RGASPI; Pedro Dalmau Naranjo, "Biografía Militar," 17 May 1937, file 590, RGASPI; Jefe de Estado Mayor to Delegación del Comité Central del P.C., 20 May 1937, file 590, RGASPI.

24. "Cuban Volunteers in Spain," *Volunteer for Liberty* 2, no. 7 (28 February 1938): 4.

25. Multiple primary sources produced by Odio Pérez himself confirm this information. Odio Pérez, "Solicitud de Paso o Ingreso en el Partido Comunista Español (Sección de la Internacional Comunista)," 9 November 1937, file 598, RGASPI;

Dr. Oscar Telge to Comarade Commandant de la Base, 8 December 1937, file 598, RGASPI; Odio Pérez, "Biografía de Militantes," 5 March 1938, file 598, RGASPI; Odio Pérez, "Biographical Statistics of the Personnel of the American Medical Bureau and Co-Workers," survey sent by Fredericka Martin, 1968, folder 5, box 2, Fredericka Martin Papers, ALBA 001. The last of these sources is undated, but correspondence indicates that Martin sent the blank survey to Odio Pérez in October 1968 and the doctor returned it completed to her in December of the same year. In contradiction with these primary sources, the book *Cuba y la defensa* gives Odio Pérez's birth year as 1901. Biographical note added by editors at the end of Eduardo Odio Pérez, "La batalla duró diez días," 115.

26. Odio Pérez, "Biografía de Militantes," 5 March 1938, file 598, RGASPI; Odio Pérez, "Biographical Statistics," 1968, folder 5, box 2, Fredericka Martin Papers, ALBA 001.

27. American Medical Bureau, press release, n.d., folder 5, box 2, Fredericka Martin Papers, ALBA 001; Odio Pérez, "Biografía de Militantes," 5 March 1938, file 598, RGASPI.

28. American Medical Bureau, press release, n.d.; Odio Pérez, "Biografía de Militantes," 5 March 1938.

29. Odio Pérez, "Biografía de Militantes," 5 March 1938, file 598, RGASPI. On the survey, he remembered the date of this event as 1929.

30. "Se oponen al homenaje a Machado," *Gráfico*, 15 February 1930, 2.

31. United Press, "Se preparaba una expedición armada a Cuba," *La Prensa*, 9 June 1932, 2.

32. Odio Pérez, "Biographical Statistics," 1968, folder 5, box 2, Fredericka Martin Papers, ALBA 001.

33. Biographical note in Odio Pérez, "La batalla duró diez días," 115.

34. Odio Pérez, "Biografía de Militantes," 5 March 1938, file 598, RGASPI.

35. R. Zubaran Capmany, "Oratoria Tropical en Nueva York," *La Prensa*, 10 October 1935, 3.

36. Odio Pérez, "Biografía de Militantes," 5 March 1938, file 598, RGASPI.

37. Odio Pérez, "Biographical Statistics," 1968, folder 5, box 2, Fredericka Martin Papers, ALBA 001; Odio Pérez, "La batalla duró diez días," 111.

38. "Recruiting Denied by Spanish Envoy," *New York Times*, 5 January 1937, 7.

39. Odio Pérez, "Biographical Statistics," 1968, folder 5, box 2, Fredericka Martin Papers, ALBA 001.

40. Odio Pérez, "La batalla duró diez días," 111.

41. Odio Pérez, "Biographical Statistics," 1968, folder 5, box 2, Fredericka Martin Papers, ALBA 001. Odio Pérez completed this survey in English, and there are also other places in which errors appear.

42. José L. Franco, Panorama Universal, *Adelante* 2, no. 21 (February 1937): 8.

43. José L. Franco, Panorama Universal, *Adelante* 2, no. 20 (January 1937): 20. In a similar *Adelante* assessment of all fascists, Mariano Salas Aranda wrote: "Culture, liberty, the law, justice, there is something there that instills fear in the fascist, for this reason when we see a Fascist state emerge the first thing put into practice is the destruction of culture, the restriction or abolition of liberties, the suppression

of the law, the absence of justice; the great literary works are incinerated on enormous pyres, their authors are assassinated, imprisoned or exiled." Mariano Salas Aranda, "Fascismo y Democracia," *Adelante* 3, no. 35 (April 1938): 8.

44. Salas Aranda, "Misión Histórica de las Revoluciones," *Adelante* 3, no. 31 (December 1937): 9. Salas Aranda acknowledged later in the article that Cuba's situation required further revolutionary action.

45. Salas Aranda, 9; Salas Aranda, "Fascismo y Democracia," *Adelante* 3, no. 35 (April 1938): 8.

46. Guillén, speech to the Second International Writers' Congress, reprinted in Guillén, *Prosa de Prisa*, 85.

47. Ferrer, *Insurgent Cuba*.

48. Guillén, speech, reprinted in Guillén, *Prosa de Prisa*, 85. Ellis notes that for Guillén, Africanism and Hispanicism "were the elements that *together* constituted the national identity." Ellis, "Nicolás Guillén and Langston Hughes," 143.

49. *Mediodía* article of 15 June 1937 discussed in Ellis, "Nicolás Guillén and Langston Hughes," 143.

50. Guillén, "Cubanos en España: Un Pelotero, Capitán de Ametralladoras," *Mediodía*, no. 45 (6 December 1937): 10; Hughes, "Harlem Ball Player Now Captain in Spain," *Afro-American*, 12 February 1938, reprinted in Mullen, *Langston Hughes*, 143–45.

51. Guillén, "Discurso del Delegado," 18.

52. Guillén, speech, reprinted in Guillén, *Prosa de Prisa*, 85.

53. Guillén, speech, 83.

54. Guillén, "España: Poema en cuatro angustias y una esperanza."

55. Guillén, "Discurso del Delegado," 18.

56. Guillén, speech, reprinted in Guillén, *Prosa de Prisa*, 84–85.

57. A directory published in the Cuban Masonic press in January 1936 lists 183 lodges. "Directorio General de Logias para 1936," *Mundo Masónico: Revista Mensual Ilustrada para el Templo y para el Hogar* 5, no. 45 (January 1936): 28–33. An article published in March in the Cuban Masonic annual report states that there were 195. Castellanos, "Informe del Gran Secretario," 593. For comparison, see Eduardo Torres Cuevas, who states that there were 67 Cuban lodges in 1909, 100 in 1919, 154 in 1924, and 334 in 1955. He does not include any figures for the 1930s or 1940s. According to his calculations, 154 lodges were home to 14,000 Masons in 1924, and 334 lodges housed 30,000 members in 1955. Torres Cuevas, "La masonería en Cuba," 518. Using these figures to calculate an estimate, we arrive at a plausible range for the number of Cuban Masons in 1936: 16,437–16,636. However, a precise number of Masons is difficult to calculate. In a later publication, Torres Cuevas states that documentation lists 189 lodges and 13,000 Masons in Cuba in 1936. Torres Cuevas, *Historia de la masonería cubana*, 240. The Masonic annual report states that the island's Grand Lodge counted only 7,967 brothers for 1936 but noted positive growth trends following a downturn in 1932–33. Castellanos, "Informe del Gran Secretario," 589–90.

58. Merriman, *History of Modern Europe*, 1225.

59. Morales Ruiz, *El discurso antimasónico*, 33–43; Pope Clement XII, "In Eminenti."

60. Morales Ruiz, *El discurso antimasónico*, 43–71; Pope Leo XIII, "Humanum Genus."

61. Morales Ruiz, *El discurso antimasónico*, 72–73.

62. "El Mensajero del Corazón de Jesús," *Rayos de Sol* 94 (1937), reproduced in Ferrer Benimeli, *La masonería española*, 147–49.

63. Editorial, *Vida Masónica* 6, no. 2 (April 1931): 17, reproduced in Ferrer Benimeli, *La masonería española*, 172. Ferrer Benimeli's citation contains an error; the volume number is 6, not 4.

64. *Boletín Oficial del Grande Oriente Español* 7, no. 73 (June 1933): 1, reproduced in Ferrer Benimeli, *La masonería española*, 173–74.

65. Morales Ruiz, *El discurso antimasónico*, 73–77.

66. "Españoles de América," 1937, Doc. 7s168, FSV-IHC.

67. "España a sus hijos en América," 1937, Doc 8s168, FSV-IHC.

68. "A todos los españoles de las Américas de habla hispana," 1937, Doc. 9s168, FSV-IHC.

69. Domingo Cuadriello, *El exilio republicano*, 39, 283; Domingo Cuadriello, *Españoles en Cuba*, 29, 34, 109. Cuban Masonic leaders considered *Mundo Masónico* a preeminent publication. They referred to ample correspondence praising it and called González Naredo "our beloved brother" in Gran Logia de la Isla de Cuba, *Anuario: 1937–1938*, 272. The issues of *Mundo Masónico* considered here are available in hardcopy at the House of the Temple Library in Washington, D.C.; the periodical is also available at the Biblioteca Nacional José Martí, Havana, Cuba.

70. González Naredo, "Puntos de Vista Por el Director: La masonería debe reaccionar ante la revolución española," *Mundo Masónico* 5, no. 52 (August 1936): 6–7.

71. Supremo Consejo Grado 33 de España, "Al Supremo Consejo Grado 33 para Cuba, Madrid, 12 de Octubre de 1936," *Mundo Masónico* 5, no. 54/55 (October–November 1936): 22.

72. Luis Martínez Reyes (Grand Secretary) and Gonzalo García Pedroso (Grand Master), "Declaración de principios sobre política internacional, Habana, 15 de Septiembre de 1937," in Gran Logia de la Isla de Cuba, *Anuario: 1937–1938*, 52.

73. González Naredo, "Continúa la Guerra Civil Española: Nuestro humilde aporte por la libertad y por la democracia del mundo," *Mundo Masónico* 5, no. 60 (April 1937): 21.

74. "La Masonería y la Guerra Civil," *Mundo Masónico* 5, no. 59 (March 1937): 31.

75. González Naredo, "La Guerra Civil Española, la Masonería y Nosotros," *Mundo Masónico* 6, no. 62/63 (June–July 1937): 4; Bolívar [pseud.], "La España de Franco, Feudo de Extranjeros," *Mundo Masónico* 6, no. 66/67 (October–November 1937): 14.

76. González Naredo, "Continúa la Guerra Civil Española, Cruel y Sangrienta Sembrando la Muerte," *Mundo Masónico* 5, no. 57/58 (January–February 1937): 19; Eduardo R. Chibás, Roberto Agramonte, Rodolfo Méndez Peñate, Miguel Coyula, Emeterio S. Santovenia, Ricardo Nuñez Portuondo, Antonio S. de Bustamante, and Emilio Roig de Leuchsenring, "La Intelectualidad Cubana y la Guerra Civil Española: A través de una interesante encuesta de la popular Revista 'Bohemia,'" *Mundo Masónico* 5, no. 59 (March 1937): 18–20.

77. Bolívar [pseud.], "El Español ante la Francia actual: De nuestro corresponsal en España," *Mundo Masónico* 5, no. 59 (March 1937): 7.

78. Luis Gertsch, "Democracía y Fascismo," *Mundo Masónico* 5, no. 59 (March 1937): 24. Author's surname is misspelled as "Gertch." Gertsch was not Spanish by birth but had resided in Spain for twenty-eight years as of 1937.

79. Antonio Penichet, "Barbarie y Civilización: Dos clases de trincheras en España," *Mundo Masónico* 6, no. 68/69 (December 1937–January 1938): 25.

80. Bolívar [pseud.], "La España de Franco, Feudo de Extranjeros," 14.

81. Ceferino González Castroverde and Hermenegildo Casas, "A todos los masones del universo," *Mundo Masónico* 5, no. 60 (April 1937): 27.

82. Bolívar [pseud.], "El Español ante la Francia actual," 8.

83. Alfredo Padrón Batista, "Civilización Enferma," *Mundo Masónico* 6, no. 61 (May 1937): 10.

84. González Naredo, "Continúa la Guerra Civil Española, Cruel y Sangrienta Sembrando la Muerte," 19.

85. Bolívar [pseud.], "El Español ante la Francia actual," 8.

86. Fabian Vidal, "Páginas Profanas: Por que el gobierno inglés es fascista y mantiene el absurdo comité de no intervención," *Mundo Masónico* 7, no. 72/73 (April–May 1938): 26.

87. Supremo Consejo Grado 33 de España, "Al Supremo Consejo Grado 33 para Cuba, Madrid, 12 de Octubre de 1936," *Mundo Masónico* 5, no. 54/55 (October–November 1936): 22.

88. Bolívar [pseud.], "Colaboración Española: Sobre la Guerra Civil en España," *Mundo Masónico* 5, no. 53 (September 1936): 28.

89. Bolívar [pseud.], "Desde Barcelona: La Guerra Civil en Esp.: La traición de las democracias," *Mundo Masónico* 5, no. 57/58 (January–February 1937): 35.

90. Luis Gertsch, "Democracía y Fascismo," *Mundo Masónico* 5, no. 59 (March 1937): 27.

91. As we have seen elsewhere, one of Republican supporters' most common warnings was directed at Spain's neighbor, France. See, for example, Bolívar [pseud.], "El Español ante la Francia actual: De nuestro corresponsal en España," *Mundo Masónico* 5, no. 59 (March 1937): 7.

92. "La Clausura de las Logias del Brasil," *Mundo Masónico* 6, no. 68/69 (December 1937–January 1938): 21; Marco Pitchón, "Informe del Presidente de la Comisión de Relaciones Exteriores," in Gran Logia de la Isla de Cuba, *Anuario: 1937–1938*, 288.

93. See, for example, González Naredo, "Continúa la Guerra Civil Española, Cruel y Sangrienta Sembrando la Muerte," 19; "El Dr. Fernando Ortiz en la Gran Logia" and "Consideraciones Masónicas, Luz y Tinieblas," *Mundo Masónico* 6, no. 68/69 (December 1937–January 1938): 10, 13.

94. Francisco Ledesma, "Y Nosotros, ¿Qué Hacemos?," *Mundo Masónico* 6, no. 66/67 (October–November 1937): 17.

95. Luis Gertsch, "Democracía y Fascismo," *Mundo Masónico* 5, no. 59 (March 1937): 24.

96. Un Ajef de Santa Clara, "Notas de Actualidad: Dios, Religión y Guerra," *Mundo Masónico* 5, no. 57/58 (January–February 1937): 22.

97. José Manuel Gallegos, Leopoldo Lobo, Enrique Monter, "Palabras de los buenos Católicos: La rebelión contra el gobierno legítimo es ilícita," *Mundo Masónico* 5, no. 60 (April 1937): 23.

98. M. F. Gómez, "Hombres sin Alma," *Mundo Masónico* 7, no. 72/73 (April–May 1938): 29.

99. "Lo que está pasando por allá: Anécdotas de la Guerra Civil Española," *Mundo Masónico* 5, no. 54/55 (October–November 1936): 26.

100. Luis Martínez Reyes and Gonzalo García Pedroso, "Declaración de Principios de la Masonería Cubana," *Facetas de la Actualidad Española* 1, no. 9 (January 1938): 44.

101. On Cubans in the Battle of Teruel, see Urcelay-Maragnès, *La leyenda roja*, 127–29.

102. Morillas Brandy, "Juan García Morales," 99–112.

103. Juan García Morales [pseud.], "Dios, es la justicia," *Mundo Masónico* 7, no. 72/73 (April–May 1938): 13.

104. González Naredo, "Puntos de Vista: De la guerra civil Española, con la Libertad y la Democracia por Escudo," *Mundo Masónico* 6, no. 68/69 (December 1937–January 1938): 6.

105. "La Masonería y la Guerra Civil," *Mundo Masónico* 5, no. 59 (March 1937): 31.

106. Antonio Penichet, "Trayectorias," *Mundo Masónico* 5, no. 54/55 (October–November 1936): 14.

107. Ceferino González Castroverde and Hermenegildo Casas, "A todos los masones del universo," *Mundo Masónico* 5, no. 60 (April 1937): 25–26.

108. Ceferino González Castroverde, "Hermanos de todo el mundo, acudid en nuestro socorro," *Mundo Masónico* 5, no. 60 (April 1937): 28.

109. Penichet, *Nuestra Responsabilidad*, 5.

110. Alfredo Padrón, "La Civilización," *Mundo Masónico* 5, no. 52 (August 1936): 20. It is probable that this individual is the same Alfredo Padrón as the furniture maker who addressed the issues of class inequality, harm done by importation of cheap foreign labor, and the establishment of Cuba's "national personality" at the August 1923 General Assembly of the Veterans and Patriots Association, as described by Whitney, *State and Revolution*, 33.

111. Alfredo Padrón, "La Civilización," 20; Bolívar [pseud.], "Colaboración Española: Sobre la Guerra Civil en España," 27; Supremo Consejo Grado 33 de España, "Al Supremo Consejo Grado 33 para Cuba, Madrid, 12 de Octubre de 1936," *Mundo Masónico* 5, no. 54/55 (October–November 1936): 22.

112. González Naredo, "Acotaciones," *Mundo Masónico* 5, no. 53 (September 1936): 29; González Naredo, "Franco y la Masonería: Trabajo leído en la 'Hora Masónica de Cuba,'" *Mundo Masónico* 6, no. 61 (May 1937): 16.

113. A. Pereira Alves, "Ni izquierda ni derecha," *Mundo Masónico* 7, no. 72/73 (April–May 1938): 13. It is likely that this individual was Alejandro Pereira Alves, a

Baptist pastor in the Cuban town of Cumanayagua and author of numerous books, including *Prominentes evangélicos de Cuba.*

114. Francisco Ledesma, "¡Masón . . . y Fascista?," *Mundo Masónico* 7, no. 70/71 (February–March 1938): 14.

115. González Naredo, "Puntos de Vista: De la guerra civil Española, con la Libertad y la Democracia por Escudo," *Mundo Masónico* 6, no. 68/69 (December 1937–January 1938): 6.

116. "Lo que está pasando por allá: Anécdotas de la Guerra Civil Española," 26; "Los Masones Españoles piden socorro," *Mundo Masónico* 5, no. 60 (April 1937): 25–26; González Naredo, "Continúa la Guerra Civil Española," 21.

117. Antonio Penichet, "Trayectorias," *Mundo Masónico* 5, no. 52 (August 1936): 11.

118. Antonio Gonzalo Pérez, "Del Supremo Consejo Gr. 33 para la Isla de Cuba a los Supremos Consejos Gr. 33, a todas las potencias de nuestra amistad, a los masones libres y aceptados de ambos hemisferios," *Mundo Masónico* 5, no. 54/55 (October–November 1936): 23.

119. González Naredo, "Franco y la Masonería: Trabajo leído en la 'Hora Masónica de Cuba,'" *Mundo Masónico* 6, no. 61 (May 1937): 16.

120. "La Masonería y la Guerra Civil," *Mundo Masónico* 5, no. 59 (March 1937): 31. Emphasis added.

121. Antonio Penichet, "¿Está actuando el Fascismo en Cuba?," *Mundo Masónico* 6, no. 66/67 (October–November 1937): 15. On European fascist agents in Latin America, see also Finchelstein, *Transatlantic Fascism,* esp. 15–41; Rock, *Latin America,* 22–23; Bulmer-Thomas, *Political Economy of Central America,* 85–86.

122. Gonzalo García Pedroso to Jesús López and José Benítez, 24 November 1937, in *Anuario: 1937–1938,* 61.

123. José Benítez to Gonzalo García Pedroso, 27 November 1937, in Gran Logia de la Isla de Cuba, *Anuario: 1937–1938,* 61–62.

124. José Benítez to Sr. Presidente del "Comité Nacionalista Español," 27 November 1937, in Gran Logia de la Isla de Cuba, *Anuario: 1937–1938,* 62–63.

125. Manuel Díaz Pérez, Cienfuegos, to Sr. Director de la Revista, Havana, 27 January 1938, in "Nuestra Actitud Antifascista: Dos cartas, dos contestaciones y un comentario," *Mundo Masónico* 7, no. 70/71 (February–March 1938): 18.

126. Mary Nieves, Havana, to Manuel Díaz Pérez, Cienfuegos, 1 February 1938, in "Nuestra Actitud Antifascista: Dos cartas, dos contestaciones y un comentario," 18. Nieves may have been a founding leader in the Masonic-affiliated women's group Hijas de la Acacia, established in Havana in 1936.

127. "Los Masones Españoles piden socorro," 25.

128. González Naredo, "Puntos de Vista: Por el Director: La revolución de España y la Masonería," *Mundo Masónico* 5, no. 53 (September 1936): 6.

129. "Los Masones Españoles piden socorro," 25.

130. Alfredo Padrón, "La Civilización," *Mundo Masónico* 5, no. 52 (August 1936): 20.

131. "La Masonería Española espera nuestra ayuda," *Mundo Masónico* 6, no. 64/65 (August–September 1937): inside cover, unnumbered.

132. Marco Pitchón, "Informe del Presidente de la Comision de Relaciones Exteriores," in Gran Logia de la Isla de Cuba, *Anuario: 1937–1938*, 296. Pitchón would go on to become founding president of B'nai B'rith in Cuba.

133. Luis Martínez Reyes, "Ayuda a la Gran Logia Española, La Habana, octubre 9 de 1938," in Gran Logia de la Isla de Cuba, *Anuario: 1938–1939*, 60–61.

134. Luis Martínez Reyes, "Informe del Gran Secretario, Habana, 26 de marzo de 1939," in Gran Logia de la Isla de Cuba, *Anuario: 1938–1939*, 229–30.

135. Luis Martínez Reyes, "Acuerdos de la Sesion Anual de 1938, Habana, 27 de marzo de 1938," in Gran Logia de la Isla de Cuba, *Anuario: 1938–1939*, 17.

136. "La Comision Pro Casa Escuela en Puigcerdá," *¡Ayuda!*, no. 4 (February–March 1938): 3.

137. "Notas y Comentarios," *¡Ayuda!*, no. 5 (May 1938): 21.

138. González Naredo, "OTRO TRIUNFO DE 'MUNDO MASONICO': No puede ser Fascista actuante y Masón a la vez, ASI LO CONFIRMA LA GRAN LOGIA," *Mundo Masónico* 7, no. 76 (November 1938): 29–30.

Chapter Six

1. Sánchez Cobos, *Sembrando Ideales*; Shaffer, *Anarchism and Countercultural Politics*; Fernández, *Cuban Anarchism*; Shaffer, "*Cuba para todos*"; Casanovas, *Bread, or Bullets!*; Stubbs, *Tobacco on the Periphery*.

2. Federación de Grupos Anarquistas de Cuba (FGAC), Secretario del Exterior, Havana, to unnamed, 20 October 1937, Correspondencia con la Federación de Grupos Anarquistas de Cuba, Habana, 20-10-1937 al 13-1-1938 (#2), Correspondencia del Comité Nacional CNT y el Comité Peninsular FAI con organizaciones anarchistas [*sic*] en el exterior, 1937–38 (Carpeta 62B), CNT-IISG. Evidencing the need to work clandestinely, there are no authors or editors identified in many of the anarchist periodicals. Therefore, citations use the organization responsible for publication rather than any individual. See also Fernández, *Cuban Anarchism*, 61–62.

3. FGAC, "A Nuestros Lectores y Simpatizantes," *Boletín Información y Propaganda* 1, no. 1 (1 September 1936): 1. The principal Spanish anarchist publications cited were *Solidaridad Obrera* and *Tierra y Libertad*.

4. FGAC Secretario del Exterior, Havana, to unnamed, 20 October 1937, #2, Carpeta 62B, CNT-IISG.

5. FGAC Secretario del Exterior, Havana, to unnamed, 20 October 1937.

6. Jesús Diéguez, Havana, to Nemesio Gálve, 16 January 1938, Correspondencia, documentos y manifiestos de la República de Cuba. 1937–38 (#6), Correspondencia con organizaciones sindicales de America del Sur, 1937–38 (Carpeta 60A), CNT-IISG.

7. Domingo Cuadriello, *El exilio republicano*, 25; "Negociado de Asociaciones, Orden Público y Elecciones Registro Especial de Asociaciones," "Centro Federalista Español—Reglamento," and other official documentation of incorporation in expediente 10402, legajo 349, RA-ANC.

8. Domingo Cuadriello, *El exilio republicano*, 59–60.

9. Adrián del Valle, "Panorama Internacional: Nacionalismo," *Rumbos Nuevos: Órgano Libertario* 1, no. 3 (1 June 1939): 1. For a succinct biographical sketch of del Valle, see Shaffer, *Anarchism and Countercultural Politics*, 15–18.

10. Del Valle, "Panorama Internacional," 1.

11. Federación de Juventudes Libertarias de Cuba (FJLC), "¡Nacionalismo! ¡Socialismo!," *Ideario* (15 January 1938): 6.

12. FJLC, "En defensa del federalismo," *Ideario* (15 January 1938): 8. Fernández lists as founding members of this group Julio Ayón Morgan, Modesto Barbeito, Floreal Barreras, Abelardo Barroso, Luis Dulzaides, Teodoro Fabel, José Fernández Martí, Gustavo López, Miguel Rivas, and another young anarchist with the unfortunately coincidental name of Gerardo Machado. Fernández indicates discord between the older anarchists of the FGAC and the FJLC youth. Fernández, *Cuban Anarchism*, 62. However, contemporary correspondence affirms the two groups' antifascist collaboration. FGAC Secretario del Exterior, Havana, to unnamed, 20 October 1937, #2, Carpeta 62B, CNT-IISG.

13. FJLC, "Bajo la Bota Asesina," *Ideario* 2, no. 3 (31 January 1938): 1.

14. FGAC, "La Democracía es Medio, No Fin," *Boletín de Información* 1, no. 1 (February 1938): 1–2; FGAC, "Sindicalismo," *Boletín de Información* 1, no. 1 (February 1938): n.p.; FJLC, "Zafra! Miseria!," *Ideario* (15 January 1938): 1.

15. FGAC, "A Nuestros Lectores y Simpatizantes," *Boletín Información y Propaganda* 1, no. 1 (1 September 1936): 1.

16. FGAC, "Militarismo," *Boletín de Información* 1, no. 1 (February 1938): n.p.; FJLC, "Bajo la Bota Asesina," *Ideario* 2, no. 3 (31 January 1938): 1; FJLC, "Notas Internacionales," *Ideario* (15 January 1938): 7; FGAC, "A Nuestros Lectores y Simpatizantes," *Boletín Información y Propaganda* 1, no. 1 (1 September 1936): 1; FGAC, untitled, *Boletín Información y Propaganda* 1, no. 1 (1 September 1936): 5.

17. FGAC, "Manifiesto a los Defensores de la Dignidad Nacional y de las Libertades Ciudadanas al Pueblo de Cuba," n.d., #6, Carpeta 60A, CNT-IISG.

18. FJLC, "Lentamente," *Ideario* 2, no. 3 (31 January 1938): 2.

19. FJLC, "Notas Internacionales," *Ideario* (15 January 1938): 7; FJLC, "Internacionales," *Ideario* 2, no. 3 (31 January 1938): 7.

20. FGAC, "Manifiesto a los Defensores de la Dignidad Nacional y de las Libertades Ciudadanas al Pueblo de Cuba," n.d., #6, Carpeta 60A, CNT-IISG; FGAC, "Mesa Redonda," *Boletín de Información* 1, no. 1 (February 1938): 3.

21. Jesús Diéguez, Havana, to Nemesio Gálve[z], 16 January 1938, #6, Carpeta 60A, CNT-IISG; FGAC Secretario del Exterior, Havana, to unnamed, 20 October 1937, #2, Carpeta 62B, CNT-IISG.

22. FGAC, "A Nuestros Lectores y Simpatizantes," *Boletín Información y Propaganda* 1, no. 1 (1 September 1936): 1; FGAC Secretario del Exterior, Havana, to unnamed, 20 October 1937, #2, Carpeta 62B, CNT-IISG; Jesús Diéguez, Havana, to Nemesio Gálve[z], 16 January 1938, #6, Carpeta 60A, CNT-IISG.

23. Juventud Libertaria, "Al Pueblo de Cuba," December 1936, 7.1, CSPDC-IISG.

24. FGAC, "Manifiesto a los Defensores de la Dignidad Nacional y de las Libertades Ciudadanas al Pueblo de Cuba," n.d., #6, Carpeta 60A, CNT-IISG; FJLC, "Editorial," *Ideario* (15 January 1938): 3.

25. FGAC, "Militarismo," *Boletín de Información* 1, no. 1 (February 1938): n.p.

26. FGAC, "Manifiesto a los Defensores de la Dignidad Nacional y de las Libertades Ciudadanas al Pueblo de Cuba," n.d., #6, Carpeta 60A, CNT-IISG.

27. FJLC, "Lentamente," *Ideario* 2, no. 3 (31 January 1938): 2.

28. FGAC, "A Nuestros Lectores y Simpatizantes," *Boletín Información y Propaganda* 1, no. 1 (1 September 1936): 1.

29. FJLC, "Editorial," *Ideario* (15 January 1938): 3; FJLC, "Editorial," *Ideario* 2, no. 3 (31 January 1938): 3; FJLC, "¡Nacionalismo! ¡Socialismo!," *Ideario* (15 January 1938): 6.

30. FJLC, "Editorial," *Ideario* (15 January 1938): 3.

31. FJLC, "Lentamente," *Ideario* 2, no. 3 (31 January 1938): 2.

32. FGAC Secretario del Exterior, Havana, to unnamed, 20 October 1937, #2, Carpeta 62B, CNT-IISG.

33. CNT, "La C.N.T. se Dirige al Mundo," 12 November 1937, #6, Carpeta 60A, CNT-IISG.

34. FGAC, "La Democracía es Medio, No Fin," *Boletín de Información* 1, no. 1 (February 1938): 1.

35. FGAC, "A Nuestros Lectores y Simpatizantes," *Boletín Información y Propaganda* 1, no. 1 (1 September 1936): 1.

36. FGAC, "La Democracía es Medio, No Fin," *Boletín de Información* 1, no. 1 (February 1938): 1–2.

37. FGAC Secretario del Exterior, Havana, to unnamed, 20 October 1937, #2, Carpeta 62B, CNT-IISG.

38. Based on 1930 U.S. Census and U.S. Social Security Administration Death Master File records cited by online genealogical research services, David Alonso of Langeloth, Pennsylvania, was born in Spain in 1901 or 1903, was married to Mary Alonso and living in Langeloth by 1930, and died there in 1982.

39. C. Llovet, Secretario del Exterior, Havana, to Secretariados Relaciones Exteriores, Barcelona, 20 February 1938, #6, Carpeta 60A, CNT-IISG.

40. Domingo Cuadriello, *El exilio republicano*, 11, 60.

41. Mariano R. Vázquez, Barcelona, to Centro Federalista Español, Havana, 19 March 1938, #6, Carpeta 60A, CNT-IISG; Jesús Diéguez, Havana, to Nemesio Gálve[z], 16 January 1938, #6, Carpeta 60A, CNT-IISG; Juan Salgado and Manuel Franco, Havana, to Mariano Vázquez, Valencia, 19 November 1937, and Juan Salgado and Manuel Franco, Havana, to Nemesio Gálvez, Paris, 19 November 1937, #6, Carpeta 60A, CNT-IISG; CNT, "La C.N.T. se Dirige al Mundo," 12 November 1937, #6, Carpeta 60A, CNT-IISG.

42. Mariano R. Vázquez, Barcelona, to Centro Federalista Español, Havana, 19 March 1938, #6, Carpeta 60A, CNT-IISG.

43. Pedro Herrera to FGAC, 30 December 1937, #8, Carpeta 58, Archivo de la Guerra Civil, Federación Anarquista Ibérica Archives, IISG.

44. C. Llovet, Secretario del Exterior, Havana, to Secretariados Relaciones Exteriores, Barcelona, 20 February 1938, #6, Carpeta 60A, CNT-IISG.

45. Pedro Herrera and Mariano R. Vázquez, Barcelona, to Federación de Grupos Anarquistas, Havana, 9 April 1938, #6, Carpeta 60A, CNT-IISG.

46. Mariano R. Vázquez, Barcelona, to Ateneo Socialista Español, Havana, 30 December 1937, #6, Carpeta 60A, CNT-IISG.

47. Pedro Herrera and Mariano R. Vázquez, Barcelona, to Federación de Grupos Anarquistas, Havana, 9 April 1938, #6, Carpeta 60A, CNT-IISG.

48. FJLC, "Pensamiento," *Ideario* 2, no. 3 (31 January 1938): 4.

49. Rojas Blaquier, *El Primer Partido Comunista*, 1:150; Alexander, *Trotskyism in Latin America*, 221.

50. Alexander, *Trotskyism in Latin America*, 222–23.

51. González Carbajal, *El Ala Izquierda Estudiantil*, 81.

52. "La Situación Politica Nacional" and "La Revolución Española," *Noticiero Bolchevique: Boletín del Partido Bolchevique Leninista* no. 1 (September 1936): 2–6. In the article on domestic politics, the anonymous author sharply criticizes the Auténticos, Joven Cuba, Sandalio Junco (for "cowardice and treason"), and, unsurprisingly, the "Stalinist Communist Party."

53. See Tennant, "Dissident Cuban Communism."

54. Tennant, 6.3.1.

55. Brea's surname is written "Brea," "Breá," and "Bréa" in various sources. Urcelay-Maragnès, *La leyenda roja*, 95, 118–119; Requena Gallego, "Compromiso político," 138; Tennant, "Dissident Cuban Communism," 6.3.1; Alexander, *Trotskyism in Latin America*, 224.

56. Tennant, "Dissident Cuban Communism," 6.3.1.

57. *Red Spanish Notebook*, quoted in Tennant, "Dissident Cuban Communism," 6.3.1.

58. Tennant, "Dissident Cuban Communism," 6.3.1.

59. See, for example, Rojas Blaquier, *El Primer Partido Comunista*, 222–39. López Civeira, after describing the failure of a general Popular Front to cohere, understates the Communist-Batista alliance, writing that in July 1938, the Communists "defined that the principal enemy was fascism and that, under the circumstances at the moment, Batista had ceased to be the center of reaction." López Civeira, *Cuba entre 1899 y 1959*, 134. Urcelay-Maragnès discusses the role of Cuban veterans of the Spanish Civil War in organizations opposing the Communist-Batista alliance. Urcelay-Maragnès, *La leyenda roja*, 231–35.

60. CC del PCC, "Llamamiento al Pueblo," 4 November 1936, número 90, legajo 1, FE-ANC.

61. Roca, "Discurso," 35–37, number 641, LAIP-LC; Roca, "¿Cómo puede Ud. mejorar su situación?," 13, 17, number 653, LAIP-LC; "Declaraciones de Unión Revolucionaria Comunista," n.d., Asignatura 1/2:3/1.1/71–72, FPPCC-IHC; Roca, *La unidad vencerá al fascismo*, 24–28, number 654, LAIP-LC.

62. José Cecilio Hernández Cárdenas ("Her-Car"), illustration, *Mediodía*, no. 13 (25 March 1937): cover.

63. Ordoqui, "Discurso," 9–10, number 641, LAIP-LC.

64. "Declaraciones de Unión Revolucionaria Comunista," n.d., Asignatura 1/2:3/1.1/71–72, FPPCC-IHC.

65. Roca, "Discurso de Francisco Calderio (Blas Roca)," *En Marcha con Todo del Pueblo*, 38, number 641, LAIP-LC.

66. "Declaraciones de Unión Revolucionaria Comunista," n.d., Asignatura 1/2:3/1.1/71–72, FPPCC-IHC.

67. Roca, "¿Cómo puede Ud. mejorar su situación? Respuestas a sus Preguntas" (Havana, June 1939), 12, 16, number 653, LAIP-LC; Roca, "Discurso," 36, number 641, LAIP-LC.

68. Roca, "¿Cómo puede Ud. mejorar su situación?," 13–16, number 653, LAIP-LC.

69. Roca, "¿Cómo puede Ud. mejorar su situación?," 15, 18, number 653, LAIP-LC. Chibás, an ally of Grau who would go on to establish the Ortodoxo Party, was strongly opposed to collaboration with the Communist Party. Caballero, *Latin America and the Comintern*, 128.

70. Roca, "Discurso," 35–36, 40–42, number 641, LAIP-LC.

71. "Declaraciones de Unión Revolucionaria Comunista," n.d., Asignatura 1/2:3/1.1/71–72, FPPCC-IHC. The antifascist character of the critique of *Diario de la Marina* would persist into the post-1959 revolutionary era, when Carlos Franqui called the publication's supporters defenders of "Maceo's killers as well as Valeriano Weyler, the Platt Amendment, Hitler, Mussolini, Franco, Trujillo, and the counterrevolution." Guerra, *Visions of Power in Cuba*, 133.

72. Sánchez Noroña, "Chibás y Pepín Rivero."

73. Comité Seccional de Luyanó del PCC, "12 DE AGOSTO," 1936, expediente 176, legajo 8, FE-ANC; CC del PCC, "Llamamiento al Pueblo," 4 November 1936, número 90, legajo 1, FE-ANC.

74. Comité Seccional de Arsenal del PCC, "¡SALVAJISMO!," n.d., expediente 202, legajo 5, FE-ANC.

75. Comité Seccional de Luyanó del PCC, "12 DE AGOSTO," 1936, expediente 176, legajo 8, FE-ANC.

76. CC del PCC, "Llamamiento al Pueblo," 4 November 1936, número 90, legajo 1, FE-ANC.

77. Rein, "Francoist Spain and Latin America," 123.

78. CC del PCC, "Llamamiento al Pueblo," 4 November 1936, número 90, legajo 1, FE-ANC.

79. Ordoqui, "Discurso de Joaquín Ordoqui," in *En Marcha con Todo del Pueblo*, 8, Number 641, LAIP-LC.

80. Marinello, "Palabras para Cuba," in *Discursos de Juan Marinello*, 15, number 629, LAIP-LC.

81. Roca, "Discurso," 35–37, number 641, LAIP-LC; Roca, "¿Cómo puede Ud. mejorar su situación?," 13, 17, number 653, LAIP-LC; "Declaraciones de Unión Revolucionaria Comunista," n.d., asignatura 1/2:3/1.1/71–72, FPPCC-IHC; Roca, *La unidad vencerá al fascismo*, 24–28, number 654, LAIP-LC.

82. "Historial breve y sincere del Don Fascismo de España y también del extranjero," 1936, Doc. 16s186, FSV-IHC.

83. Ford, "Discurso de James W. Ford," in *En Marcha con Todo del Pueblo*, 19–21, number 641, LAIP-LC.

84. CC del PCC, "Llamamiento al Pueblo," 4 November 1936, número 90, legajo 1, FE-ANC.

85. "Historial breve y sincere del Don Fascismo de España y también del extranjero," 1936, Doc. 16s186, FSV-IHC.

86. CC del PCC, "Llamamiento al Pueblo," 4 November 1936, número 90, legajo 1, FE-ANC.

87. Roca, "Discurso," 48, number 641, LAIP-LC.

88. Ford, "Discurso," 20–23, number 641, LAIP-LC.

89. Alonso and Chávez Alvarez, *Memorias inéditas del censo de 1931*, 74.

90. Roca, "Intervención del compañero Blas Roca en la discusión del caso Martín Castellanos," in PCC, *Cuidemos la unidad*, 5, number 644, LAIP-LC.

91. Roca, *La unidad vencerá*, 80, number 654, LAIP-LC.

92. Comité Seccional de Luyanó del PCC, "12 DE AGOSTO," 1936, expediente 176, legajo 8, FE-ANC; CC del PCC, "Llamamiento al Pueblo," 4 November 1936, número 90, legajo 1, FE-ANC.

93. Alexander, *Trotskyism in Latin America*, 222.

94. Comité Directivo, "Editorial: Asociación de Auxilio al Niño del Pueblo Español," *¡Ayuda!*, no. 1 (July 1937): 4.

95. "Comité de Recepción a los Niños Españoles Al Pueblo de Cuba," 1937, Doc. 12s168 1938, FSV-IHC.

96. CC del PCC, "Defendamos al Pueblo Abisinio," 11 October 1935, signatura 53, caja 1, FE-ANC.

97. CC del PCC, "Llamamiento al Pueblo," 4 November, 1936, número 90, legajo 1, FE-ANC.

98. Ford, "Discurso," 15, number 641, LAIP-LC; Roca, *La unidad vencerá*, 4, number 654, LAIP-LC.

99. Roca, *La unidad vencerá*, number 654, LAIP-LC; Manuel Luzardo, *El Camino de la Victoria Popular*, 23, number 615, LAIP-LC; Roca, "Discurso," 49, number 641, LAIP-LC.

100. Whitney, *State and Revolution*, 147–48.

101. The following four constituent groups of the Frente Democrático Español are listed in a flyer for a public event the organization held in April 1937: Frente Democrático Español, "Asista a la Conmemoración del Aniversario de la República Española," 14 April 1937, Doc. 5s168, FSV-IHC. See also Naranjo Orovio, *Cuba, otro escenario*, 59.

102. FGAC Secretario del Exterior, Havana, to unnamed, 20 October 1937, #2, Carpeta 62B, CNT-IISG.

103. FGAC Secretario del Exterior, Havana, to unnamed, 20 October 1937.

104. Ignacio González Cobos and Francisco Alvarez Fernández, "Circulo Español Socialista: Sociedad de Cultura y Subsidios: Reglamento General," 24 December 1933, expediente 6269, legajo 237, RA-ANC.

105. Círculo Español Socialista, Correspondencia, 1934–37, AH-71-49, PSOE-AO-FPI.

106. FGAC Secretario del Exterior, Havana, to unnamed, 20 October 1937, #2, Carpeta 62B, CNT-IISG. Contradicting the anarchist characterization, Domingo Cuadriello states that the ASE was of a "more moderate ideological character" than the CES. He cites expediente 6740, legajo 250, RA-ANC; however, this file was re-

ported missing by archive staff during the research for this book. Domingo Cuadriello, *El exilio republicano*, 11, 304.

107. FGAC Secretario del Exterior, Havana, to unnamed, 20 October 1937, #2, Carpeta 62B, CNT-IISG.

108. FGAC Secretario del Exterior, Havana, to unnamed, 20 October 1937.

109. Asociación Nacional de Ayuda al Pueblo Español, *Estatutos*, asignatura 454 1938, fondo unnamed, IHC.

110. Otero to Méndez Peñate, 28 June 1938, 20.39/87, RG-IHC; "Ejecutivo Nacional de la Asociación de Ayuda al Pueblo Español," n.d, 1/12:196/2.1/11, FPPCC-IHC. Information on the Federación de Trabajadores de la Provincia de la Habana found in Alexander, *History of Organized Labor in Cuba*, 80. Information on the Hermandad de Jóvenes Cubanos and Jóvenes del Pueblo found in de la Fuente, *Nation for All*, 227. Information on the Casa de Cultura found in Domingo Cuadriello, *El exilio republicano*, 26.

111. "N. de la R.," *España: Revista de textos y documentos* 1, no. 4 (15 December 1938): 5. Monetary amounts rounded up to the nearest dollar by author. See also the recurring column "Nota de la Asociación Nacional de Ayuda al Pueblo Español" in the Communist daily *Noticias de Hoy* during these months, as well as "Gran Triunfo de la Ayuda al P. Español," *Noticias de Hoy* 1, no. 45 (6 July 1938): 1, 8.

112. Introduction to Rosa P. Leclerc, "Los Niños de edad Escolar y la Colonias," *¡Ayuda!* 2, no. 6 (September 1938): 16.

113. "Ejecutivo Nacional de la Asociación de Ayuda al Pueblo Español," n.d., asignatura 1/12:196/2.1/11, FPPCC-IHC; Domingo Cuadriello, *El exilio republicano*, 55–56.

114. Whitney, *State and Revolution*, 167–68; Farber, *Revolution and Reaction*, 82–83. Accounts produced in post-revolutionary socialist Cuba reinforce the idea that the Communist Party was largely responsible for Cuban antifascism. See Bello and Pérez Díaz, *Cuba en España*; Instituto de Historia, *Cuba y la defensa*.

Conclusion

1. Ángel Augier, "Cómo era Julio Antonio Mella," *Bohemia* (23 and 30 January 1949), excerpted in Cairo, *Mella 100 años*, 1:206.

2. Thomas, *Cuba*, 706–7; Fernando Mires, *La rebelión permanente*, 293.

3. "El Nuevo presidium de la Asociación Nacional de Ayuda al Pueblo Español," *España* 1, no. 4 (15 December 1938): 6–7.

4. "El Nuevo presidium de la Asociación Nacional de Ayuda al Pueblo Español," 6–7.

5. Luis Martínez Reyes (Grand Secretary) and Gonzalo García Pedroso (Grand Master), "Declaración de principios sobre política internacional, Habana, 15 de Septiembre de 1937," in *Anuario: 1937–1938*, 52; Gonzalo García Pedroso to Jesús López and José Benítez, 24 November 1937, in Gran Logia de la Isla de Cuba, *Anuario: 1937–1938*, 61.

6. González Naredo, "OTRO TRIUNFO DE 'MUNDO MASONICO': No puede ser Fascista actuante y Masón a la vez, ASI LO CONFIRMA LA GRAN LOGIA," *Mundo Masónico* 7, no. 76 (November 1938): 29–30.

7. "El Nuevo presidium de la Asociación Nacional de Ayuda al Pueblo Español," 6–7.

8. Historical documentation indicates that Juan Marinello was a member of the Communist Party in 1938. Ana Suárez Díaz, personal communication, 30 January 2019.

9. "El Nuevo presidium de la Asociación Nacional de Ayuda al Pueblo Español," 6–7.

10. "El Nuevo presidium de la Asociación Nacional de Ayuda al Pueblo Español," 6–7.

11. Pérez, *Cuba: Between Reform and Revolution*, 218; Whitney, "Constitution of 1940," 64.

12. Grant Watson, quoted in Whitney, *State and Revolution*, 149.

13. Fulgencio Batista, quoted in Whitney, *State and Revolution*, 149.

14. Whitney, "Constitution of 1940," 64.

15. Farber, *Revolution and Reaction*, 84.

16. Tabares del Real, "Fulgencio Batista," 51.

17. Kiddle, "Repúblicas Rojas," 81–82. This work examines in depth the ways in which Mexico's pro-Republican policy affected its relations with the rest of Latin America.

18. "Notas Editoriales: Vida de la A.A.N.P.E.," *¡Ayuda!*, no. 4 (February/March 1938): 21.

19. Argote-Freyre, *Fulgencio Batista*, 254.

20. Argote-Freyre, 256.

21. Argote-Freyre, 254.

22. Argote-Freyre, 251.

23. Pérez, *Cuba: Between Reform and Revolution*, 217; Argote-Freyre, *Fulgencio Batista*, 253–254; Alexander, *History of Organized Labor in Cuba*, 81–83; Sims, "Cuba," 220–21; Farber, *Revolution and Reaction*, 85.

24. Harold Sims writes: "Labor support for an elected President Batista depended on his continuing responsiveness to union demands." Sims, "Cuba," 224.

25. Roca, "Discurso," 39, number 641, LAIP-LC; Roca, "Discurso de Francisco Calderio (Blas Roca) en el acto del recibimiento," in P.C.C., *El recibimiento*, 5, no. 648, LAIP-LC; Roca, "Discurso," 5, number 648, LAIP-LC.

26. Roca, "Discurso," 5, number 648, LAIP-LC.

27. "Una Amenaza a la Paz," *Mediodía*, no. 87 (26 September 1938): 3.

28. U.S. Chargé d'Affaires Albert Nufer to secretary of state, quoted in Caballero, *Latin America and the Comintern*, 144.

29. Nufer to secretary of state, quoted in Caballero, *Latin America and the Comintern*, 144.

30. Roca, *La unidad vencerá*, 11, number 654, LAIP-LC.

31. Abed Brooks, "Perspectives," *World News and Views* 18, no. 60 (24 December 1938): 60, cited in Whitney, *State and Revolution*, 169.

32. "Una Amenaza a la Paz," *Mediodía*, no. 87 (26 September 1938): 3.

33. Domingo Cuadriello, *El exilio republicano*, 52; Argote-Freyre, *Fulgencio Batista*, xi.

34. Caballero, *Latin America and the Comintern*, 129.

35. Whitney, *State and Revolution*, 172.

36. Ford, "Discurso," 18, number 641, LAIP-LC.

37. Jaffe, "The Rise and Fall," 28.

38. Roca, "Discurso," 38–39, number 641, LAIP-LC.

39. Caballero, *Latin America and the Comintern*, 61–62. Though willing to ally with former enemies such as Batista and Roosevelt, the Communists declared in their manifesto their continuing virulent opposition to Trotskyists, who, they implied, would bring fascism and war to the Americas. For a Cuban example of virulent anti-Trotskyist rhetoric—calling Trotskyists terrorists and fascists—in relation to Spain, see Joaquín Cardoso, "Los Trotskistas y la Guerra," *Mediodía*, no. 77 (18 July 1938): 20.

40. One of the anonymous readers for the University of North Carolina Press points out an enormous and mutual failing of Batista in his "progressive" turn and of the Cuban Communist Party: the forcible deportation during the late 1930s of thousands of Haitians and British West Indians from the island of Cuba, which Batista oversaw and about which the PCC was notably silent despite a respectable history of antiracist activism and cross-racial worker solidarity. In the words of this reader, the Cuban antifascism of Batista and the Communists had a "racist blind spot when it came to Haitians and British West Indians on the island."

41. As Farber notes, the Communist-Batista alliance weathered the Nazi-Soviet Pact (August 1939) with no perceivable impact, which, he asserts, "was rather unusual, considering the many other Popular Front alliances ruined after the Ribbentrop-Molotov agreement." Farber, *Revolution and Reaction*, 86.

42. Comité Pro-Repatriación de Cubanos en Francia, "Al Pueblo de Cuba," *¡Ayuda!*, no. 10 (April 1939): 9.

43. Comité Pro-Repatriación de Cubanos en Francia, "Al Pueblo de Cuba," 9.

44. Octavio S. Martínez, "Informe de la Comisión de Relaciones Exteriores," in Gran Logia de la Isla de Cuba, *Anuario: 1938–1939*, 264.

45. Morales Ruiz, *El discurso antimasónico*, 305–6.

46. Ramiro Valdés Daussá to the Government and People of Cuba in General, 11 January 1939, 1/12:196/2.1/9–10, FPPCC-IHC.

47. "Editoriales," *¡Ayuda!*, no. 9 (January/February 1939): 3.

48. "La 'Asociación de Auxilio al Niño del Pueblo Español' ha recibido desde París el siguiente despacho," n.d., 1/12:196/2.1/12, FPPCC-IHC.

49. Jacques Honore, "El Martirio Español: Exodo Trágico," *¡Ayuda!*, no. 10 (April 1939): 8; cover of *¡Ayuda!*, no. 10 (April 1939); Nini Haslund, "Madrid," *¡Ayuda!*, no. 10 (April 1939): 12; Francisco Pelayo, "Francisco Pelayo, niño de la Colonia Pueblo de Cuba, refugiado en Francia, escribe a Rosa Pastora Leclerc," *¡Ayuda!*, no. 10 (April 1939): 14.

50. "Editoriales," *¡Ayuda!*, no. 9 (January/February 1939): 3.

51. "Relación de la ayuda prestada por esta Asociación hasta la fecha," *¡Ayuda!*, no. 10 (April 1939): 3.

52. M. L. M., "La obra del 'Office Internacional Pour L'Enfance,'" *¡Ayuda!*, no. 10 (April 1939): 24.

53. Rafael Marquina, "Un llamado a la conciencia de la mujer cubana," *¡Ayuda!*, no. 10 (April 1939): 13.

54. "La A.A.N.P.E. continuará su ayuda á la infancia," *¡Ayuda!*, no. 10 (April 1939): 31.

55. Back cover of *¡Ayuda!*, no. 10 (April 1939).

56. Ramiro Valdés Daussá, Havana, to Henri Wallon, Paris, 17 April 1940, 34.1/2005(16–17), Serie Asociación de Auxilio al Niño del Pueblo Español, Sección Otros Instituciones Nacionales, RG-IHC.

57. Ramiro Valdés Daussá, Havana, to María Uria, Cahartre-Evre-Loir, France, 18 April 1940, 34.1/2005(22), Serie Asociación de Auxilio al Niño del Pueblo Español, Sección Otros Instituciones Nacionales, RG-IHC.

58. "Nuestros Objetivos," *Rumbos Nuevos* 1, no. 1 (1 April 1939): 2.

59. Del Valle, "La Reacción en Marcha," *Rumbos Nuevos* 1, no. 1 (1 April 1939): 1; "El sindicalism y sus tácticas," *Rumbos Nuevos* 1, no. 1 (1 April 1939): 4; "La Asociación Internacional de Trabajadores se dirige al proletariado," *Rumbos Nuevos* 1, no. 1 (1 April 1939): 5; Solidaridad Internacional Antifascista de Cuba, "Solidaridad Internacional Antifascista de Cuba S.I.A., se Dirije al Pueblo: Manifiesto a los antifascistas todos," 15 February 1939, in *Rumbos Nuevos* 1, no. 1 (1 April 1939): 6.

60. "La Verdad Sobre la Tragedia Española," *Rumbos Nuevos* 1, no. 2 (1 May 1939): n.p.

61. Del Valle, "Panorama Internacional: Nacionalismo," *Rumbos Nuevos* 1, no. 3 (1 June 1939): 1.

62. Del Valle, "La Reacción en Marcha," *Rumbos Nuevos* 1, no. 1 (1 April 1939): 1; del Valle, "Panorama Internacional: Nacionalismo," *Rumbos Nuevos* 1, no. 3 (1 June 1939): 1.

63. "Traición a Espaldas de los Libertarios," *Rumbos Nuevos* 1, no. 1 (1 April 1939): 3; "La Verdad Sobre la Tragedia Española," n.p.; Comité Nacional, Movimiento Libertario, C.N.T., F.A.I., F.I.J.L., "La Verdad Sobre la Guerra y la Revolución en España: ¡A los trabajadores del mundo!," *Rumbos Nuevos* 1, no. 3 (1 June 1939): n.p.

64. "La Verdad Sobre la Tragedia Española," n.p.

65. "Nuestros Objetivos," *Rumbos Nuevos* 1, no. 1 (1 April 1939): 2; XX [pseud.], "El Hombre," *Rumbos Nuevos* 1, no. 2 (1 May 1939): 6.

66. "Una lección que debe aprender el proletariado del mundo entero," *Rumbos Nuevos* 1, no. 1 (1 April 1939): 4–5; "Dos palabras a las juventudes," *Rumbos Nuevos* 1, no. 1 (1 April 1939): 6.

67. Del Valle, "La Fuerza es el Unico Derecho Internacional," *Rumbos Nuevos* 1, no. 2 (1 May 1939): n.p.

68. Joaquín Ochotorena, "Secretaria de Gobernación: Resolución," 21 April 1939, Falange Español Tradicionalista de las JONS, expediente 10768, legajo 357, RA-ANC.

69. Domingo Cuadriello, *El exilio republicano*, 52–53; Naranjo Orovio, *Cuba, otro escenario*, 111–15; Chase, *Falange*, esp. 67–78.

70. Domingo Cuadriello, *El exilio republicano*, 53–54.

71. Comité Central de las Organizaciones Hebreas de Cuba, "Al Pueblo de Cuba," 27 May 1939, Doc. 1s133 1939 Mayo, FSV-IHC. See also Edith Garcia Buchaca, "La

Mujer Cubana contra los Odios Raciales: A la opinión pública: El Congreso Nacional Femenino condena la campaña anti-semita," 1939, Doc. 3s51, FSV-IHC.

72. Gert Caden and E. Julio Wolff, "Estatutos del Comité Alemán Antifascista," 27 April 1943, and "Acta de Constitución," 17 June 1943, Comité Alemán Antifascista, expediente 10668, legajo 355, RA-ANC.

73. Domingo Cuadriello, *El exilio republicano*.

74. Domingo Cuadriello, 62.

75. Julio C. Cabarrocas and Alberto Monteagudo, "Reglamento," 5 June 1940, and Cabarrocas, "Acta de Constitución," 20 June 1940, Asociación Cultural de Ex-Combatientes Antifascistas, expediente 6951, legajo 257, RA-ANC. Members listed are Alberto Monteagudo [Seoane], Manuel Romero, Julio C[onstantino] Cabarrocas, Gustavo Rodríguez [Malagamba], Abelardo Iglesia[s Saavedra], Oscar Gonzalez, Pedro Fajardo [Boheras], Francisco Villanueva, Orlando [León] Lemus, Martinez Cubielle, Antonio Torres, and Tito Peña [López]. According to Domingo Cuadriello, the majority of members were anarchists. Domingo Cuadriello, *El exilio republicano*, 62–64. Frank Fernández, historian of Cuban anarchism, lists the following as anarchists who fought for the Republic: Iglesias, Malagamba, Monteagudo, Fajardo Boheras, and Cabarrocas.

76. Mario Alvarez Izquierdo to Sr. Gobernador de la Provincia, Havana, 9 October 1942, Formación de Excombatientes Antifascistas, expediente 10055, legajo 335, RA-ANC.

77. Alvarez and Norberto Hernández Nodal, "Estatutos de la 'Formación de Ex-combatientes Antifascistas' F.E.A.," 8 October 1942, Formación de Excombatientes Antifascistas, expediente 10055, legajo 335, RA-ANC.

78. "Acta de Constitución: Elecciones de Ejecutivo," 7 November 1942, Formación de Excombatientes Antifascistas, expediente 10055, legajo 335, RA-ANC. Members listed are Norberto H. Nodal, Mario A. Izquierdo, Carlos V. Bravo, Gilberto Galán, Andrés G. Lanuza, Rogelio Rodríguez, Dr. Fernando R. V., Segundo Collar M., Juan A. Izquierdo, Oscar G. Ancheta, Mario Morales M., Alberto Monteagudo, Ramón Rey Ravelo, Carlos Cañizares, Juan Palacios H., Mario Sánchez, José H. Rizo, Héctor Morales, Arístides Saavedra, Manuel Alonso, Gustavo Malagamba, Dr. C. F. Arratte, Justo B. Quintana, Dagoberto F. Vera, Ramón L. Alvarez, and Agustín B. Abad.

79. Manuel Rivero Setien and Roberto Casals Otero, "Reglamento," 12 September 1944, Asociación de Ex-Combatientes Anti-Fascistas Revolucionarios, expediente 5721, legajo 225, RA-ANC.

80. Norberto Hernández Nodal, "Fiche Individuelle," 26 June 1937, file 595, RGASPI; Gustavo Rodríguez Malagamba and Enrique Gregori Barbó, "Acta de Constitución," 3 July 1946, expediente 5721, legajo 225, RA-ANC; Domingo Cuadriello, *El exilio republicano*, 314n163.

81. Domingo Cuadriello, *El exilio republicano*, 52.

82. Frente Nacional Anti-Nazi Fascista, "Estatutos y Reglamento de la Asociación 'Frente Nacional Anti-Nazifascista," 8 July 1941, Frente Nacional Anti-Nazi Fascista, expediente 10624, legajo 354, RA-ANC.

83. Whitney, "Constitution of 1940," 64.

84. British embassy, quoted in Whitney, *State and Revolution*, 174.

85. Whitney, "Constitution of 1940," 64–65; Suárez Díaz, *Retrospección Crítica*, 5–6; Tabares del Real, "Fulgencio Batista," 47–48, 54.

86. Pérez, *Cuba: Between Reform and Revolution*, 220.

87. Whitney, "Constitution of 1940," 65–66.

88. Whitney lists the influence of the Spanish Republic on the 1940 Cuban constitution, along with "Cuba's own historical and political traditions," New Deal liberalism, and "anti-imperialist and populist ideologies in Peru, Mexico, Venezuela, Argentina, and Chile." Whitney, "Constitution of 1940," 65.

89. Whitney, *State and Revolution*, 148.

90. Whitney, 175.

91. Whitney, "Constitution of 1940," 65–66.

92. Suárez Díaz, *Retrospección Crítica*, 3; Tabares del Real, "Fulgencio Batista," 47.

Postscript

1. Smith, *Closest of Enemies*, 38.

2. Hennessy, "Cuba," 101.

3. Academy of Sciences, *International Solidarity*, 106.

4. Fredericka Martin to Eduardo Odio Pérez, 6 June 1970, folder 4, box 2, The Fredericka Martin Papers, ALBA 001.

5. Whitney, "Constitution of 1940," 66.

6. Pérez, *Cuba: Between Reform and Revolution*, 224.

7. Pérez, 224–27.

8. Bethell and Roxborough, *Latin America*, 2.

9. Casuso, *Cuba and Castro*, 87.

10. Casuso, 81.

11. Casuso, 81.

12. Casuso, 93, 99.

13. Casuso, 94–95.

14. Casuso, 101, 103.

15. Casuso, 102–5.

16. Casuso, 144.

17. Casuso, 80–83. I am indebted to one of the anonymous readers for the University of North Carolina Press for pointing out, for example, that Roa was a vocal critic of the USSR in the 1950s, such as during the Soviet invasion of Hungary (1956).

18. Instituto de Historia, *Cuba y la defensa*, 225, 269–73, 277–80, 281, 291.

19. Guerra López, "Cuba y la Asociación," 40, 43–45.

20. Though much documentation of the work is undated, some is marked with the year 1963. The records indicate that much work had already been completed seeking out veterans' information prior to the dating of these documents.

21. I am indebted to one of the anonymous readers for the University of North Carolina Press for pointing out that this term was not always applied accurately and in fact could simply be used as an insult.

22. Doc. RG 4.12/2005(1–279), Serie Fichas de Datos de Combatientes Cubanos de la Guerra Civil Española, Sección Personalidades Cubanas, RG-IHC. Another assessment document called each of these three men traitors and noted that the latter two were executed. "Relación de excombatientes cubanos de la Guerra civil española," n.d., Doc. 1/2:1.10/31–33, FPPCC-IHC. A third stated, regarding both Feria Pérez and Fernández Ortega: "Executed [or shot] by the Rev. TRAITOR." Doc. RG 4.11/2005(102–150), Serie Doc. Relacionada con la Guerra Civil Española, Sección Personalidades Cubanas, RG-IHC.

23. "Relación de excombatientes cubanos de la Guerra civil española," n.d., Doc. 1/2:1.10/31–33, FPPCC-IHC.

24. Doc. RG 4.12/2005(1–279), Serie Fichas de Datos de Combatientes Cubanos de la Guerra Civil Española, Sección Personalidades Cubanas, RG-IHC.

25. Instituto de Historia, *Cuba y la defensa*, 293–301; Bello and Pérez Díaz, *Cuba en España*, 259–67.

26. Federico Chao Rodríguez, "INFORME: Sobre el trabajo realizado por el compañero Federico Chao Rodríguez en las provincias de Villaclara y La Habana," n.d., Doc. 4.2/2005(14–15), Serie PCC, Sección PCC(1965), RG-IHC; Chao Rodríguez, "Biografía de Militantes," 30 December 1938, file 589, RGASPI.

27. De la Cova, *Moncada Attack*, 158.

28. Doc. RG 4.12/2005(1–279), Serie Fichas de Datos de Combatientes Cubanos de la Guerra Civil Española, Sección Personalidades Cubanas, RG-IHC.

29. "Mártires del Moncada," *Granma*, accessed 28 June 2010, www.granma .cubaweb.cu/marti-moncada/gm10.html.

30. De la Cova, *Moncada Attack*, 158.

31. Commission Judiciaire, "Rapport No. 1731," 7 September 1937, file 588, RGASPI. The record does not indicate whether or not detention was in fact enforced.

32. Rosa Hilda Zell to Fredericka Martin, 28 July 1968, folder 4, box 2, The Fredericka Martin Papers, ALBA 001. The subject of a good deal of intrigue and speculation in nonacademic sources, Masferrer has not garnered much scholarly attention; brief mentions in the literature serve generally to illustrate either the political gangsterism of the 1940s or the brutality of Batista's government during the 1950s. However, Domingo Cuadriello provides a useful biographical summary in a footnote. Domingo Cuadriello, *El exilio republicano*, 614–15n4.

33. Sims, "Cuba," 226.

34. Domingo Cuadriello, *El exilio republicano*, 591–92, 614–15; de la Cova, *Moncada Attack*, 3–4.

35. Farber, *Revolution and Reaction*, 121; Thomas, "Cuba," 148; Ameringer, "The Auténtico Party," 343; Domingo Cuadriello, *El exilio republicano*, 289, 615n4; Garza C., "Causas y desarrollo," 358.

36. Domingo Cuadriello, *El exilio republicano*, 615n4.

37. Domingo Cuadriello, 591–92; de la Cova, *Moncada Attack*, 26–27, 288. This view is expressed by numerous non-scholarly sources as well.

38. Thomas, "Cuba," 148.

39. Domingo Cuadriello, *El exilio republicano*, 615n4.

40. Instituto de Historia, *Cuba y la defensa*, 293–301; Bello and Pérez Díaz, *Cuba en España*, 259–67.

41. Rafael Chao Santana, "Reseña y Testimonios Complementarios," 15 February 1996, expediente 1/122, legajo Cuba, caja 63184, AHP.

42. Chao Santana, "Biografía de Militantes, 28 December 1938, file 589, RGASPI.

43. Comité Central, Partido Comunista de España, untitled assessment form, 7 November 1938, file 589, RGASPI.

44. "Campo de Concentración Internacional (Grupo Cubano)," n.d. but probably 26 May 1939, Doc. 1/2:1/1.10/58–64, and "Lista de Embarque: Repatriados en el vapor 'Orduna' el 13 de mayo de 1939," n.d. but probably 26 May 1939, Doc. 1/2:1/1.10/51–57, FPPCC-IHC. Date assessment based on related documents in archive.

45. Chao Santana, "Reseña y Testimonios Complementarios," 15 February 1996, expediente 1/122, legajo Cuba, caja 63184, AHP.

46. "Agrupación de Veteranos Internacionalistas Cubanos: España 1936–1939," n.d. but probably 1987, legajo Cuba, caja 63189, and Chao Santana, "Reseña y Testimonios Complementarios," 15 February 1996, expediente 1/122, legajo Cuba, caja 63184, AHP.

47. Fursenko and Naftali, *One Hell of a Gamble*, 11–12. I am indebted to one of the anonymous readers for the University of North Carolina Press for reminding me of this fact.

48. Bello and Pérez Díaz, *Cuba en España*.

49. Instituto de Historia, *Cuba y la defensa*, 1–6.

50. Bray, *Antifa*, 51.

51. Bray, xv. That said, it is important to note that in contrast to the many liberals and moderates portrayed as ardent Cuban antifascists in this book, liberals and moderates stand substantially apart from antifa, defined specifically as leftist, in Bray's book.

52. Personal observations at La Marcha Memorial de la Batalla del Jarama, 26 February 2011, Jarama Valley, Spain.

53. Hugo García, "Fallace último matancero defensor de la República Española," *Juventud Rebelde*, 15 August 2009, www.juventudrebelde.cu/cuba/2009-08-15/fallece-ultimo-matancero-defensor-de-la-republica-espanola; Isabel Munera, "El 'brigadista' que luchó en tres guerras," *El Mundo*, 23 August 2009, www.elmundo.es/elmundo/2009/08/23/opinion/18960598.html; Michel Porcheron, "Universo Lípiz: último matancero defensor de la República Española," *Granma*, 3 February 2010, www.granma.cu/espanol/2010/febrero/mier3/universo.html.

54. Porcheron, "Universo Lípiz."

55. Arcadio Ríos, *Fuego en la sangre* (Matanzas: Ediciones Matanzas, 2004), quoted in Porcheron, "Universo Lípiz."

56. See only Doc. 1/2:1/1.10/203–214, Fondo Primer Partido Comunista de Cuba, IHC. Document contains no title, date, or other identifying information.

57. Porcheron, "Universo Lípiz."

58. Maydel Santana, "Teresa Casuso, Maestra, Diplomática, Escritora, a los 82," *El Nuevo Herald*, Miami (30 July 1994): 4B.

Bibliography

Archives and Libraries

Cuba

Archivo Nacional de Cuba, Havana
    Fondo Especial (FE-ANC)
    Registro de Asociaciones (RA-ANC)
Biblioteca Nacional José Martí, Havana [*Accessed via digital reproduction*]
Instituto de Historia de Cuba, Havana
    Fondo Primer Partido Comunista de Cuba (FPPCC-IHC)
    Fondo Salvador Vilaseca (FSV-IHC)
    Registro General (RG-IHC)

Netherlands

Internationaal Instituut voor Sociale Geschiedenis, Amsterdam [*Accessed via digital reproduction*]
    CNT (España) Archives (CNT-IISG)
    Cuba Social and Political Developments Collection (CSPDC-IISG)
    Federación Anarquista Ibérica Archives
    Latin American Anarchist and Labour Periodicals, 1880–1940
    Ugo Fideli Papers

Russia

Russian Center for the Preservation and Study of Recent History, Moscow [*Accessed via microfilm reproduction*]
    Comintern Archives (RGASPI)

Spain

Archivo General Militar de Ávila, Ávila
Archivo Histórico Provincial de Albacete, Albacete (AHP)
Archivos de Organizaciones, Fundación Pablo Iglesias, Madrid [*Accessed via digital reproduction*]
    Partido Socialista Obrero Español (PSOE-AO-FPI)
Biblioteca Nacional de España, Madrid
Centro de Estudios y Documentación de las Brigadas Internacionales, Universidad de Castilla–La Mancha, Albacete (CEDOBI)
Centro Documental de la Memoria Histórica, Salamanca

United States

Abraham Lincoln Brigade Archive, Tamiment Library, New York University,
New York, N.Y.

The Carl Geiser Papers

The Fredericka Martin Papers

The Harry Randall Fifteenth International Brigade Photograph Collection

Roll Call—American Volunteers in the Spanish Civil War

The Veterans of the Abraham Lincoln Brigade Records, 1933–2006

Butler Library, Columbia University, New York, N.Y.

Camden County Historical Society, Camden, N.J.

The John Tisa / Cedric W. Fowler Labor Union & Spanish Civil War Materials
Collection

Centro de Estudios Puertorriqueños, Hunter College, City University of New York,
New York, N.Y.

The Erasmo Vando Papers, 1917–1996

The Jesús Colón Papers, 1901–1974

Homer Babbidge Library, University of Connecticut, Storrs, Conn.

Hoover Library, Stanford University, Stanford, Calif. [*Accessed via microfilm
reproduction*]

House of the Temple Library, Scottish Rite of Freemasonry Southern Jurisdiction,
Washington, D.C.

Library of Congress, Washington, D.C.

Latin American and Iberian Pamphlets (LAIP-LC)

Masonic Library and Museum, Grand Lodge of Free and Accepted Masons of
Pennsylvania, Philadelphia, Pa.

New York Public Library, New York, N.Y.

Rutgers University Libraries, New Brunswick, N.J.

The Robert J. Alexander Papers

Spanish Civil War Oral History Project, University of South Florida, Tampa, Fla.
[*Accessed via digital reproduction*]

Sterling Memorial Library, Yale University, New Haven, Conn.

Van Gorden-Williams Library and Archives, National Heritage Museum,
Lexington, Mass.

Newspapers and Periodicals

Adelante
The Afro-American
Alma Mater
¡Ayuda! Órgano oficial de la Asociación de Auxilio al Niño del Pueblo Español
Bohemia
Boletín de Información (Federación de Grupos Anarquistas de Cuba)
Boletín Información Comisariado (35th Division)
Boletín Información y Propaganda (Federación de Grupos Anarquistas de Cuba)
Boletín Oficial del Grande Oriente Español

Diario de la Marina
España
Facetas de Actualidad Española
Foreign Relations of the United States: The American Republics
Frente Único
Gráfico
Granma
Ideario
Insurrexit: Órgano de la Juventud Libertaria de la Habana
Juventud Rebelde
Línea
El Machete
Masas
Mediodía
El Mundo
Mundo Masónico: Revista Mensual Ilustrada para el Templo y para el Hogar
New Masses
New York Times
Nosotros: Por la Libertad del Pueblo Español
Noticias de Hoy
Noticiero Bolchevique: Boletín del Partido Bolchevique Leninista
Nuestra Palabra
El Nuevo Herald
La Prensa
Rayos de Sol
Reconquista
República
Rumbos Nuevos: Órgano Libertario
Solidaridad Obrera
Tiempo en Cuba
¡Tierra!
Tierra y Libertad
The Volunteer for Liberty
World News and Views

Books and Articles

Academy of Sciences of the U.S.S.R. *International Solidarity with the Spanish Republic: 1936–1939*. Moscow: Progress, 1974.

Agrupación Revolucionaria de Cuba. "Proclama al Pueblo de Cuba." In *Documentos para la historia de Cuba*, edited by Hortensia Pichardo, vol. 4, pt. 1. Havana: Editorial de Ciencias Sociales, 1980.

Aguilar, Luis E. *Cuba 1933: Prologue to Revolution*. New York: W. W. Norton, 1972.

Ala Izquierda Estudiantil. "Manifiesto programa del Ala Izquierda Estudiantil a los estudiantes y clase trabajadora de Cuba." In *Documentos de Cuba Republicana*, edited by Felicia Villafranca, 200–208. Havana: Instituto Cubano del Libro, 1972.

Alexander, Robert J. *A History of Organized Labor in Cuba.* Westport, Conn.: Praeger, 2002.

———. *Trotskyism in Latin America.* Stanford: Hoover Institute Press, 1973.

Alonso, Gladys, and Ernesto Chávez Alvarez, eds. *Memorias inéditas del censo de 1931.* Havana: Editorial de Ciencias Sociales, 1978.

Alvarez Blanco, Ernesto. "Recuerdan en Sitges, Cataluña, la labor realizada durante la Guerra Civil Española por la cardenense Rosa Pastora Leclere, primera maestra internacionalista cubana." *El Cardenense* (blog), 10 February 2014. http://elcardenense.blogspot.com/2014/02/recuerdan-en-sitges -cataluna-la-labor.html.

Ameringer, Charles D. "The Auténtico Party and the Political Opposition in Cuba, 1952–57." *Hispanic American Historical Review* 65, no. 2 (May 1985): 327–51.

Arboleya, Jesús. *The Cuban Counterrevolution.* Translated by Rafael Betancourt. Athens, Ohio: Ohio University Center for International Studies, 2000.

Argote-Freyre, Frank. *Fulgencio Batista: From Revolutionary to Strongman.* New Brunswick, N.J.: Rutgers University Press, 2006.

Arnedo-Gómez, Miguel, "Debates on Racial Inequality and Afro-Cuban Culture in *Adelante.*" *Bulletin of Spanish Studies* 88, no. 5 (2011): 711–35.

Barchino, Matías, and María Rubio Martín, eds. *Nicolás Guillén: Hispanidad, vanguardia y compromiso social.* Cuenca: Ediciones de la Universidad de Castilla–La Mancha, 2004.

Barker, A. J. *The Civilizing Mission: A History of the Italo-Ethiopian War of 1935–1936.* New York: Dial Press, 1968.

Bauerkämper, Arnd, and Grzegorz Rossoliński Liebe, eds. *Fascism without Borders. Transnational Connections and Cooperation between Movements and Regimes in Europe from 1918 to 1945.* New York, Berghan Books, 2017.

Baumann, Gerold Gino. *Los voluntarios latinoamericanos en la Guerra Civil Española.* Cuenca: Ediciones de la Universidad de Castilla–La Mancha, 2009.

Bayor, Ronald H., ed. *The Columbia Documentary History of Race and Ethnicity in America.* New York: Columbia University Press, 2004.

Beals, Carleton. *The Crime of Cuba.* Philadelphia: J. B. Lippincott, 1933.

Bello, Alberto Alfonso. *El Mártir de Majadahonda, Pablo de la Torriente Brau y su época.* Havana: Editorial de Ciencias Sociales, 2003.

Bello, Alberto Alfonso, and Juan Pérez Díaz. *Cuba en España: Una gloriosa página de internacionalismo.* Havana: Editorial de Ciencias Sociales, 1990.

Bethell, Leslie, and Ian Roxborough, eds. *Latin America between the Second World War and the Cold War, 1944–1948.* Cambridge: Cambridge University Press, 1992.

Binns, Niall. "La matanza de los inocentes: Intelectuales cubanas en defensa del niño español." *Anuario Colombiano de Historia Social y de la Cultura* 38, no. 2 (July–December 2011): 83–110.

Bisso, Andrés, ed. *El antifascismo argentino.* Buenos Aires: Buenos Libros-CeDinCi, 2007.

Bowen, Wayne H. *Spaniards and Nazi Germany: Collaboration in the New Order.*
Columbia: University of Missouri Press, 2000.

Bray, Mark. *Antifa: The Antifascist Handbook.* Brooklyn: Melville House, 2017.

Bronfman, Alejandra. *Measures of Equality: Social Science, Citizenship, and Race in Cuba, 1902–1940.* Chapel Hill: University of North Carolina Press, 2004.

Broué, Pierre, and Emile Témime. *The Revolution and the Civil War in Spain.*
Translated by Tony White. Chicago: Haymarket Books, 2008. First published in France in 1961.

Bueno, Salvador, and Vivian Lechuga, eds. *Órbita de Raúl Roa.* Havana: Ediciones Unión, 2004.

Bulmer-Thomas, Victor. *The Political Economy of Central America since 1920.*
Cambridge: Cambridge University Press, 1987.

Caballero, Manuel. *Latin America and the Comintern, 1919–1943.* Cambridge: Cambridge University Press, 1986.

Cabrera, Olga, ed. *Antonio Guiteras: Su pensamiento revolucionario.* Havana: Editorial de Ciencias Sociales, 1974.

———. *Mella: Documentos y artículos.* Havana: Editorial de Ciencias Sociales, 1975.

Cairo, Ana, ed. *Mella 100 años.* 2 vols. Santiago de Cuba: Editorial Oriente and Havana: Ediciones Memoria, 2003.

Callaba Torres, Juana Rosa. "La alternativa oligárquico-imperialista: Machado."
In *Historia de Cuba: La Neocolonia: Organización y crisis desde 1899 hasta 1940,* edited by José Cantón Navarro et al., 240–81. Havana: Editora Política, 1998.

Cantón Navarro, José, Oscar Zanetti Lacuona, Pedro Álvarez-Tabío Longa, Federico Chang Pon, and Alejandro García Álvarez, eds. *Historia de Cuba: La Neocolonia: Organización y crisis desde 1899 hasta 1940.* Havana: Editora Política, 1998.

Carr, Barry. "'Across Seas and Borders': Charting the Webs of Radical Internationalism in the Circum-Caribbean, 1910–1940." In *Exile and the Politics of Exclusion in the Americas,* edited by Luis Roniger, Pablo Yankelevich, and James Green, 217–40. Eastbourne and Portland, Ore.: Sussex Academic Press, 2012.

———. "Review: *Julio Antonio Mella: Una biografía,*" *Hispanic American Historical Review* 91, no. 1 (1 February 2011): 194–96.

Carrillo, Justo. *Cuba 1933: Students, Yankees, and Soldiers.* Translated by Mario Llerena. New Brunswick, NJ: Transaction, 1994.

Casanovas, Joan. *Bread, or Bullets! Urban Labor and Spanish Colonialism in Cuba, 1850–1898.* Pittsburgh: University of Pittsburgh Press, 1998.

Casaus, Víctor. *Pablo, 100 años después.* Havana: Centro Cultural Pablo de la Torriente Brau, Ediciones La Memoria, 2001.

Castellanos, José F. "Informe del Gran Secretario, Sesion Annual, Habana, 22 de marzo de 1936." In *Anuario de la Gran Logia de la Isla de Cuba.* Havana: Molina y Compañía, 1938.

Castells, Andreu. *Las Brigadas Internacionales de la Guerra de España.* Barcelona: Editorial Ariel, 1974.

Casuso, Teresa. *Cuba and Castro*. Translated by Elmer Grossberg. New York: Random House, 1961.

Chase, Allan. *Falange: The Axis Secret Army in the Americas*. New York: G. P. Putnam's Sons, 1943.

Cohen, Robin. *Global Diasporas: An Introduction*. London: Routledge, 2001.

Collazo Pérez, Gregorio E., and Carlos del Toro González. "Primeras manifestaciones de la crisis del sistema neocolonial (1921–1925)." In *Historia de Cuba: La Neocolonia: Organización y crisis desde 1899 hasta 1940*, edited by José Cantón Navarro et al., 194–239. Havana: Editora Política, 1998.

Collier, Ruth Berins. "Labor Politics and Regime Change: Internal Trajectories versus External Influences." In *Latin America in the 1940s: War and Postwar Transitions*, edited by David Rock, 59–88. Berkeley: University of California Press, 1994.

Commissariat of War. *The Book of the XV Brigade: Records of British, American, Canadian, and Irish Volunteers in the XV International Brigade in Spain, 1936–1938*. Madrid: Commissariat of War, XV Brigade, 1938.

Copsey, Nigel. *Anti-Fascism in Britain*. Basingstoke: Palgrave Macmillan, 2000.

———. Preface to *Varieties of Anti-Fascism: Britain in the Inter-War Period*, edited by Nigel Copsey and Andrzej Olechnowicz, xiv–xxi. Basingstoke: Palgrave Macmillan, 2010.

Copsey, Nigel, and Andrzej Olechnowicz, eds. *Varieties of Anti-Fascism: Britain in the Inter-War Period*. Basingstoke: Palgrave Macmillan, 2010.

Córdova, Efrén. *Clase trabajadora y movimiento sindical en Cuba*. Miami: Ediciones Universal, 1995.

Cuevas, Yazmín, and Guadalupe Olivier. "Julio Antonio Mella." In *Movimientos estudiantiles en la historia de América Latina*, edited by Renate Marsiske, vol. 3, 105–40. Mexico City: Universidad Nacional Autónoma de México, 2006.

Cushion, Steve. *A Hidden History of the Cuban Revolution: How the Working Class Shaped the Guerrilla Victory*. New York: Monthly Review Press, 2016.

Davies, Hywel M. *Fleeing Franco: How Wales Gave Shelter to Refugee Children from the Basque Country during the Spanish Civil War*. Cardiff: University of Wales Press, 2011.

De Bernardi, Alberto, and Paolo Ferrari, eds. *Antifascismo e identità europea*. Rome: Carocci, 2004.

De la Cova, Antonio Rafael. *The Moncada Attack: Birth of the Cuban Revolution*. Columbia: University of South Carolina Press, 2007.

De la Fuente, Alejandro. *A Nation for All: Race, Inequality, and Politics in Twentieth-Century Cuba*. Chapel Hill: University of North Carolina Press, 2001.

Díaz-Quiñones, Arcadio. "1898." *Hispanic American Historical Review* 78, no. 4 (November 1998): 577–81.

Domingo Cuadriello, Jorge. "El ABC fue otra esperanza de Cuba." *Espacio Laical* 8, no. 32 (October–December 2012): 82–88.

———. *El exilio republicano español en Cuba*. Madrid: Siglo XXI, 2009.

———. *Españoles en Cuba en el siglo XX*. Seville: Iluminaciones Renacimiento, 2004.

Drake, Paul W. "International Crises and Popular Movements in Latin America: Chile and Peru from the Great Depression to the Cold War." In *Latin America in the 1940s: War and Postwar Transitions*, edited by David Rock, 109–36. Berkeley: University of California Press, 1994.

Dugan, James, and Laurence Lafore. *Days of Emperor and Clown: The Italo-Ethiopian War, 1935–1936*. Garden City, N.Y.: Doubleday, 1973.

Dumpierre, Erasmo. *Julio Antonio Mella: Biografía*. Havana: Instituto Cubano del Libro, 1975.

Eatwell, Roger. *Fascism: A History*. London: Penguin, 1996.

Eby, Cecil D. *Comrades and Commissars: The Lincoln Battalion in the Spanish Civil War*. University Park: Pennsylvania State University Press, 2007.

Ellis, Keith. "Nicolás Guillén and Langston Hughes: Convergences and Divergences." In *Between Race and Empire: African-Americans and Cubans Before the Cuban Revolution*, edited by Lisa Brock and Digna Castaneda Fuertes, 129–67. Philadelphia: Temple University Press, 1998.

Esquenazi-Mayo, Roberto. *A Survey of Cuban Revistas, 1902–1958*. Washington: Library of Congress, 1993.

Falcoff, Mark. Preface to *The Spanish Civil War, 1936–1939: American Hemispheric Perspectives*, edited by Mark Falcoff and Fredrick B. Pike, ix–xvi. Lincoln: University of Nebraska Press, 1982.

Falcoff, Mark, and Fredrick B. Pike, eds. *The Spanish Civil War, 1936–1939: American Hemispheric Perspectives*. Lincoln: University of Nebraska Press, 1982.

Farber, Samuel. *Revolution and Reaction in Cuba, 1933–1960: A Political Sociology from Machado to Castro*. Middletown, Conn.: Wesleyan University Press, 1976.

Featherstone, David. "Black Internationalism, Subaltern Cosmopolitanism, and the Spatial Politics of Antifascism." *Annals of the Association of American Geographers* 103, no. 6 (2013): 1406–20.

Federación Obrera de la Habana. *El Sindicado General de Empleados del Comercio de Cuba, frente al IV Congreso Obrero Nacional*. 12 January 1934.

Fernández, E. "La razón del 4 de Septiembre." *Revista de la Biblioteca Nacional de Cuba José Martí* 104, no. 2 (2013): 145–74.

Fernández, Frank. *Cuban Anarchism: The History of a Movement*. Translated by Charles Bufe. Tucson: See Sharp Press, 2001.

Fernández, James D. "Nueva York: The Spanish-Speaking Community Responds." In *Facing Fascism: New York and the Spanish Civil War*, edited by Peter N. Carroll and James D. Fernández, 84–91. New York: New York University Press, 2007.

Fernández Muñiz, Áurea Matilde. *La Guerra Civil Española en la sociedad cubana: Aproximación a una época*. Havana: Editorial de Ciencias Sociales, 2010.

Ferrao, Luis A. *Puertorriqueños en la Guerra Civil Española: Prensa y Testimonios, 1936–1939*. San Juan: La Editorial, Universidad de Puerto Rico, 2009.

Ferrer, Ada. *Freedom's Mirror: Cuba and Haiti in the Age of Revolution*. New York: Cambridge University Press, 2014.

———. *Insurgent Cuba: Race, Nation, and Revolution, 1868–1898*. Chapel Hill: University of North Carolina Press, 1999.

Ferrer Benimeli, José Antonio, ed. *La masonería en la España del siglo XX*. 2 vols. Toledo: Centro de Estudios Históricos de la Masonería Española, 1996.

———. *La masonería española: La historia en sus textos*. Madrid: Ediciones Istmo, 1996.

Finchelstein, Federico. *Transatlantic Fascism: Ideology, Violence, and the Sacred in Argentina and Italy, 1919–1945*. Durham, N.C.: Duke University Press, 2010.

Fisher-Thompson, Jim. "Ethiopia and U.S. Celebrate 100 Years of Diplomatic Relations." 18 December, 2003. https://allafrica.com/stories/200312190063.html.

Fronczak, Joseph. "Local People's Global Politics: A Transnational History of the Hands Off Ethiopia Movement of 1935." *Diplomatic History* 39, no. 2 (2015): 245–74.

Fursenko, Aleksandr, and Timothy Naftali. *One Hell of a Gamble: Khrushchev, Castro, Kennedy, 1958–1964: The Secret History of the Cuban Missile Crisis*. New York: W. W. Norton, 1997.

García, Gervasio Luis. "I Am the Other: Puerto Rico in the Eyes of North Americans, 1898." *Journal of American History* 87, no. 1 (June 2000): 39–64.

García, Hugo. "Transnational History: A New Paradigm for Anti-Fascist Studies?" *Contemporary European History* 25, no. 4 (2016): 563–72.

———. "Was There an Antifascist Culture in Spain during the 1930s?" In *Rethinking Antifascism: History, Memory and Politics, 1922 to the Present*, edited by Hugo García, Mercedes Yusta, Xavier Tabet, and Cristina Clímaco, 92–113. New York: Berghahn, 2016.

García, Hugo, Mercedes Yusta, Xavier Tabet, and Cristina Clímaco, eds. *Rethinking Antifascism: History, Memory and Politics, 1922 to the Present*. New York: Berghahn, 2016.

García Álvarez, Alejandro. "La consolidación del dominio imperialista." In *La Neocolonia: Organización y crisis desde 1899 hasta 1940*, edited by José Cantón Navarro et al., 90–141. Vol. 3 of *Historia de Cuba*. Havana: Editora Política, 1998.

García Passalacqua, Juan. "The Dilemmas of Puerto Rican Intellectuals." In *Unity in Variety: The Hispanic and Francophone Caribbean*, edited by Alistair Hennessy. Vol. 2 of *Intellectuals in the Twentieth-Century Caribbean*. London: Macmillan, 1992.

Garza C., Lucinda. "Causas y desarrollo del conflicto cubano-norteamericano de enero de 1959 a julio de 1960." *Foro Internacional* 9, no. 4 (April–June 1969): 354–86.

Gentile, Emilio. "I Fasci Italiani All'Estero: The 'Foreign Policy' of the Fascist Party." In *Fascism Outside Europe: The European Impulse against Domestic Conditions in the Diffusion of Global Fascism*, edited by Stein Ugelvik Larsen, 95–115. Boulder, Colo.: Social Science Monographs, 2001.

Gómez Álvarez, Maximino. *U-Boats del III Reich en Cuba*. Madrid: Entrelíneas Editores, 2009.

González Carbajal, Ladislao. *El Ala Izquierda Estudiantil y su época*. Havana: Editorial de Ciencias Sociales, 1974.

———. *Mella y el movimiento estudiantil*. Havana: Editorial de Ciencias Sociales, 1977.

Gran Logia de la Isla de Cuba. *Anuario de la Gran Logia de la Isla de Cuba*. Havana: Molina y Compañía, 1938.

———. *Anuario de la Gran Logia de la Isla de Cuba: 1937–1938.* Guanabacoa: Imp. Alejandro López, 1941.

———. *Anuario de la Gran Logia de la Isla de Cuba: 1938–1939.* Guanabacoa: Imp. Alejandro López, 1941.

Griffin, Roger. *International Fascism: Theories, Causes, and the New Consensus.* London: Arnold, 1998.

———. *The Nature of Fascism.* London: Routledge, 1991.

Grip, Lina, and John Hart. "The Use of Chemical Weapons in the 1935–36 Italo-Ethiopian War." *SIPRI Arms Control and Non-proliferation Programme,* October 2009, 1–7.

Gronbeck-Tedesco, John A. *Cuba, the United States, and Cultures of the Transnational Left, 1930–1975.* New York: Cambridge University Press, 2015.

Guerra, Lillian. *The Myth of José Martí: Conflicting Nationalisms in Early Twentieth-Century Cuba.* Chapel Hill: University of North Carolina Press, 2005.

———. *Visions of Power in Cuba: Revolution, Redemption, and Resistance, 1959–1971.* Chapel Hill: University of North Carolina Press, 2012.

Guerra López, Dolores. "Cuba y la Asociación de Auxilio al Niño del Pueblo Español." In *La Guerra Civil Española en la sociedad cubana: Aproximación a una época,* edited by Áurea Matilde Fernández Muñiz, 40–52. Havana: Editorial de Ciencias Sociales, 2010.

Guillén, Nicolás. *Prosa de Prisa.* Vol. 1, *1929–1972.* Havana: Editorial Arte y Literatura, 1975.

———. "Soldados en Abisinia." In *¡Patria o muerte! The Great Zoo and Other Poems by Nicolás Guillén,* edited by Robert Márquez, 178–83. New York: Monthly Review Press, 1972.

Guillén, Nicolás, and Juan Marinello. *Hombres de la España leal.* Havana: Editorial Facetas, 1938.

Guridy, Frank Andre. "'Enemies of the White Race': The Machadista State and the UNIA in Cuba." *Caribbean Studies* 31, no. 1 (January–June 2003): 107–37.

———. "From Solidarity to Cross-Fertilization: Afro-Cuban/African American Interaction during the 1930s and 1940s." *Radical History Review,* no. 87 (Fall 2003): 19–48.

Gutiérrez Coto, Amauri. "Izquierda cubana y republicanismo español." In *El Atlántico como frontera: Mediaciones culturales entre Cuba y España,* edited by Damaris Puñales Alpízar, 69–90. Madrid: Editorial Verbum, 2014.

Hagemann, Albrecht. "The Diffusion of German Nazism." In *Fascism outside Europe: The European Impulse against Domestic Conditions in the Diffusion of Global Fascism,* edited by Stein Ugelvik Larsen, 88–92. Boulder, Colo.: Social Science Monographs, 2001.

Hatzky, Christine. *Julio Antonio Mella (1903–1929): Una biografía.* Santiago de Cuba: Editorial Oriente, 2008.

Hennessy, Alistair. "Cuba." In *The Spanish Civil War, 1936–1939: American Hemispheric Perspectives,* edited by Mark Falcoff and Fredrick B. Pike, 101–58. Lincoln: University of Nebraska Press, 1982.

Hughes, Langston. "Harlem Ball Player Now Captain in Spain: Basilio Cueria, Head of Machine Gun Company Called One of Best Officers." In *Langston Hughes in the Hispanic World and Haiti*, edited by Edward J. Mullen, 196–98. Hamden, Conn.: Archon Books, 1977.

———. "Mussolini, Don't You 'Mess' with Me: Ballad of Ethiopia." *Afro-American*, 28 September 1935, 3.

Ibarra Guitart, Jorge Renato. *Mediación del 33: ocaso del machadato*. Havana: Editorial Política, 1999.

Instituto de Historia del Movimiento Comunista y de la Revolución Socialista de Cuba. *Cuba y la defensa de la República Española (1936–1939)*. Havana: Editora Política, 1981.

Jackson, Gabriel. *Concise History of the Spanish Civil War*. New York: John Day, 1974.

Jacoby, Karl. "Between North and South: The Alternative Borderlands of William H. Ellis and the African American Colony of 1895." In *Continental Crossroads: Remapping U.S.-Mexico Borderlands History*, edited by Samuel Truett and Elliot Young, 209–39. Durham, N.C.: Duke University Press, 2004.

———. *The Strange Career of William Ellis: The Texas Slave Who Became a Mexican Millionaire*. New York: W. W. Norton, 2016.

Jaffe, Philip J. "The Rise and Fall of Earl Browder." *Survey* 18, no. 12 (Spring 1972): 14–65.

Jiménez Trujillo, José F. "Protection of Childhood during the Spanish Civil War: Art and Propaganda on the Republican Side." In *Children and Youth at Risk: Historical and International Perspectives*, edited by Christine Mayer, Ingrid Lohmann, and Ian Grosvenor, 49–70. New York: Peter Lang, 2009.

Kelley, Robin D. G. "'Africa's Sons with Banner Red': African American Communists and the Politics of Culture, 1919–1934." In *Race Rebels: Culture, Politics, and the Black Working Class*, 103–22. New York: Free Press, 1994.

———. "'This Ain't Ethiopia, but It'll Do': African Americans and the Spanish Civil War." In *Race Rebels: Culture, Politics, and the Black Working Class*, 123–58. New York: Free Press, 1994.

Kiddle, Amelia M. "Repúblicas Rojas." In *Mexico's Relations with Latin America during the Cárdenas Era*, 81–108. Albuquerque: University of New Mexico Press, 2016.

Kirk, John M. *José Martí: Mentor of the Cuban Nation*. Tampa: University Presses of Florida, 1983.

Kirk, Tim, and Anthony McElligot. *Opposing Fascism: Community, Authority and Resistance in Europe*. Cambridge: Cambridge University Press, 1999.

Kulístikov, Vladímir. "América Latina en los planes estratégicos del Tercer Reich." *América Latina* 10 (1984): 46–56.

Lafita, María Luisa. *Dos héroes cubanos en el 5to. regimiento*. Havana: Editorial de Ciencias Sociales, 1980.

———. *Rodolfo Ricardo Ramón de Armas y Soto (1912–1937): Héroe del internacionalismo proletario*. Havana: Departamento de Orientación Revolucionaria del Comité Central del Partido Comunista de Cuba, 1975.

Lambe, Ariel Mae. "Who Is the Mysterious 'Cuba Hermosa'? New Evidence Comes to Light." *The Volunteer*, 22 November, 2016, www.albavolunteer.org/2016/11 /who-is-the-mysterious-cuba-hermosa-new-evidence-comes-to-light.

Landis, Arthur H. *The Abraham Lincoln Brigade*. New York: Citadel Press, 1967.

Larsen, Stein Ugelvik, Bernt Hagtvet, and Jan Petter Myklebust. *Who Were the Fascists: Social Roots of European Fascism*. Oslo: Universitetsförlaget, 1980.

Lavin, Raul. Interview by Ana M. Varela-Lago. Spanish Civil War Oral History Project, Florida Studies Center, University of South Florida, Tampa, Florida. 8 December 1997. Digital Object Identifier S64-00011.

Legarreta, Dorothy. *The Guernica Generation: Basque Refugee Children of the Spanish Civil War*. Reno: University of Nevada Press, 1984.

Leiva, Juan Chongo. *El fracas de Hitler en Cuba*. Havana: Editorial Letras Cubanas, 1989.

Linz, Juan J. "Some Notes towards a Comparative Study of Fascism in Sociological Historical Perspective." In *Fascism: A Reader's Guide*, edited by Walter Laqueur, 3–121. Berkeley: University of California Press, 1976.

Liss, Sheldon B. *Roots of Revolution: Radical Thought in Cuba*. Lincoln: University of Nebraska Press, 1987.

López, Kathleen. *Chinese Cubans*. Chapel Hill: University of North Carolina Press, 2013.

López Civeira, Francisca. *Cuba entre 1899 y 1959: Seis décadas de historia*. Havana: Editorial Pueblo y Educación, 2007.

López Civeira, Francisca, Oscar Loyola Vega, and Arnaldo Silva León. *Cuba y su historia*. Havana: Instituto Cubano del Libro, 1998.

López Isla, Mario Luis. *En la primera línea: Cubanos en la Guerra Civil Española*. Santa Cruz de Tenerife: Editorial Benchomo, 2005.

López Sánchez, José. *Pablo: imagen y leyenda*. Havana: Centro Cultural Pablo de la Torriente Brau, Ediciones La Memoria, 2003.

Luzardo, Manuel. *El Camino de la Victoria Popular*. Havana: Ediciones Sociales, n.d.

Marinello, Juan. *Discursos de Juan Marinello al servicio de la causa popular*. Havana: Ediciones Páginas, n.d.

Mason, Tim. *Nazism, Fascism and the Working Class*. Edited by Jane Caplan. Cambridge: Cambridge University Press, 1995.

Mastellari Maecha, Pía. "El pueblo español se mantuvo cada vez más firme." In *Cuba y la defensa de la República Española (1936–1939)* by Instituto de Historia del Movimiento Comunista y de la Revolución Socialista de Cuba. Havana: Editora Política, 1981.

McLeod, Marc C. "'Sin dejar de ser cubanos': Cuban Blacks and the Challenges of Garveyism in Cuba." *Caribbean Studies* 31, no. 1 (January–June 2003): 75–115.

Mella, Julio Antonio. "Los universitarios contra el imperialismo yanqui y el servilismo del gobierno cubano." In *Documentos de Cuba Republicana*, edited by Felicia Villafranca, 174–75. Havana: Instituto Cubano del Libro, 1972.

Merriman, John. *A History of Modern Europe from the Renaissance to the Present*. New York: W. W. Norton, 1996.

Miller, Daniel A., dir. *Crucible of Empire: The Spanish-American War*. New York: Great Projects Film Company, 1999. DVD.

Ministerio de Cultura, Biblioteca Nacional José Martí. *Índice de Mediodía, 1936–1939*. Havana: Editorial Orbe, 1979.

Mintz, Sidney. "Review." *American Anthropologist* (New Series) 59, no. 6 (December 1957): 1138–39.

Mires, Fernando. *La rebelión permanente: Las revoluciones sociales en América Latina*. 3rd ed. Mexico D.F.: Siglo XXI Editores, 2005.

Montejo Arrechea, Carmen V. *Sociedades Negras en Cuba, 1878–1960*. Havana: Editorial de Ciencias Sociales, 2004.

Morales Ruiz, Juan José. *El discurso antimasónico en la Guerra Civil Española (1936–1939)*. Zaragoza: Diputación General de Aragón, 2001.

Morgan, Philip. *Fascism in Europe, 1919–1945*. London: Routledge, 2003.

Morillas Brandy, José Antonio. "Juan García Morales: Un cura republicano: Obrero de la pluma." *Cuadernos Republicanos* 23 (1995): 99–112.

Mosse, George L. "Introduction: Toward a General Theory of Fascism." In *International Fascism: New Thoughts and New Approaches*, 1–41. London: Sage, 1979.

Mullen, Edward J. *Langston Hughes in the Hispanic World and Haiti*. Hamden, Conn.: Archon Books, 1977.

Naranjo Orovio, Consuelo. *Cuba, otro escenario de lucha: La guerra civil y el exilio republicano español*. Madrid: Consejo Superior de Investigaciones Científicas, Centro de Estudios Históricos, Departamento de Historia de América, 1988.

Nicolau González, Ramón. "La organización y traslado de los combatientes cubanos a la República Española." In *Cuba y la defensa de la República Española (1936–1939)* by Instituto de Historia del Movimiento Comunista y de la Revolución Socialista de Cuba. Havana: Editora Política, 1981.

Nurhussein, Nadia. "Ethiopia in the Verse of the Late Harlem Renaissance." In *A Companion to the Harlem Renaissance*, edited by Cherene Sherrard-Johnson, 423–39. Malden, Mass.: Wiley Blackwell, 2015.

Odio Pérez, Eduardo. "La batalla duró diez días." In *Cuba y la defensa de la República Española (1936–1939)* by Instituto de Historia del Movimiento Comunista y de la Revolución Socialista de Cuba. Havana: Editora Política, 1981.

Olivares B., Edmundo. *Pablo Neruda: Los caminos de América*. Santiago: Editorial LOM, 2004.

Orwell, Geroge. *Homage to Catalonia*. 1952; San Diego: Harcourt Brace, 1980.

Padrón, Pedro Luis. *Julio Antonio Mella y el movimiento obrero*. Havana: Editorial de Ciencias Sociales, 1980.

Pankhurst, Richard. "Invasion, Occupation and Liberation." In *The Ethiopians*, 219–49. Oxford: Blackwell, 1998.

———. "William H. Ellis—Guillaume Enriques Ellesio: The First Black American Ethiopianist?" *Ethiopia Observer* 15 (1972): 89–121.

Pappademos, Melina. *Black Political Activism and the Cuban Republic*. Chapel Hill: University of North Carolina Press, 2011.

Partido Bolchevique Leninista. *Estatutos*. Havana: 1933.

———. *Programa del Partido Bolchevique Leninista*. Havana: Imprenta O'Reilly, 1934.

Partido Comunista de Cuba. *Cuidemos la unidad: El caso del Dr. Martín Castellanos*. Havana: 1938.

———. *El recibimiento del Coronel Batista*. Havana: Ediciones Sociales, 1938.

———. *En Marcha con Todo del Pueblo*. Havana: Ediciones Sociales, 1938.

Passmore, Kevin. *Fascism*. New York: Oxford University Press, 2002.

Paxton, Robert O. *The Anatomy of Fascism*. New York: Vintage Books, 2004.

Payne, Stanley G. *Falange: A History of Spanish Fascism*. Stanford: Stanford University Press, 1961.

———. *Fascism in Spain, 1923–1977*. Madison: University of Wisconsin Press, 1999.

———. *A History of Fascism, 1914–1945*. Madison: University of Wisconsin Press, 1995.

Penichet, Antonio. *Nuestra Responsibilidad ante la Próxima Guerra*. Havana: Logia Minerva, 1936.

Pereira Alves, Alejandro. *Prominentes evangélicos de Cuba*. El Paso: Casa Bautista de Publicaciones, 1936.

Pérez, Louis A., Jr. *Cuba: Between Reform and Revolution*. 5th ed. New York: Oxford University Press, 2015.

———. *Cuba under the Platt Amendment, 1902–1934*. Pittsburgh: University of Pittsburgh Press, 1986.

———. *The Structure of Cuban History: Meanings and Purpose of the Past*. Chapel Hill: University of North Carolina Press, 2013.

Pérez Díaz, Máximo. *Indice de Mediodía, 1936–1939*. Havana: Editorial ORBE, 1979.

Pérez Montfort, Ricardo. *Hispanismo y falange: Los sueños imperiales de la derecha española y México*. Mexico: Fondo de Cultura Económica, 1992.

Pérez-Stable, Marifeli. *The Cuban Revolution: Origins, Course, and Legacy*. 2nd ed. New York: Oxford University Press, 1999.

Pichardo, Hortensia. *Documentos para la historia de Cuba*. 4 vols. Havana: Editorial de Ciencias Sociales, 1980.

Pike, Fredrick B. "The Background to the Civil War in Spain and the U.S. Response to the War." In *The Spanish Civil War, 1936–39: American Hemispheric Perspectives*, edited by Mark Falcoff and Fredrick B. Pike, 1–49. Lincoln: University of Nebraska Press, 1982.

———. "Making the Hispanic World Safe from Democracy: Spanish Liberals and Hispanismo." *Review of Politics* 33, no. 3 (July 1971): 307.

Pons Prades, Eduardo. *Los niños republicanos en la guerra de España*. Madrid: Oberon, 2004.

Pope Clement XII. "In Eminenti: Papal Bull Dealing with the Condemnation of Freemasonry." 28 April 1738.

Pope Leo XIII. "Humanum Genus: On Freemasonry." 20 April 1884.

Porcheron, Michel. "Alberto Bello y 'su' guerra: La de más de 1000 voluntarios cubanos en el bando de los republicanos españoles (1936–1939)." *Rebelión*, 28 April 2008.

Preston, Paul. *A Concise History of the Spanish Civil War*. London: Fontana, 1996.

Rein, Raanan. "Francoist Spain and Latin America, 1936–1953." In *Fascism Outside Europe: The European Impulse against Domestic Conditions in the Diffusion of Global Fascism*, edited by Stein Ugelvik Larsen, 116–52. Boulder, Colo.: Social Science Monographs, 2001.

Requena Gallego, Manuel. "Compromiso político de la cultura cubana con el gobierno de la República Española durante la guerra civil." In *Nicolás Guillén: Hispanidad, vanguardia y compromiso social*, edited by Matías Barchino and María Rubio Martín, 135–48. Cuenca: Ediciones de la Universidad de Castilla–La Mancha, 2004.

Richet, Isabelle. "Marion Cave Roselli and the Transnational Women's Anti-fascist Networks." *Journal of Women's History* 24, no. 3 (2012): 117–39.

Roa, Raúl. "Los últimos días de Pablo de la Torriente Brau." In *Órbita de Raúl Roa*, edited by Salvador Bueno and Vivian Lechuga, 331–48. Havana: Ediciones Unión, 2004.

———. "Presidio Modelo." In Bueno and Lechuga, *Órbita de Raúl Roa*.

———. "Rafael Trejo y el 30 de septiembre." In Bueno and Lechuga, *Órbita de Raúl Roa*.

———. "Reacción versus Revolución: Carta a Jorge Mañach, Hospital Militar de Columbia, November 1931." In Bueno and Lechuga, *Órbita de Raúl Roa*.

———. "Tiene la palabra el camarada Máuser." In Bueno and Lechuga, *Órbita de Raúl Roa*.

Robinson, Richard. "The Parties of the Right and the Republic." In *The Republic and the Civil War in Spain*, edited by Raymond Carr, 46–78. London: MacMillan, 1970.

Roca, Blas. *¿Cómo puede Ud. mejorar su situación? Respuestas a sus Preguntas*. Havana, 1939.

———. *La unidad vencerá al fascismo: Informe ante la Tercera Asamblea Nacional del Partido Comunista de Cuba, efectuada en la ciudad de Santa Clara los días 10, 11, 12, 13, 14 y 15 de Enero de 1939*. Havana: Ediciones Sociales, 1939.

Rock, David, ed. *Latin America in the 1940s: War and Postwar Transitions*. Berkeley: University of California Press, 1994.

Rodríguez, Elizabet, and Idania Trujillo, eds. *Papeles de familia: Compilación, presentación y notas*. Havana: Centro Cultural Pablo de la Torriente Brau, Ediciones La Memoria, 2006.

Rodríguez, Pedro Pablo. *De los dos Américas: Aproximaciones al pensamiento martiano*. Havana: Centro de Estudios Martianos, 2002.

———. "La idea de liberación nacional en José Martí." *Pensamiento Crítico* no. 49–50 (February–March 1971): 120–69.

Roig de Leuchsenring, Emilio. *Historia de la Enmienda Platt: Una interpretación de la realidad cubana*. 1935; Havana: Editorial de Ciencias Sociales, 1973.

———. *La España de Martí*. Havana: Editorial Páginas, 1938.

Rojas Blaquier, Angelina. *El Primer Partido Comunista de Cuba: Sus tácticas y estrategias*. Vol. 1, *1925–1935*. Santiago de Cuba: Editorial Oriente, 2005.

———. "Nicolás, a 50 años de un soneto histórico." *Periódico Cubarte*. 26 May 2009. http://archivo.cubarte.cult.cu/periodico/print/articulo/8133.html. Accessed 26 May 2016.

Rojas Blaquier, Angelina, and Núñez Machín, eds. *Asela mía: Cartas de Rubén Martínez Villena a su esposa*. Santiago de Cuba: Editorial Oriente, 2000.

Ruiz, Eduardo Ramón. *Cuba: The Making of a Revolution*. Amherst: University of Massachusetts Press, 1968.

Ryan, Lorraine. "The Sins of the Father: The Destruction of the Republican Family in Franco's Spain." *History of the Family* 14, no. 3 (2009): 245–52.

Sánchez Cobos, Amparo. *Sembrando Ideales: Anarquistas españoles en Cuba (1902–1925)*. Seville: Consejo Superior de Investigaciones Científicas, 2008.

Sánchez Noroña, Ivonne. "Chibás y Pepín Rivero en torno a la guerra civil española." *Perfiles de la Cultura Cubana: Revista del Instituto Cubano de Investigación Cultural Juan Marinello* 15. September–December 2014. www.perfiles.cult.cu/article_c.php?numero=15&article_id=350.

Schoonover, Thomas D. *Hitler's Man in Havana: Heinz Lüning and Nazi Espionage in Latin America*. Lexington: University of Kentucky Press, 2008.

Scott, William D. "Motivos of Translation: Nicolas Guillén and Langston Hughes." *CR: The New Centennial Review* 5, no. 2 (2005): 35–71.

Scott, William R. "Black Nationalism and the Italo-Ethiopian Conflict 1934–1936." *Journal of Negro History* 63, no. 2 (April 1978): 118–34.

———. *The Sons of Sheba's Race: African-Americans and the Italo-Ethiopian War, 1935–1941*. Bloomington: Indiana University Press, 1993.

Seidman, Michael. *Antifascismos, 1936–1945: La lucha contra el fascismo a ambos lados del Atlántico*. Translated by Hugo García. Madrid: Alianza, 2017.

———. *Transatlantic Antifascisms: From the Spanish Civil War to the End of World War II*. Cambridge: Cambridge University Press, 2017.

Selassie, Haile. "Appeal to the League of Nations." June 1936. www.mtholyoke.edu/acad/intrel/selassie.htm.

Shaffer, Kirwin. *Anarchism and Countercultural Politics in Early Twentieth-Century Cuba*. Gainesville: University Press of Florida, 2005.

———. "*Cuba para todos*: Anarchist Internationalism and the Cultural Politics of Cuban Independence, 1898–1925." *Cuban Studies* 31 (2000): 45–75.

———. "Freedom Teaching: Anarchism and Education in Early Republican Cuba, 1898–1925." *The Americas* 60, no. 2 (October 2003): 151–83.

———. "The Radical Muse: Women and Anarchism in Early-Twentieth-Century Cuba." *Cuban Studies* 34 (2003): 130–53.

Shinn, David H. Introduction to *The 1903 Skinner Mission to Ethiopia*, by Robert P. Skinner. 1903; Hollywood, Calif.: Tsehai, 2003.

Sims, Harold. "Cuba." In *Latin America between the Second World War and the Cold War, 1944–1948*, edited by Leslie Bethell and Ian Roxborough, 217–42. Cambridge: Cambridge University Press, 1992.

Sluga, Glenda. "Fascism and Anti-Fascism." In *The Palgrave Dictionary of Transnational History*, edited by Akira Iriye and Pierre-Yves Saunier, 381–82. Basingstoke: Palgrave, 2009.

Smith, Wayne S. *The Closest of Enemies: A Personal and Diplomatic Account of U.S.-Cuban Relations since 1957.* New York: W. W. Norton, 1987.

Soler Martínez, Rafael. "El Partido Bolchevique Leninista Cubano." *Estudios de historia social y económica de América* no. 15 (July–December 1997): 271–90.

Soto, Lionel. *La Revolución del 33.* Vol. 1–2. Havana: Editorial de Ciencias Sociales, 1977.

———. *La revolución precursora de 1933.* Havana: Editorial Si-Mar, 1995.

Stavans, Ilan, and Iván Jaksić. *What Is* la hispanidad? *A Conversation.* Austin: University of Texas Press, 2011.

Sternhell, Zeev. "Fascist Ideology." In *Fascism: A Reader's Guide,* edited by Walter Laqueur, 315–76. Berkeley: University of California Press, 1976.

Stubbs, Jean. *Tobacco on the Periphery: A Case Study in Cuban Labour History, 1860–1958.* Cambridge: Cambridge University Press, 1985.

Suárez Díaz, Ana. *Escapé de Cuba: El exilio neoyorquino de Pablo de la Torriente Brau (marzo, 1935–agosto, 1936).* Havana: Editorial de Ciencias Sociales, 2008.

———. "La Centuria Guiteras: De Nueva York al Frente de Jarama (1937)." *Caliban: Revista Cubana de Pensamiento e Historia* 7 (April–June 2010).

———, ed. *Retrospección Crítica de la Asamblea Constituyente de 1940.* Havana: Editorial de Ciencias Sociales, 2011.

Suchlicki, Jaime. *University Students and Revolution in Cuba, 1920–1968.* Coral Gables, Fla.: University of Miami Press, 1969.

Sullivan, Frances Peace. "Radical Solidarities: U.S. Capitalism, Community Building, and Popular Internationalism in Cuba's Eastern Sugar Zone, 1919–1939." PhD diss., New York University, 2012.

Tabares del Real, José A. "Fulgencio Batista y la Asamblea Constituyente de 1940." In *Retrospección Crítica de la Asamblea Constituyente de 1940,* edited by Ana Suárez Díaz, 47–59. Havana: Editorial de Ciencias Sociales, 2011.

———. *La revolución del 30: Sus dos últimos años.* Havana: Editorial de Ciencias Sociales, 1975.

Tarrow, Sidney. *Power in Movement: Social Movements and Contentious Politics.* 2nd ed. Cambridge: Cambridge University Press, 1998.

Tennant, Gary Andrew. "Dissident Cuban Communism: The Case of Trotskyism, 1932–1965." PhD diss., University of Bradford, 1999. www.marxists.org/history/etol/document/fi/cuba/tennent/PhD/contents.html.

Thomas, Hugh. "Cuba: La revolución y sus raíces históricas." *Estudios Internacionales* 4, no. 16 (January–March 1971): 126–57.

———. *Cuba, or The Pursuit of Freedom.* New York: Da Capo Press, 1998.

Tilly, Charles, and Sidney Tarrow. *Contentious Politics.* Boulder, Colo.: Paradigm, 2007.

Tisa, John. *Recalling the Good Fight: An Autobiography of the Spanish Civil War.* South Hadley, Mass.: Bergin and Garvey, 1985.

———[unattributed]. *The Story of the Abraham Lincoln Battalion: Written in the Trenches of Spain.* New York: Friends of the Abraham Lincoln Battalion, 1937.

Torres Cuevas, Eduardo. *Historia de la masonería cubana: Seis ensayos.* Havana: Imagen Contemporanea, 2004.

———. "La masonería en Cuba durante la Primera República (1902–1933)." In *La masonería en la España del siglo XX.* Vol. 1, edited by José Antonio Ferrer Benimeli. Toledo: Centro de Estudios Históricos de la Masonería Española, 1996.

Torriente Brau, Pablo de la. *Adventuras del soldado desconocido Cubano.* Havana: Centro Cultural Pablo de la Torriente Brau, Ediciones La Memoria, 2000.

———. "América frente al fascismo." In *Cartas y crónicas*, 278–79. Havana: Ediciones La Memoria, Centro Cultural Pablo de la Torriente Brau, 1999.

———. "¡Arriba muchachos!" In *¡Arriba muchachos!*, edited by Emilio Hernández Valdés, 5–6. Havana: Centro Cultural Pablo de la Torriente Brau, Ediciones La Memoria, 2001.

———. *Cartas Cruzadas.* Edited by Víctor Casaus. Vol. 2. Havana: Ediciones La Memoria, Centro Cultural Pablo de la Torriente Brau, 2012.

———. *Cartas y crónicas de España.* Edited by Víctor Casaus. Havana: Centro Cultural Pablo de la Torriente Brau, Ediciones La Memoria, 1999.

———. "En el parapeto: Polémica con el enemigo." In *Cartas y crónicas*, 222–27.

———. "Hasta después de muerto . . . ." In Hernández Valdés, *¡Arriba muchachos!*, 16–17.

———. "La revolución española se refleja en Nueva York." In *Cartas y crónicas*, 269–77.

———. "Las mujeres contra Machado." In *Testimonios y reportajes*, edited by Emilio Hernández Valdés, 87–115. Havana: Centro Cultural Pablo de la Torriente Brau, Ediciones La Memoria, 2001.

———. "Me voy a España." In *Peleando con los milicianos*, 9–12. México, 1938. Havana: Ediciones Nuevo Mundo, 1962.

———. *Peleando con los milicianos.* México, 1938. Havana: Ediciones Nuevo Mundo, 1962.

———. "We Are from Madrid." In *Cartas y crónicas*, 238–44.

Torriente Brau, Zoe de la. "Pablo de la Torriente Brau." In *Papeles de familia: Compilación, presentación y notas*, edited by Elizabet Rodríguez and Idania Trujillo, 13–32. Havana: Centro Cultural Pablo de la Torriente Brau, Ediciones La Memoria, 2006.

Turton, Peter. *José Martí: Architect of Cuba's Freedom.* Avon: Bath Press, 1986.

Urcelay-Maragnès, Denise. *La leyenda roja: Los voluntarios cubanos en la guerra civil española.* León: Lobo Sapiens, 2011.

———. "Los voluntarios cubanos en la Guerra Civil Española (1936–1939): La leyenda roja." *Historia Social*, no. 63 (2009): 41–58.

Vera Jiménez, Fernando. "Cubanos en la Guerra Civil española. La presencia de voluntarios en las Brigadas Internacionales y el Ejército Popular de la República." *Revista Complutense de Historia de América* 25 (1999): 295–321.

Vergnon, Gilles. *L'antifascisme en France, de Mussolini à Le Pen.* Rennes: Presses Universitaires de Rennes, 2009.

Vials, Christopher. *Haunted by Hitler: Liberals, the Left and the Fight against Fascism in the United States.* Amherst: University of Massachusetts Press, 2014.

Villafranca, Felicia, ed. *Documentos de Cuba Republicana*. Havana: Instituto Cubano del Libro, 1972.

Vinyes, Ricard, Montse Armengou, and Ricard Belis. *Los niños perdidos del franquismo*. Barcelona: Debolsillo, 2003.

Vogeley, Nancy. "Spanish-Language Masonic Books Printed in the Early United States." *Early American Literature* 43, no. 2 (2008): 337–60.

Weber, Eugen. *Varieties of Fascism: Doctrines of Revolution in the Twentieth Century*. New York: Van Nostrand Reinhold, 1964.

Whitney, Robert. "The Architect of the Cuban State: Fulgencio Batista and Populism in Cuba, 1937–1940." *Journal of Latin American Studies* 32, no. 2 (May 2000): 435–59.

———. "Constitution of 1940." In *Cuba*, vol. 1. Detroit: Gale, Cengage Learning, 2012.

———. *State and Revolution in Cuba: Mass Mobilization and Political Change, 1920–1940*. Chapel Hill: University of North Carolina Press, 2001.

Yates, James. *Mississippi to Madrid: Memoir of a Black American in the Abraham Lincoln Brigade*. Seattle: Open Hand, 1989.

Young, Robert J. C. *Postcolonialism: An Historical Introduction*. Malden, Mass.: Blackwell, 2001.

Zeitlin, Maurice. "Political Generations in the Cuban Working Class." *American Journal of Sociology* 71, no. 5 (March 1966): 493–508.

Zimmermann, Adrian. "The International Labour Movement's Struggle Against Fascism: Some Starting Points for a Research Project in Transnational Labour History." Paper presented at the 10th European Social Science History Conference, Vienna, 23–26 April 2014. www.academia.edu/6802568.

Index

ABC (revolutionary society), 229n69; in Batista government, 47; Communist criticism of, 174; proto-fascism accusations against, 230n69; in Welles mediations, 40

Abeal, Victor, assassination of, 154

Abraham Lincoln Battalion (International Brigade XV), 94–95, 242n98; in Battle of Jarama, 99; Centuria Antonio Guiteras of, 95–98, 132, 134. *See also* International Brigades (IBs)

Abyssinia. *See* Ethiopia

activism: African American, 62; women's and children's, 104

activism, Cuban: AANPE's, 101–30; Communist, 3, 9, 11, 31, 41; continuity in, 206, 208, 211; diversity of, 94, 96; in exile, 77; familial consequences of, 105; following strike of 1935, 3, 11, 222n7; humanitarian, 102; interpersonal relationships of, 17; radicalization of, 27; reimagining of, 2; resilience of, 17; transformations to, 206; unity within, 2; water and fire metaphors for, 77; worker, 49–50

—anti-Batista, 47–53; among Republican volunteers, 95–96; Casuso's, 47–48; students', 48–49, 51; Trotskyists', 171

—anti-Machado, 28–29; Batista's, 231n87; Casuso's, 32–37, 209; at Club Mella, 93; Communist, 31, 41; deaths in, 39; exile for, 39–40; following Mella's death, 31; imprisonment for, 39; intellectuals', 31, 35; middle class in, 40; resilience in, 40; sabotage in, 37; students', 29–30, 31, 35–38; during Sumner mediation, 41; Torriente's, 32–37; of traditional political class, 31; in uprising of 1932, 139–40; vengeance in, 42

—black: for New Cuba, 60; pan-Africanism of, 60–61, 65, 141; rejection of strongmen, 59–60; renovation of, 60; support for Spanish Republic, 21, 73, 74–75, 142; transnational, 21, 60, 141–42. *See also* antifascism, Cuban: black

—domestic: antifascism and, 2, 16; International Communism and, 56; for New Cuba, 10, 16

—Spanish Republican, 76–100; continuity of struggle in, 94–100, 132–33, 142–43; opposition to Batista, 95–96; Torriente's, 76–87; transnational, 94, 132–41. *See also* antifascism, Cuban; Cuba, New

Adelante (periodical), 60, 68, 234n23; antifascism of, 66, 142, 251n43; on bombing of Ethiopia, 70; on Ethiopia, 65, 72; on indifference to fascism, 74; Spanish conflict in, 74

Africa: black nationhood in, 65; European colonization of, 64, 69. *See also* diaspora, black; Ethiopia

Afro-American (periodical), Hughes's writings for, 144

Agramonte, Ignacio, 87

Agramonte, Roberto, 88

Agrupación de Veteranos Internacionalistas Cubanos, 216

Agrupación Revolucionaria de Cuba, New Cuba proclamation, 44

Aguilar, Luis E., 232n106

211, 213–14; official status of, 186, 205; on "Old Spain," 12; and opposition to Franco, 95–96; organic nature of, 179; pan-Hispanic identity in, 17; popularity of, 187; in Republican army, 20; revolutionary ambiguity concerning, 218; role in Cuban politics, 19, 138, 184, 186; social/cultural progress in, 142; Spanish antifascists in, 201; Spanish Republican, 3, 14, 20, 91–92, 97, 104, 235n40; transnational, 8, 11, 20, 52, 131, 161, 162, 179, 216–17; Trostskyist, 170–72; unity in, 19, 21, 180–84; versus U.S. antifascism, 198–99; value for Revolution of 1959, 216; during World War II, 198–204

—black, 58–72, 131; African identity in, 144; anticolonialism in, 67, 69; of black diaspora, 17, 20, 60; defense of Spanish Republic, 21, 73, 74–75, 142; diasporic identity in, 17; diversity in, 234n22; fight against racism, 69; on global complacency, 72; on slavery, 68; transnational solidarity of, 146. See also activism, Cuban: black

—Communist, 9, 11, 12, 172–81, 191, 263n114; of Popular Front, 173, 179–81, 184; popular politics and, 138

—Masonic, 131, 147–61, 185, 194; moderate, 160; organizing in, 158; philosophical arguments for, 153–56; religious arguments for, 153–54; self-defense arguments for, 150, 156, 157, 158–59, 185; during World War II, 201

antifascism, transnational, 8; AANPE in, 125; aid to Spanish children, 196; of black Cubans, 146; in Cuban activism, 8, 11, 20, 52, 131, 161, 179, 216–17; diversity of, 16; divisions within, 182; as global left, 17; goals and values of, 15; local antifascism and, 16; networks for, 92; pan-Africanist, 60–61; scholarship on,

225n67; support for Spanish Republic, 129. See also transnationalism

anti-imperialism, Cuban, 9, 10, 30; during Government of 100 Days, 45; in Machado activism, 41; military, 138. See also Liga Anti-Imperialista de Cuba

Aponte, José Antonio, 64, 66; Rebellion of 1812, 63–64

Argote-Freyre, Frank, 189

Arocena, Berta, 112, 124, 186

Arredondo, Alberto, 68, 69

Asociación Cultural de Ex-Combatientes Antifascistas, 201; anarchists in, 202, 267n75; members of, 267n75

Asociación de Amigos de las Brigadas Internacionales (AABI), 218

Asociación de Auxilio al Niño del Pueblo Español (AANPE), 101–30; activist/charitable balance for, 106, 114, 123; advertising posters of, 108, 114; anarchist influence on, 103–4; antifascism of, 104, 106–11, 113, 123, 125; anti-Nationalist propaganda of, 110; Batista's banning of, 102; building of solidarity, 114–15, 117; Camagüey delegation, 109, 127; campaign accomplishments of, 122–29; campaign finances of, 117–21, 247nn79–81; centralized fund-raising, 119–21, 247n81; children's committees, 115–16, 130; Christian imperative of, 107, 109–11, 113; clothing drives of, 111, 123–24, 126–27, 238n111; Comité Directivo, 107, 117, 122; on cultural responsibility, 113; definition of fascism, 127; demoralization affecting, 120; diversity of supporters, 107; donors to, 117–21; end of, 196–97; at end of Civil War, 195–96; expenses of, 118, 119; founding of, 20, 101, 129, 243n3; Freemasons in, 185;

207, 211; deportations under, 265n40; discontent under, 188; election of, 189–90; Falange and, 191, 199–200; Franco and, 80, 141, 175; inauguration (1940), 199; ouster of Grau, 46; political legitimacy of, 190, 191, 204–5; populism of, 204–5; pro-labor policies of, 187, 264n24; reformist stance of, 205; rise to power, 1, 9, 19, 44, 46, 76, 105; rivalry with Grau, 189; and F. D. Roosevelt, 191–92; during Sergeants' Revolt, 43–44, 45; social programs of, 187; strongman governance of, 46, 187; understanding of popular politics, 188; veterans supporting, 214–15; visit to U.S., 192. *See also* antifascism, Cuban: anti-Batista

Battle of Brunete (Spanish Civil War), 100

Battle of Jarama (Spanish Civil War): commemoration of (2011), 218; Cuban volunteers in, 98–100, 121, 242n115

Baumann, Gerold Gino, 240n68

Bayo, Alberto, 208, 209

Bay of Pigs invasion (1961), 208

Beals, Carleton, 28, 140, 226n11

Black Legend, Spanish, 14, 18

Blanco, Edelmiro, 171

Blanco, Tomás, 110–11, 245n37

Bofill, Jaime, work with Torriente, 83, 86, 101, 239n44, 243n1

Bohemia (weekly magazine): Chibás's writings for, 175; coverage of Hitler, 54, 55; on Mussolini, 54; Torriente's writings for, 78, 83

Bolaños, María Josefa, 126

Boletín Información y Propaganda (FGAC publication), 163

The Book of the XV Brigade, 94–95

Borroto Mora, Tomás, "Sintesis," 69–70

Brau, Graciela, 33

Brau, Salvador, 33

Bray, Mark, *Antifa*, 217, 270n51

Brazil, Vargas coup d'état in, 152

Brea Landestoy, Juan Ramón, 171; Communist harassment of, 172

Bronfman, Alejandra, 74

Broué, Pierre, 7

Browder, Earl, 241n84; Cuban Communists and, 92

Brunet, Arsenio, 132

businesses, Cuban, support for Spanish Republic, 91–92

Cabarrocas, Julio Constantino, 201

Caden, Gert, 201

Caffery, Jefferson, 57, 233n9

Cahartre-Evre-Loir camp, Spanish refugee children in, 197

Cala Reyes, Manuel (Niño Cala), 214

Calvo (Nationalist spokesman), 84–85

Camp de Gurs (France), Cuban volunteers in, 136, 250n15

Cárdenas, Lázaro, 240n53; Batista and, 188, 191; welcoming of Republican children, 115

Carmona de Gordón Ordas, Consuelo, 112, 113, 126

Carpentier, Alejo, 63

Carrera Justiz, Pablo, 186

Casa de la Cultura y Asistencia Social (Cuba), 184; AANPE display at, 127; support of Spanish Republic, 91

Casa-Escuela Pueblo de Cuba (Sitges, Spain), 102, 124–26, 248n99; Club Mella visit to, 125; contributors to, 124, 125; Masonic support of, 160

Casaus, Víctor, 221n3

Castro, Fidel: Casuso and, 22, 210–11, 212; conflict with Masferrer, 215; *Granma* expedition, 208, 216; Moncada barracks attack, 214; with Ortodoxos, 208

Casuso, Teresa "Teté," 19; activism in 1950s, 208; Alzheimer's of, 219; anti-Batista activism, 47–48; anticommunism of, 114; anti-Machado activism, 32–37, 209; on

child-saving movements: international, 102; Progressive, 102, 103, 243n8. *See also* Asociación de Auxilio al Niño del Pueblo Español

China: Cuban antifascism and, 237n79; Japanese occupation of, 73

Christianity: in AANPE rhetoric, 107, 109–11, 113; as avenue to peace, 245n33; in Ethiopia, 63; Marxism and, 112. *See also* Catholic Church; Vatican

Círculo Español Socialista (CES), support for Spanish Republic, 91

Círculo Republicano Español (Cuba): in FDE, 181; founding of, 9; support for Spanish Republic, 91

Civil War, Spanish, 5, 20; aid to children in, 101–30; as anticolonial struggle, 142; antifascist nostalgia for, 217; Battle of Brunete, 100; Battle of Jarama, 98–100, 121, 242n115; black diaspora and, 75; black volunteers for, 75, 144–45; continuity of struggle in, 94–100; domestic causes of, 7; effect on Cuban Left, 162, 163–64; Ethiopian volunteers in, 75; fall of Barcelona in, 195; fatalities of, 7; foreign fascist aid to, 6–7, 84, 85–86, 152; foreign volunteers in, 7; Masonic martyrs in, 153–54; *milicianos* of, 83, 87, 111; Nationalist shelling in, 83; Non-Intervention Agreement for, 6–7, 91, 152, 187–88; Old versus New Spain in, 14; PCE in, 100, 135; Puerto Rican volunteers in, 89; Republican defeat in, 126, 127–28, 135–36; Republican losses in, 120; significance for Spanish America, 80; soldiers' interchange in, 83–84; Spanish American volunteers in, 89–90; Spanish Cubans and, 74; Torriente's journalism on, 80–81, 83–85; Torriente's participation in, 83–87; U.S. volunteers in, 89; and world war threat, 152. *See also* Spanish Republic, Second; volunteers, Cuban

clases populares, Cuban, Batista and, 188, 189, 191–92, 205

Clement XII, Pope, "In Eminenti," 148

Club Atenas, 59, 60; support for AANPE, 121

Club Cubano Julio Antonio Mella (Barcelona), 93; transnational exchanges at, 93, 138; visit to Casa-Escuela, 125, 248n102

Club Cubano Julio Antonio Mella (New York City), 10, 11; anti-Machado struggle at, 93; celebration of Guiteras, 97; Communist recruitment at, 137–38; Odio Pérez in, 140; pro-Republican recruitment at, 92; refugees from Batista at, 93; Torriente in, 40, 229n64

Club José Martí (New York City), 77

CMCD (Havana radio), anti-Freemason broadcasts, 157–58

Cold War, Batista coup during, 209

colonialism: racism as, 62–63; rescue of Ethiopia from, 62; slavery in, 68

colonialism, Spanish: as forerunner of fascism, 176; of Old Cuba, 24

Comité Alemán Antifascista (Havana), 201

Comité Central de las Organizaciones Hebreas de Cuba, 200

Comité Nacionalista Español de Cuba (CNE), 14; anti-Freemason broadcasts, 157–58

Comité Pro-Abisinia (Cuba), 66, 73

Comité Pro-Repatriación de Cubanos en Francia, 193–94

Committee for Spanish Children (Paris), 107, 127

Committee of Proletarian Defense, 51–52

communism: black radicalism and, 74; Cuban Freemasons' opposition to, 155–56; as Judeo-Masonic, 149

Communist International (Comintern), 222n8; antifascism of, 172; Cuban domestic problems and, 96; goals of,

Communist International (Comintern)
(*continued*)
91; organizing of Republican
volunteers, 90–91, 137–38, 173, 180;
Popular Front of, 3, 55–56, 57, 180;
Seventh World Congress (1953), 56;
Third Period, 50, 56, 57, 173, 180;
transnational antifascism of, 3
Communist Party, Cuban. *See* Partido
Comunista de Cuba
Communist Party, French, 89
Communist Party of the United States
of America (CPUSA), pro-Spanish
Republican support of, 92
Communists, Cuban: alienation of
leftists, 172, 173; alliance with
anarchists, 168; alliance with Batista,
173, 180, 189, 190, 205, 260n59;
anarcho-syndicalists and, 11;
antifascism of, 9, 11, 12, 138, 172–81,
184, 191, 263n114; coalition building
by, 173, 180–81; conception of fascism,
173; conflict with anarchists, 41–42;
conflict with Trotskyists, 50–51, 172,
265n39; on domestic fascism, 175;
domestic political groups and, 57, 58;
effect of anarchism on, 163; on
Falange, 174; on Italo-Ethiopian War,
20, 21, 56–57, 74, 180; nationalists'
distrust of, 173; on New Cuba, 178,
179; Polar Stadium assembly, 136;
records of, 241n73; F. D. Roosevelt
and, 192; on Soviet Union, 178, 179; on
Spanish colonialism, 176; on Spanish
Nationalists, 176; in strike of 1935, 52;
support for Chinese revolutionaries,
237n79; on threat of Old Cuba, 177;
transnationalism of, 179; and world
war threat, 193. *See also* Partido
Comunista de Cuba; Popular Front,
Cuban Communist
Confederación de Trabajadores de Cuba
(CTC), Batista and, 190
Confederación Nacional del Trabajo
(CNT): alliance with UGT, 169–70;

anarchism of, 164, 168; FGAC and,
170; New York members of, 169
Confederación Nacional Obrera de
Cuba (CNOC): conflict with FOH,
50; in strike of 1925, 32; in strike of
1935, 52
Consejo Nacional de la Infancia
Evacuada (Barcelona), 127
Corcho Díaz, Manuel, 213
Corzo, María Luisa, 122
Crisis (NAACP journal), 75
Crowder, Enoch H., reforms to Cuba,
25, 26
Cuba: in Allied Forces, 192; Axis spies
in, 200; capitalist exploitation of,
66, 67; circular migration in, 131;
civilizing rhetoric for, 69;
Commission on Foreign Relations,
159; constituent assembly (1939),
205; constitution (first), 24;
constitution of 1940, 205–6, 268n88;
Cuba y la defensa, 251n25; Department
of State, 136; European fascist threat
to, 12–13; Falange affiliates in, 14;
fascist agents in, 166; foreign labor
in, 231n94, 255n110; *gangsterismo* in,
208, 215, 269n32; as gateway to
Americas, 13; during Great Depression,
28–31, 40, 42; indigenous mortality
in, 68; instability of 1920s, 25;
internment of foreign nationals, 200;
Nationalists in, 14, 157, 199; "national
personality" of, 255n110; Nazi agents
in, 13, 200; obligatory military
service in, 200; pro-Republican
Spaniards in, 9; relations with Soviet
Union, 200; Republic of 1902, 206;
Spanish immigrants in, 17; special
relationship with Spain, 17–18,
78, 90, 107, 111–13, 128, 145–476;
strongman governance in, 2, 9, 12, 79,
80; Supreme Council of, 156–57; ties
to Mexico, 188, 191; U.S. intervention
in, 19, 24, 25–27; U.S. loan to, 25–26;
during World War II, 13, 198–204.

Directorio Estudiantil Universitario
(DEU), 30; AIE split from, 38;
imprisonment of members, 37;
political program of, 37; in Sumner
mediation, 41
Directorio Social Revolucionario
"Renacimiento," 60
Domenech, Francisco, 102
Domingo Cuadriello, Jorge, 215,
230n69, 262n106; on AANPE, 102; on
anarchist veterans, 267n75; *El exilio
republicano español en Cuba*, 201
Durruti, Buenaventura, 217

economy, Cuban: under Batista, 188;
crisis of 1920s, 25–26; during
Government of 100 Days, 45
education, Cuban: racially segregated,
144; U.S. influence on, 243n9
Eliseo, Guillermo Enrique (William H.
Ellis), 65
Ellis, Keith, 252n48
Ethiopia: as "African Jerusalem," 61;
Aponte rebellion and, 63; bombing
of, 70, 71, 75, 85, 236n75; capitalist
exploitation of, 67; Christianity in,
63; Cuban Garveyites on, 66; Cuban
knowledge of, 58; defeat of, 72–73;
global indifference toward, 73;
redemption of black race, 61;
resonance for diaspora, 61;
sovereignty of, 61, 64; symbolism
of, 61–62, 63, 66, 179; Treaty of
Friendship with Italy (1928), 72.
See also Italo-Ethiopian War, Second
Ethiopians: accusations of decapitations
against, 70, 236n71; humanity of, 70

Fabal, Gustavo, 112, 247n90
Facetas de Actualidad Española
(periodical), 10, 88; on Sánchez
Menéndez, 100
Falange Española, 5–6; Batista and, 191,
199–200; in Cuba, 14, 174; under
Decreto No. 3411, 199; *hispanismo* of,

19; influence in Americas, 13–14;
JONS and, 5–6; journalistic exposés
of, 14; Masonic members of, 160;
neocolonialism of, 14–15; neo-
imperialism of, 19; propaganda in
Americas, 14; support for Nationalists,
91; *tribunal de urgencia* on, 200
Falcoff, Mark, 89–90
Farber, Samuel, 265n41
fascism: Argentine, 222n14; attacks on
exploited people, 144; authoritarian
male leadership of, 4; "chosen
people" of, 4; as colonialism, 62–63;
Comintern policy on, 172; definitions
of, 3–4, 9, 83; democratic antidote to,
143–44; dictatorship and, 8; emotional
experience of, 4; empirical
comparisons for, 222n11; failure to
contain, 73–74; global struggle
against, 89; imperialism and, 8, 9;
international threat of, 79; Japanese,
73–74, 166; LAI on, 7, 223n34;
military tactics of, 155; nationalism
of, 165; parallel government of, 4;
proletariat alliance against, 172;
racist, 62–63, 144; as reactionary, 14;
scholarship on, 3, 222n12; in South
America, 152, 222n14; threat to Latin
America, 143
fascism, Cuban: censorship of, 200; in
dictatorship, 8; domestic, 174, 175;
foreign, 173–74, 199; imperialism in,
8, 9; nationalism in, 165; Spanish
fascism and, 175–76
fascism, European: American fear of,
224n51; Cuban anarchists on, 197;
Cuban attacks on, 4; propaganda in
Americas, 12, 14; rise of, 54; versus
Spanish fascism, 176; threat to Cuba,
12–13; Torriente's concern over, 79;
workers' struggle against, 10
fascism, German, threat to Cuba,
177–78. *See also* Nazism, German
Fascism, Italian: barbarism of, 71–72;
capitalist exploitation in, 67;

civilizing rhetoric of, 68–69, 70; Cuban opposition to, 8; Cuban-U.S. relations and, 66–67; expansionism of, 57; German Nazism and, 3; PCC on, 56; technical perfection of, 67

fascism, Spanish: authoritarian nationalism of, 6; Catholicism in, 6; as composite of enemies, 14; Cuban anarchists on, 165; Cuban fascism and, 175–76; versus European fascism, 176; military dictatorship of, 4; neocolonialist, 15; traditionalists', 175, 195. *See also* Nationalists, Spanish

Faupel, Wilhelm von, Spanish American intelligence operation, 13

Federación Anarquista Ibérica (FAI), 172; FGAC and, 170

Federación de Grupos Anarquistas de Cuba (FGAC), 163, 224n44; anticommunist manifesto of, 41; and antifascist left, 181–82; CNT and, 170; transnationalism of, 169

Federación de Juventudes Libertarias de Cuba (FJLC), 165; founding members of, 258n12

Federación Estudiantil Universitaria (FEU), 183

Federación Médica Cubana, on Machado, 139

Federación Obrera de La Habana (FOH): anarcho-syndicalism of, 26; conflict with CNOC, 50; in general strike, 41, 52; Trotskyist leadership of, 41

Feria Pérez, Armentino, 212, 269n22

Fernández, Frank, 258n12

Fernández, James D., 93

Fernández Ortega, Eufemio, 212–13, 269n22

Fernández Sánchez, Leonardo, 137

Ferrer, Ada, 63

Figueroa, Isidro, 36

Ford, James W., 92; anti-imperialism of, 178; on de Armas, 99; on Soviet Union, 178; on U.S.-Cuban relations, 192; on volunteer characteristics, 132

Formación de Excombatientes Antifascistas, 202, 212

France: concentration camps in, 136, 193–95, 196, 197, 216, 218, 250n15; provisional government of, 200; Spanish Republican warnings to, 254n91

Franco, Francisco, 15; anti-Freemasonry of, 156; Batista and, 80, 141, 175; Cuban antifascism and, 95–96; Falange support for, 6; family policy of, 243n8; German/Italian support for, 6, 12; *hispanismo* of, 19; military aircraft of, 114; neo-imperialism of, 19; overthrow of legitimate government, 143; Union Square rally opposing, 1, 78–79, 238n12

Franco, José Luciano, 67, 142; on capitalism, 66; on Italian Fascists, 68–69; publication of *Adelante*, 72–73

Franqui, Carlos, 261n69

Freemasonry: aid to Spanish Republic, 159; authoritarian opposition to, 148; belief in reason, 155; Catholic prohibitions on, 148; challenge to secular rulers, 148; fascist persecution of, 149–50; fight for civilization, 155; ideological plurality of, 194; political involvement tradition, 150; as pro-democratic, 150; respect for legal government, 150–51; Russian opposition to, 150

Freemasonry, Cuban: in AANPE, 185; aid to Spanish children, 160; aid to Spanish Masons, 159; in ANAPE, 183; anticommunism of, 155–56; conception of Christianity, 153; conciliation with Franco, 194–95; condemnation of Vatican, 153; dissension within, 160–61; Falange members, 160; and fall of Spanish Republic, 194–95; fascists in, 160;

Llera de Sánchez Govín, Evangelina de la, 186

López, Alfredo, 39

López, Kathleen, 237n79

López Civeira, Francisca, 8, 260n59

López Rodríguez, José, 185

Low, Mary, 171, 172

Lüning, Heinz August, 13, 200

Maceo, Antonio, 73

Machadato: executions under, 39; exiles from, 39–40, 43; mainstream opposition to, 37; PCC collaboration with, 56, 181; police violence in, 39, 41; resistance to, 29–48; rise of, 28–32; uprising against (1932), 139–40; Welles mediation and, 40–42

Machado, Gerardo: antifascist opposition to, 8; commemoration of fall, 82; and death of Mella, 23; downfall of, 42–43, 60, 76, 82; early support for, 227n17; elections of, 19, 28, 35; fall of, 1, 9; loss of control, 40; military rule of, 37; Mussolini and, 227n31; nationalism of, 28; PCC collaboration with, 56; "Platform of Regeneration," 28; reform rhetoric of, 28, 29; secret police of, 39; strongman governance of, 29. See also activism, Cuban: anti-Machado

El Machete (Communist periodical), sponsorship of Torriente, 83

Marinello, Juan, 10, 35, 77, 221n3; and AANPE, 128, 186; Communism of, 249n118, 264n8; on ties to Spain, 177

Martí, José, 18, 24; activists' adoption of, 225n77; on aid to children, 107; La Edad de Oro, 33; legacy of, 225n79; Spanish characterizations of, 73; Torriente and, 128

Martin, Fredericka, 133, 136, 251n25

Martínez, Armando, 112

Martínez, Carlos, 77, 78

Martínez, Georgina, 109

Martínez, Octavio S., 194; on Republican violence, 110

Martínez, Vicente, 70–71

Martínez de Marcilla, Don Diego, 154

Martínez Marquez, Guillermo, 186

Marxism: black radicalism and, 74; Christianity and, 112

Masas (LAI periodical), 9–10, 11, 137, 223n34; domestic problems in, 30

Masferrer, Rolando, 214, 269n32; conflict with Castro, 215; paramilitary gang of, 215

Masons. See antifascism, Cuban: Masonic; Freemasonry

Mastellari Maecha, Pía, 135

May Day unrest (Cuba, 1930), 32

Mayobre, Fancisco, 184

Mazas Garbayo, Gonzalo, 83

McCarthyism, 198

media, Cuban: as fascist, 167; Hitler in, 54, 55; Spanish Republic in, 55

Mediodía (periodical), 10; on AANPE, 107; on Batista, 191; on Club Mella, 93; on fascists in Cuba, 174; on Ford, 92; Haile Selassie interview in, 142; homage to Torriente in, 88; Hughes's writings for, 144–45; Torriente's writings for, 83; world events in, 142. See also Guillén, Nicolás

Mella, Julio Antonio, 47; anarchists' mentorship of, 103; antifascism and, 7–9, 19, 24; collaboration with leftists, 96; on dictatorship, 9; early life of, 23–24; legacy of, 31; as martyr, 23, 38, 39, 45–46; Marxism of, 29–30; murder of, 23, 24, 30–31, 226n1; repatriation of remains, 45–46; student activism of, 29; transnational identities of, 24; in Veterans and Patriots Movement, 29

Mendieta, Carlos: anti-Machado activism of, 31, 140; Machado's capture of, 37; presidency of, 46–47

Revolution of 1933, 32, 167, 174; anarchists on, 167; Batista's beliefs and, 187; change following, 206. *See also* Government of 100 Days

Revolution of 1959, 184; antifascist legacy of, 22, 212; Casuso and, 210–11; defeat of Batista, 207; Generation of 1930s and, 208, 212, 216; Spanish Republican ideal for, 207–8

Reyes Spíndola, Octavio, 190

Riestra, Genaro, 199

Ríos, Fernando de los, 120; New York reception for, 141; at Polar Stadium event, 127, 128–29

Rivera, Diego, 23

Rivero, Don Nicolás, 175

Rivero Setien, Manuel, 212, 215; death of, 213

Rivero y Alonso, José Ignacio "Pepín," 175

Roa, Raúl, 35, 88; in AIE, 38; Communism of, 211; founding of ORCA, 77; imprisonment of, 38; on Lípiz Rodríguez, 219; "Rafael Trejo y el 30 de septiembre," 38; on Soviet Union, 268n17; on Torriente, 82, 87

Roca, Blas (Francisco Calderio), 174–75, 185; depiction of Cuban fascism, 177–78; on FDR, 192; on "Soviet Cuba," 178

Rodó, José Enrique, *Ariel*, 18

Rodríguez, Avelino, 122

Rodríguez, Carlos Rafael, 88, 185

Rodríguez, Gustavo, 132

Rodríguez, José López, 8

Rodríguez, Luis Felipe, 117

Rodríguez, Pedro Pablo, 18

Rodríguez Barco, Berta, 115

Rodríguez Malagamba, Gustavo, 202

Rodríguez Miranda, Augusto, 185

Rodríguez y Serrano, Ana, 121

Roig de Leuchsenring, Emilio, 10, 88, 101; on Martí, 249n119

Rome, fascist violence of, 70

Romero Salicrup, Manasés, 213

Roosevelt, Franklin Delano: antifascist fight of, 191; Batista and, 191–92; "Good Neighbor" policy of, 40; U.S. imperialism and, 230n70; view of Mexico, 188

Roosevelt, Theodore, 40; Menelik II and, 65

Ropero Invernal del Niño Español (AANPE, 1937–38), 123–24, 126–27; food supplies in, 127, 248n111

Rufo, Angel, 121

Rumbos Nuevos (anarchist periodical), 197–98

Rural Guard, Cuban, 37

Russia, opposition to Freemasonry in, 150

Russian Revolution, 25; Cuban Left on, 162

Sabas Alomá, Mariblanca, 117

Saenz, José M., "Menelik y Cuba," 65

Salas Aranda, Mariono, 72; on Fascist state, 251n43; support for Spanish Republic, 142–44

Sánchez Menéndez, Alberto, death in battle, 100

Schoonover, Thomas D., 224n51

Scott, William R., 75

Segura, Doña Isabel de, 154

Sergeants' Revolt (1933), 43–44. *See also* Revolution of 1933

Sierra de Guadarrama (Spain), Torriente at, 83

Sims, Harold, 264n24

slavery: in colonization, 68; under Haile Selassie, 235n57

Smith, Wayne, 207

Sociedad de Marineros Pescadores de Batabano, donation to AANPE, 121

Sociedades Hispanas Confederadas de Ayuda a España (New York City), 93

societies, black Cuban, 58–60, 234n22; discontent in, 59

Soler, Oscar, 133–34; in Camp de Gurs, 136; transnational identity of, 136–37

South America, fascism in, 152

Soviet Union: Cuban Communists on, 178, 179; Cuban relations with, 200; and Italo-Ethiopian War, 57, 233n12; pact with Nazis (1939), 265n41; PCC on, 57–58

Spain: as antifascist model, 177; Cuban antifascism and, 2, 217–18; as Cuban motherland, 18–19, 78, 90; disaster relief for Cuba, 111; domestic problems of, 89; Great Depression in, 5; loss of colonies, 5, 18; Nazi influence in, 13, 75; neutrality in World War II, 5; as proxy for Ethiopia, 75, 141

Spain, New: generational interpretation of, 104; New Cuba and, 100

Spain, Old: association with Nationalism, 143, 165; Cuban antifascists on, 12

Spanish America: relationship with motherland, 79; significance of Spanish Civil War for, 80; strongman governments of, 79

Spanish-American War, U.S. imperialism in, 18, 64

Spanish Empire, pan-Hispanic identity in, 17–18

Spanish Republic, First (1873–75), 4–5

Spanish Republic, Second (1931–39), 5; Anglo-American aid to, 85–86; black Cubans support for, 21, 73, 74–75, 142; "bourgeoisie," 172; children's health under, 108; Cuban anarchists on, 165; Cuban antifascists' support for, 3, 14, 91–92, 97, 104, 235n40; in Cuban media, 55; Cuban opinions on, 223n33; Cuban unity and, 21; defeat of, 126, 127–28, 193–98; as democracy, 150, 151–52, 156; establishment of, 9; fascism in, 165; French Communist aid to, 89; global support for, 128–29; influence on Cuba, 9, 206; influence on Cuban constitution, 268n88; inspiration for Revolution of 1959,

207–8; legitimacy of, 143, 150–51, 175; Masonic philosophical arguments for, 153–56; Masons' belief in, 149, 150; Ministerio de Instrucción Pública, 127, 248n99; Nationalist attack on, 74; as New Spain, 14; Union Square rally for, 1, 78–79, 238n12. See also Civil War, Spanish; volunteers, Cuban

Spanish Supreme Council, on Spanish democracy, 150

Stalinism, 260n52; Cuban Left on, 162

strikes: following Machado departure, 42; Havana bus drivers', 49; during Mendieta presidency, 49–50. See also general strike

Suárez Díaz, Ana, 229n64, 243n1, 249n118

Suárez Solis, Rafael, 245n33

Suchlicki, Jaime, 231n87, 232n106

sugar industry, Cuban: Batista and, 191; crises in, 34; effect of Hawley-Smoot Act on, 30

Tabares del Real, José A., 187, 227n17

Tacón, Miguel, 176

Tafari, Ras. See Haile Selassie, Emperor

Témime, Emile, 7

Thomas, Hugh, 215

Tiempo en Cuba (newspaper), 215

¡Tierra! (anarchist periodical), 11

Tisa, John: on Club Julio Mela, 93; on Cuban volunteers, 94–95; on de Armas, 98, 99; editorship of *Volunteer for Liberty*, 242n98; *The Story of the Abraham Lincoln Battalion*, 242n98; on volunteer language problems, 132

Torres Cuevas, Eduardo, 252n57; on example of Spain, 177

Torriente Brau, Pablo de la, 10, 19; in AIE, 38; anti-Batista activism of, 140; antifascism of, 76, 79, 84–85; anti-Machado activism of, 32–37; celebration of Guiteras, 97; childhood activism of, 34–35; commemorations of, 88, 96, 129; core identity of, 78; courtship of Casuso, 33; in Cuban domestic struggle, 20; Cuban identity of, 84; death of, 20, 87, 105; definition of fascism, 83; early life and family of, 33–34; exchange with Nationalists, 84–85; exile in New York, 40, 52, 76–82, 90, 229n64; first meeting with Casuso, 33; imprisonment of, 38; leadership of, 35; legacy of, 87–88; letters from Spain, 86–87, 239n44; love of music, 85–86; marriage to Casuso, 48, 51, 228n35; Martí and, 128; as martyr, 88, 101, 128; and Mella, 39, 45–46; on military power, 79; multinational background of, 34; pessimism concerning Civil War, 86–87; on post-1935 politics, 76; resilience of, 48; return to Cuba, 43; on revolutionary Mexico, 240n53; sense of duty, 79; during Sergeants' Revolt, 43; in Spanish Civil War, 83–87; on Spanish Republic, 1–2; in strike of 1935, 52–53; as transnational activist-writer, 80; transnationalism of, 87; transnational readership of, 83; travel to Spain, 81–82, 83; at Union Square rally, 1, 78–79, 238n12; volunteer recruitment and, 137; writings for *Bohemia*, 78; writings from Spain, 80–81, 83–85, 101, 130; writings in New York, 239n42. Works: "¡Arriba muchachos!," 36–37; *Aventuras del soldado desconocido Cubano*, 82, 239n36; "Las mujeres contra Machado," 228n46; "We Are from Madrid," 231n97

Torriente Brau, Zoe de la, 34; on Mella, 39; on Pablo's death, 87; on Pablo's marriage, 228n36; on strike of 1935, 52; on unrest of 1930, 36

Torriente Garrido, Félix de la, 33

transnationalism, Cuban: anarchists', 164–65; of black Cubans, 21, 60, 141–42; Communist organizing and, 137; in Cuban identity, 21, 131; domestic aspects of, 63; Freemasons', 21, 148; multiple sources of, 131; pan-Africanist, 60–61, 141; the personal/political in, 105; of Republican volunteers, 131, 132–41. *See also* antifascism, transnational

Trejo González, Rafael: death of, 36, 37, 38, 228n45; as martyr, 38, 39

Trotskyists, Cuban: AIE and, 50–51; anti-Batista activism of, 171; antifascism of, 170–72; conflict with Communists, 50–51, 172, 265n39; defeat of, 170–71; of Guantánamo, 171; leadership of FOH, 41; in strike of 1935, 170, 171, 232n122. *See also* Oposición Comunista de Cuba

Unión General de Trabajadores (UGT), 169–70

Unión Nacionalista (UN), 31; decimation of, 36; military allegiance to, 47; opposition to Grau, 46; Rebellion of Río Verde, 37, 38; strikebreakers, 49; in Welles mediations, 40

United States: entry into World War II, 198; influence in, 174, 243n9; intervention in Cuba, 19, 24, 25–27; loan to Cuba, 25–26; relationship with Batista, 188–89. *See also* imperialism, U.S.; intervention, U.S.

"The Universal Ethiopian Anthem," 66, 235n50

Universal Negro Improvement Association (UNIA), 65

University of Havana: Alma Mater statue, 54; decree of autonomy for, 47–48, 232n106; representation in AANPE, 186; student unrest at, 29–30, 35–37, 54

Urcelay-Maragnès, Denise, 91, 240n68, 260n59

Valdés Cofiño, "Don" Julio, 138
Valdés Daussá, Ramiro, 81, 197; murder
 of, 209; and refugee children, 122;
 and relief for Barcelona, 195
Vargas, Getúlio, coup d'état of, 152
Varona, Enrique José, 35
Vatican, and invasion of Ethiopia, 70,
 71, 236n65. *See also* Catholic Church
veterans, Cuban (Spanish Civil War):
 commemoration in Spain, 216;
 execution of, 212–13, 269n22;
 obituaries of, 219; official records of,
 212–16, 218–19, 240n68, 268n20,
 269n22; pro-Batista, 214–15;
 revolutionary erasure of, 218–19;
 training of revolutionaries, 208, 209,
 216. *See also* volunteers, Cuban
Veterans and Patriots Movement
 (Cuba), 31; defeat of, 27–28; rebellion
 of 1924, 27; repression of, 29
veterans' organizations (Spanish Civil
 War), antifascist, 201–2
Vincent, Sténio, 166
Volunteer for Liberty (Spanish
 Republican periodical), 88, 95, 138
volunteers, Cuban (Spanish Civil War),
 20; in Abraham Lincoln Battalion, 94,
 95; anti-Batista, 94–95; in Battle of
 Jarama, 98–100, 121, 242n115;
 bilingual, 132–34; black, 75, 144–45;
 blending in with Spaniards, 134–35;
 in Centuria Antonio Guiteras, 95–98,
 132, 134; Comintern support for, 90;
 Communist organization of, 90–91,
 137–38, 173, 180; continuity of
 domestic struggle, 132–33;
 coordinated mobilization of, 92;
 deaths of, 100; departure for Spain,
 88, 138; diversity among, 94–95; in
 French concentration camps, 136,
 193–95, 216, 218, 250n15;
 intelligentsia among, 132; in
 International Brigades, 88, 89;
 medical skills of, 132; military men
 among, 138–39, 250n22; music of,

132; positions held by, 88; rapport
 with villagers, 134–45; in regular
 Spanish army, 135; restrictions on, 91;
 return from Spain, 135–36, 193, 216;
 Spanish Cubans, 89; support
 networks for, 91–92; Torriente's
 inspiration for, 90; as translators, 21,
 132–34; transnationalism of, 131,
 132–41; veterans, 260n59. *See also*
 Civil War, Spanish; Spanish Republic;
 veterans' organizations

wars of independence, Cuban, 24;
 causes of, 64; of 1868, 142–43; of
 1895–98, 15, 64; Italo-Ethiopian wars
 and, 64–65, 67; Masons in, 147–48;
 Spanish solidarity and, 111–12;
 veterans of, 27
Welles, Sumner, 1; during Government
 of 100 Days, 45; and Machado
 departure, 42–43; mediation with
 Cuba, 40–42, 229n68; replacement
 of, 233n9
Weyler, Valeriano, 15, 142, 176
Whitney, Robert, 25, 30, 206; on Cuban
 constitution, 268n88; on political
 cynicism, 208
women, Cuban: in AANPE, 116–17, 123,
 126; antifascism of, 104
women, Spanish Republican, defense of
 Republic, 104
World War II: Cuban antifascism
 during, 198–204; Cuban
 counterintelligence in, 13; Cuban
 military service during, 200; Cuban
 wartime propaganda in, 201;
 mainstream antifascism of, 21;
 Spanish neutrality in, 5; U.S. entry
 into, 198

Yates, James, 63

Zayas, Alfredo, 25
Zayas government, corruption of, 26,
 28, 226n11

ENVISIONING CUBA

Ariel Mae Lambe, *No Barrier Can Contain It: Cuban Antifascism and the Spanish Civil War* (2019).

Henry B. Lovejoy, *Prieto: Yorùbá Kingship in Colonial Cuba during the Age of Revolutions* (2018).

A. Javier Treviño, *C. Wright Mills and the Cuban Revolution: An Exercise in the Art of Sociological Imagination* (2017).

Antonia Dalia Muller, *Cuban Émigrés and Independence in the Nineteenth-Century Gulf World* (2017).

Jennifer L. Lambe, *Madhouse: Psychiatry and Politics in Cuban History* (2017).

Devyn Spence Benson, *Antiracism in Cuba: The Unfinished Revolution* (2016).

Michelle Chase, *Revolution within the Revolution: Women and Gender Politics in Cuba, 1952–1962* (2015).

Aisha K. Finch, *Rethinking Slave Rebellion in Cuba: La Escalera and the Insurgencies of 1841–1844* (2015).

Christina D. Abreu, *Rhythms of Race: Cuban Musicians and the Making of Latino New York City and Miami, 1940–1960* (2015).

Anita Casavantes Bradford, *The Revolution Is for the Children: The Politics of Childhood in Havana and Miami, 1959–1962* (2014).

Tiffany A. Sippial, *Prostitution, Modernity, and the Making of the Cuban Republic, 1840–1920* (2013).

Kathleen López, *Chinese Cubans: A Transnational History* (2013).

Lillian Guerra, *Visions of Power in Cuba: Revolution, Redemption, and Resistance, 1959–1971* (2012).

Carrie Hamilton, *Sexual Revolutions in Cuba: Passion, Politics, and Memory* (2012).

Sherry Johnson, *Climate and Catastrophe in Cuba and the Atlantic World during the Age of Revolution* (2011).

Melina Pappademos, *Black Political Activism and the Cuban Republic* (2011).

Frank Andre Guridy, *Forging Diaspora: Afro-Cubans and African Americans in a World of Empire and Jim Crow* (2010).

Ann Marie Stock, *On Location in Cuba: Street Filmmaking during Times of Transition* (2009).

Alejandro de la Fuente, *Havana and the Atlantic in the Sixteenth Century* (2008).

Reinaldo Funes Monzote, *From Rainforest to Cane Field in Cuba: An Environmental History since 1492* (2008).

Matt D. Childs, *The 1812 Aponte Rebellion in Cuba and the Struggle against Atlantic Slavery* (2006).

Eduardo González, *Cuba and the Tempest: Literature and Cinema in the Time of Diaspora* (2006).

John Lawrence Tone, *War and Genocide in Cuba, 1895–1898* (2006).

Samuel Farber, *The Origins of the Cuban Revolution Reconsidered* (2006).

Lillian Guerra, *The Myth of José Martí: Conflicting Nationalisms in Early Twentieth-Century Cuba* (2005).

Rodrigo Lazo, *Writing to Cuba: Filibustering and Cuban Exiles in the United States* (2005).

Alejandra Bronfman, *Measures of Equality: Social Science, Citizenship, and Race in Cuba, 1902–1940* (2004).

Edna M. Rodríguez-Mangual, *Lydia Cabrera and the Construction of an Afro-Cuban Cultural Identity* (2004).

Gabino La Rosa Corzo, *Runaway Slave Settlements in Cuba: Resistance and Repression* (2003).

Piero Gleijeses, *Conflicting Missions: Havana, Washington, and Africa, 1959–1976* (2002).

Robert Whitney, *State and Revolution in Cuba: Mass Mobilization and Political Change, 1920–1940* (2001).

Alejandro de la Fuente, *A Nation for All: Race, Inequality, and Politics in Twentieth-Century Cuba* (2001).

CPSIA information can be obtained
at www.ICGtesting.com
Printed in the USA
LVHW031953150720
660785LV00007B/556

9 781469 652856